First published in Great Britain in 2008 by
The Breedon Books Publishing Company Limited
Breedon House, 3 The Parker Centre,
Derby, DE21 4SZ.

A catalogue record for this book is available from the British Library.

ISBN 978-1–85983–671-2

Printed and bound Cromwell Press Ltd., Trowbridge, Wiltshire.

CONTENTS

AUTHOR'S NOTES

Aldershot FC/Aldershot Town FC

There seems to be a split among fans of Aldershot Town as to whether what many describe as the 'old' and 'new' clubs are actually the same club. While it can never be denied (nor should it ever be forgotten) that Aldershot FC and Aldershot Town FC are inextricably linked, my own personal view (having supported both clubs) is that they are two separate entities, and they have been treated as such in this book.

Factual accuracy

While every effort has been made to ensure that the facts within this book are accurate, some players have had careers that have been difficult to track. In the case of these, their career trail 'goes cold' at various points (some very early on). Furthermore, some reference sources have contradicted others, so I have had to make a 'judgement call' as to which information is correct.

There have also been a few instances of there being more than one player with the same name. This in itself is problematic, but it becomes even more of a problem when said players have played for the same club(s) at the same time.

Signing dates

The signing date (shown in brackets in playing career) was hard to establish for some players, as signings are often made in the last few days of one month or within the first few days of another. Where applicable, some quoted dates have been taken from media reports and various club resources. Where a player's specific signing date within a season is not known, the season in which he signed is quoted.

Loans, trials and work experience

When a player's loan move immediately becomes a permanent move, the signing date quoted in the playing career section is that on which the initial loan began. However, when a player has returned to their parent club and/or a close season has preceded a permanent move, both moves are shown in their own right.

When a player has been on trial at a club and then remains permanently, the signing date quoted is that on which the player ceased to be a trialist. However, as before, when a player has returned to their parent club and/or a close season has preceded a permanent move, both moves are shown in their own right.

Different sources have often listed a specific move by the same player as 'work experience loan', some as 'work experience' and some as 'loan'. As my perception of work experience is something that one does while at school, I have opted for 'loan' in all such cases.

Transfer fees

Transfer fees have been quoted where relevant/known. The two main sources of this information have been press reports and club websites. It should be noted that in the non-League pyramid, players often move for little or no fee.

Player source

Some clubs have applied various names to their junior, scholarship, apprentice and youth training schemes. Where possible, the name that has been used is the one documented in official club-related information or from reliable independent media sources.

Names of Leagues, Cups, etc

I am a bit of a traditionalist, so I have referred to Leagues, Cups, etc under their historical names, such as the Isthmian League as opposed to using the names of sponsors and naming it the Diadora League or Ryman League. Also, several Leagues have had changes of sponsor over the years, so I did not want to mislead the reader by listing the same League under several different sponsors' names. As with all rules, there are exceptions, one of which is unique: sponsored competitions that were/will be discontinued on cessation of the competition sponsorship, such as Dan Air Elite Cup and Setanta Shield.

The divisions within the Football League were rebranded in preparation for the 2004–05 season, at which time Divisions One, Two and Three became the Championship, League One and League Two respectively.

Allocation of League title-winners' medals

I have taken the view of the majority of club secretaries that I have spoken to, i.e. if a player has played in at least 10 games in a title-winning campaign, he is awarded a medal. I have applied the same theory to players being involved in promotion and relegation, with the exception that all the 'signed' players involved in Aldershot Town's Isthmian League Division Three title-winning season received a medal. Tim Read was the only loanee to receive a medal that season. Another exception is the 2007–08 season when (I believe) all the players that played in the Conference Premier-winning campaign were awarded a medal.

Allocation of Cup-winners' medals

Details of past Finals of some minor Cups are difficult to find, with some clubs and football associations not keeping records at all. Even where records were kept, the non-playing substitutes (who are awarded medals) were not always listed. Due to the fact that there is so much 'minor silverware' played for in non-League football, not all instances of players winning these have been documented in their profiles. However, they have been listed in club honours where relevant/known.

Appearances and goals

The figures quoted pertaining to players' Aldershot Town careers relate to all senior competitions and not just League appearances. Where X +Y appears in *ATFC Apps*, this indicates X starts plus Y substitute appearances.

All facts and figures quoted are correct as of 30 June 2008.

2007–08 season

Unless otherwise stated, the last club listed in *Playing Career* is the club with which a player finished the 2007–08 season. Furthermore, I have tried to provide a summary of how those clubs performed in their relevant Leagues plus documenting any Cup Finals that were reached. However, due to the sparsity of reporting within the lower reaches of the non-League game and the fact that some clubs either do not have the resources to maintain up-to-date websites or do not have a website at all, some minor silverware may not be accounted for in my summaries.

Abbreviations

M = Monthly contract
NC = Non-contract
1ML = One-month loan
2ML = Two-month loan
3ML = Three-month loan
4ML = Four-month loan
5ML = Five-month loan
6ML = Six-month loan
7ML = Seven-month loan
DR = Dual registration
DRL = Dual registration loan
L = Loan of unknown length
SLL = Season-long loan
STL = Short-term loan
W = Weekly contract
YTS = Youth training scheme

ACKNOWLEDGEMENTS

Firstly, I would like to acknowledge two basic facts:
1. Without the efforts of an extremely dedicated group of people in 1992 we would have no club to support, so a heartfelt 'thanks' goes to all those involved. (See The Formation of Aldershot Town Football Club, elsewhere in this book.)
2. Without the 350 players that have donned the Shots shirt plus the five 'permanent' and six caretaker managers that the club has had, I would have had no subject matter to write about, so a big 'thank you' to you all for the joy, ecstasy and happy memories that you have brought me.

The following people merit a special 'thank you' for the big part they played in this book:
Aldershot Town FC board of directors – for officially sanctioning this project. I would also like to thank Bob Bowden for his part in this.
Graham Brookland – not only did Graham provide me with some information pertaining to players' careers and write the excellent Aldershot Town Managers section of this book, but his support and encouragement was invaluable.
Martin Gooday and Karl Prentice – both of whom provided me with several photographs.
Gordon Macey – my literary mentor and adviser, who gave me lots of encouragement.
Ian Morsman – Ian is both the official club photographer and a very close friend of mine. We spent many a long hour looking through thousands of photos in order to source the vast majority of the pictures that have been used in this book. In addition, Ian's personal support and endless encouragement during this project have been priceless.
Alan Platt – provided me with some excellent information pertaining to players' careers.
Jack Rollin (literary legend of the football world) – for providing me with some excellent information pertaining to players' careers. He also advised me where necessary and has kindly written the foreword for this book.
Dale Walker – not only is Dale an ex-Shots player, he is also one of my best friends. His help with player information and his personal support have contributed greatly to this project.
Gary Waddock – for granting me access to the players that won the 2007–08 Conference Premier title.

I am very grateful to the following people/organisations, whose help, knowledge and contribution of information has been central in the compilation of this book:
Aldershot Military Museum, Aldershot News Group, Keith Allen, Cheryl Angell, Mike Appleby, John Aulsberry, James Avenell, Andy Awbery, Bruce Badcock, Carole Bailey, Ann Marie Ballantrye, Chris Blackie, Phil Blakey, Mark Broad, Keith Broughton, Luke Brown, Patricia Brown, Chester Browton, Carolyne Buckhurst-Matravers, Phillip Burkinshaw, Terry Byfield, Neil Cassar, Rob Challis, Tim Clark, Mike Clement, Gareth Coates, Jake Collinge, Alan Constable, Heather Cook, Jon Couch, Roy Couch, Ben Cranston, Roger Creed, Dane Cross, Phil Davison, Sally Day, Tony Dolbear, Mark Doyle, Pat Drake, Craig Dunbar, Eric Durrant, Leigh Edwards, Roly Edwards, Alan Evans, Russell Evans, Bob Fisher, David Fowkes, John Fryer, Nick Fryer, Chris Gay, Michael Gegg, Andy Gillard, Paul Godfrey, Paul Griffin, Simon Grigor, Tony Hampford, John Harman, Anthony Herlihy, Richard Hooker, Terry Hunt, Steve Hutson, Kelly Ingleson, Neil Jensen, Nobby Johnson, Ali Kazemi, Chris Keenan, Simon Kelly, Alan King, Howard Krais, Nigel Kyte, Kevin Lamb, Eddie Larkham, John Leyden, Edward Lucas, Simon Lynch, Alistair McKail, Keith Maddocks, Phil Malcolm, John Marchment, Eric Marsh, Craig Matthews, Ed Miller, Kerry Miller, Jason Mills, Paul Milton, Andy Morgan, Terry Morris, Glenn Moulton, Andy Muckle, Dave Munday, Ray Murphy, Kevin O'Byrne, Charlie Oliver, Steve Parsons, Alan Payne, Colin Peake, Ray Peploe, Lee Peskett, Andrew Poole, Tony Pope, Norman Posner, Craig Pottage, Gary Pratt, Les Rance, Mervyn Rees, Stuart Reeves, Les Reynolds, Steve Rogers, Mike Robins, David Ruffles, Ann Sandford, David Selby, Steve Shimwell, Adam Silver, Alan Smith, Graham Smith, Mark Smith, Cliff Sparkes, David Stanley, Ceri Stennett, Ian Stewart, Emma Storey, Joe Sullivan, Andy Sutton, Dave Tavener, Steve Taylor, Gordon Tennant, Steve Thompson, David Thomson, Noel Tilbrook, Malcolm Tombs, Dave Tomlinson, Ken Tomlinson, Paul Trenter, Jason Tull, Brian Turrell, Andrew Vaughan, Mark Venables, Peter Wade, Dell Ward, Garry Ward, Eric Warner, Gareth Watmore, Alan Watson, Chris Watts, Bob Weaver, Dawn Webb, Mark Wells, Mark Williams, Mike Williams, Vince Williams, Mike Wilson, Rob Wilson and Robin Woolman.

Finally, I would like to thank the following players for willingly giving me their time and help (plus a few anecdotes that I dare not use):
Gary Abbott, Nana Achamfour, Mark Anderson, Darren Angell, Will Antwi, Danny Bailey, Keith Baker, Neil Baker, Darren Barnard, Richard Barnard, Trevor Baron, Simon Bassey, Steve Beeks, Nicky Bell, Steve Benitez, Paul Bennett, Mark Bentley, Darren Brodrick, Ian Brooks, Brian Broome, Steve Buckingham, Michael Bullen, Phil Burns, Nick Burton, Mark Butler, Tony Calvert, Stuart Cash, Lewis Chalmers, Anthony Charles, Jason Chewins, Dwain Clarke, Tony Cleeve, Les Cleevely, Sam Cobbett, Owen Coll, Brett Cooper, Matt Crossley, Jimmy Dack, Scott Davies, Richard Dean, Scott Donnelly, Roscoe D'Sane, Koo Dumbuya, Adam Dunsby, Rob Elvins, Gavin Evans, Nathan Fealey, Colin Fielder, Mark Frampton, Luke Garrard, Marcus Gayle, Luke Gedling, Andy Glasspool, Jamie Gosling, Andrew Grace, Mark Graham, Joel Grant, John Grant, Andy Guppy, Mark Hammond, Ben Harding, George Hardy, Paul Harford, Mark Harper, Steve Harris, Stuart Harte, Johnson Hippolyte, Danny Holmes, Lee Holsgrove, Jon Horsted, Jamie Horton, Gareth Howells, Kirk Hudson, Josh Huggins, John Humphrey, Otis Hutchings, Danny Hylton, Mikhael Jaimez-Ruiz, Nigel James, Nick Jansen, Miles Jones, Ian Jopling, Darren Keown, Ryan Kirby, Marc Kleboe, Martin Kuhl, Dean Larkham, Jayson Lay, Dave Lee, Brian Lucas, Barry McCoy, Fiston Manuella, James Mariner, Shaun May, Junior Mendes, Gavin Mernagh, Jason Milletti, Neil Musgrove, Andy Nunn, Dave Osgood, Steve Osgood, Andy Pape, Adam Parker, Kevin Parkins, Grant Payne, Gary Phillips, Lewis Phillips, Lee Protheroe, Mark Pye, Dan Read, Paul Read, Tim Read, Jon Richards, Jim Rodwell, Andy Russell, Emmanuel Sackey, Will Salmon, Neil Selby, Jason Short, Paul Shrubb, Daniel Simmonds, Oliver Squires, Steve Stairs, Dominic Sterling, Anthony Straker, Jimmy Sugrue, Andy Sullivan, Steve Talboys, Stuart Tanfield, Nathan Tapley, Anthony Thirlby, Paul Thompson, Chris Tomlinson, Jason Tucker, Mark Turkington, Phil Turrell, Stuart Udal, Luke Walker, Steve Watson, Dan Weait, Neil Webb, Darren Wheeler, Ryan Williams, Jeff Wood, Paul Wooller, Lloyd Wye and Roy Young.

FOREWORD

'They never come back' was the old boxing maxim. But it is not true for Aldershot Football Club, left in ruins through disgraceful financial mismanagement and unceremoniously kicked out by the Football League in March 1992 – the first club to be dealt with in this manner since Leeds City in 1919. Yet, whereas the Yorkshire team disappeared, there were more than crumbs of comfort as the Shots reformed and began a new life at the broken biscuit end of the non-League pyramid food chain.

Thus you have the bare facts. The reality was a tentative start in the Diadora-sponsored Isthmian League Division Three, at the same Recreation Ground that had been the former club's home since 1927. Expectations for the opening fixture against Clapton were modest enough, with a crowd of some 750 on the predicted budget. Twice as many turned up, and that proved the lowest attendance of the season. There was a scare when the visitors went two goals ahead, only for Aldershot Town to run out 4–2 winners. Later in the season there was a 6,000 gate for the Hampshire Cup local derby with Farnborough Town. The phoenix was already rising from the ashes.

Sixteen years on, the town of Aldershot had a Football League team again. There had been several high fives – promotions, managers and Hants Cups – and plenty of happy clapping on the way, with the odd share of disappointment as expectations rose too quickly. During the old club's reign, Reading had been the chief local rivals. In non-League football it was Farnborough and later, when successive promotions brought Conference football to Aldershot, the main rivals became Woking.

There had been no giant-killing FA Cup performances but certainly one victory that should have been against Bristol Rovers at the Rec and a replay in which we were not disgraced. Twice so near in the trophy, including last season of course at the same semi-final stage. Reaching the Conference while still part-time and battling through to the Play-off Final at Stoke, only to lose in the lottery of the penalty shoot-out. The next season, as full-timers, it was a similar departure in the semi-final.

Yet 2007–08 was the icing on the cake. After a slow beginning to the campaign, it increased in tempo and finished with statistics that will prove hard to beat in the future: 101 points and 31 wins. The defining moments were arguably the win at Torquay United and the week of four matches in eight days with only two points dropped. The clinching point was secured at Exeter City. As a bonus there was a double, this time the penalty shoot-out going the Shots' way in the Setanta Shield. Pleasing, too, that having won the Championship title, the team remained unbeaten in their last 18 games.

In the interim, a new generation of youthful support has become the solid backbone of Aldershot Town Football Club, along with many of those who followed the Shots in their earlier existence. Many people who give time and energy outside the green, green grass of home have contributed immensely to the success of the club, but the essential ingredients have been the 350 first-team players whose personal sketches have been faithfully recorded on the following pages. The future beckons for those who will follow them on the field of play, the lads in Red and Blue.

Jack Rollin

THE FORMATION OF ALDERSHOT TOWN FOOTBALL CLUB

The vast majority of the following text is taken from the excellent The Rise & Rise of Aldershot Town – Champions *publication compiled by Graham Brookland and Karl Prentice and has been reproduced with the kind permission of Adline...*

The town's football club was finally laid to rest. The high court had finally conceded that the club was hopelessly insolvent after countless battles with the liquidator over the previous five years. Week after week false promises were made by the board of directors of rescue packages and, by the end, some of the directors couldn't even be bothered to turn up and watch the football being played by their own players, who eventually had to endure 12 weeks without receiving payment.

The final game on Friday 20 March 1992 at Ninian Park, Cardiff, was an emotional setting as the Shots fans were coming to terms with the fact that this was to be the final match. At the end, the players and supporters embraced each other, knowing that the curtain was coming down. The players had to look elsewhere for employment – and the supporters?

The Shots had won only 25 League games in their previous 128 attempts and had a highest League position of 22nd in that time. The ultimate game at the Recreation Ground attracted 1,374 spectators to see a 3–0 defeat by Lincoln City; however, despite the result and the fact that the struggling side scored just three goals in the final 16 matches, acquiring just three points in that time, there was a ray of light beckoning.

Local businessman Terry Owens, in conjunction with the supporters' club, called a public meeting to 'discuss the formation and infrastructure of the proposed Aldershot Town Football Club' for Wednesday 22 April. The turnout of 600 proved that football returning to Aldershot was practical and the enthusiasm was never doubted. Owens and the supporters' club had to get to work, and quickly! An application to join the Diadora League (the sponsored guise of the Isthmian League) was made, and negotiations with Rushmoor Borough Council began for the possibility of playing on the Recreation Ground, the home of Aldershot FC for 66 years.

A financial structure was set up with the assistance of David Brookland – who became the club's financial advisor – and he, Terry Owens and a 5,500-signature petition organised by the supporters' club, in favour of football at the Recreation Ground, took off to the council offices on 30 April. They were given a three-year licence to play at the Rec after three cases were considered. Terry Owens stated at the time:

> the outcome of the meeting was very positive. They indicated at 10.15am the following morning that we would be granted a one-year licence to play at the Rec, but by one o'clock the licence was turned into a three-year deal. I'm very proud and pleased for the people of Aldershot. Handing in a petition with nearly 6,000 names in support went a long way. There's no time for rest, though. The biggest hurdle we had to jump was the Beecher's Brook. That was the Rushmoor Borough Council fence. We've jumped that, but we have several more hurdles to jump. We've got to sort out status in the Diadora League, appoint a manager, form a board of directors. It now gets harder. People say you'll never get everything up and running by August. I'll prove them wrong.

Next on the agenda was the formation of the company. This occurred on 6 May 1992, when Owens together with supporters' club chairman Graham Brookland were appointed directors of the newly formed company with Peter Bridgeman, the company secretary.

With every item in order, the next task was to appoint a manager. Ian McDonald and Steve Wignall were the last management team of the defunct club, ironically for McDonald in his testimonial year. Both had expressed an interest in working together at the new club even though they had not been accepted into a League as yet. It was an enormous task, but both men lived in the town and worked well together. Then, out of the blue, McDonald was offered the job as Millwall reserve-team manager, and it was a job he could not refuse. The way was open for Wignall to become manager, and on Saturday 23 May he was offered the opportunity at a meeting with the two directors and secretary. He gladly accepted, saying:

> This is a great opportunity for myself. It's going to be a very difficult job; it's a new club, fresh club, CLEAN club. We've got honest people working in it. Dropping out of the Football League after 20 years is going to be difficult, but I'm on the ladder of the management side of things now and I'm really looking forward to it...One of the main things I've learnt in the past few months is the financial side of things. How things are NOT to be done. As far as players are concerned, I've learnt it is possible to surround yourself with loyal players, which we had at the end of Aldershot FC. If the new players give as much effort as those players gave over the last three months, I don't think there will be any problems at all...It'll be fantastic to get back to the Recreation Ground. I thought when I walked out on the final day when they locked the gates that that was it. Once again, it's a new club, some of the old faces will be there but there'll be some new faces. Hopefully, there will be plenty of the old faces in the crowd who supported us superbly for the last three months. I hope they come back again, give us a bit of a chance. It's not going to all happen at once

> but hopefully we'll be successful…When Ian McDonald phoned and told me of his appointment at Millwall, my initial reaction was ecstatic really. I know if anybody deserves anything, he does. I've met a lot of honest people in the game and I've met a lot of dishonest people in the game. He's one of the most honest I've ever met and it's a great opportunity for him.

Now the battle was on to find players, as Wignall only had one, local lad Chris Tomlinson. On Wednesday 3 June, a seven-man board of directors of local origin was formed at a meeting at the Hogs Back Hotel near Farnham. Joining Terry Owens, made chairman, and Graham Brookland – who was involved in making it a requirement that whoever is supporters' club chairman shall automatically become a director – were John McGinty, Karl Prentice, Peter Bloomfield, Malcolm Grant and, later in the summer, Kevin Donegan.

The seed was sown on 15 June when the Diadora League formally accepted Aldershot Town into its structure in Division Three, where the average attendance the previous season had been 92! It now needed a further packed public meeting the following night to inform the supporters of the news that Aldershot Town were 'alive and kicking'!

THE BEGINNING OF THE DREAM

On Saturday 22 August 1992 (just five months after the demise of the 'old' club) Aldershot Town played their first-ever competitive game – an Isthmian League Division Three fixture against Clapton at the Recreation Ground. A crowd of 1,493 saw the Shots go 2–0 down to an Ian Scott double after 27 minutes. However, the team fought hard, and a 34th-minute goal from Mark Butler plus strikes by Steve Stairs in the 36th and 42nd minutes ensured the home side went into half-time in the lead. A further goal from Butts on the hour mark secured an historic 4–2 victory.

The Aldershot Town line up that day was:

1	Tim Read (aged 21), goalkeeper signed on loan from Woking.
2	Kevin Parkins (31), right-back previously with Windsor and Eton.
3	Steve Buckingham (25), left-back signed from Farnham Town.
4	Stuart Udal (20), centre-back from Ash United.
5	Chris Tomlinson (22), centre-back, who played in Aldershot FC's last-ever match.
6	Keith Baker (37), centre-back, whose last club was Farnborough Town.
7	Brian Lucas (31), ex-Aldershot FC midfielder signed from Basingstoke Town.
8	Dave Osgood (25), midfielder, who joined from Maidenhead United.
9	Steve Stairs (24), forward previously with Farnham Town.
10	Shaun May (27), midfielder signed from Farnham Town.
11	Mark Butler (27), forward from Egham Town.
12	Koo Dumbuya (21), midfielder previously with Staines Town.
14	Paul Bennett (29), midfielder, whose last club was Basingstoke Town.

Note: Koo Dumbuya was an unused substitute in this match, and Paul Bennett replaced the injured Steve Buckingham after 86 minutes. Full details of the above players can be found elsewhere in this book.

Aldershot Town Football Club, with the Simpsonair Challenge Trophy and Skol Challenge Trophy, 1992–93. Back row, left to right: 'Ginge' McAllister (physio), Steve Stairs, John Nibbs, Steve Harris, Tim Read, Chris Tomlinson, Shaun May, Stuart Udal, Steve Wignall (manager). Front row: Tony Calvert, Mark Butler, Steve Benitez, Craig Wright, Brian Lucas, Kevin Parkins, Koo Dumbuya.

A TO Z OF ALDERSHOT TOWN PLAYERS

Ben Abbey — Forward

Born: 13 May 1977, Pimlico.

Aldershot Town FC record:

Debut:	v Sutton United (h), Isthmian League Premier Division, 19 August 2000.
Last appearance:	v Walton and Hersham (a), Isthmian League Cup first round, 12 September 2000.
Appearances:	4 + 2
Goals:	1

Playing career:
Osterley, Maidenhead United (February 1997), Crawley Town (September 1997), Reading (trial, November 1998), Reading (trial, March 1999), Oxford United (October 1999), Aldershot Town (1ML, August 2000), Southend United (October 2000), Brentford (trial, July 2001), Leyton Orient (trial, July 2001), Stevenage Borough (November 2001), Crawley Town (November 2001), Woking (August 2002), Macclesfield Town (March 2003), Barnet (trial, July 2003), Gravesend and Northfleet (July 2003), Hertford Town (summer 2004), St Albans City (September 2004), Northwood (November 2004), Farnborough Town (August 2005), Hampton and Richmond Borough (October 2005), Metropolitan Police (March 2006), Tooting and Mitcham United (February 2007).
Ben has made 33 Football League appearances, scoring seven goals.

Club honours:
Isthmian League Full Members' Cup (Maidenhead United 1997), Sussex Floodlight Cup (Crawley Town 1999), Surrey Senior Cup (Tooting and Mitcham United 2007), London Senior Cup (Tooting and Mitcham United 2008 [unused substitute]), Isthmian League Division One South Play-off Final (Tooting and Mitcham United 2008).

Ben is the cousin of ex-Shot Nigel James and started his career at Osterley before following manager Alan Devonshire to Maidenhead United in February 1997. He finished the season with an Isthmian League Full Members' Cup-winners' medal and moved to Southern League Premier Division side Crawley Town in September of that year. His 46 goals for Crawley (including 31 in the 1998–99 season) led to a couple of trials at Reading before progression into the Football League was achieved, with a £35,000 move to Oxford United in September 1999.

Ben made his Oxford debut as a substitute against Bristol City the following month but never managed to hold down a regular place. He joined Aldershot Town on a one-month loan deal in August 2000 but failed to make an impact at the Rec during that spell. He returned to the Kassam Stadium when his loan finished but was transferred to Southend United shortly afterwards – his time at Oxford had yielded a solitary goal in 13 appearances.

Ben's impact at Roots Hall was almost immediate, as he scored twice in only his second appearance (against Macclesfield Town), finishing that season as top scorer (13 goals), and was a member of the side that lost the Southern Area Final of the Football League Trophy to Brentford. He was surprisingly released by Southend that summer, and he returned to Crawley Town in November 2001 following trials at Leyton Orient and Brentford plus a short stint at Stevenage Borough.

Ben joined Woking in August 2002 and scored the only goal of the game on his debut against Forest Green Rovers. He went on to score nine more goals that season before getting another stab at League football when joining Macclesfield Town in March 2003. However, he was released two months later and subsequently played for Gravesend and Northfleet, St Albans City, Northwood and Farnborough Town before joining Hampton and Richmond Borough in the summer of 2005.

A move to Metropolitan Police came in the summer of 2006 before he signed for Tooting and Mitcham United in February 2007. He was a regular in the Tooting side until he damaged his groin in December 2007 and subsequently missed a month of the season. Tooting eventually finished as runners-up to Dover Athletic in the League and won promotion to the Isthmian League Premier Division by virtue of a Play-off Final victory over Cray Wanderers. They also won that season's London Senior Cup.

Gary Abbott — Forward

Born: 7 November 1964, Catford.

Aldershot Town FC record:

Debut:	v Purfleet (a), Isthmian League Premier Division, 22 August 1998.

Gary's achievements at Aldershot Town include:

* Winning the non-League Player of the Year and Adidas Predator of the Year (awarded to the top scorer in senior non-League football) in 2000.
* Scoring 10 hat-tricks, including four goals on two occasions and five goals once.
* Holding the club record for most hat-tricks in a season – four, which he achieved in 1998–99 and 1999–2000.
* Scoring in 11 consecutive League games between 22 January 2000 and 1 April 2000.
* Being the only player to score five goals in the Hampshire Senior Cup Final.
* Winning the Isthmian League Golden Boot in 1998–99, 1999–2000 and 2000–01.

Last appearance: v Heybridge Swifts (a), Isthmian League Premier Division, 5 May 2001.
Appearances: 148 + 8
Goals: 120 (second in all-time top 10)

Playing career:
Welling United (November 1981), Barnet (December 1987), Gillingham (trial, 1988), Enfield (February 1989), Welling United (August 1990), Enfield (June 1994), Slough Town (June 1996), Aldershot Town (June 1998), Welling United (May 2001), Grays Athletic (August 2002), Gravesend and Northfleet (November 2002), Chesham United (January 2003), Welling United (January 2003), Fisher Athletic (London, player-coach, June 2003, player-manager from October 2003), Walton and Hersham (February 2004), Hornchurch (March 2004), Braintree Town (player-assistant manager, June 2004), Cray Wanderers (player-coach, June 2005).

Representative honours:
England Semi-Professional XI (3 caps), FA XI, Middlesex Wanderers, Isthmian League XI.

Club honours:
Southern League Premier Division (Welling United 1985–86), Kent Senior Cup (Welling United 1986), London Challenge Cup (Welling United 1992), Isthmian League Premier Division (Enfield 1994–95), Isthmian League Charity Shield (Aldershot Town 1999), Isthmian League Cup (Aldershot Town 1999), Hampshire Senior Cup (Aldershot Town 1999, 2000).

Post-playing coaching/management career:
Manager of Sittingbourne (November 2007).

Gary is a prolific goal machine whose goalscoring record in non-League football is second-to-none, having amassed just over 550 goals in 1,117 games. With a record like that, it is rather surprising that he never played in the Football League, although Millwall, Southampton, Charlton Athletic and Queen's Park Rangers reportedly showed interest in him early in his career.

Gary started out at Welling United, signing for them on his 17th birthday, and spent six seasons there. His goals fired them to the Southern League Premier Division title in 1985–86 and contributed to him winning the first of his England Semi-Professional XI caps (as a substitute) against Italy in May 1987 before a fee of £15,000 took him to Barnet in December 1987. During his time at Underhill, Tottenham Hotspur and Newcastle United made enquiries and he trialled at Gillingham, but nothing came of their interest. As the 1987–88 season drew to a close, Gary looked set to make the move into the Football League via promotion from the Conference, but Barnet lost out to Lincoln City in the title race on the final day of the season.

Gary began the following season at Underhill but, having scored 16 goals in 40 games, he joined Conference rivals Enfield on loan in February 1989. He scored a hat-trick on his debut against Weymouth and made his move permanent a month later for a fee of £40,000. At the time, this was a non-League record and was still Enfield's record purchase when the club was liquidated in 2007. Unfortunately, the move did not turn out to be successful, as the club were relegated the following season. This resulted in Gary returning to Welling for his second spell in August 1990 for a £30,000 fee (still a record for an incoming Wings player).

He scored twice on his debut on the opening day of the 1990–91 season and went into the FA Cup record books in October 1991 when he headed all five goals in Wings' 5–1 victory over Alvechurch in a fourth qualifying-round tie. He again scored five goals later that season while playing for an FA XI against an Isthmian League XI.

Gary was Welling United's top scorer in 1991–92 (25 goals) and 1992–93 (19 goals) and stayed at Park View Road until the summer of 1994, when Enfield paid out £12,000 to bring him back to Southbury Road. His 34 goals contributed to the Es winning the Isthmian League Premier Division in 1994–95, and he scored in six rounds of that season's FA Cup – one of his goals knocked out Second Division Cardiff City in round one. Enfield were runners-up to Hayes in the Isthmian League Premier Division in 1995–96, and Gary finished top scorer (26 goals).

After bringing his Enfield career goals tally to 89 in 120 appearances, his next port of call was Slough Town, whom he joined in August 1996. He stayed there for two seasons during which time he was top scorer in 1996–97 (18 goals) and scored a total of 35 goals in 94 appearances. He was also a member of the Rebels side that reached the 1997–98 FA Trophy semi-final against Southport.

Many people were surprised when Aldershot Town paid £8,000 to bring Gary to the Rec in June 1998 (a few months short of his 34th birthday). However, by the end of a season that yielded both a career-best and a club-record 48 goals in all competitions, including a last-gasp winner against local rivals Basingstoke Town in the Hampshire Senior Cup Final, it was seen as a bargain.

Aside from scoring goals, another attribute that Gary possessed was the ability to hold the ball up while waiting for his teammates to arrive, and this enabled him to set up several goals. He was the Shots' top scorer in 1999–2000 (45 goals) and also in 2000–01 (27 goals), but that was to be his last contribution in a Shots shirt. After scoring 120 goals in 156 games and attaining 'legend' status (his goals total is second only to Mark Butler's), he embarked on his third spell at Welling in May 2001, finishing top scorer there in 2001–02 with 31 goals – a total that included the 10 goals in three games that earned him the accolade of overall top scorer in that season's FA Trophy.

Brief spells at Grays Athletic, Gravesend and Northfleet and Chesham United in 2002–03 followed but yielded just two goals in 15 games before he returned to Welling for a fourth spell in January 2003.

Having achieved the accolade of Welling's all-time record goalscorer (241 goals in 557 matches), Gary left for Fisher Athletic (London) as player-coach and had a brief spell as player-manager at Walton and Hersham and Hornchurch before becoming George Borg's player-assistant manager at Braintree Town in the summer of 2004. Seventeen appearances produced four goals before Gary took up the role of player-coach at Cray Wanderers in July 2005, and he finished joint top scorer (13 goals) with Leigh Bremner that season. He had totalled 25 goals in 72 appearances when he suffered two prolapsed discs in his neck against Maidstone United in January 2007 – an injury that forced Gary to retire.

In 2007 Gary's phenomenal goalscoring record was duly rewarded when he was voted the Most Outstanding non-League Player of the Era by readers of the *Non-League Club Directory*. In November that year, Gary took his first step into management when he was appointed manager of Isthmian League Division One South side Sittingbourne, leading the Brickies to a very commendable ninth-place finish in the League.

Nana Achamfour — Forward

Born: 15 August 1981, Lambeth.

Aldershot Town FC record:

Debut: as substitute v Newport (Isle of Wight) (a), Hampshire Senior Cup third round, 25 January 2000.
Last appearance: v Newport (Isle of Wight) (a), Hampshire Senior Cup third round, 15 November 2000.
Appearances: 3 + 2

Playing career:
Egham Town (youth), Aldershot Town (youth, January 2000), UWIC Inter Cardiff (August 2001), Grange Harlequins (August 2002).

Nana was originally part of the youth set-up at Egham Town (while also playing for Hazlehurst AFC in the Croydon Sunday League) but never played for the first team. He joined the Aldershot Town youth team in January 2000 and was one of a number of youth players who played for the first team in minor Cup competitions. He left in November 2000 to pursue his educational studies, and it was during those studies that he signed for League of Wales side UWIC Inter Cardiff.

Nana's last-known club was Welsh League side Grange Harlequins, for whom he signed in August 2002.

Darren Adams — Forward

Born: 12 January 1974, Bromley.

Aldershot Town FC record:

Debut:	v Bognor Regis Town (h), Isthmian League Division One, 17 August 1996.
Last appearance:	as substitute v Whyteleafe (a), Isthmian League Division One, 15 February 1997.
Appearances:	30 + 3
Goals:	13

Playing career:

Danson Furness (August 1993), Cardiff City (January 1994), Woking (1ML) (March 1996), Aldershot Town (August 1996), Dover Athletic (February 1997), Welling United (November 1998), Hampton and Richmond Borough (September 1999), Fisher Athletic (London, June 2000), Erith and Belvedere (February 2001), Chatham Town (October 2004), Erith and Belvedere (August 2005), Eton Manor (February 2006).

Darren has made 34 Football League appearances, scoring four goals.

Club honours:

Kent Senior Cup (Welling United 1999).

Darren is a fleet-of-foot forward who began his career in the Kent League with Danson Furness. He got his Football League break in January 1994 when Division Two side Cardiff City came calling, and he made his debut against Barnet later that month.

Unfortunately, his first season at Ninian Park ended in disappointment, as the Bluebirds were relegated to Division Three. Unable to secure a first-team place, Darren was loaned to Woking in March 1996 but failed to make an impression.

He was released by Cardiff at the end of the 1995–96 season and came to the Rec as a pre-season trialist, playing under a pseudonym so as not to alert other clubs of his availability. He impressed sufficiently to be offered a contract, but a spectacular long-range scissor-kick in a League game against Whyteleafe and a hat-trick in the FA Cup against Merstham were the only memorable contributions that he made.

In February 1997 he moved to Conference side Dover Athletic for a £3,000 fee, after which he moved to Welling United. Darren scored the only goal to secure the 1999 Kent Senior Cup for the Wings before having a spell at Hampton and Richmond Borough and joining Erith and Belvedere in February 2001. He was the Deres' top scorer in 2001–02 (29 goals) as well as their Player of the Year and finished as top scorer again at Park View Road (which they shared with Welling United) in 2002–03 (22 goals).

Darren joined Chatham Town in October 2004 and then returned to Erith and Belvedere in August 2005. Having scored 82 goals in his two spells for the Deres, he left to join Eton Manor in the Essex Senior League in February 2006.

Ollie Adedeji — Centre-back

Born: 15 July 1970, Lewisham.

Aldershot Town FC record:

Debut:	v Hendon (a), Isthmian League Premier Division, 14 August 1999.
Last appearance:	v Billericay Town (a), Isthmian League Premier Division, 2 March 2002.
Appearances:	109 + 14
Goals:	1

Playing career:

Finchley (summer 1989), Bromley (September 1991), Boreham Wood (August 1993), Bromley (January 1994), Aldershot Town (May 1999), Farnborough Town (trial, March 2002), Canvey Island (May 2002), Billericay Town

(October 2002), Hornchurch (May 2003), Braintree Town (May 2004), AFC Hornchurch (November 2007), Boreham Wood (January 2008; player-caretaker assistant manager from February 2008).

Representative honours:
Isthmian League XI.

Club honours:
London Challenge Cup (Bromley 1996), Isthmian League Charity Shield (Aldershot Town 1999), Hampshire Senior Cup (Aldershot Town 2000), Isthmian League Premier Division (Braintree Town 2005–06).

Ollie is a solid defender who started his career at Finchley before moving on to Bromley and Boreham Wood in August 1993. He returned to Hayes Lane in January 1994, and his consistency was rewarded with three Player of the Year awards (1994, 1995 and 1996). That same consistency earned him a move to Aldershot Town in May 1999 (reportedly in preference to more than one offer to play in the Conference), and it was no surprise that he won the Player of the Year award at the end of his first season.

Ollie's time at the Rec ended controversially in March 2002 when both he and teammate Mark Graham were sacked for fighting each other during a League game at Billericay Town. Following his departure, Ollie trialled at neighbours Farnborough Town before joining Canvey Island in May of that year. In a quirk of fate, he joined Billericay in October 2002 (for whom Mark Graham was also playing) and was immediately named as captain. He linked up with ex-Shots boss George Borg in May 2003 when he signed for Hornchurch and was part of the Urchins side that were defeated by Tranmere Rovers in the second round of the following season's FA Cup.

In May 2004 Ollie followed Borg to Braintree Town where, as captain, he played a major role in them winning the Isthmian League Premier Division in 2005–06. He was also a member of the side that reached the FA Cup first round (where they lost to Shrewsbury Town) for the first time.

In December 2006 he was named as Borg's player-assistant and finished the season as the club's Player of the Year. In October 2007 Ollie left Cressing Road (when Borg was dismissed) and played briefly for AFC Hornchurch before rejoining Boreham Wood in January 2008. The following month, ex-Shots boss George Borg arrived at Meadow Park as caretaker manager and immediately named Ollie as player-caretaker assistant manager. Boreham Wood finished the season in 19th place in the Isthmian League Premier Division, which saw them relegated (on goal difference) before Halifax Town's ejection from the Conference Premier threw them a lifeline. They did beat Ware in order to win the 2008 Hertfordshire Senior Cup, but Ollie was not in the squad.

Mazin Ahmad — Forward

Born: 2 February 1985, Bucharest, Romania.

Aldershot Town FC record:

Debut:	as substitute v Gravesend and Northfleet (a), Conference National, 1 April 2006.
Last appearance:	v Southport (a), Conference National, 29 April 2006.
Appearances:	2 + 5

Playing career:
Woking, Molesey (summer 2002), Yeovil Town (trial, May 2003), Walton and Hersham (August 2003), Epsom and Ewell, Kingstonian (August 2004), Mansfield Town (trial, August 2005), Yeovil Town (trial, August 2005), Aldershot Town (March 2006), Farnborough Town (trial, July 2006), Yeovil Town (trial, July 2006), Basingstoke Town (trial, August 2006), Kingstonian (September 2006), Molesey (December 2006), Dulwich Hamlet (January 2007), Godalming Town (November 2007).

Mazin was born in Romania and started out at Woking before signing for Molesey in the summer of 2002. Following a trial at Yeovil Town and spells at Walton and Hersham and Epsom and Ewell, he signed for Kingstonian in August 2004. While at Kingsmeadow he gained a reputation as a quick forward who could score goals out of nothing, and this led to trials at Mansfield Town and Yeovil (again) before a move to Aldershot Town in March 2006. However, he displayed neither of his Ks traits and left in the summer of 2006, trialling at Farnborough Town, Yeovil (yet again) and Basingstoke Town (for whom he made just one substitute appearance) before moving back to Kingstonian. But he was on the move again in December (to Molesey) and again in January (to Dulwich Hamlet).

Mazin started the 2007–08 season at Champion Hill and moved to Godalming Town in November but had to wait until mid-January to make his debut against Oxford City. Godalming finished the 2007–08 season in 12th place in the Southern League Division One South and West.

Chris Allen — Winger

Born: 18 November 1972, Oxford.

Aldershot Town FC record:

Debut:	v Heybridge Swifts (h), Isthmian League Premier Division, 30 March 2002.
Last appearance:	v Havant and Waterlooville, Hampshire Senior Cup Final (at Southampton FC), 1 May 2002.
Appearances:	8 + 1
Goals:	1

Playing career:
Oxford United (from trainee, May 1991), Nottingham Forest (1ML, February 1996), Nottingham Forest (July 1996), Luton Town (3ML, November 1997), Cardiff City (2ML) (October 1998), Port Vale (March 1999), Stockport County (October 1999), Slough Town (July 2000), Brighton & Hove Albion (NC, March 2001), Cambridge United (NC, September 2001), Dover Athletic (September 2001), Leyton Orient (trial, January 2002), Aldershot Town (NC) (March 2002), North Leigh (August 2006).
Chris has made 217 FA Premier League and Football League appearances, scoring 15 goals.

Representative honours:
Football League Under-21, England Under-21 (two caps).

Club honours:
Hampshire Senior Cup (Aldershot Town 2002), Oxfordshire Senior Cup (North Leigh 2008), Hellenic League Premier Division (North Leigh 2007–08).

Post-playing coaching/management career:
Under-14 coach at Oxford United, first-team coach at Oxford United (2003 to 2006).

Like many before and since, Chris failed to deliver what the Aldershot Town fans had expected based on his pre-Shots career. He was a trainee at Oxford United and signed full professional forms in May 1991. He made his Oxford debut as a substitute against Leicester City in February 1992 and represented the Football League and England at Under-21 level before tasting relegation from Division One with the Us in 1993–94.

Chris was loaned to Nottingham Forest for a month in February 1996 and returned to the Manor Ground to play a bit-part in helping the club finish runners-up to Swindon Town in that season's Division Two title race. A fee of £500,000 took him to the City Ground on a permanent basis in the summer, but Forest were relegated from the FA Premier League at the end of that season and Chris's career took a downward turn. He had loan spells at Luton Town and Cardiff City before joining Port Vale in March 1999, moving to Stockport County in October 1999 and then Slough Town (following a successful trial) during the summer of 2000. Non-contract spells at Brighton & Hove Albion and Cambridge United followed before he moved to Dover Athletic in September 2001. A trial at Leyton Orient preceded Chris moving to the Rec in March 2002, with his last game for the Shots being the victory over Havant and Waterlooville in the Hampshire Senior Cup Final that year.

Chris subsequently retired and returned to Oxford United, where he was Under-14s coach as well as being on the first-team coaching staff from 2003 to 2006. He came out of retirement in August 2006 to play for Hellenic League Premier Division side North Leigh, and his 20 goals that season helped the club finish as runners-up to Slimbridge in the League.

In 2007–08 he scored 23 goals in 29 appearances, which greatly assisted in the winning of the League title (on goal difference from Almondsbury Town). He also scored North Leigh's second goal as they celebrated their centenary year by beating Banbury United 2–1 in that season's Oxfordshire Senior Cup Final – the first time the club had ever won the Cup. During 2007–08 Chris combined his playing with his post as an Under-9s coach at Oxford United.

Mark Anderson **Forward**

Born: 7 April 1976, Frimley.

Aldershot Town FC record:

Debut:	v Walton and Hersham (h), Diadora League Cup second round, 1 November 1994.
Last appearance:	v Kingstonian (at Aldershot Town FC), Isthmian League Cup Final, 6 May 1996.
Appearances:	4 + 27
Goals:	6

Playing career:
Farnborough Town (youth), Aldershot Town (October 1993), Wokingham Town (1ML, September 1996), Bracknell Town (October 1996), Chertsey Town (July 1999), Cove (July 2002), Sandhurst Town (October 2002), Bracknell Town (July 2006), Godalming Town (July 2007), Fleet Town (October 2007).

Club honours:
Russell Cotes Cup (Fleet Town 2008), Basingstoke Senior Cup (Fleet Town 2008), Aldershot Senior Cup (Fleet Town 2008).

Mark started as a youth player at Farnborough Town before making the move across the county to the Rec in October 1993, but he had to wait just over a year to make his Shots debut. A one-month loan at Wokingham Town in September 1996 was followed immediately by a three-month loan to Bracknell Town, which became permanent in January 1997 for a fee of £1,000.

Mark was Bracknell's top scorer the following season and eventually left Larges Lane in July 1999 to join Chertsey Town. Unfortunately, he sustained a bad knee injury in November 2000 and this sidelined him until the summer of 2002, when he signed for Cove before moving on to Sandhurst Town three months later.

During his time at Yorktown Road, he was Fizzers' joint top scorer along with Peter Mulvaney in 2002–03 (31 goals) and the top scorer in his own right in 2003–04 (20 goals) and 2004–05 (39 goals). The latter tally also won him the Combined Counties League Golden Boot, and his overall tally that season in all competitions was 60 goals.

Having scored more than 250 goals for Sandhurst Town, Mark rejoined Bracknell in July 2006 and was their top scorer that season (23 goals). A move to Godalming Town followed in July 2007 and he scored three goals in his first three games, including two debut strikes against Farnborough on the opening day of the season. Having scored six goals for the Gs, Mark joined Fleet Town in October 2007 and went on to score 21 goals in 47 appearances in what could be described as a 'busy' 2007–08 season.

The Blues finished as runners-up to Farnborough in Southern League Division One South and West before losing to Uxbridge in the resultant Play-off semi-final. They then experienced treble Cup Final joy, as New Milton Town were beaten to win the Russell Cotes Cup, Alresford Town were defeated to claim the Basingstoke Senior Cup and Badshot Lea were overturned to win the Aldershot Senior Cup. Fleet's only Final defeat of the season came against Tadley Calleva in the North Hants Cup.

Phil Anderson **Defender**

Born: 1 March 1987, Upney.

Aldershot Town FC record:

Debut:	as substitute v Gravesend and Northfleet (h), Conference National, 12 August 2006.
Last appearance:	v Fleet Town (at AFC Bournemouth), Hampshire Senior Cup Final, 5 May 2007.
Appearances:	12 + 8

Playing career:
Southend United (trainee, July 2003), Aldershot Town (August 2006), Thurrock (summer 2007).

Club honours:
Hampshire Senior Cup (Aldershot Town 2007).

Phil could play at centre-back but performed better as a left-back. He worked his way up through the youth and reserve teams at Southend United but never made a first-team appearance. He joined Aldershot Town on trial in

July 2006, was awarded a contract shortly afterwards and played sporadically during the season. Having appeared in the Shots' victory over Fleet Town in the 2007 Hampshire Senior Cup Final, Phil was released and subsequently joined Thurrock, who finished the 2007–08 season in 12th place in the Conference South.

Paul Andrews — Left-back/Centre-back

Born: 3 December 1983, Frimley.

Aldershot Town FC record:

Debut: as substitute v Cheshunt (a), Isthmian League Cup second round, 19 November 2002.
Appearances: 0 + 1

Playing career:

Aldershot Town (youth), Uxbridge (January 2003), Aldershot Town (trial, July 2003), Holmer Green (summer 2004), Flackwell Heath (February 2005), Bisley (August 2005), Farnborough (July 2007), Guildford City (September 2007).

Club honours:

Hellenic League Division One East (Bisley 2006–07).

Paul was a youth-team player whose sole appearance for the Shots was in November 2002. A couple of months later, he joined Uxbridge before returning to the Rec in the summer of 2003 as a trialist.

He signed for Holmer Green in the summer of 2004 before moving to Flackwell Heath and then Bisley, where he was captain during their 2006–07 Hellenic League Division One East title-winning season.

He joined the newly formed Farnborough FC in July 2007 and, despite scoring on his debut against Bridgwater Town, found that his first-team opportunities were limited. As a result of this, he joined Guildford City a couple of months later and was a member of the side that finished the season as runners-up to Merstham in the Combined Counties League Premier Division.

Wayne Andrews — Forward

Born: 25 November 1977, Paddington.

Aldershot Town FC record:

Debut: v Aylesbury United (h), Isthmian League Premier Division, 19 February 2000.
Last appearance: v Harrow Borough (h), Isthmian League Premier Division, 6 March 2001.
Appearances: 34 + 12
Goals: 12

Playing career:

Watford (from trainee, July 1996), Cambridge United (1ML, October 1998), Peterborough United (2ML, February 1999), St Albans City (July 1999), Aldershot Town (February 2000), Chesham United (August 2001), Oldham Athletic (May 2002), Colchester United (July 2003), Crystal Palace (August 2004), Coventry City (June 2006), Sheffield Wednesday (1ML, November 2006), Bristol City (2ML, January 2007), Leeds United (1ML) (October 2007), Bristol Rovers (1ML, March 2008).
Wayne has made 221 Football League appearances, scoring 45 goals.

On his day, Wayne could scare defences when running at full tilt towards them. However, he sometimes failed to 'produce' when in vital areas.

Wayne started as a trainee at Watford and signed full pro forms in July 1996, making his debut as a substitute against AFC Bournemouth the following month. Unfortunately, his progress was halted when he broke his ankle, which caused him to miss the rest of the season. A one-month loan spell at Cambridge United in October 1998 was followed by a two-month loan spell at Barry Fry's Peterborough United in February 1999.

Wayne's impact at London Road was immediate, as he scored four goals on his debut in a televised match against Barnet. He was released by Watford at the end of the 1998–99 season and joined St Albans City, scoring 16 goals in his first 27 games before joining Aldershot Town with teammate Simon Ullathorne in February 2000. Wayne formed a good partnership with Gary Abbott, but his performances became inconsistent and he was sold to Chesham United for £3,000 in August 2001. His 26 goals in his only season at the Meadow not only made him the club's top scorer but also brought him to the attention of Oldham Athletic, who were managed by Iain Dowie (brother of Chesham manager Bob). An agreement between the brothers saw Wayne move up to Lancashire in May 2002, and his 11 goals in the 2002–03 season helped the Latics reach the Play-off semi-finals before losing to Queen's Park Rangers.

In September 2004, after a year's spell with Colchester United, he was reunited with Iain Dowie (this time at FA Premier League new boys Crystal Palace) in a swap deal involving Gareth Williams, but his time at Selhurst Park was disappointing, with the Eagles being relegated that season and beaten by Watford in the following season's Championship Play-off semi-finals.

Wayne moved on to Coventry City in June 2006, but limited opportunities saw him loaned out to Sheffield Wednesday, Bristol City and Leeds United. In March 2008 Coventry announced that Wayne was one of a number of players to be released at the end of season, so he was allowed to join Bristol Rovers on loan until the end of the season. Unfortunately, he was stretchered off with a knee ligament injury after just 17 minutes of his debut against Yeovil Town and did not play again that season. In total, Wayne played just 10 League and Cup games that season but failed to score in any of them. At the time of writing, it is believed that Wayne is without a club.

Aside from playing football, Wayne has tried his hand at acting and had a minor role in the 2001 film *Mean Machine* alongside footballer-turned-actor Vinnie Jones.

Darren Angell — Centre-back

Born: 19 January 1967, Marlborough.

Aldershot Town FC record:

Debut: v Egham Town (a), Isthmian League Division Two, 22 January 1994.
Last appearance: v Malden Vale (h), Isthmian League Division Two, 19 April 1994.
Appearances: 15
Goals: 2

Playing career:
Reading (youth), Newbury Town (summer 1983), Portsmouth (June 1985), Colchester United (1ML, December 1987), Cheltenham Town (February 1988), Lincoln City (July 1988), Barnet (September 1988), Staines Town (1ML, March 1989), Chesham United (July 1989), Kintbury Rangers (summer 1990), Hungerford Town (player-coach, September 1993), Aldershot Town (January 1994).
Darren has made one Football League appearance.

Representative honours:
Berkshire Youth, Isthmian League XI.

Post-playing coaching/management career:
Coach at Hungerford Town (August 1994), manager of Kintbury Rangers (summer 2006).

Towering centre-back Darren is the older brother of ex-Stockport County scoring legend Brett Angell and the younger brother of ex-Newbury Town right-back Warren. He started as a youth player at Reading and then moved to Newbury Town before joining brother Brett at Portsmouth in June 1985.

In December 1987 he joined Colchester United on a month's loan but got injured after half an hour of his debut against Tranmere Rovers. He moved to Conference outfit Cheltenham Town in February 1988 and played there for the remainder of the season before moving to Lincoln City for a brief stint and then on to Barnet in September 1988. A month's loan at Staines Town was followed by a move to Chesham United in July 1989 and then a summer 1990 move to Hellenic League side Kintbury Rangers.

Darren took on the role of player-coach at Hungerford Town in September 1993 and moved to Aldershot Town in January 1994, having impressed while playing against the Shots earlier in the season. His appearances for the Shots were restricted by injury, but he still contributed to the club being promoted from Isthmian League Division Two before retiring just prior to the start of the following season.

He went back to Hungerford Town as coach in August 1994 before returning to Kintbury Rangers as manager in the summer of 2006. Darren resigned from his post a year later and currently works as a bricklayer.

Will Antwi — Right-back/Centre-back/Midfielder

Born: 19 October 1982, Ashford, Kent.

Aldershot Town FC record:

Debut: v Northwich Victoria (a), Conference, 3 January 2004.
Last appearance: v Carlisle United (a), Conference National Play-off semi-final second leg, 6 May 2005.
Appearances: 56 + 10

Playing career:

Crystal Palace (from trainee, July 2002), Queen's Park Rangers (trial, May 2003), Wycombe Wanderers (trial, July 2003), Ljungskile SK (Sweden, July 2003), Aldershot Town (January 2004), Wycombe Wanderers (June 2005).
Will has made 46 Football League appearances, scoring one goal.

Representative honours:

Ghana Under-23 (one cap), Ghana full international (one cap).

Will started as a trainee at Crystal Palace, signing full contract forms in July 2002. He made his debut as a substitute in a 7–0 demolition of Cheltenham Town in a League Cup tie in October of that year but found his first-team opportunities few and far between in South London. However, that did not prevent him from winning his sole cap for Ghana against Nigeria in the LG Four Nation Tournament in May 2003. Strangely, this came just two weeks after his sole Under-23 cap.

Will was released by Palace in May 2003 and had pre-season trials at Queen's Park Rangers and Wycombe Wanderers before a three-month spell playing for Swedish Second Division side Ljungskile SK. Although Will is not renowned as a goalscorer, his time in Scandinavia yielded seven goals from 10 games.

He returned to the UK, but FIFA's registration rules meant that that he could not sign for another club until the year was out. He duly signed for Aldershot Town on 1 January, and his versatility allowed him to fill the right-back, centre-back and defensive midfielder roles in the sides that lost to Hednesford Town over two legs in the 2003–04 FA Trophy semi-finals and the side that lost that season's Conference Play-off Final on penalties to Shrewsbury Town (Will scored the winning penalty in the semi-final shoot-out victory over Hereford United). The attendance of 19,216 for the latter game is a record for a non-Wembley-staged Conference Play-off Final.

Will made a slow start to the 2004–05 season, but his form improved noticeably as a result of Terry Brown transfer-listing him towards the end of the year. This upturn in form contributed greatly to the Shots reaching the Conference National Play-offs before losing on penalties to Carlisle United in the two-leg semi-final. In fact, Will's form had improved so much that it paved the way for a move to Wycombe Wanderers in June 2005. Unfortunately, he picked up a groin injury shortly after joining and did not make his debut until the following April.

Will's injury jinx struck again on New Year's Day 2007 when he was injured against Hereford United. He struggled through to the League Cup semi-final against Chelsea later that month, but that was where his season ended and he did not play again until October 2007, being named as captain on his return. Will got injured again in the December and made just five appearances all season (the last one coming at the end of April) as Wycombe finished seventh in League Two and then lost to Stockport County in the Play-off semi-finals.

Lovelace Asare — Left-back

Born: 15 August 1983, London.

Aldershot Town FC record:

Debut: v Slough Town (a), Isthmian League Full Members' Cup first round, 24 October 2000.
Last appearance: v Newport, Isle of Wight, (a), Hampshire Senior Cup second round, 15 November 2000.
Appearances: 2

Playing career:

Tooting and Mitcham United (youth), Aldershot Town (youth, summer 2000), Egham Town (August 2002), Clapton, AFC Hornchurch (2005–06 season).

Lovelace started as a youth player at Tooting and Mitcham before joining the Shots' youth side in the summer of 2000. He played youth and reserve-team football before making two first-team appearances in 2000–01. He moved to Egham Town in August 2002 and later played for Clapton before spending part of the 2005–06 season at AFC Hornchurch. Nothing else is known about Lovelace's career or current whereabouts.

Jon Ashwood — Goalkeeper

Born: 15 May 1985, Ashford, Middlesex.

Aldershot Town FC record:

Debut: v Corinthian-Casuals (h), Isthmian League Cup third round, 27 February 2002.
Last appearance: v Brockenhurst (h), Hampshire Senior Cup second round, 21 October 2003.
Appearances: 2

Playing career:
Chelsea (youth), Wimbledon (youth), Millwall (youth trial), Wigan Athletic (youth trial), Portsmouth (youth trial), Cove (youth), Aldershot Town (youth), Camberley Town (1ML, April 2003), Metropolitan Police (1ML, September 2003), Farnborough Town (February 2004), Harrow Borough (October 2004), Cove (February 2005), Farnborough Town (March 2005), Kingstonian (September 2005), Molesey (October 2005), Hayes (trial, July 2006), Uxbridge (August 2006), Ash United (October 2006), Beaconsfield SYCOB (December 2006), Molesey (summer 2007).

Representative honours:
Isthmian League XI.

Club honours:
Hampshire Senior Cup (Aldershot Town 2002 [unused substitute]), Isthmian League Charity Shield (Aldershot Town 2003 [unused substitute]).

Jon was a young 'keeper who played for the youth teams at Chelsea, Wimbledon and Cove as well as having youth trials at Millwall, Wigan Athletic and Portsmouth before coming to the Rec. He made his first-team debut for the Shots at the end of February 2002 before being loaned out to Camberley Town in April 2003. He was an unused substitute in the Shots' first-ever Conference game against Accrington Stanley in August 2003 before moving to Metropolitan Police on a one-month loan the following month.

In February 2004 Jon joined Farnborough Town on a month's loan, signing permanently the following month. Moves to Harrow Borough and Cove preceded him returning to Cherrywood Road in March 2005. However, he played just once before making a solitary appearance for Kingstonian and then joining Molesey in October 2005.

Jon left Walton Road at the end of the 2005–06 season and trialled at Hayes before signing for Uxbridge in August 2006. He moved to Ash United two months later and then Beaconsfield SYCOB a couple of months after that. That season ended in disappointment for Jon, as the Rams were relegated, and he left shortly afterwards to rejoin Molesey. Unfortunately, the Moles finished rock bottom of Isthmian League Division One South and were relegated in 2007–08.

Danny Bailey — Midfielder

Born: 25 March 1982, Aldershot.

Aldershot Town FC record:

Debut: as substitute v Worthing (a), Isthmian League Full Members' Cup second round, 2 February 1999.
Appearances: 0 + 1

Playing career:
Aldershot Town (youth), AFC Guildford (2003–04 season), Badshot Lea (summer 2005).

Club honours:
Combined Counties League Division One (AFC Guildford 2003–04), Hellenic League Supplementary Cup (Badshot Lea 2006).

The son of ex-Aldershot Town director Aiden Whelan, Danny is a young midfielder with a sweet left foot who was involved at the Rec as early as the 1992–93 season, when he was playing for the Shots' colts side. As he got older, he captained the youth team and made his only senior appearance during 1998–99. He left the Rec during the 2002–03 season, taking some time out of the game. On his return he played for AFC Guildford and Badshot Lea, helping the latter club gain promotion to the Hellenic League Premier Division in 2006–07 and to finish in 11th place in that League in 2007–08. The club were also runners-up to Fleet Town in the Aldershot Senior Cup Final that season.

Keith Baker — Defender

Born: 19 February 1955, Hounslow.

Aldershot Town FC record:

Debut: v Clapton (h), Isthmian League Division Three, 22 August 1992.
Last appearance: v Barking (a), Isthmian League Division One, 7 January 1995.
Appearances: 137
Goals: 2

Playing career:
Crystal Palace (youth trial), Fulham (youth trial), Ipswich Town (youth trial), Hounslow Town (August 1971), Ruislip Manor (August 1972), Leyton Orient (trial, March 1973), Molesey (August 1973), Southall and Ealing Borough (December 1975), Staines Town (August 1977), Egham Town (November 1978), Farnborough Town (September 1984), Egham Town (summer 1988), Farnborough Town (March 1989), Chesham United (summer 1989), Farnborough Town (December 1990), Aldershot Town (player-assistant manager, July 1992), Farnborough Town (January 1995), Fleet Town (August 1996).

Representative honours:
Isthmian League XI.

Club honours:
Isthmian League Division One (Farnborough Town 1984–85), Hampshire Senior Cup (Farnborough Town 1986, 1991), Southern League Premier Division (Farnborough Town 1990–91), Isthmian League Division Three (Aldershot Town 1992–93).

Keith was a very experienced and popular defender within the footballing community and is the father of ex-Shots defender Neil Baker. Having had youth trials at Crystal Palace, Fulham and Ipswich Town, he signed as a youth player at Hounslow Town in August 1971 and had his debut for them as a 16–year-old. Keith stayed for a year before joining Ruislip Manor, trialling at Leyton Orient and signing for Molesey in August 1973. He then played for Southall and Ealing Borough, Staines Town and Egham Town before joining Farnborough Town in September 1984, and Keith's experience and calmness was a major factor in them winning the Isthmian League Division One in his first season.

He left Cherrywood Road to rejoin Egham in the summer of 1988 but returned the following March and helped the club reach the Conference for the first time in their history at the end of the season. Although they had finished as runners-up to Leytonstone and Ilford in the Isthmian League Premier Division, Boro were promoted because the Essex side's ground failed to meet the Conference's grading criteria.

That summer, Keith joined Chesham United and stayed until December 1990 when he re-signed for Farnborough. Again, he played a major part in a title-winning side – the Southern League Premier Division – and was also in the Boro side that took First Division West Ham United to a replay (which the Hammers won 1–0) in the FA Cup third round in January 1992. Earlier in that run, he had been part of television history (along with Brian Broome, Danny Holmes and Jamie Horton) when Boro's second-round replay victory over Division Three strugglers Torquay United became the first-ever FA Cup tie televised by the now ubiquitous Sky Sports.

When Aldershot Town were formed in 1992, Keith joined as player-assistant manager and wore the number-six shirt in the club's first-ever game against Clapton. Not for the first time in his career, his influence that season resulted in a League title being won, and he was central to the Shots reaching the FA Vase quarter-final and getting promoted again the following season, as well as being the joint winner of the Player of the Year award with Steve Harris.

The 1993–94 season also yielded a record for Keith, as he became the oldest-ever Shots goalscorer (39 years and 35 days) against Leatherhead in March. Keith returned to Cherrywood Road for a fourth spell in January 1995 before joining Fleet Town in August 1996. His stay at Calthorpe Park was short-lived though, as he decided to hang up his boots after playing some pre-season friendlies.

Keith currently works as a cabin steward for a well-known airline.

Neil Baker — Centre-back

Born: 4 September 1979, Ashford, Middlesex.

Aldershot Town FC record:

Debut:	v Aylesbury United (a), Isthmian League Premier Division, 7 September 1999.
Last appearance:	v Carshalton Athletic (a), Isthmian League Premier Division, 6 May 2000.
Appearances:	17 + 6
Goals:	1

Playing career:

Southampton (youth), Wycombe Wanderers (trainee, July 1996), Farnborough Town (March 1997), Aldershot Town (July 1999), Boreham Wood (July 2000), Sutton United (December 2000), Bracknell Town (July 2001), Portland Timbers (US, trial, January 2003), Bracknell Town (March 2003), Sandhurst Town (March 2007), Leatherhead (June 2007), Bracknell Town (October 2007).

Club honours:

Hampshire Senior Cup (Aldershot Town 2000), Isthmian League Division One (Boreham Wood 2000–01).

Neil is a centre-back who began playing at Southampton at the age of 12. From there, he joined Wycombe Wanderers as a trainee in July 1996 and then Farnborough Town in March 1997. Neil was part of the Boro side that lost the two-leg Conference League Cup Final to Doncaster Rovers in May 1999 before marking his arrival at the Rec with an own-goal on his debut two months later.

Neil did not get the run in the team that he might have hoped for, so it was not too surprising that he left to join Boreham Wood the following summer. His stay there only lasted until the December (when he joined Sutton United), but he still managed to play enough games there to be awarded a medal in respect of the Wood winning the Isthmian League Division One title.

He performed steadily at Gander Green Lane but left in the summer of 2001 to begin his association with Bracknell Town. The Robins finished in fourth spot in the Isthmian League that season, gaining them a place in the Isthmian League Division One South when the League was restructured.

In January 2003 Neil's work commitments took him to America, where he trialled at USL side Portland Timbers. He returned home after two months whereupon he immediately re-signed for Bracknell and was appointed captain. He remained at Larges Lane until March 2007 when he joined Berkshire neighbours Sandhurst Town, but his stay lasted just two games before he left.

Neil signed for Leatherhead in June 2007 and was appointed as captain but was affected by a change of management in the October so left to re-sign for Bracknell Town. Reappointed as captain, it was hoped that Neil could help turn the club's fortunes around as, at the time of his rejoining, the Robins had drawn three and lost eight of their opening 11 Southern League Division One South and West games! Despite being troubled by injury, Neil contributed six goals to the cause; however, he could not prevent the club from struggling for the rest of the season, as 20th place was secured, with the margin of survival being a mere two points!

Umarr Bangura — Left-back

Born: 18 July 1983, Freetown, Sierra Leone.

Aldershot Town FC record:

Debut:	v Forest Green Rovers (a), Conference Challenge Cup Southern Section quarter-final, 15 February 2005.
Appearances:	1

Playing career:

Chertsey Town, Harrow Borough, Aldershot Town (NC, February 2005).

Umarr was one of those players who left Aldershot Town almost as soon as they arrived! Very little was known about him prior to his arrival (other than that he had reportedly played for Chertsey Town and Harrow Borough), and even less is known of him since his departure.

Joe Banks — Midfielder

Born: 26 January 1981, Bracknell.

Aldershot Town FC record:

Debut:	as substitute v Worthing (a), Isthmian League Full Members' Cup second round, 2 February 1999.
Appearances:	0 + 1

Playing career:
Aldershot Town (youth), Cove, Fleet Town (October 2002), Farnham Town (2006–07 season).

Joe is one of a number of youth players to have made a first-team appearance for Aldershot Town in what were often considered to be 'minor' Cup competitions. Following his sole Shots appearance, he went on to play for Cove, Fleet Town and Farnham Town. The latter finished the 2007–08 season in fifth place in the Combined Counties League Division One, but it is not known whether Joe remained at the Memorial Ground for the entire season.

Darren Barnard — Left-back

Born: 30 November 1971, Rinteln, Germany.

Aldershot Town FC record:

Debut:	v York City (h), Conference National, 14 August 2004.
Last appearance:	v Fleet Town (at AFC Bournemouth), Hampshire Senior Cup Final, 5 May 2007.
Appearances:	121 + 5
Goals:	23

Playing career:
Wokingham Town (August 1988), Chelsea (July 1990), Reading (1ML) (November 1994), Bristol City (October 1995), Barnsley (August 1997), Northampton Town (trial, July 2002), Grimsby Town (August 2002), Kilmarnock (trial, July 2004), Mansfield Town (trial, July 2004), Aldershot Town (August 2004), Camberley Town (July 2007; player-director of football).
Darren has made 344 FA Premier League and Football League appearances, scoring 49 goals.

Representative honours:
Aldershot, Farnborough and District Schoolboys, England Schoolboys, England Under-18s (eight caps, one goal), Isthmian League XI, Wales full international (22 caps), Wales Non-League XI (two caps).

Club honours:
Hampshire Senior Cup (Aldershot Town 2007).

Darren brought a wealth of experience (as well as a cultured left foot) to the left-back position for the Shots. He started as a youth-team player with his local club Wokingham Town, where his manager was Terry Brown, who would later sign him for the Shots.

Having helped the Town to the runners'-up spot in the Isthmian League Premier Division in 1989–90, Darren joined Chelsea for a fee of £100,000 (a record for a Wokingham sale). However, he had to wait nearly two years to make his debut, doing so as a substitute against West Ham United in April 1992. He adapted well to top-flight football (despite often being played out of position) but was never a regular.

Following a one-month loan at Reading (during an 18-month period in which he did not play a first-team game for Chelsea), Darren joined Bristol City for £175,000 in October 1995 and was part of the squad that reached the Division Two Play-offs in 1996–97 (where they lost to Brentford) before moving to FA Premier League new boys Barnsley for £750,000 in August 1997. Many observers would say that this move was the turning point of Darren's career, as it led to him making his full international debut for Wales against Jamaica in March 1998. However, his first season at Oakwell was to end with the disappointment of relegation. Furthermore, he had an accident that has been mentioned in several 'strange injury' listings over the years: having already been out for three months with a knee ligament problem, he aggravated the injury when he slipped in a puddle of his puppy's urine, which put him out for a further two months! With those two 'events' behind him, Darren was an integral part of the much-improved Barnsley side that lost the 1999–2000 Division One Play-off Final to Ipswich Town before suffering his second relegation with the Yorkshire side the following season.

Darren joined Grimsby Town in August 2002, but his luck did not improve, as he endured successive relegations with the Mariners in 2002–03 and 2003–04, after which he left Blundell Park. He won the last of his 22 caps for Wales in a friendly against Norway in May 2004 before joining Aldershot Town in the August, after trials at Kilmarnock and Mansfield.

Darren contributed some spectacular long-range goals for the Shots, a good proportion of which came from set-pieces. One such goal gave the Shots a last-minute victory in the local derby against Woking in August 2004. He immediately became a crowd favourite, and his goal haul that season helped the club reach the Conference National Play-off semi-finals. That summer, he won two Wales non-League XI caps (both as captain), thus becoming the only Shots player to captain Wales at that level.

Despite having suffered from the condition known as Gilmore's Groin for some time, Darren continued to play and was an integral part in the Shots' best-ever FA Cup run in 2006–07, when they reached the third round before being beaten by League One side Blackpool.

In July 2007 Darren joined Combined Counties League Premier Division side Camberley Town in the role of player-director of football, and he contributed 13 goals in all competitions as the Krooners finished the season in third place. When he is not playing his 'regular' football, Darren partcipates on the 'masters' circuit.

Richard Barnard — Goalkeeper

Born: 27 December 1980, Frimley.

Aldershot Town FC record:

Debut: v Yeading (h), Isthmian League Charity Shield, 19 August 2003.
Last appearance: v Wycombe Wanderers (h), LDV Vans Trophy Southern Section first round, 28 September 2004.
Appearances: 28 + 4

Playing career:

Aldershot Town (youth), Millwall (from trainee, May 1999), Hereford United (trial, August 2000), Bristol Rovers (trial, August 2000), Maidenhead United (August 2000), Aldershot Town (June 2003), Queen of the South (November 2004), Sutton United (trial, July 2006), Crawley Town (trial, October 2006), Slough Town (September 2007; player-caretaker assistant manager from November 2007; player-assistant manager from January 2008), Carshalton Athletic (March 2008).
Richard has made 29 Scottish League appearances.

Representative honours:

England Under-17s.

Club honours:

Berks and Bucks Senior Cup (Maidenhead United 2002, 2003), Isthmian League Charity Shield (Aldershot Town 2003).

Richard began his career as a youth-team player at Aldershot Town before becoming a trainee at Millwall. Following his release from the Den, he trialled at Hereford United before signing for Maidenhead United in August 2000. He always played well against the Shots, so the fans knew what to expect when he came to the Rec in June 2003 in preparation for the club's debut season in the Conference. That season, he was a member of the Shots side that lost to Hednesford Town in the FA Trophy semi-finals, as well as being an unused substitute when the Shots lost in the Conference Play-off Final.

By October 2004 Richard was finding his first-team chances limited due to the excellent form of Nikki Bull. In addition to this, he was planning to move to Scotland for personal reasons, so he asked to be released from his contract. Despite speculation that Scottish First Division outfit St Johnstone were interested in signing him, he joined their divisional rivals Queen of the South in the November. He spent two seasons there before leaving in the summer of 2006, trialling at Sutton United and Crawley Town. Richard was hoping to sign for Crawley but fate dealt him a cruel blow, as he broke his leg in training a week before the season started and subsequently missed the entire campaign.

In August 2007 Richard joined Slough Town but missed his scheduled debut due to being stuck in traffic! Three months later, the club were already struggling near the foot of the Southern League Division One South and West table, which resulted in the double resignation of manager Darren Wilkinson and his assistant Nick Roddis. Richard then took up the role of player-caretaker assistant manager to caretaker manager Mark Betts, with both being appointed permanently towards the end of January 2008. However, despite their best efforts, Slough continued to struggle (they eventually finished 21st but escaped relegation thanks to Halifax Town's expulsion from the Conference Premier) and both incumbents left in March 2008.

Richard joined Carshalton Athletic and helped them with a 2–0 victory over Tonbridge Angels on the final day of the season, securing their place in the Isthmian League Premier Division on goal difference.

Matthew Barnes-Homer — Midfielder

Born: 25 January 1986, Dudley.

Aldershot Town FC record:

Debut: as substitute v Hereford United (a), Conference, 21 September 2004.
Last appearance: v Wycombe Wanderers (h), LDV Vans Trophy Southern Section first round, 28 September 2004.
Appearances: 1 + 2

Playing career:
Wolverhampton Wanderers (trainee, July 2002), Syracuse Salty Dogs (US) (April 2004), Aldershot Town (NC, September 2004), Virginia Beach Mariners (US) (December 2004), Hednesford Town (February 2005), Bromsgrove Rovers (April 2005), Tividale (February 2006), Willenhall Town (August 2006), Wycombe Wanderers (March 2007), Kidderminster Harriers (August 2007).
Matthew has made one Football League appearance.

Matthew spent two years as a trainee at Wolverhampton Wanderers, playing regularly in their reserve side during the 2003–04 season before joining the quirkily named Syracuse Salty Dogs in the American A-League. He returned to the UK in September 2004 and signed for the Shots, but probably the only memory that Shots fans will have of him is his gold-coloured boots! He left the Shots after making just three appearances and went back to the A-League with Virginia Beach Mariners before returning to the UK and trialling at a number of clubs.

Matthew signed and played only one game for Hednesford Town in February 2005 before joining Bromsgrove Rovers in the April, scoring on his debut against Brackley Town. Spells at Tividale and Willenhall Town followed before he trialled at Wycombe Wanderers, signing permanently in March 2007. He made just one substitute appearance (against Bristol Rovers) before being released and signing for Kidderminster Harriers in the August.

Matthew scored six goals in the 2007–08 season (including the third-minute opener against the Shots at the Rec in March) as the Harriers finished in 13th spot.

Trevor Baron — Defender

Born: 27 April 1959, Slough.

Aldershot Town FC record:

Debut: v Bracknell Town (a), Isthmian League Division Three, 13 March 1993.
Last appearance: v Farnborough Town (h), Hampshire Cup semi-final, 16 March 1993.
Appearances: 2
Goals: 1

Playing career:
Chertsey Town (August 1975), Burnham (August 1977), Marlow (August 1979), Windsor and Eton (March 1981), Slough Town (August 1984), Windsor and Eton (December 1984), Woking (January 1986), Aldershot Town (1ML, March 1993), Marlow (August 1993), Slough Town (June 1994), Woking (March 1996), Walton and Hersham (July 1996), Chesham United (player-coach, summer 1999), Windsor and Eton (player-assistant manager, August 2000), Wokingham Town (player-caretaker manager, March 2003; left May 2003).

Representative honours:
Isthmian League XI.

Club honours:
Isthmian League Division One (Windsor and Eton 1983–84), Isthmian League Cup (Woking 1991), Isthmian League Premier Division (Woking 1991–92), Isthmian League Charity Shield (Woking 1991, 1992), Berks and Bucks Senior Cup (Marlow 1994), Surrey Senior Cup (Woking 1996).

Post-playing coaching/management career:
Joint caretaker manager of Walton and Hersham (December 1998 to March 1999), assistant manager of Flackwell Heath (May 2001), joint caretaker manager of Flackwell Heath (April 2002), assistant manager of Wokingham Town (June 2002).

Trevor spent his early years at Chertsey Town, Burnham and Marlow before joining Geoff Chapple's Windsor and Eton in March 1981, where his strength in the air and calmness on the ball contributed greatly to the club winning the Isthmian League Division One title in 1983–84.

A brief spell at Slough Town followed before he returned to Stag Meadow, going on to make more than 200 appearances for the Royalists.

In January 1986 he was reunited with Chapple when he joined Woking, where he became hugely popular with the fans during his 360-plus appearances. During his time at Kingfield, the club finished the 1989–90 season as Isthmian League Division One runners-up (to Wivenhoe Town) and also reached the fourth round of the 1990–91 FA Cup, where they lost 1–0 to First Division Everton. During that run, the Cards defeated Conference sides Bath City, Kidderminster Harriers and Merthyr Tydfil before famously beating Second Division West Bromwich Albion, which led to the sacking of Albion manager (and future Aldershot FC boss) Brian Talbot. Trevor was also a key member of the sides that won the Isthmian League Premier Division in 1991–92 and the Charity Shield in 1992 (a game in which Trevor scored twice against Redbridge Forest).

In March 1993 Trevor joined Aldershot Town on a one-month loan and scored on his debut against Bracknell Town, thus becoming the first loanee to make a scoring debut. Unfortunately, he sustained a knee ligament injury in the second game of this spell and missed the remainder of the season.

Having recovered from his injury, Trevor joined Marlow in the summer of 1993 and ended the season as Blues' Player of the Year and a winner in the Berks and Bucks Senior Cup Final. Again, he won the Player of the Year award in 1994 after rejoining Slough and making a significant contribution as they gained Conference status.

Trevor returned to Kingfield in March 1996 and helped the Cards finish as runners-up to Stevenage Borough in that season's Conference before joining Walton and Hersham in the summer. He captained Walton to promotion to the Isthmian League Premier Division that season before his time at Stompond Lane sadly ended in September 1988 when he ruptured his achilles tendon and was forced to retire. In December of that year, he took up the role of joint caretaker manager of the Swans with Mark Hill – a role he carried out until March 1999. That summer, he briefly came out of retirement and joined Chesham United as player-coach but retired again in the September due to ongoing problems with his achilles.

In August 2000 Trevor again came out of retirement to join Windsor and Eton as player-assistant manager, and he was inspirational in securing promotion. In May 2001 he undertook the role of assistant manager to Neil Catlin at Flackwell Heath and then, when Catlin resigned the following summer, took on the role of joint caretaker manager with Mark Fiore until June 2002, when he resumed his working relationship with Catlin (this time at Wokingham Town). With the club lurching from crisis to crisis, Catlin resigned in March 2003 and Trevor took on the mantle of player-caretaker manager for the rest of the season. Trevor retired that summer and currently works as a courier.

David Bass — Midfielder

Born: 29 November 1974, Frimley.

Aldershot Town FC record:

Debut:	v Billericay Town (h), Isthmian League Division One, 18 August 1994.
Last appearance:	v Whyteleafe (a), Isthmian League Division One, 10 October 1994.
Appearances:	13
Goals:	6

Playing career:
Reading (from trainee, July 1993), Aldershot Town (2ML, August 1994), Basingstoke Town (1ML, August 1996), Rotherham United (July 1997), Farnborough Town (1ML, February 1999), Carlisle United (March 1999), Scarborough (August 1999), Stevenage Borough (1ML, April 2000), Kingstonian (August 2000), Hitchin Town (November 2001).
David has made 38 Football League appearances.

David was a very talented midfielder who made his senior debut for Reading as a substitute against AFC Bournemouth while still a trainee. He signed full professional forms at Reading in July 1993 and joined Aldershot Town on a two-month loan in August 1994, with his class being immediately apparent. However, his loan spell was cut short by a cruciate ligament injury that he sustained against Whyteleafe in the October. Once recovered, he struggled to get back into the Reading first team and was eventually released after being loaned to Basingstoke Town in August 1996.

In July 1997 David signed for Rotherham United but played less than 20 games for the Millers before being loaned to Farnborough Town and then joining Carlisle United in March 1999. He only stayed at Brunton Park for five months before moving on to Conference side Scarborough.

David moved to fellow Conference side Stevenage Borough on a month's loan in April 2000 before trialling at and signing for Kingstonian in the August. While at Kingsmeadow, he was part of the Ks side that took Division Two side Bristol City to a replay in the fourth round of the 2000–01 FA Cup.

He joined Hitchin Town in November 2001 and was appointed as captain for the season, but injury continued to limit his appearances. He was appointed as Hitchin's football in the community officer in October 2002, a role he combined with that of scholarship scheme coach at Top Field.

David eventually had to admit defeat in his battle against injury and so retired from playing in the summer of 2003. He currently works as a lecturer at a college in Hertfordshire.

Simon Bassey — Midfielder

Born: 5 February 1976, Lambeth.

Aldershot Town FC record:

Debut:	v Worthing (h), Isthmian League Division One, 6 December 1997.
Last appearance:	v Hitchin Town (a), Isthmian League Premier Division, 11 March 2000.
Appearances:	41 + 8
Goals:	1

Playing career:
Charlton Athletic (trainee, July 1992), Carshalton Athletic (August 1994), Aldershot Town (December 1997), Carshalton Athletic (July 2000), Dulwich Hamlet (October 2000), Carshalton Athletic (July 2001), Crawley Town (January 2002), Tooting and Mitcham United (February 2002), AFC Wimbledon (August 2002).

Club honours:
Isthmian League Division One (Aldershot Town 1997–98), Combined Counties League Premier Division (AFC Wimbledon 2003–04).

Post-playing coaching/management career:
Reserve-team coach at AFC Wimbledon (summer 2005), first-team coach at AFC Wimbledon (May 2007).

Simon was a combative central-midfielder who could also play at full-back. He started out as a trainee at Charlton Athletic before signing for Carshalton Athletic in August 1994.

In December 1997 he signed for the Shots and his tenacity played a big part in securing the Isthmian League Division One title that season. He sustained a bad knee injury in only the third League match of the 1998–99 season (against Gravesend and Northfleet) and did not play again until October 1999.

Simon left the Rec in July 2000 and rejoined Carshalton Athletic but soon moved on to Dulwich Hamlet. A return to Carshalton came in July 2001, with moves to Crawley Town and Tooting and Mitcham United following soon after.

Simon's knee injury forced him to retire in the summer of 2002, but he was persuaded to reverse the decision and join the newly formed AFC Wimbledon. A strong end-of-season run saw the club finish third in the Combined

Counties League before Simon helped them win the newly designated Premier Division title the following season.

In October 2004 he was appointed as player-coach at Kingsmeadow but did not play any games in that season's Isthmian League Division One title-winning campaign. Following two further operations, he finally retired in the summer of 2005 and took up the role of reserve-team coach at Kingsmeadow. He was promoted to first-team coach under Terry Brown in May 2007 and helped achieve a third-place finish in the Isthmian League Premier Division and victory over Staines Town in the subsequent Play-off Final. Away from football, Simon works as a taxi driver.

Karl Beckford — Midfielder

Born: 4 June 1985, Lambeth.

Aldershot Town FC record:

Debut:	v Stevenage Borough (a), Conference National, 1 January 2007.
Last appearance:	as substitute v Kidderminster Harriers (a), Conference National, 17 April 2007.
Appearances:	13 + 9
Goals:	1

Playing career:

Charlton Athletic (from trainee, July 2001), Sheffield Wednesday (trial, July 2004), Gillingham (July 2004), Welling United (1ML, September 2004), Lewes (July 2005), Stevenage Borough (trial, December 2006), Aldershot Town (December 2006), AFC Wimbledon (June 2007, 2 February 2008), Bromley (1ML, March 2008).

Karl is an attacking midfielder who signed professional forms at Charlton Athletic in July 2001, having previously been a trainee. He left the Valley in the summer of 2004 and trialled with Sheffield Wednesday before joining Gillingham in the July. Brief loans followed at Welling United in September 2004 and Lewes in July 2005 (where he signed permanently) before he trialled briefly at Stevenage Borough and signed for Aldershot Town in December 2006.

Karl arrived at the Rec with a reputation as a goalscoring midfielder, and he made a scoring debut but failed to live up to his reputation after that. He was released at the end of the season and signed for Isthmian League Premier Division side AFC Wimbledon, who were managed by the Shots' immensely popular ex-boss Terry Brown.

In March 2008 Karl was loaned to Bromley for a month, before returning to Kingsmeadow and playing in the Play-off semi-final victory over AFC Hornchurch. However, he was not in the squad for the Final victory over Staines Town and was released shortly after. At present, it is believed that Karl is still looking for a club.

Steve Beeks — Midfielder

Born: 10 April 1971, Ashford, Middlesex.

Aldershot Town FC record:

Debut:	v Tooting and Mitcham United (h), Isthmian League Division One, 21 December 1996.
Last appearance:	v Carshalton Athletic (a), Isthmian League Full Members' Cup second round, 22 December 1997.
Appearances:	46 + 3
Goals:	9

Playing career:

Aldershot FC (from trainee, July 1989), Woking (August 1991), Sutton United (September 1991), Staines Town (January 1992), Egham Town (October 1996), Aldershot Town (December 1996), Basingstoke Town (January 1998), Maidenhead United (March 1999), Cove (player-manager, June 1999), AFC Totton (September 2001), Cobham (September 2001), Wokingham Town (September 2001), Fleet Town (player-manager, October 2001), Winchester City (October 2002), Frimley Green (August 2003), Molesey (player-manager, September 2003), Wraysbury (summer 2007), Godalming Town (DR, November 2007).

Steve has made three Football League appearances.

Representative honours:

Surrey Youth, Hampshire FA XI, Middlesex FA XI, Combined Counties League XI.

Club honours:
El Cañuelo Trophy (Staines Town 1993, 1995), Middlesex Senior Cup (Staines Town 1994), Middlesex Senior Charity Cup (Staines Town 1994), Isthmian League Full Members' Cup (Staines Town 1995), Isthmian League Division One (Aldershot Town 1997–98), Berks and Bucks Senior Cup (Maidenhead United 1999), Combined Counties League (Cove 2000–01), Combined Counties League Cup (Cove 2001), Southern Counties Floodlit Cup (Fleet Town 2002).

Steve is one of the elite group of seven players who have played competitively for both Aldershot clubs, the others being Colin Fielder, Brian Lucas, Steve Osgood, Paul Shrubb, Chris Tomlinson and Jason Tucker. He is primarily a midfielder but has also played at centre-back.

Steve was a trainee with Aldershot FC, signed full pro forms in July 1989 and made his senior debut as a substitute against Hereford United in May 1990. He had stints at Woking and Sutton United before joining Staines Town in January 1992, with whom he experienced relegation from the Isthmian Premier League in 1992–93 (their first relegation by virtue of League position in 63 years). He was then top scorer at Wheatsheaf Lane in 1993–94 (26 goals), 1994–95 (27 goals) and 1995–96 (24 goals), helping the club win various Cups before gaining promotion back to the Isthmian League Premier Division in the 1995–96 season and being voted Swans' Player of the Year too.

In total, Steve played 298 games for Staines and scored 81 goals before having a brief spell with Egham Town and then returning to the Rec in December 1996. While with the Shots, he played up until December 1997 in the side that would eventually win the Isthmian League Division One title. He moved on to Basingstoke Town and then had a short spell at Maidenhead United, where he scored in extra-time to secure victory over Wycombe Wanderers in the 1999 Berks and Bucks Senior Cup Final.

That summer, Steve joined Cove as player-manager and led them to the Combined Counties League and Cup double and a club-best progression to the last 16 of the FA Vase the following season. He (rather surprisingly) left Squirrels Lane that summer and played a handful of games for AFC Totton, Cobham and Wokingham Town.

In October 2001 he was appointed player-manager of Fleet Town, with success being achieved in his first season, as he guided the club to promotion from the Wessex League to the Southern League Eastern Division and to victory in the Southern Counties Floodlit Cup. He resigned in September 2002 and subsequently played for Winchester City and Frimley Green.

In September 2003 Steve got back on the managerial ladder at Isthmian League Division One South side Molesey, where he stayed until tendering his resignation in May 2007. He played for Wraysbury (in the Middlesex County League Premier Division) and Godalming Town (Southern League Division One South and West) during the 2007–08 season as well as unofficially 'managing' Ruislip Manor for a couple of games (to help them out) in the early part of that season. Godalming finished their season in 12th place while Wraysbury occupied the seventh spot in their league.

Aside from playing, Steve currently runs his own soccer school as well as being the head coach of Wealdstone's academy side.

Nicky Bell — Midfielder

Born: 18 December 1978, Reading.

Aldershot Town FC record:

Debut:	v Bromley (a), Isthmian League Full Members' Cup first round, 26 October 1999.
Last appearance:	v Abingdon Town (a), Isthmian League Cup second round, 23 November 1999.
Appearances:	2 + 3
Goals:	1

Playing career:
Nottingham Forest (youth trial), Reading (trainee, July 1995), Wokingham Town (October 1996), Fleet Town (July 1997), Aldershot Town (NC, October 1999), Burnham (September 2000), Slough Town (October 2000), Camberley Town (November 2000), Wokingham Town (March 2001).

Club honours:
Isthmian League Charity Shield (Aldershot Town 1999 [unused substitute]).

Nicky is the son of ex-Aldershot FC forward Terry Bell. He had a youth trial at Nottingham Forest (where his father began his career) before joining another of his dad's clubs as a trainee at Reading in July 1995.

Nicky moved to Wokingham Town on his release from Elm Park and then signed for Fleet Town in July 1997.

Unfortunately, injury and fatigue syndrome ended his time there in the summer of 1998, and he was out of football until he signed for the Shots in October 1999.

Sadly, Nicky's syndrome and injuries again forced him to leave the Rec. He was out of the game until he signed for Burnham the following September, but he never fully recovered from his illness. In November 2001 Nicky retired from playing just short of his 23rd birthday and currently works as an account manager for a courier company.

Steve Benitez — Forward

Born: 10 August 1969, Harlesden.

Aldershot Town FC record:

Debut:	as substitute v Horsham (h), Isthmian League Division Three, 29 August 1992.
Last appearance:	v Northwood (h), Isthmian League Division Three, 31 October 1992.
Appearances:	0 + 7

Playing career:

Brentford (schoolboy and youth), Cadiz CF (Spain)(summer 1988), Portimenence (Portugal)(summer 1990), Aldershot Town (summer 1992), ADO Den Haag (Holland), St Albans City (July 1995), Hendon (trial, October 2001), FC Hasental (US, september 2007).

Club honours:

Isthmian League Division Three (Aldershot Town 1992–93).

Steve was a forward whose career was plagued by knee and groin injuries. He played schoolboy and youth-team football at Brentford before playing for Cadiz CF in Spain (a country familiar to him due to his parentage) and Portimenence in Portugal.

He joined the newly formed Aldershot Town in the summer of 1992 and played in the majority of the Shots' pre-season games, but his seven appearances in the season 'proper' were all as a substitute. Finding his opportunities limited at the Rec due to the last-minute arrival of Steve Stairs (who had quickly formed a formidable partnership with Mark Butler), Steve left and joined Dutch side ADO Den Haag. He then played for a handful of other Dutch sides on non-contract terms. A solitary appearance for St Albans City and a trial at Hendon followed before he decided to leave his footballing career behind to concentrate on martial arts.

Since then, he has become a world famous practitioner of the Indonesian art of Pencak Silat and has attained the title of 'Pendekar' – one of few people outside Indonesia to be awarded this title. He has worked as a bodyguard for several film stars and has acted as a fight adviser and choreographer on several feature films. He also runs a health, fitness and life school studio in London and writes a regular magazine column in *Martial Arts* magazine. At present, Steve is working on an Anglo-Indonesian film project entitled *Dark Eden* and is based in southern California, where he has been playing for FC Hasental who play in the Tri County Soccer League.

Paul Bennett — Midfielder/Winger

Born: 16 January 1963, Nakuru, Kenya.

Aldershot Town FC record:

Debut:	as substitute v Clapton (h), Isthmian League Division Three, 22 August 1992.
Appearances:	0 + 1

Playing career:

Bass Alton (summer 1981), Liphook (summer 1985), Alton Town (summer 1986), Basingstoke Town (summer 1990), Aldershot Town (summer 1992), Alton Town (summer 1993), Fareham Town (October 1993), Lindford Royal Exchange (summer 1994).

Club honours:

Isthmian League Division Three (Aldershot Town 1992–93).

Paul came to the Rec in the summer of 1992 and has the distinction of being the first-ever player to make a substitute appearance for Aldershot Town, doing so wearing the number-14 shirt four minutes from the end of their first-ever game against Clapton.

With work commitments hampering his chances at the Rec, Paul went to Australia and trained with Sydney Olympic but was unfortunate to get injured virtually as soon as he got there. On his return to the UK, he rejoined Alton Town but soon signed for Fareham Town.

Paul finished his career playing lower league Saturday football for Lindford RE and local Sunday football for Barnwood and Holroyd. He retired in the summer of 2005 and currently works in the sales department of a well-known mobile phone network provider.

Mark Bentley — Midfielder

Born: 7 January 1978, Hertford.

Aldershot Town FC record:

Debut:	v Hendon (a), Isthmian League Premier Division, 14 August 1999.
Last appearance:	v Havant and Waterlooville, Hampshire Senior Cup Final (at Southampton FC), 1 May 2002.
Appearances:	105 + 9
Goals:	25

Playing career:

Enfield (from youth, August 1996), Aldershot Town (August 1999), Southampton (trial, September 1999), Crewe Alexandra (trial, March 2000), Gravesend and Northfleet (May 2002), Dagenham and Redbridge (June 2003), Southend United (January 2004), Gillingham (May 2006).

Mark has made 185 Football League appearances, scoring 21 goals.

Representative honours:

FA XI.

Club honours:

Hampshire Senior Cup (Aldershot Town 2000, 2002), Division Two Play-off Final (Southend United 2005), Division One (Southend United 2005–06).

Mark is a skilful attacking midfielder who started out as a youth player at Enfield. He signed a full contract in August 1996 and was part of the Es side that finished as runners-up in the Isthmian League Premier Division that season.

Mark signed for the Shots (under former boss George Borg) in August 1999 and made a positive contribution to the club finishing the season as runners-up in the Isthmian League Premier Division. He also scored a hat-trick in the 9–1 thrashing of Andover in that season's Hampshire Senior Cup Final. His performances caught the eye of scouts from Southampton and Crewe Alexandra, and although he had trials nothing came of them.

He represented the FA XI during the 2000–01 season (the only Shots player to do so) and won the supporters' Player of the Year in 2001. He was again voted Player of the Year in 2002 after a move to newly promoted Gravesend and Northfleet.

With Gravesend having avoided relegation by just two points, it was not surprising that Mark joined fellow Conference side Dagenham and Redbridge in the summer, where he improved sufficiently to finally make a move into the Football League in January 2004, when a £25,000 fee took him to Southend United. He was a member of the side that lost to Wrexham in the 2005 Football League Trophy Final and the side that beat Lincoln City to win that season's League Two Play-off Final. Mark followed that up the following season with a League One-winners' medal, and although he was offered a one-year contract in May 2006 he opted for the extra security of a two-year deal with Gillingham, even though it meant that he would remain in League One.

Mark scored four League goals as the Gills finished the 2006–07 season in 16th place, but things got worse for both parties in 2007–08, as he managed just two League strikes in a season that saw the club relegated by virtue of their 22nd-place finish.

Mark Biggins — Midfielder

Born: 18 April 1963, Middlesbrough.

Aldershot Town FC record:

Debut:	v AFC Lymington (h), Hampshire Senior Cup first round, 27 September 1994.

Last appearance: v Chertsey Town (a), Isthmian League Division One, 22 October 1994.
Appearances: 6

Playing career:
Hampton, Hanwell Town, Feltham, Maidenhead United (November 1984), St Albans City (December 1985), Windsor and Eton (August 1987), Woking (December 1987), Aldershot Town (September 1994), Wealdstone (December 1994), Harrow Borough (July 1995), St Albans City (December 1995), Hendon (July 1996), Hampton (December 1996), Kingstonian (January 1997), Hampton (July 1997), Ashford Town (January 1998), Carshalton Athletic (March 1998), Bedfont (July 1998).

Representative honours:
FA XI, Isthmian League XI.

Club honours:
Isthmian League Division One (St Albans City 1985–86), Hertfordshire Charity Cup (St Albans City 1987), Isthmian League Cup (Woking 1991), Surrey Senior Cup (Woking 1991), Isthmian League Premier Division (Woking 1991–92), Isthmian League Charity Shield (Woking 1991, 1992), London Senior Cup (Bedfont 2000).

Mark was an experienced attacking midfielder who helped St Albans City to the Isthmian League Division One title in 1985–86 before moving to Windsor and Eton for £2,500 in August 1987. His stay was brief, and he joined Woking a few months later for £2,000. His career took off at Kingfield, and he was the Cards' Player of the Year in 1988–89 and part of the side that finished the 1989–90 season as runners-up in the Isthmian League Division One.

However, it was during the 1990–91 season that Mark and his Woking teammates came to prominence, as they reached the fourth round of the FA Cup where they lost 1–0 to First Division Everton – a run that included them famously beating Second Division West Bromwich Albion in the third round.

The following season, he won the Isthmian League Premier Division with Woking and scored one of the goals that enabled the Cards to beat Redbridge Forest to win the 1992 Isthmian League Charity Shield.

Mark joined Aldershot Town in September 1994 but only lasted a couple of months before departing for Wealdstone. From there, he moved to a number of clubs, including Carshalton Athletic and Bedfont (with whom he won the London Senior Cup in 2000) before retiring in the summer of 2001.

Mark Blake — Centre-back

Born: 19 December 1967, Portsmouth.

Aldershot Town FC record:
Debut: v Slough Town (h), Isthmian League Premier Division, 25 March 2000.
Last appearance: v Basingstoke Town (a), Isthmian League Premier Division, 27 February 2001.
Appearances: 38 + 2
Goals: 1

Playing career:
Southampton (from apprentice, December 1985), Colchester United (1ML, September 1989), Shrewsbury Town (July 1990), Fulham (September 1994), AS Cannes (France, July 1998), Aldershot Town (March 2000), Andover (March 2001), Bashley (October 2001), Winchester City (January 2002; player-assistant manager from December 2004), Eastleigh (player-coach, January 2005), Winchester City (STL, March 2005).
Mark has made 304 Football League appearances, scoring 23 goals.

Representative honours:
England Youth, Hampshire FA XI.

Club honours:
Division Three (Shrewsbury Town 1993–94), Hampshire Senior Cup (Aldershot Town 2000), Wessex League (Winchester City 2003–04), Wessex League Cup (Winchester City 2004), FA Vase (Winchester City 2004).

Post-playing coaching/management career:
Head coach at Eastleigh (summer 2006).

Mark was a commanding centre-back who signed full professional forms at Southampton in December 1985 and made his senior debut against Tottenham Hotspur in May 1986. Following a loan spell at Colchester United during the 1989–90 season, he joined Shrewsbury Town in July 1990 for a fee of £100,000 (a Shrews record).

Unfortunately, Mark was at Gay Meadow when the club suffered relegation from Division Three in 1992, but he was also part of the side that came back up in 1994 by winning the Division Three title.

With Fulham, Mark played a part in reaching the Division Two Play-off semi-finals where they lost to Grimsby Town in 1997–98. He was released from Craven Cottage at the end of that season and joined French Ligue 2 side AS Cannes.

In March 2000 Mark returned to the UK and signed for Aldershot Town, bringing a steadiness to the back four. He was part of the Hampshire Cup-winning side that season, before leaving the Rec in October 2001 to join Andover. Three months later, he joined Winchester City and was a member of the side that completed the Wessex League, Wessex League Cup and FA Vase treble in 2004. He assumed the role of player-assistant manager at Hillier Way in December that year but left to join Isthmian League Premier Division Eastleigh as player-coach the following month.

In March 2005 he returned to Winchester on an emergency loan and played for his injury-ravaged former side in their Hampshire Senior Cup semi-final victory over Gosport Borough. Ironically, that victory meant that they would play the Shots in the Final but Mark played no part in that game, as he had returned to Eastleigh.

Mark retired in the summer of 2006 and stayed at the Silverlake Stadium as head coach, but he left in the September due to the increasing demands of his job with an IT company.

Andre Boucaud — Midfielder

Born: 9 October 1984, Enfield.

Aldershot Town FC record:

Debut: v Stevenage Borough (h), Conference National, 17 September 2005.
Last appearance: as substitute v Gravesend and Northfleet (h), Conference National, 12 November 2005.
Appearances: 12 + 1

Playing career:

Queen's Park Rangers (youth), Reading (trainee, summer 2002), Peterborough United (1ML, March 2003) Peterborough United (2ML, August 2003), Walsall (trial, November 2003), Peterborough United (May 2004), Aldershot Town (2ML, September 2005), Kettering Town (July 2006), Wycombe Wanderers (August 2007).
Andre has made 49 Football League appearances, scoring two goals.

Representative honours:

Trinidad and Tobago full international (six caps).

Andre is one of several loanees who have failed to impress at the Rec. He made his senior debut as a substitute for Peterborough against Mansfield Town in March 2003 and later won his first international cap in May 2004 against Iraq. Shortly afterwards, Andre joined Peterborough on a permanent basis but was unfortunate enough to experience relegation from Division One at the end of that season.

Andre joined the Shots on a two-month loan in September 2005 but was disappointing and so returned to Peterborough, where he made just two further appearances before joining Kettering Town in July 2006.

He joined Wycombe Wanderers on trial in July 2007 and impressed sufficiently to sign permanently the following month. However, Andre made just 11 appearances in all competitions during the 2007–08 season, and a seventh-place finish in League Two was followed by defeat to Stockport County in the Play-off semi-finals (he played no part in the Play-offs). Shortly after that defeat, Andre was one of several players released by Wycombe and, at the time of writing, he is still believed to be clubless.

Dave Boyce — Forward

Born: 15 February 1966.

Aldershot Town FC record:

Debut: v Molesey (a), Isthmian League Division One, 22 February 1997.

Last appearance: v Worthing (h), Isthmian League Division One, 12 April 1997.
Appearances: 6 + 1
Goals: 1

Playing career:
Crystal Palace (from trainee, July 1984), Fisher Athletic (July 1986), Dover Athletic (August 1987), Crawley Town (July 1988), Waterlooville (June 1990), Gravesend and Northfleet (November 1993), Havant Town (March 1995), Salisbury City (September 1996), Aldershot Town (February 1997), Wrecclesham (summer 1997).

Club honours:
Sussex Senior Cup (Crawley Town 1990).

Dave came to the Rec with a reputation as a goalscorer, but he was never given the chance to prove it during his short time with the Shots.

He began his career as a trainee with Crystal Palace and signed full professional forms in July 1984, moving to Fisher Athletic in July 1986 and then Dover Athletic the following summer. While at the Crabble, Dave scored in seven successive games during the 1987–88 season before he joined Crawley Town in July 1988. He finished his first season there as the club's top scorer (with 37 goals) and shared the top scorer's prize with Damian Webber the following season (both scored 18 goals). The latter season ended with Dave scoring the winning goal in the Sussex Senior Cup Final before departing for Waterlooville that summer.

Dave was Waterlooville's top scorer in 1991–92 and earned himself a £6,000 move to Gravesend and Northfleet in November 1993 – a record fee for an outgoing player at Jubilee Park and, at the time, a record for an incoming player at Stonebridge Road.

Dave was on the move again in March 1995 and later joined Aldershot Town in 1997. He never really got a run in the side and was released after just two months due to work commitments. Dave joined Wrecclesham that summer, but details of his subsequent career are unknown.

Bertie Brayley — Midfielder/Forward

Born: 5 September 1981, Brentwood.

Aldershot Town FC record:
Debut: v Tamworth (h), Conference National, 13 August 2005.
Last appearance: as substitute v Grays Athletic (a), Conference National, 29 August 2005.
Appearances: 2 + 3

Playing career:
West Ham United (trainee, July 1998), Tottenham Hotspur (trial, January 2000), Queen's Park Rangers (August 2000), Swindon Town (August 2001), Southend United (trial, July 2002), Canvey Island (August 2002), Heybridge Swifts (1ML, August 2003), Hornchurch (January 2004), Braintree Town (1ML, August 2004), Billericay Town (1ML, September 2004), Heybridge Swifts (November 2004), Farnborough Town (February 2005), Thurrock (March 2005), Aldershot Town (M, June 2005), Grays Athletic (September 2005), Margate (December 2005), Eastleigh (September 2006), Braintree Town (November 2006), Chelmsford City (July 2007).
Bertie has made seven Football League appearances.

Representative honours:
England Learning Disability XI.

Club honours:
Isthmian League Premier Division (Chelmsford City 2007–08).

An attacking midfielder or striker, Bertie joined West Ham United as a trainee in July 1998. He was a member of the team (along with Michael Carrick and Joe Cole) that won the 1999 FA Youth Cup, with Bertie scoring three goals in the two-leg Final. A trial at Tottenham Hotspur preceded a summer 2000 move to Queen's Park Rangers, but he did not appear for the first team during his only season at Loftus Road.

Following a trial at Southend, he joined Swindon Town in August 2001, making his senior debut as a substitute against Peterborough United on the opening day of the 2001–02 season. After seven League appearances for the

Robins (all as a substitute), he joined Canvey Island in August 2002. One achievement of note for Bertie is that he scored Gulls' fastest-ever League hat-trick (in under four minutes) in a 10–1 victory over Enfield in April 2003, which contributed to them finishing as runners-up to the Shots in the Isthmian League Premier Division that season.

A £17,500 fee took Bertie from a loan at Heybridge Swifts to Hornchurch in January 2004. The following season, however, the Urchins struggled (eventually going into administration), and Bertie went on loan to Braintree Town and Billericay Town (for whom he played in their best-ever FA Cup run as they reached the first round). After several club spells, Bertie signed for Aldershot Town in June 2005 but did not stay long before moving on to Grays Athletic and Margate.

In the summer of 2006 Bertie earned international honours when he was part of the England learning disability team that reached the World Cup quarter-finals in Germany. In that tournament, he scored five goals in an 11–1 opening-game victory over Mexico, with his first goal coming after just 38 seconds!

Bertie later joined his ex-Canvey boss Jeff King at Chelmsford City in the summer of 2007 and proceeded to score 16 goals in all competitions, 14 of which greatly contributed towards the winning of the Isthmian League Premier Division title. The Clarets also reached that season's Essex Senior Cup Final but lost out to Southend United.

Darren Brodrick — Centre-back

Born: 14 December 1973, Hammersmith.

Aldershot Town FC record:

Debut: v Whyteleafe (h), Isthmian League Division One, 21 September 1996.
Last appearance: v Hampton (a), Isthmian League Division One, 31 January 1998.
Appearances: 65 + 3
Goals: 5

Playing career:

Fulham (trainee, July 1990), Woking (September 1992), Kingstonian (October 1992), Carshalton Athletic (July 1994), Kingstonian (December 1994), Walton and Hersham (August 1995), Hendon (March 1996), Aldershot Town (September 1996), Gravesend and Northfleet (February 1998), Walton and Hersham (1ML, March 1999), Croydon (September 1999), Sutton United (January 2000), Croydon (March 2000), Carshalton Athletic (August 2000), Geylang United (Singapore, trial, January 2002).

Club honours:

Isthmian League Division One (Aldershot Town 1997–98), Isthmian League Full Members' Cup (Croydon 2000).

Darren was a giant centre-back who started his footballing life as a trainee with Fulham. He moved to several clubs before his arrival at the Rec in September 1996.

Darren was a regular in the 1997–98 season, and he made a significant contribution to the Shots winning the Isthmian League Division One title even though he left to join Gravesend and Northfleet in February 1998.

After several club spells, Darren returned to former club Croydon, where he was a member of the side that won the 2000 Isthmian League Full Members' Cup. He rejoined Carshalton Athletic in August 2000 but struggled with a shoulder injury and was released in February 2001.

Darren had his injury operated on, and a family connection led to him trialling with Singapore S-League side Geylang United in January 2002. However, his shoulder injury was still causing problems, so he returned to the UK and subsequently retired. Darren currently works as a sales consultant for an IT company near Oxford.

Ian Brooks — Midfielder

Born: 17 May 1986, Reading.

Aldershot Town FC record:

Debut: as substitute v Locksheath (h), Hampshire Senior Cup third round, 2 December 2003.
Last appearance: as substitute v Fareham Town (h), Hampshire Senior Cup second round, 2 November 2004.
Appearances: 0 + 2

Playing career:
Reading (youth), Aldershot Town (youth), Chertsey Town (3ML, March 2005), Hayes (September 2005), Reading Town (December 2006), Bracknell Town (July 2007), Reading Town (October 2007).

Representative honours:
Hampshire Youth.

Ian can play in the centre or on the right of midfield, but his career progress has been rather curtailed by his university studies. He played in Reading's youth team before joining the Shots, where he was one of a number of youth-team players to make their first-team debuts for the Shots in minor Cup competitions.

Ian left the Rec in September 2005 and joined Hayes then Combined Counties League side Reading Town before moving on to Bracknell Town in July 2007. However, his stay at Larges Lane was a short one, and he returned to Reading Town a couple of months later, with the club finishing 13th in the Combined Counties League Premier Division.

Brian Broome — Midfielder

Born: 14 April 1960, Reading.

Aldershot Town FC record:

Debut:	v Kingsbury Town (a), Isthmian League Division Three, 2 March 1993.
Last appearance:	v Cove (a), Isthmian League Division Three, 1 May 1993.
Appearances:	9
Goals:	3

Playing career:
Aldershot FC (apprentice, 1975–76), Camberley Town (youth, summer 1977), Farnborough Town (summer 1980), Wokingham Town (summer 1987), Farnborough Town (summer 1990), Basingstoke Town (September 1992), Bracknell Town (October 1992), Aldershot Town (February 1993), Farnborough Town (July 1993), Bracknell Town (June 1994; player-manager from summer 1996), Wokingham Town (November 1998).

Representative honours:
Isthmian League XI, FA XI.

Club honours:
Isthmian League Division One (Farnborough Town 1984–85), Hampshire Senior Cup (Farnborough Town 1982, 1984, 1986, 1991), Southern League Premier Division (Farnborough Town 1990–91, 1993–94), Isthmian League Division Three (Aldershot Town 1992–93).

Brian was a very experienced midfielder who played briefly for the Shots near the end of the 1992–93 season. He was originally an apprentice at Aldershot FC before joining the youth team at near neighbours Camberley Town in the summer of 1977.

Brian began his association with Farnborough Town in the summer of 1980, scoring on his debut against Clapton in the August. He was a member of the sides that won the Isthmian League Division One title in 1981–82 as well as the Hampshire Senior Cup in 1982, 1984 and 1986.

He joined Wokingham Town in the summer of 1987 and was a member of the side that reached that season's FA Trophy semi-finals and also finished runners-up to Slough Town in the Isthmian League Premier Division in 1989–90.

Brian rejoined Farnborough in the summer of 1990, and further honours followed that season in the form of the Southern League Premier Division title and his fourth Hampshire Senior Cup triumph. He was also involved when Boro took First Division West Ham United to a replay (which the Hammers won 1–0) in the FA Cup third round in January 1992.

A move to Basingstoke Town in September 1992 was quickly followed by one to Bracknell Town, and it was from there that he joined Aldershot Town in February 1993. Brian's most memorable contribution in a Shots shirt was his goal in the 2–1 home victory over Thame United in April 1993, as it secured the Isthmian League Division Three title. The other scorer that day was (unsurprisingly) Mark Butler!

A second return to Cherrywood Road followed that summer, with this move culminating in him being part of a Southern League Premier Division title-winning side for a second time. He bade a final farewell to Boro in the summer of 1994, having amassed a club-record 529 appearances over the course of his three spells there.

He was appointed captain at newly promoted Bracknell Town and finished his first season at Larges Lane as the joint winner of the Player of the Year with Justin Day, before being appointed as player-manager in the summer of 1996.

In November 1998, Brian made an unexpected return to Wokingham and played in the club's last-ever game at Finchampstead Road against Bedford Town in May 1999. He retired that summer and currently runs a vending machine company.

John Brough — Centre-back

Born: 8 January 1973, Ilkeston.

Aldershot Town FC record:

Debut:	v Tamworth (h), Conference National, 13 August 2005.
Last appearance:	v Hereford United (a), Conference National, 21 February 2006.
Appearances:	17 + 3
Goals:	1

Playing career:
Notts County (from trainee, July 1991), Shrewsbury Town (July 1992), Telford United (August 1994), Hereford United (November 1994), Cheltenham Town (July 1998), Aldershot Town (June 2005), Newport County (March 2006), Bishops Cleeve (player-coach, July 2007).
John has made 231 Football League appearances, scoring 10 goals.

Club honours:
Conference (Cheltenham Town 1998–99), Division Three Play-off Final (Cheltenham Town 2001–02).

Post-playing coaching/management career:
Youth-team manager of Cheltenham Town (November 2007).

John is best known as a centre-back, but he played as a forward in the early part of his career. He was a trainee at Notts County and signed full professional forms in July 1991 but did not make his senior debut until the opening day of the 1992–93 season, when he was with Shrewsbury Town. A brief spell at Telford United followed his release from Gay Meadow in the summer of 1994 before he joined Hereford United in November 1994.

During his time at Edgar Street, he was part of the squads that lost to Darlington in the Division Three Play-off semi-finals in 1995–96 and that dropped out of the Football League in 1997. At the end of Hereford's first season in the Conference, John signed for Cheltenham Town, where he was part of side that won the Conference in 1998–99. He was part of the Robins side that beat Rushden and Diamonds to win the Division Three Play-off Final in 2002 and the side that got relegated the following season.

John joined Aldershot Town in June 2005 but his appearances were restricted by injury, and he was released in March 2006. He immediately signed for Newport County, where he was appointed as captain before playing on the losing side in the 2007 FAW Premier League Cup Final.

In July 2007 John joined Southern League side Bishops Cleeve as player-coach but made only a handful of appearances before leaving in the November to take up the position of youth-team manager at his former club Cheltenham Town.

Tony Brown — Midfielder

Born: 7 March 1961.

Aldershot Town FC record:

Debut: as substitute v Whyteleafe (h), Isthmian League Division One, 21 September 1996.
Appearances: 0 + 1

Playing career:

Hameln (Germany), Aldershot Town (September 1996), Basingstoke Town (September 1996), Chertsey Town (September 1997), Fleet Town (November 1997), Wokingham Town (February 1998).

Representative honours:

British Army.

'Bomber' was a soldier who appeared for a handful of clubs in Germany prior to his arrival at the Rec. He won the Army Cup in 1996 with the 28th Regiment Royal Engineers and, after a lengthy process of obtaining international clearance, made his sole appearance for Aldershot Town as a substitute against Whyteleafe in September of that year. Unfortunately, Tony was one of several players that the club had in his position, so he moved to Basingstoke Town later that month. Moves to Fleet Town and Wokingham Town followed, with him leaving the latter club in October 1998 and reportedly retiring.

Stafford Browne — Forward

Born: 4 January 1971, Haywards Heath.

Aldershot Town FC record:

Debut: v Grays Athletic (h), Isthmian League Premier Division, 7 October 2000.
Last appearance: as substitute v Purfleet (a), Isthmian League Premier Division, 3 May 2003.
Appearances: 79 + 26
Goals: 53 (fifth in all-time top 10)

Playing career:

Ringmer, Lewes (1994–95 season), Horsham (August 1996), Hastings Town (August 1997), Brighton & Hove Albion (M, August 1998), Welling United (November 1998), Billericay Town (August 1999), Yeovil Town (September 1999), Billericay Town (September 1999), Dagenham and Redbridge (September 2000), Aldershot Town (October 2000), Grays Athletic (June 2002), St Albans City (October 2002), Aldershot Town (NC, December 2002), Kingstonian (June 2003), Wivenhoe Town (August 2004), Chelmsford City (1ML, March 2005), Worthing (August 2005), Wivenhoe Town (October 2006), Heybridge Swifts (July 2007).
Stafford has made three Football League appearances.

Representative honours:

Isthmian League XI.

Club honours:

Hampshire Senior Cup (Aldershot Town 2002, 2003 [unused substitute]), Isthmian League Premier Division (Aldershot Town 2002–03).

Stafford began his career at Sussex County League side Ringmer before moving to neighbours Lewes, where he was top scorer in 1994–95 and 1995–96 (28 goals). His goalscoring brought about moves to Horsham and then Hastings United, where he was top scorer in 1997–98 with a club-record 29 goals. He signed for Brighton & Hove Albion on a month-to-month contract in August 1998 and made his debut against Carlisle United on the opening day of 1998–99. Unfortunately, his Football League career lasted just two months before he signed for Welling United, where he finished as the club's top League goalscorer (seven goals) that season.

After several club spells, Stafford signed for Aldershot Town in October 2000, where his goalscoring rate was virtually a goal every other game as he finished the season having netted 17 times in 33 games. The following season, he scored a hat-trick in the 3–1 win against Havant and Waterlooville in the Hampshire Senior Cup Final (at Southampton FC), thus becoming the first player to score a competitive hat-trick at the newly built Saint Mary's Stadium. He also finished the season as top scorer with 30 goals.

That summer, Stafford left the Shots for short stints at Grays Athletic and St Albans City before returning to the Rec in December 2002. However, his return did not go down well with the Shots faithful and his six goals that season did not really do much to change their minds.

Stafford moved to Kingstonian that summer, scoring on his debut against Thurrock, and his 14 goals that season helped the Ks reach the Isthmian League Play-offs, where they lost to Lewes in the Final.

Stafford finished top scorer (with 18 goals) at Wivenhoe Town in August 2004 and then at Worthing in 2005 (with 28 goals). And, after a two-year absence, he again finished as Wivenhoe's top scorer for the 2006–07 season (with eight goals) before moving to Heybridge Swifts in July 2007. He finished the 2007–08 season as Player of the Year and top scorer (24) at Scraley Road, with the club finishing in 12th spot in the Isthmian League Premier Division.

Liam Buchan — Midfielder

Born: 18 January 1987, Crawley.

Aldershot Town FC record:

Debut: as substitute v Newport, Isle of Wight (h), Hampshire Senior Cup third round, 30 November 2004.

Last appearance: v Forest Green Rovers (a), Conference Challenge Cup Southern Section quarter-final, 15 February 2005.

Appearances: 2 + 1

Playing career:

Gillingham (youth), Millwall (youth, February 2003), Southend United (youth, March 2003), Crawley Town (youth, March 2003), Aldershot Town (NC, November 2004), Oakwood (summer 2005), Three Bridges, Oakwood (January 2007).

Liam was a young midfielder who appeared briefly for Aldershot Town during the 2004–05 season. Having played youth football at Gillingham, Millwall and Southend United, he joined Crawley Town in March 2003. He joined the Shots in November 2004 but could not break into the first team for any length of time and so left to sign for Oakwood. A spell at fellow Sussex side Three Bridges (where he was popular with the fans) followed before he rejoined Oakwood in January 2007. It is not known who Liam played for in the 2007–08 season.

Steve Buckingham — Utility defender/Midfielder

Born: 5 February 1967, Guildford.

Aldershot Town FC record:

Debut: v Clapton (h), Isthmian League Division Three, 22 August 1992.

Appearances: 1

Playing career:

Cranleigh (summer 1982), Godalming and Guildford (summer 1983), Cranleigh (summer 1985), Wrecclesham (summer 1987), Ash United (summer 1988), Farnham Town (summer 1990), Aldershot Town (August 1992), Godalming and Guildford (October 1992), Basingstoke Town (summer 1993), Cranleigh (DR, January 1995), Sheerwater (summer 1996).

Club honours:
Combined Counties League (Farnham Town 1990–91, 1991–92), Dan Air Elite Cup (Farnham Town 1992), Combined Counties Premier Challenge Cup (Farnham Town 1992), Isthmian League Division Three (Aldershot Town 1992–93).

Steve is often the 'forgotten man' of the quartet that joined Aldershot Town in the summer of 1992 following the unfortunate demise of Farnham Town – the others being Steve Harris, Shaun May and Steve Stairs. He started his career as a 15-year-old playing reserve-team football at Combined Counties League side Cranleigh before joining Godalming and Guildford in the summer of 1983, making his first-team debut for the club the following season. He then returned to Cranleigh before playing for Wrecclesham and Ash United.

Steve's career took a step up in the summer of 1990 when he moved to Farnham Town, where he was to be an integral part of the side that won back-to-back Combined Counties League titles. The latter of those titles formed part of a record treble-winning season that also saw the club win the Dan Air Elite Cup and the Combined Counties Premier Challenge Cup.

Steve was an 11th-hour signing for the Shots in August 1992, having signed the day before their first-ever match. He wore the number-three shirt and got injured four minutes from the end. Although he recovered relatively quickly from this injury, the combination of being unable to regain his place in the team and the fact that the club had no reserve side resulted in him signing for Godalming and Guildford in October 1992.

After moves to Basingstoke Town, where he played mainly for the reserves, Cranleigh and then Sheerwater, he retired in the summer of 1997 and currently works as a deputy financial director in UK Government.

Paul Buckle — Midfielder

Born 16 December 1970, Hatfield.

Aldershot Town FC record:

Debut:	v Aylesbury United (a), Isthmian League Premier Division, 5 October 2002.
Last appearance:	v Bashley (at Southampton FC), Hampshire Senior Cup Final, 3 May 2003.
Appearances:	41 + 1
Goals:	5

Playing career:
Brentford (from trainee, July 1989), Wycombe Wanderers (1ML, December 1992), Torquay United (February 1994), Exeter City (October 1995), Cambridge United (trial, August 1996), Northampton Town (August 1996), Aylesbury United (October 1996), Wycombe Wanderers (NC, October 1996), Colchester United (November 1996), Exeter City (July 1999), Aldershot Town (July 2002), Weymouth (player-coach, August 2003), Exeter City (December 2004), Tiverton Town (December 2004), Exeter City (player-coach, March 2005; player-assistant manager from February 2006).
Paul has made 336 Football League appearances, scoring 24 goals.

Representative honours:
Isthmian League XI.

Club honours (as player): Division Three (Brentford 1991–92), Division Three Play-off Final (Colchester United 1998), Isthmian League Premier Division (Aldershot Town 2002–03), Hampshire Senior Cup (Aldershot Town 2003).

Post-playing coaching/management career:
Manager of Torquay United (May 2007).

Paul started his career in Brentford's academy side who were, at the time, managed by Colin Lee (who would later be Paul's chief executive at Torquay United during his managerial spell there). While still a trainee, he made his senior debut for Brentford as a substitute against York City in May 1988, signing full professional forms at Griffin Park in July 1989.

Paul was part of the Bees sides that reached the Division Three Play-offs in 1990–91 (although he did not actually take part in the semi-final defeat to Tranmere Rovers) and the Southern Area Final of the

Associate Members' Cup, where they lost to Birmingham City. Paul played sporadically in the side that won the Division Three title the following season and made five appearances in 1992–93 when the club came straight back down. He also had a one-month loan spell in the Conference with Wycombe Wanderers that season, as well as being a member of the Bees side that lost to Derby County in the Anglo-Italian Cup semi-final.

Paul moved to Torquay United in February 1994 and was part of the squad (together with Nick Burton) that reached the Division Three Play-offs before losing to Preston North End in the semi-finals.

In October 1995 he moved to Exeter City in a deal that took Russell Coughlin in the opposite direction. The following summer, he was one of several players forced to leave Exeter due to the club suffering serious financial problems. Paul had a trial at Cambridge United plus short spells at Northampton Town, Aylesbury United and Wycombe before he joined Colchester United in November 1996. He played on the losing side of the 1997 Auto Windscreens Shield Final against Carlisle United at Wembley, before returning there the following year and winning the Division Three Play-off Final by beating Torquay.

Colchester struggled the following season and narrowly avoided relegation before Paul returned to St James Park in July 1999. He sustained an ankle injury in the opening game of the 1999–2000 season against Hull City and missed the next three months as a result.

In July 2002 Paul signed for Aldershot Town, and his competitive style of play combined with his experience greatly contributed to the winning of the Isthmian League Premier Division title that season. However, he left to be player-coach at Weymouth in August 2003, helping the club finish that season as runners-up to Crawley Town in the Southern League Premier Division, thus gaining entry into the newly formed Conference South.

After short spells at Exeter (reportedly playing for free) and Tiverton Town, the lure of St James was too great and Paul was back there for a fourth time in 2005, this time as player-coach. Towards the end of the following season, he stepped up to become player-assistant manager and was an unused substitute for the Grecians in the second leg of the 2005–06 FA Trophy semi-final, which they lost to Grays Athletic.

Paul retired from playing in May 2007, became manager of Torquay United later that month and attained his UEFA A licence in March 2008. Paul nearly achieved success on two fronts in 2007–08, as the Gulls challenged the Shots throughout the season for the League title but finished third, failing to win any of their last four games, and then lost the subsequent Play-off semi-final to neighbours Exeter. Paul's first managerial season ended on a losing note, as Torquay were beaten by Ebbsfleet United in the FA Trophy Final.

Nikki Bull — Goalkeeper

Born: 2 October 1981, Hastings.

Aldershot Town FC record:

Debut: v Hitchin Town (a), Isthmian League Premier Division, 17 August 2002.
Appearances: 277 + 1 (third in all-time top 10).
Goals: 1

Playing career:

Brighton & Hove Albion (schoolboy trials), Aston Villa (schoolboy), Queen's Park Rangers (from trainee, July 1999), Hayes (2ML, March 2002), Aldershot Town (May 2002).

Representative honours:

Sussex Schoolboys, England National Game XI (four caps).

Club honours:

Isthmian League Premier Division (Aldershot Town 2002–03), Hampshire Senior Cup (Aldershot Town 2003, 2007 [unused substitute]), Conference Premier (Aldershot Town 2007–08).

Prior to Aldershot Town's promotion into the Football League, Nikki was widely regarded as one of the best goalkeepers in non-League football. He has improved markedly during his time with the Shots and is a very popular figure among the fans at the Rec. Having turned down the offer of a schoolboy contract at Brighton & Hove Albion, Nikki started as a schoolboy at Aston Villa. He was offered the chance of a traineeship there but decided that he wanted to find a club nearer to his Sussex home and so accepted an offer from Queen's Park Rangers. Nikki signed full professional forms at Loftus Road in July 1999 and was the substitute 'keeper for the first team on several occasions without actually making an appearance.

The 2000–01 season ended in disappointment as QPR were relegated from Division One, and that relegation saw many of the top players leave. Nikki hoped that this would be an opportunity for him to earn a starting place but it was not to be, as the club signed Chris Day to fill the number-one spot.

Nikki spent the last two months of the 2001–02 season on loan at Conference outfit Hayes, but his efforts could not prevent the Middlesex club being relegated. He was released by QPR that summer and, despite being offered the chance to return to Church Road on a permanent basis, opted to sign for Aldershot Town instead.

His performances in his first season at the Rec earned him international recognition, and he made his England National Game XI debut as a substitute against Belgium in February 2003, thus becoming the first-ever Shots player to win international honours. That season he also became the only Shots 'keeper to score a goal, doing so in a memorable 6–2 victory against Hendon in the final home game of the season. The Shots had already secured the Isthmian League Premier Division title (and promotion to the Conference for the first time in the club's history) a few days previously and, as the game entered the last quarter of an hour, they were awarded a penalty. The chant of 'Give it to Bully' started to reverberate around the Rec and usual penalty-taker Roscoe D'Sane entered into the spirit of the occasion and handed the spot-kick over to Nikki, who duly despatched his kick past Dave Hook. Nikki's season was then rounded off nicely by him winning the Player of the Year award.

The following season, he played in the club's first-ever Conference game against Accrington Stanley and was a member of the side that lost to Hednesford Town in the FA Trophy semi-finals, the side that lost the 2004 Conference Play-off Final to Shrewsbury Town and the side that was beaten on penalties by Carlisle United in the semi-finals the following season. Nikki was part of the England National Game XI squad that won the Four Nations Tournament in 2005, and he won the Player of the Year award at the Rec (for the second time) in 2006.

During the 2006–07 season, he played in the side that reached the FA Cup third round, where they lost to Blackpool. His importance to Aldershot is illustrated by the fact that he was an ever present in the League in 2004–05, 2005–06 and 2006–07. The number of times that Nikki's performances saved points is incalculable, and that level of consistency fuelled countless rumours that he would join a Football League side, but he resisted the temptation and stayed at the Rec. That decision turned out to be the right one, as he had a fantastic 2007–08 season, during which he helped the club reach the FA Trophy semi-finals before bowing out to Ebbsfleet United. More importantly, he was a major factor in winning the Conference Premier title to earn promotion into the Football League. Although it is hard to single out any one of Nikki's saves that season, many would say that the wonder save he made in the dying minutes of the title-winning draw at Exeter was a defining moment.

Nikki's season was nicely rounded off, as he became the first-ever Shots player to win the Player of the Year award three times, which is a fitting testimony to his popularity among the Rec faithful. A double accolade followed shortly after the season's end, when he was crowned the non-League Goalkeeper of the Year and non-League Player of the Year at the National Game Awards. Following protracted negotiations and an apparent stalemate, Nikki signed a new two-year contract at the Rec at the end of May 2008. Shortly after he was named in the Conference Premier Team of the Year (along with four of his Shots teammates) and was voted Goalkeeper of the Year at the League's annual awards ceremony.

Michael Bullen — Goalkeeper

Born: 5 January 1974, Chertsey.

Aldershot Town FC record:

Debut: v Barking (h), Isthmian League Division One, 6 April 1996.
Last appearance: v Hitchin Town (a), Isthmian League Cup first round, 8 September 1998.
Appearances: 59

Playing career:

Wimbledon (trainee, July 1990), Portsmouth (trial, August 1992), Walton and Hersham (November 1992), Staines Town (summer 1993), Aldershot Town (August 1995), Yeading (1ML, February 1998), Gravesend and Northfleet (1ML, March 1998), Chesham United (1ML, September 1998), Chertsey Town (October 1998), Hampton (November 1998), Banstead Athletic (August 1999), Woking (March 2000).

Representative honours:

South of England Youth XI, British Universities.

Club honours:

El Cañuelo Trophy (Staines Town 1994), Isthmian League Division One (Aldershot Town 1997–98).

Michael was a sizeable 'keeper who started out as a trainee at Wimbledon before trialling at Portsmouth and then signing for Walton and Hersham in November 1992. Unfortunately, his career from hereon was dogged by injury. He tore a quadricep muscle a couple of months after signing for Walton and this kept him out of action until June 1993.

Michael then signed for Staines Town, but his bad luck continued, as he broke his arm in a car accident soon afterwards and was out for a further seven months. Having helped Staines attain a sixth-place finish in Isthmian League Division One in 1994–95, Michael signed for Aldershot Town in August 1995, but the performances of Mark Watson meant that he had to wait until the following April to make his debut. However, this worked in his favour, as it enabled him to go to China to represent British Universities in the World Student Games the month after he signed.

Michael was first-choice 'keeper for the Shots in 1996–97 and made 36 appearances as seventh place in Isthmian League Division One was achieved. He then picked up a finger injury in the 1997–98 pre-season and a shoulder injury early that same season, and these combined to keep him out again. He was loaned out to Yeading and Gravesend and Northfleet that season but still managed to make enough appearances for the Shots to earn himself a League-winners' medal.

Michael had a one-month loan at Chesham United before leaving the Rec in October 1998, going on to play for several clubs, including Hampton, Banstead Athletic and Woking. He made his debut for the Cards in March 2000 as a substitute against Scarborough, but his persistent shoulder problems meant it would be his only appearance for the Surrey side. He had a second shoulder operation in the summer of 2000, which kept him out for 10 months. However, by the time he had recovered, his work commitments dictated that he would have to quit playing. Michael currently works as an IT specialist within a firm of solicitors.

Phil Burns — Goalkeeper

Born: 18 December 1966, Stockport.

Aldershot Town FC record:

Debut:	v Egham Town (h), Isthmian League Division Two, 21 August 1993.
Last appearance:	v Worthing (a), Isthmian League Division One, 14 April 1995.
Appearances:	74

Playing career:

Manchester United (youth trial, 1982), Huddersfield Town (apprentice, July 1982), army (February 1985), Reading (March 1989), Ipswich Town (trial, summer 1991), Slough Town (August 1991), Airdrieonians (£20,000, November 1991), Portsmouth (2ML, October 1992), Sheffield United (2ML, December 1992), Wycombe Wanderers (trial, summer 1993), Aldershot Town (August 1993), Chesham United (2ML, February 1995), Wokingham Town (July 1995), Bordon WMC (January 1996), Aldershot Town (summer 1996).

Phil has made 12 Football League and Scottish Premier League appearances.

Representative honours:

British Army, Combined Services.

Phil was not scared to run at oncoming forwards in order to protect his goal, and this was a trait that made him popular with the Shots fans. Having trialled at Manchester United as a 15-year-old, he joined Huddersfield Town as an apprentice in July 1982. Two years later, he was told that he had no future at Leeds Road – a decision that left him feeling disappointed and disillusioned. Despite having several offers from other clubs, Phil decided that his immediate future lay away from football so he joined the army in February 1985.

Phil spent the next four years in the Royal Electrical and Mechanical Engineers, during which time he played for both the Army and the Combined Services representative sides. In early 1989 fate intervened when a scout from Reading was watching an army game with a particular player (not Phil) as his 'target'. However, the scout was unimpressed and so recommended Phil to Reading.

He left the army and signed for the Royals in March 1989 and made his debut (ironically) against Huddersfield Town in September 1990. By the end of that season, it was clear that he was not going to become a regular at Elm Park, so he signed for Conference side Slough Town in August 1991. However, the Berkshire side were suffering financially, and Phil left to join Scottish Premier Division side Airdrieonians in the November for £20,000.

The Diamonds reached the Scottish Cup Final in his first season but, although he played in some of the earlier rounds, Phil played no part in the Final. In October 1992 he was loaned to Portsmouth for two months, during which time he played in an Anglo-Italian Cup tie in Bari.

Phil was then loaned to Sheffield United before leaving Broomfield Park. He joined the Shots in August 1993, after a pre-season trial at Wycombe Wanderers, and missed just one League game in the 1993–94 campaign, as promotion from Isthmian League Division Two was achieved. He also kept a club-record 23 clean sheets in the League and played an important part in the club reaching the quarter-finals of the FA Vase (where they lost to Atherton Laburnum Rovers), playing in all bar one of the games.

In February 1995 Phil went on a two-month loan to Chesham United before leaving the Rec that summer and signing for Wokingham Town. At the turn of the year, he decided that he had had enough of being a 'keeper, so he left Wokingham, signed for Bordon WMC (a lower league side near his home) and played the rest of that season as a centre-half!

Phil returned to the Rec in the summer of 1996 in his traditional goalkeeping role but only ever made it onto the substitutes' bench. He left the Rec (and subsequently retired) in October 1996 and currently runs a builders' merchants in Alton.

Nick Burton — Centre-back/Midfielder

Born: 10 February 1975, Bury St Edmunds.

Aldershot Town FC record:

Debut: as substitute v Leyton Pennant (a), Isthmian League Division One, 10 February 1996.
Last appearance: v Bournemouth Poppies (h), Hampshire Senior Cup third round, 18 November 1997.
Appearances: 73 + 6
Goals: 3

Playing career:

Portsmouth (trainee, July 1991), Torquay United (August 1993), Yeovil Town (May 1995), Aldershot Town (January 1996), Hampton/Hampton and Richmond Borough (December 1997), Gravesend and Northfleet (October 2001), Farnborough Town (May 2003), Crawley Town (March 2005), Eastleigh (June 2005), St Albans City (November 2005), Staines Town (March 2006), Farnborough Town (July 2006), Basingstoke Town (trial, July 2007), Harrow Borough (August 2007).
Nick has made 16 Football League appearances, scoring two goals.

Club honours:

Isthmian League Division One (Aldershot Town 1997–98), Middlesex Charity Cup (Hampton 1998, 1999), Middlesex Super Cup (Hampton and Richmond Borough 2000), Isthmian League Premier Division (Gravesend and Northfleet 2001–02), Hampshire Senior Cup (Farnborough Town 2004).

Nick is best known as a quality centre-back, but he has occasionally played as a central midfielder. He started out as a trainee at Portsmouth but never made the first team at Fratton Park.

In August 1993 he joined Torquay United and made a scoring debut (with an overhead kick) against Carlisle United later in the month. Later that season, he was part of the squad that reached the Division Three Play-off semi-finals before losing to Preston North End.

He spent the first part of the 1995–96 season with Yeovil Town before joining Aldershot Town in January 1996. The Shots pushed harder for promotion the following season, and by the time Nick left in December (to sign for Hampton) he had already performed consistently enough to put the club into a strong position from which they would eventually go on to win that season's Isthmian League Division One title.

During his time at the Beveree, Nick was Player of the Year (in 2000) as well as captaining the side to minor Cup success. He was also part of the Beavers side that achieved a club-best progression in the FA Cup in 2000–01 before being knocked out by Barnet in the first round.

In October 2001 Nick joined Gravesend and Northfleet and finished the season as an Isthmian League Premier Division winner. In May 2003 he moved to Farnborough Town, becoming the first signing made by the newly appointed Tommy Taylor. The club struggled and were heading for relegation by the turn of the year, which resulted in several players (including Nick) departing. Nick joined Crawley Town in March 2005 in a straight swap deal involving Kevin Hemsley, but he left in the summer to join Eastleigh. However, despite being appointed as joint captain with Martin Thomas, his stay there lasted just five months before he joined St Albans City and then Staines Town.

Nick returned to Cherrywood Road in July 2006, but it was not a happy return as the club went into administration and suffered a 10-point deduction before being liquidated. The only good thing to happen to him that season was the Player of the Year award, but that turned out to be cold comfort in light of the club's demise.

That summer, Nick trialled at Basingstoke Town before signing for Harrow Borough (whose coach was his ex-Boro teammate Ken Charlery). The club finished the season in 16th place in the Isthmian League Premier Division, avoiding relegation by just two points.

Mark Butler — Forward

Born: 23 May 1965, Aldershot.

Aldershot Town FC record:

Debut: v Clapton (h), Isthmian League Division Three, 22 August 1992.
Last appearance: v Berkhamsted Town (h), Isthmian League Division One, 2 May 1998.
Appearances: 271 + 32 (second in all-time top 10)
Goals: 155 (first in all-time top 10)

Playing career:
Tongham (summer 1981), Ash United (August 1985), Egham Town (summer 1986), Wycombe Wanderers (March 1989), Chesham United (October 1989), Egham Town (summer 1990), Aldershot Town (July 1992), Modbury (Australia, STL, summer 1994), Staines Town (June 1998, caretaker manager from April 2003), Fleet Town (DR, August 2002), Chertsey Town (player-coach, August 2003), Ashford Town (player-assistant manager from June 2004; player-manager from December 2004).

Representative honours:
FA XI, Isthmian League XI.

Club honours:
Isthmian League Division Three (Aldershot Town 1992–93), Isthmian League Division One (Chesham United 1990–91, Aldershot Town 1997–98), Jim Lawford Memorial Cup (Staines Town 2000).

Post-playing coaching/management career:
Manager of Ashford Town (May 2005).

Managerial Honours: Isthmian League Cup (Ashford Town 2007).

Mark's achievements at Aldershot Town include:
* Winning Player of the Year in 1993.
* Scoring eight hat-tricks.
* Being top scorer in three of his six seasons (1993–94, 1994–95 and 1995–96).

Mark was the first Aldershot Town player to:
* Score on his debut.
* Score a hat-trick.
* Make 50, 100, 150, 200, 250 and 300 appearances. The 50-appearance milestone was shared with Steve Harris.
* Score 50, 100 and 150 goals.
* Gain representative honours.
* Be sent off – a fact that he has since stated he deeply regrets and which, as countless people can testify, was completely out of character.

Mark was a prolific forward and one of a handful of players who can truly lay claim to being an Aldershot Town 'legend'. During his time at the Rec, he became extremely popular with the fans to the extent that some called for him to be given a testimonial when he departed – even though he had only been at the club for six seasons.

Mark began playing with local sides Tongham and Ash United before moving up the non-League ladder to join Egham Town in the summer of 1986. His career path then took him into the Conference with Wycombe Wanderers in March 1989 for a fee of £4,200 (a record for a player departing Tempest Road), but he still ended the season as Egham's top scorer (21 goals).

While at Loakes Park, he was part of the Wycombe side that reached the FA Trophy quarter-finals (where they lost to Hyde United) in 1988–89 before joining Chesham United in October 1989 for £5,000. He was joint-top scorer that season along with Dermot Drummy, with a paltry seven goals.

Mark returned to Egham in the summer of 1990 for £3,000 (still the Sarnies' record purchase) and ended the season as the club's top scorer (37 goals). The following season, he scored a club-record 50 goals in all competitions, as well as being the top scorer in the entire Isthmian League that season (31 goals). Mark is also Egham's all-time record scorer with 168 goals.

In July 1992 Mark made the move to the newly formed Aldershot Town and wore his customary number-11 shirt in the club's first-ever League game. He scored two of the Shots goals in the 4–2 victory over Clapton in that game, the first of which earned him the distinction of being the club's first-ever goalscorer. By the end of the campaign, in which he missed just one League game, Mark had an Isthmian League Division Three-winners' medal. He was always a consistent performer for the Shots, and this was rewarded when he played for the Isthmian

League XI against the Combined Services in February 1994, thus becoming the first Shots player to win representative honours.

The following season, he was a member of the side that was defeated by Atherton Laburnum Rovers in the FA Vase quarter-finals and the side that gained promotion. He also finished the season as the club's top scorer (again) with 35 goals, two of which contributed to the 3–0 home victory over Hampton that clinched promotion.

Mark jetted off to Australia for a few months in the summer of 1994 and played in the South Australia Premier Division for Modbury before returning to be the Shots' top scorer in 1994–95 (33 goals) and 1995–96 (33 goals).

In August 1997 Mark got his first taste of what management was like when he was part of a caretaker management triumvirate at the Rec (along with Andy Meyer and Joe Roach) following the departure of Steve Wigley. His final contribution to the club's rise was scoring 13 goals in the 1997–98 season, which saw the club win the Isthmian League Division One title.

Having played 303 games (second only to his close friend Jason Chewins) and scored a club record 155 goals, Mark moved on to Staines Town in June 1998 and proceeded to be the club's top scorer for the next four seasons, which included scoring 14 goals in 1998–99 and 22 in 1999–2000. He was part of the side that won the Jim Lawford Memorial Cup in 2000, as well as being in the veterans' side that won the Brover Vets Challenge Vase against Spanish side CD Mijas in 2002 and 2004.

In August 2002 he made a solitary appearance for Fleet Town on a dual-registration basis before taking over as caretaker manager at Staines for the last seven games of the season following the resignation of Ken Ballard. He applied for the vacant manager's job but was beaten to the position by Steve Cordery, after which he joined Chertsey Town as player-coach.

Mark's next move was to become player-assistant manager to Nathan Wharf at Ashford Town (Middlesex) in June 2004, and he made the step up to player-manager at Short Lane in December 2004 following Wharf's resignation. Under his stewardship, the club progressed well, being beaten in the 2004–05 Southern League Play-offs by Evesham United, although getting to that stage was a momentous feat in itself.

Mark retired from playing that summer to concentrate on his managerial duties, and in 2005–06 he led Ashford Town to the runners'-up spot behind Clevedon Town in the Southern League Division One West, thus securing promotion to the Isthmian League Premier Division for the first time in the club's history. In 2006–07 he led them to the FA Trophy first round (where they lost to Braintree Town) for the first time in their history and to victory in the Isthmian League Cup Final by beating Dover Athletic. Mark continued his excellent work at Short Lane in 2007–08, as he led the club to a fantastic sixth-place finish in the Isthmian League Premier Division, missing the Play-offs by just one place and two points.

Adrian Caceres — Winger

Born: 10 January 1982, Buenos Aires, Argentina.

Aldershot Town FC record:

Debut:	v Barnet (a), Conference National, 26 February 2005.
Last appearance:	v Stevenage Borough (h), Conference National, 19 March 2005.
Appearances:	6

Playing career:

Boca Juniors (Argentina, youth), Velez Sarsfield (Argentina, youth), Perth SC (Australia, 1999–2000), Southampton (September 2000), Brentford (1ML, September 2001), Hull City (March 2002), Perth Glory (Australia, April 2002), Yeovil Town (July 2004), Aldershot Town (NC, February 2005), Wycombe Wanderers (March 2005), Perth Glory (Australia, summer 2005), Melbourne Victory (Australia, February 2006), Central Coast Mariners (Australia, February 2008).

Adrian has made 38 Football League appearances, scoring four goals.

Club honours:

National Soccer League Championship (Perth Glory 2002–03, 2003–04), Division Two (Yeovil Town 2004–05), A-League Championship (Melbourne Victory 2006–07), A-League Premiership (Melbourne Victory 2006–07).

Adrian is a dual national (Australian/Argentinian) left-winger, who was fairly anonymous during his short spell at the Rec. He played youth-team football at Boca Juniors and Velez Sarsfield in his birthplace before moving to Perth SC in Australia. Southampton paid £25,000 to bring him to the UK for the first time in September 2000, but he never made it into the first team.

Adrian joined Brentford on a month's loan in September 2001, with his debut coming against Tranmere Rovers later that month. A short spell at Hull City followed before he returned to Australia in April 2002 to sign for Perth Glory. This proved to be a successful move, as the Glory won back-to-back National Soccer League Championships in 2002–03 and 2003–04.

Adrian returned to the UK in July 2004 and signed for Yeovil Town, scoring on his debut against Bury on the opening day of the 2004–05 season. Having played a part in putting the Glovers in a position from which they would win that season's Division Two title, he joined Aldershot Town in February 2005. A month later, he left the Rec relatively unnoticed and made a return to the Football League by signing for Wycombe Wanderers.

At the end of the season, Adrian re-signed for Perth Glory and created club history by scoring their first-ever A-League goal in the League's inaugural season, and he has since developed a reputation for scoring spectacular goals.

In February 2006 Adrian joined fellow A-League side Melbourne Victory and played a crucial role in them winning the 2006–07 A-League Premiership and Championship double (the only time this has been achieved). However, having reportedly become disgruntled at often being used (with, it should be noted, great success) as an 'impact player' from the bench or regularly substituted when he started matches, he signed for fellow A-Leaguers Central Coast Mariners in February 2008. It was agreed that he would remain with the Victory side for the initial stages of the AFC Champions League (which began the following month) before linking up with the Mariners.

Tony Calvert — Midfielder

Born: 20 May 1964, Wokingham.

Aldershot Town FC record:

Debut:	as substitute v Leatherhead (h), Isthmian League Cup preliminary-round replay, 16 September 1992.
Last appearance:	v Ruislip Manor (a), Isthmian League Division One, 6 February 1995.
Appearances:	120 + 5
Goals:	22

Playing career:

Broadmoor (summer 1981), Sandhurst Town (summer 1983), Cove (December 1984), Maidenhead United (1ML, February 1985), Ash United (December 1985), Frimley Green (summer 1987), Camberley Town (DR, August 1987), Farnborough Town (November 1988), Cove (March 1989), Leatherhead (September 1989), Hartley Wintney (January 1990), Farnborough Town (February 1990), Sandhurst Town (summer 1990), Frimley Green (DR, December 1991), Aldershot Town (August 1992), Hampton (March 1995), Wokingham Town (August 1996), Ash United (January 1997), Bracknell Town (August 2001), Ash United (June 2002, player-manager from July 2003), Wokingham and Emmbrook (player-manager, summer 2005), Binfield (November 2007).

Representative honours:

Combined Counties League XI (captain).

Club honours:

Combined Counties League (Ash United 1986–87, 1998–99), Isthmian League Division Three (Aldershot Town 1992–93), Combined Counties Premier Challenge Cup (Ash United 1998), Aldershot Senior Cup (Ash United 1999).

Tony was well known in local footballing circles, both for his playing skills and for his reputation as a practical joker. He began playing for local league side Broadmoor in the summer of 1981 before playing for Combined Counties League sides Sandhurst Town, Cove and Ash United, winning the League title with Ash in 1986–87.

Tony later joined Frimley Green, Camberley Town – with whom he was dual registered – then Farnborough Town, where he was part of the side that was promoted to the Conference for the first time in the club's history, replacing Leytonstone and Ilford; however, Tony left to rejoin Cove before the season's end.

September 1989 saw Tony move to Leatherhead before linking up again with ex-Ash United and ex-Camberley Town boss Mick Wollen at Hartley Wintney the following January. Returns to Farnborough, Sandhurst and Frimley Green (on a dual-registration basis) followed before he signed for Aldershot Town in the summer of 1992. However, a 10-match ban picked up while playing local Sunday league football meant that his debut did not come until mid-September. He soon got into his stride, and his mastery of the midfield was instrumental in the club winning the Isthmian League Division Three title that season.

The following season saw the Shots reach the FA Vase quarter-final before losing to Atherton Laburnum Rovers in a second replay, although the disappointment was offset by securing a second successive promotion (a campaign in which Tony missed just one League game).

Tony left the Rec in March 1995 and joined Hampton, where he helped achieve a top-three finish in the Isthmian League Division Two in 1995–96 before moving on to Wokingham Town in August 1996. He returned for a second spell at Ash in January 1997 and captained the club to victory in the 1998 Combined Counties Premier Challenge Cup Final, plus the Combined Counties League and Aldershot Senior Cup double the following season.

Tony joined Bracknell Town in August 2001 before returning to Shawfields Road for a third spell in the summer of 2002, taking on the role of player-manager in July 2003 and leaving the following May. He then took a year out of the game before taking on the role of player-manager at Hellenic League Division One East side Wokingham and Emmbrook in the summer of 2005. He resigned from his post the following May but was persuaded to return shortly after; however, he had a change of heart and finally left Lowther Road a few weeks before the start of the 2006–07 season.

Tony then retired from regular football, but the lure of playing was too much for him to resist and he came out of retirement in November 2007 to sign for Wokingham's divisional rivals Binfield. Tony has also played veterans' football and was part of the Flackwell Heath Vets side that won the FA Over-40s Cup in 2004, 2005 and 2006, as well as the Vets Junior Cup in 2007. He also played in the Heathens' European title decider defeat against Real Madrid in Spain in October 2005.

Dave Carroll — Midfielder

Born: 20 September 1966, Paisley, Scotland.

Aldershot Town FC record:

Debut:	v Heybridge Swifts (h), Isthmian League Premier Division, 30 March 2002.
Last appearance:	v Chesham United (h), Isthmian League Premier Division, 19 October 2002.
Appearances:	15 + 7
Goals:	2

Playing career:

Chelsea (schoolboy, 1980), Fulham (youth, 1983), Crystal Palace (trial, August 1985), Wembley (August 1985), Ruislip Manor (summer 1986), Wycombe Wanderers (May 1988), Aldershot Town (NC, March 2002), Windsor and Eton (November 2002; player-manager from December 2004).

Dave has made 302 Football League appearances, scoring 40 goals.

Representative honours:

England Schoolboys, FA XI, Middlesex Wanderers.

Club honours:

Berks and Bucks Senior Cup (Wycombe Wanderers 1990), FA Trophy (Wycombe Wanderers 1991, 1993), Championship Shield (Wycombe Wanderers 1991), Bob Lord Trophy (Wycombe Wanderers 1992), Conference (Wycombe Wanderers 1992–93), Division Three Play-off Final (Wycombe Wanderers 1994), Hampshire Senior Cup (Aldershot Town 2002), Isthmian League Premier Division (Aldershot Town 2002–03).

Dave played as a wide midfielder and is a Wycombe Wanderers legend. He played 602 games for the Chairboys and scored more than 100 goals, which led their fans to dub him 'Jesus'. He began as a schoolboy at Chelsea and moved on to play for the youth and reserve teams at Fulham. He turned down the offer of a professional contract at Craven Cottage in favour of going to America on a soccer scholarship. However, he was unable to settle in the States and returned home and then took a break from the game.

Dave's association with Wycombe began in May 1988 when they paid Grosvenor Vale a fee of £8,000 (a record fee for a player leaving Ruislip Manor) to bring him to Loakes Park. He was part of the side that beat Kidderminster Harriers to win the FA Trophy in 1991 and scored in their 1993 Trophy victory over Runcorn. He also played a huge part in winning the Conference in 1992–93, which led to him appearing in their first-ever Football League game against Carlisle United in August 1993.

Dave is currently Wycombe's third-highest Football League appearance-maker (302 games) as well as being their second-highest Football League goalscorer (41 goals). He was a member of the Wycombe side that beat

Preston North End in the Division Three Play-off Final in 1994, with his second goal in the 4–2 victory at Wembley probably ranking as one of the greatest goals ever seen. He also played in the Wycombe side that progressed to the semi-finals of the 2000–01 FA Cup before being beaten 2–1 by Liverpool.

In March 2002 Dave joined Aldershot Town and scored on his debut. Despite being plagued by injuries during his time at the Rec, he still managed to make enough appearances in that Isthmian League Premier Division title-winning season to earn a medal before leaving in November 2002 to join Windsor and Eton. He took on the role of player-manager at Stag Meadow in December 2004 but was sacked in May 2006 after the club were relegated from the Isthmian League Premier Division. Following his sacking, he retired from playing and, in 2007, was voted as the greatest-ever Wycombe player, thus gaining a place in the PFA Hall of Fame.

Stuart Cash — Left-back

Born: 5 September 1964, Tipton.

Aldershot Town FC record:

Debut:	v Leyton Pennant (a), Isthmian League Division One, 24 September 1997.
Last appearance:	v Sutton United (h), Isthmian League Charity Shield, 6 December 1999.
Appearances:	37 + 12
Goals:	3

Playing career:

Wolverhampton Wanderers (youth), Bilston Town, Stourbridge, Halesowen Town, Nottingham Forest (September 1989), Rotherham United (3ML, March 1990), Brentford (3ML, September 1990), Wycombe Wanderers (2ML, March 1991), Shrewsbury Town (2ML, September 1991), Chesterfield (August 1992), Wycombe Wanderers (August 1994), Stevenage Borough (October 1994), Chertsey Town (player-assistant manager, November 1994), Slough Town (January 1997), Chesham United (February 1997), Halesowen Town (March 1997), Enfield (July 1997), Aldershot Town (player-assistant manager, September 1997).

Stuart has made 56 Football League appearances, scoring two goals.

Club honours:

FA Trophy (Wycombe Wanderers 1991), Isthmian League Division One (Aldershot Town 1997–98), Isthmian League Charity Shield (Aldershot Town 1999).

Post-playing coaching/management career:
Assistant manager of Aldershot Town (January 2000), caretaker manager of Aldershot Town (February 2002–March 2002), manager of St Albans City (November 2004), assistant manager of Lewes (June 2005), assistant manager of AFC Wimbledon (May 2007).

Stuart started his career playing youth-team football at Wolverhampton Wanderers before playing senior football for West Midlands sides Bilston Town, Stourbridge and Halesowen Town.

Stuart made his senior debut at Rotherham United in March 1990 against Leyton Orient. A year later, he joined Wycombe Wanderers on a two-month loan – a spell that included him playing in the Chairboys' FA Trophy victory over Kidderminster Harriers. A loan at Shrewsbury Town preceded his leaving the City Ground and signing for Chesterfield in August 1992.

Following a brief return to Wycombe and an even briefer spell at Stevenage Borough, he joined Chertsey Town as player-assistant manager to Allan Cockram. It was at Chertsey that Shots fans first became aware of Stuart, as it was he that scored a late winning goal for the Curfews against Basingstoke Town on the final day of the 1994–95 Isthmian League Division One season to secure the third promotion spot at the expense of the Shots.

After several club stints, Stuart followed manager George Borg to Aldershot Town and was appointed as player-assistant manager. Despite denying them promotion in 1994–95, he quickly became popular with the Shots faithful as he helped oversee the club's winning of the Isthmian League Division One title that season. He gave up playing at the end of 1999 and concentrated on the task of getting the Shots into the Conference, yielding a runners'-up spot that season and fourth place the following season.

Borg departed the Rec in January 2002, and Stuart acted as caretaker manager before reverting to his role as assistant when Terry Brown was appointed as manager in March 2002. The season ended with a third-place finish, but the duo achieved the feat of getting the club into the Conference for the first time ever at the end of the 2002–03 season. The following season, as well as reaching the FA Trophy semi-final, the Shots exceeded all expectations by reaching the Conference Play-off Final. However, the fairytale did not reach its desired conclusion, as they lost on penalties to Shrewsbury Town.

Having been involved in two promotions and five Cup Final victories, Stuart left the Rec in November 2004 to take on the manager's role at St Albans City. However, his stay at Clarence Park lasted just eight days (and two matches) after which he resigned, reportedly due to work and family commitments.

Stuart returned to football in June 2005 when he became assistant manager to Steve King at Conference South side Lewes, helping the club finish in a creditable fourth place. The following season, the Rooks equalled their best-ever FA Cup run by reaching the first round, where they were knocked out by Darlington.

In May 2007 Stuart renewed his managerial partnership with Terry Brown when he joined his ex-Shots boss at AFC Wimbledon. The duo led the Dons to a third-place finish in the Isthmian League Premier Division and to victory over Staines Town in the subsequent Play-off Final. This granted them entry into the Conference South and continued the club's meteoric climb up the pyramid. Away from football, Stuart works as a bailiff.

Jon Challinor — Midfielder

Born: 2 December 1980, Northampton.

Aldershot Town FC record:

Debut:	v Accrington Stanley (h), Conference, 10 August 2003.
Last appearance:	v Carlisle United (a), Conference National Play-off semi-final second leg, 6 May 2005.
Appearances:	87 + 10
Goals:	24

Playing career:
Rushden and Diamonds (from trainee, June 1998), Stamford (February 2000), Cambridge City (February 2001), Kalamazoo Kingdom (US, April 2002), St Albans City (August 2002), Kalamazoo Kingdom (US, April 2003), Aldershot Town (August 2003), Exeter City (May 2005), Rushden and Diamonds (May 2007).

Representative honours:
England National Game XI (one cap).

Jon is an attacking midfielder with a penchant for scoring some spectacular goals. He is the twin brother of Rothwell Town midfielder Richard Challinor and began as a trainee at Rushden and Diamonds, signing a full contract in June 1998. However, he struggled to break into the first team and so moved on to Stamford in February 2000.

Jon's performances brought him to the attention of Southern League Premier Division side Cambridge City, and he moved to Milton Road in February 2001. Again, his performances attracted other sides and, after a spell at United States Soccer League side Kalamazoo Kingdom, he joined St Albans City in August 2002.

He revisited the Kingdom in May 2003 and coached at their summer soccer camps before returning to the UK. He was expected to return to Clarence Park but decided to sign for the Shots instead and played in the club's first-ever Conference game against Accrington Stanley on the opening day of the 2003–04 season before making his only England National Game XI appearance (against Italy) in February 2004.

Jon weighed in with his fair share of goals as the Shots reached the FA Trophy semi-finals but lost in that season's Conference Play-off Final. However, his season did end on a bright note, as he was named in the non-League Team of the Year.

Jon struggled to command a regular starting place the following season, but he continued to contribute goals as the club reached the Play-off semi-finals again (he appeared as a substitute in both legs against Carlisle United).

Jon left the Rec in May 2005 to join Exeter City, and subsequent media reports about his reasons for departing led to him becoming one of the few ex-players to be vehemently disliked by the Shots faithful. He was part of the Exeter side that lost to Grays Athletic in the two-leg semi-final of the 2005–06 FA Trophy, and his performances and goals were also instrumental in helping the Grecians reach the Conference National Play-off Final in 2007, where they lost to Morecambe.

Shortly after the Trophy Final, Jon re-signed for Rushden, for whom he scored eight goals in the 2007–08 season as they reached the Setanta Shield Final (where they lost to the Shots) and attained a 16th-place finish in the Conference Premier.

Lewis Chalmers — Midfielder

Born: 4 February 1986, Manchester.

Aldershot Town FC record:

Debut:	v Kidderminster Harriers (a), Conference Premier, 11 August 2007.
Appearances:	49 + 3
Goals:	3

Playing career:
Manchester United (schoolboy), Manchester City (youth), Accrington Stanley (youth), Altrincham (from youth, November 2004), Aldershot Town (June 2007).

Representative honours:
England National Game XI/England C (ten caps).

Club honours:
Setanta Shield (Aldershot Town 2008), Conference Premier (Aldershot Town 2007–08).

Lewis is the archetypal box-to-box central midfielder, but he also possesses the ability to play as an emergency centre-back. He is very capable of playing the ball around, is not afraid to tackle when required and has a fantastic long throw, all of which contributed to him quickly becoming a crowd favourite at the Rec.

Having played schoolboy football at Manchester United, Lewis went on to play youth-team football at Manchester City and Accrington Stanley before joining Altrincham during the 2002–03 season, eventually making his senior debut for the Robins in March 2005.

Lewis made his England National Game XI debut against Holland in November 2006 and was part of the squad that won the 2005–07 European Challenge Trophy and the Four Nations Tournament in 2007. In June of that year (having played nearly 100 games for the Robins), Lewis got a taste of full-time football when he became Gary Waddock's first Shots signing, after which he stated that the vociferous support that the fans displayed was one of the reasons he decided to join.

His superb performances during the season led to him adding to his tally of England C caps, as well as being one of the leading nominees for the Player of the Year award. He was also part of the Shots side that reached the FA Trophy semi-finals before losing to Ebbsfleet United and the side that won the club's first-ever piece of national silverware, as Rushden and Diamonds were beaten on penalties to win the 2008 Setanta Shield. The 'ultimate prize' followed a couple of weeks later, as the Conference title and promotion into the Football League was achieved.

Shortly after the season's end, Lewis signed a new two-year deal at the Rec, helped England C retain their Four Nations crown and was named in the Conference Premier Team of the Year.

Paul Chambers — Centre-back

Born: 14 January 1965, Wolverhampton.

Aldershot Town FC record:

Debut:	v Billericay Town (h), Isthmian League Division One, 13 August 1994.
Last appearance:	v Marlow (a), Isthmian League Division One, 4 March 1997.
Appearances:	115 + 4
Goals:	9

Playing career:
Plymouth Argyle (from apprentice, January 1983), Saltash United (July 1984), Torquay United (October 1984), Bristol Rovers, Basingstoke Town (December 1990), Aldershot Town (August 1994), Fleet Town (July 1997), Overton United (player-manager, summer 2000).
Paul has made two Football League appearances.

Representative honours:
Isthmian League XI.

Post-playing coaching/management career:
Manager of Overton United (summer 2004).

Paul was a commanding centre-back who began as an apprentice at Plymouth Argyle before signing full professional forms in January 1983. Eighteen months later, he joined Western League side Saltash United before making a return to the Football League with Torquay United in October 1984. He made his senior debut against Colchester United later that month and made one more Football League appearance before having a short spell with Bristol Rovers.

Details of Paul's career immediately after leaving Rovers are unknown, but it is known that he signed for Basingstoke Town in December 1990 and was their captain in 1991–92 and 1992–93. He also won the Player of the Year award at the Camrose in the latter season.

Paul joined Aldershot Town in July 1994 for a then club record £5,000 and was immediately appointed captain. However, even though he performed consistently well, he was never fully accepted by the Shots faithful, who saw him as a poor substitute for Steve Harris (who had made the opposite journey for £2,000 as part of the deal).

Paul eventually left the Rec in July 1997 and joined Hampshire neighbours Fleet Town but only stayed there for four months. He later joined Overton United as player-manager, leading them to promotion to Hampshire League Division One in 2002–03. A knee injury caused him to retire in the summer of 2004, and he resigned his position in April 2005. Paul was last heard of working in the IT department of a Basingstoke-based company.

Neil Champion — Midfielder

Born: 5 November 1975, Farnborough, Hampshire.

Aldershot Town FC record:

Debut:	v Chertsey Town (h), Isthmian League Division One, 16 August 1997.
Last appearance:	v Carshalton Athletic (a), Isthmian League Premier Division, 6 May 2000.
Appearances:	91 + 26
Goals:	1

Playing career:
AFC Bournemouth (trainee, August 1992), Torquay United (trial), Havant Town, Petersfield United (August 1994), Fareham Town (October 1995), Aldershot Town (July 1997), Havant and Waterlooville (May 2000), Chichester City United (1ML, September 2006), Winchester City (October 2006), Farnborough (July 2007), AFC Totton (2007–08 season).

Club honours:
Isthmian League Division One (Aldershot Town 1997–98), Isthmian League Cup (Aldershot Town 1999), Hampshire Senior Cup (Aldershot Town 1999), Russell Cotes Cup (Havant and Waterlooville 2004), Wessex League (AFC Totton 2007–08).

Neil is a battling midfielder who began as a trainee at AFC Bournemouth before financial problems caused him to be released, after which he trialled at Torquay United and played for Havant Town and Petersfield United.

In October 1995 he joined Fareham Town and it soon became evident that he could play at a higher level. That chance came in July 1997 when he joined Aldershot Town, earning the distinction of being Steve Wigley's last-ever signing before he departed the Rec.

Neil's calmness on the ball contributed greatly to the Shots winning the Isthmian League Division One title that season, and that influence carried on the following season when the club won the Isthmian League Cup and Hampshire Senior Cup double. He was unfortunate to be sent off early in the latter Final (against Basingstoke Town), following what appeared to be an innocuous tackle on Toby Redwood, which resulted in the defender's leg being broken. Neil's last appearance for the Shots sticks in supporters' minds, as he saved a penalty after taking over in goal following 'keeper Stuart Searle's dismissal early in the second half.

Neil joined Havant and Waterlooville in May 2000 and was their goalscorer in the 3–1 Hampshire Senior Cup Final defeat by the Shots in 2002. He was also part of the Hawks side that lost to Tamworth over two legs in the 2003 FA Trophy semi-final. The end of Neil's time at Westleigh Park was signalled by a one-month loan to Chichester City United in September 2006, after which he immediately joined Winchester City. He signed for the newly formed Farnborough FC in July 2007 but left shortly after appearing in the opening game of the 2007–08 season. He signed for AFC Totton, where he was part of the side that won that season's Wessex League Premier Division with a whopping 106 points!

Anthony Charles — Defender

Born: 11 March 1981, Isleworth.

Aldershot Town FC record:

Debut:	v Hitchin Town (a), Isthmian League Premier Division, 17 August 2002.
Appearances:	92 + 9
Goals:	4

Playing career:
Brook House, Crewe Alexandra (September 1999), Hyde United (3ML, December 2000), Hayes (1ML, October 2001), Hayes (March 2002), Aldershot Town (July 2002), Lewes (1ML, September 2003), Farnborough Town (October 2003), Barnet (January 2005), Aldershot Town (3ML, February 2007), Aldershot Town (July 2007).
Anthony has made 57 Football League appearances.

Representative honours:
Isthmian League XI, England National Game XI (two caps).

Club honours:
Isthmian League Premier Division (Aldershot Town 2002–03), Hampshire Senior Cup (Farnborough Town 2004), Conference Premier (Aldershot Town 2007–08).

Anthony is primarily a centre-back, but he has been utilised as a left-back on several occasions by the Shots. He started out at Brook House before Crewe Alexandra paid £5,000 for him in September 1999. Unable to get into the first team at Gresty Road, he was loaned out to Northern Premier League side Hyde United and Conference side Hayes before signing permanently at Church Road in March 2002.

Following Hayes' relegation at the end of that season, he joined Aldershot Town for a fee of £1,100, and his defensive versatility played a major part in the club securing that season's Isthmian League Premier Division title. However, by the start of the following season, he had fallen out of favour and joined Lewes on a month's loan in September 2003. The loan was cut short when he reportedly broke club rules prior to an FA Cup tie, so he returned to the Rec and almost immediately signed for Farnborough Town.

Apart from winning the Hampshire Senior Cup in 2004, Anthony's time at Cherrywood Road was fairly unproductive, with the club only avoiding relegation from the Conference in 2003–04 as a result of other qualifying clubs being denied after failing to meet ground grading criteria. Even though he was playing in a struggling side, Anthony still managed to make his England National Game XI debut against Belgium in November 2003, and a second cap followed three months later.

With Boro looking destined for relegation for a second successive season, he left to join that season's eventual champions Barnet for a fee of £12,000, although he did not play enough games for the Bees following his arrival to be awarded a medal.

Anthony made his Football League debut against Bristol Rovers in the opening game of the 2005–06 season and had a steady season and a half before returning to the Rec on a three-month loan in February 2007. The much-improved Anthony Charles quickly became a crowd favourite and was seen as a welcome permanent signing in the summer following his release from Underhill.

During 2007–08, Anthony was part of the Shots side that equalled a club-best progression to the FA Trophy semi-finals and won the Conference Premier title, with the latter achievement making him a 'history maker' – he is the only player to win a title with the Shots, leave and then return to win a second title. Anthony's importance to the side was confirmed when he signed a new two-year contract just after the 2007–08 season finished, and shortly afterwards he was named in the Conference Premier Team of the Year.

Lee Charles **Forward**

Born: 20 August 1971, Hillingdon.

Aldershot Town FC record:

Debut:	v Hitchin Town (a), Isthmian League Premier Division, 17 August 2002.
Last appearance:	as substitute v Shrewsbury Town (at Stoke City FC), Conference Play-off Final, 16 May 2004.
Appearances:	55 + 29
Goals:	22

Playing career:

Yeading, Chertsey Town (December 1993), Queen's Park Rangers (August 1995), Barnet (1ML, September 1995), Cambridge United (1ML, February 1998), Hayes (July 1998), Nuneaton Borough (June 2000), Aldershot Town (July 2002), Weymouth (July 2004), St Albans City (December 2004), Worthing (February 2005), Windsor and Eton (1ML, December 2005), King's Lynn (February 2006), North Greenford United (2006–07 season), Slough Town (July 2007).

Lee has made 28 FA Premier League and Football League appearances, scoring two goals.

Representative honours:

Isthmian League XI, FA XI, England Semi-Professional XI (three caps, one goal).

Club honours:

FA Vase (Yeading 1990), Isthmian League Associate Members' Trophy (Chertsey Town 1994), Isthmian League Cup (Chertsey Town 1994), Isthmian League Premier Division (Aldershot Town 2002–03), Isthmian League Charity Shield (Aldershot Town 2003), Hampshire Senior Cup (Aldershot Town 2003).

'Chippy' – a name that he reportedly got at school because of his love of chips – is predominantly a striker, but he has also played on either side of midfield. He started as a youth player at Yeading and was an 18-year-old substitute in their 1990 FA Vase Final victory against Bridlington. He was also on the fringes of the side that won the Isthmian League Division Two South that season but played a bigger part the following season when the Ding missed promotion by just three points.

In 1991–92 Lee was part of the side that was promoted as a result of finishing as runners-up to Stevenage Borough in Isthmian League Division One, and he finished the 1992–93 season as the club's top scorer (15 goals).

Lee joined Chertsey Town in December 1993, and his 28 goals that season helped the Curfews finish as runners-up to Newbury Town in Isthmian League Division Two (thus securing promotion along with the third-placed Shots). His goals also greatly assisted in the winning of both the Isthmian League Associate Members' Trophy (he scored the only goal in the Final against Hornchurch) and the Isthmian League Cup (he also scored in the victory over Enfield).

He had an even better 1994–95 season at Alwyns Lane, finishing the season having scored 35 goals and being part of the side that pipped the Shots to the third promotion spot on the last day of the season, as well as winning the Player of the Year award. Lee's achievements paved the way for a £67,500 move to FA Premier League side Queen's Park Rangers in August 1995 but he was loaned out to Barnet the following month, and it was for the Bees that he made his senior debut (against Bury). Lee returned to QPR and made his debut for them as a substitute against West Ham United in November 1995. That was to be one of just four appearances that he made that season – a season that was to end in relegation.

Unable to establish himself at Loftus Road with Kevin Gallen, Mark Hateley and John Spencer as competition, Lee was loaned out to Cambridge United in February 1998 before joining Hayes in July 1998. He made a scoring debut for the England Semi-Professional XI (as a substitute) against Italy in March 1999 and finished that season as Hayes' top scorer (21 goals) and Player of the Year. The following season, he was part of the Missioners side knocked out of the FA Cup second round in a replay by Hull City (he scored in both games) and was top scorer again with 18 goals.

In June 2000 Lee joined fellow Conference side Nuneaton Borough but only managed a paltry five League goals that season. He was the club's top scorer the following season (14 goals) before joining Aldershot Town in July 2002. Having scored on his debut, he went on to became the scorer of the Shots' fastest-ever goal, when he netted after just 14 seconds at Andover in a Hampshire Senior Cup semi-final second-leg tie in March 2003.

In 2003–04 he was a member of the side that lost to Hednesford Town in the FA Trophy semi-finals, and his goal in the 1–1 draw against Tamworth in the final game of the 'regular' season confirmed the Shots' place in that season's Conference Play-offs.

Having been part of the side that lost the Play-off Final to Shrewsbury Town, Lee left the Shots after they went full-time that summer. Following spells at several clubs, he signed for Slough Town in July 2007 after a successful trial, but he only played sporadically in a season that saw the Rebels relegated (and later reprieved as Halifax Town were expelled from the Conference Premier) before reportedly retiring at the end of the season. Lee is currently employed as a postal worker.

Gary Cheeseman — Utility defender/Midfielder

Born: 18 January 1974, Guildford.

Aldershot Town FC record:

Debut:	v Worthing (a), Isthmian League Full Members' Cup second round, 2 February 1999.
Appearances:	1

Playing career:

Aldershot Town (January 1999), Farnborough Town (September 1999), Staines Town (July 2000).

Gary could play on either side of the pitch and was comfortable as a defender or as a midfielder. Very little is known about his early career, but he signed for the Shots in January 1999 and made his sole appearance the following month. He signed for Farnborough Town in September 1999 and then moved to Staines Town the following summer but did not make his debut until the following April. He left Staines in April 2003 due to work commitments, and details of his subsequent career are unknown.

John Cheesewright — Goalkeeper

Born: 12 January 1973, Romford.

Aldershot Town FC record:

Debut:	v Croydon (h), Isthmian League Division One, 20 September 1997.
Last appearance:	v Croydon Athletic (h), Isthmian League Cup first round, 21 October 1997.
Appearances:	8

Playing career:

Tottenham Hotspur (from trainee, August 1990), Southend United (March 1991), Birmingham City (November 1991), Kingsbury Town (January 1992), Redbridge Forest (March 1992), Cobh Ramblers (June 1992), Billericay Town (August 1992), Braintree Town (October 1992), Colchester United (January 1994), Wimbledon (STL, July 1995), unknown Hong Kong club (September 1995), Wycombe Wanderers (March 1996), Romford (August 1997), Aldershot Town (September 1997), Heybridge Swifts (November 1997), St Albans City (March 1998), Barnet (NC, April 1998), Gravesend and Northfleet (August 1998), Leyton Pennant (October 1998), Braintree Town (January 1999), Heybridge Swifts (August 1999), Eton Manor (January 2000), Ford United (March 2000). John has made 59 Football League appearances.

Representative honours:
Essex schoolboys, Essex youth.

John was a goalkeeper who was renowned for having an enormous kick. He started out as a trainee at Tottenham Hotspur and signed full contract forms in August 1990 but did not make any first-team appearances at White Hart Lane.

In March 1991 he joined Southend United before moving on to Birmingham City in December of that year. He made his senior debut against AFC Bournemouth that same month and then had brief spells elsewhere before joining Braintree Town in October 1992, where he stayed until January 1994 when Colchester United paid £10,000 to take him to Layer Road. This fee equalled the record for a player leaving the Iron (Matt Metcalf had joined Brentford for the same fee in September 1993).

John made the 'keeper's jersey his own until December 1994, and he joined Wimbledon on a short-term loan in July 1995, playing in three of the Dons' four Intertoto Cup games before going out to play in Hong Kong (it is not known who he played for there).

On his return to the UK in March 1996, he signed for Wycombe Wanderers but did not make an appearance that season. He started the following season as second-choice 'keeper, but a run of poor results saw him claim the number-one spot from Brian Parkin in October 1996. Parkin reclaimed the jersey the following March which led to John leaving Adams Park in August 1997 to join Romford. However, after playing just three games, he signed for Aldershot Town and stayed for two months before joining Heybridge Swifts. He then had several brief spells, including a second spell at Heybridge Swifts in August 1999, which preceded moves to Eton Manor and Ford United, whom he left in May 2000. Details of his subsequent career are unknown.

Jason Chewins — Left-back

Born: 22 October 1970, Portsmouth.

Aldershot Town FC record:

Debut:	v Billericay Town (h), Isthmian League Division One, 13 August 1994.
Last appearance:	as substitute v Hereford United (a), Conference Play-off semi-final second leg, 3 May 2004.
Appearances:	461 + 28 (first in all-time top 10)
Goals:	15

Playing career:
Southampton (youth trial, summer 1985), Newcastle United (youth trial, November 1986), Exeter City (youth trial, May 1987), Alton Town (summer 1987), Basingstoke Town (February 1991), Wealdstone (February 1994), Aldershot Town (July 1994), Havant and Waterlooville (June 2004), Ashford Town (November 2005), Alton Town (September 2007), Cambridge (New Zealand, April 2008).

Representative honours:
Hampshire Under-18s, Isthmian League XI.

Club honours:
Isthmian League Division One (Aldershot Town 1997–98), Isthmian League Cup (Aldershot Town 1999), Hampshire Senior Cup (Aldershot Town 1999, 2000, 2002, 2003), Isthmian League Charity Shield (Aldershot Town 1999, 2003), Isthmian League Premier Division (Aldershot Town 2002–03), Isthmian League Cup (Ashford Town 2007).

Jason is another of the chosen few regarded as legendary by the Shots faithful. He holds the club's appearance record and is widely regarded as a gentleman by countless people within the game.

He began his career with Hampshire League side Alton Town before moving to Isthmian League Premier Division side Basingstoke Town in February 1991 and winning the Player of the Year award in his first season. Following a brief spell at Wealdstone, he joined Aldershot Town in July 1994; however, if fate and, more specifically, caretaker manager Paul Shrubb had not intervened, he may not have lasted as long at the Rec as he did. In January 1995 Jason was due to go out on loan to Bognor Regis Town, but this move was cancelled by Shrubby, who had just taken temporary charge following Steve Wignall's departure. The rest, as they say, is history!

During his time at the Rec, Jason won the Isthmian League Division One (he missed just one League game in 1997–98) and Premier Division titles, as well as four Hampshire Senior Cups, two Isthmian League Charity Shields and an Isthmian League Cup. He also represented the Isthmian League on four occasions and was the first Shots player to reach the 350, 400 and 450-appearance milestones. His consistency also saw him win the supporters' Player of the Year award in 1999 and 2002 – the first time a player had won it twice.

Jason's popularity among the Shots fans led to a public outcry when they felt he was being singled out for criticism by manager George Borg during a run of bad results in the 2001–02 season. Jason was an unused substitute in the club's first-ever Conference game against Accrington Stanley in August 2003 but was in the side that reached that season's FA Trophy semi-finals.

In 2004 he was granted a 10-year testimonial (the only Shots player ever to be given that honour), and his last Shots involvement was as an unused substitute in the 2004 Conference Play-off Final. Jason left the Rec in July 2004 and joined Havant and Waterlooville, and his customary consistency led to him winning the Player of the Year award that season.

In November 2005 he moved to Ashford Town (Middlesex), who were managed by his close friend, former teammate and fellow Shots legend Mark Butler. His experience and coolness was evident throughout a season that culminated in Ashford finishing as runners-up to Clevedon Town in the Southern League Division One West, thus securing promotion to the Isthmian League Premier Division.

Jason returned to his footballing roots in September 2007, re-signing for Alton Town (by now playing in the Wessex League Premier Division) where he stayed until February 2008, when he emigrated to New Zealand. Shortly after arriving on the North Island, Jason signed for Cambridge, who play in Division One of the country's Northern League.

Dwain Clarke — Winger/Forward

Born: 9 April 1978, Hillingdon.

Aldershot Town FC record:

Debut:	as substitute v Canvey Island (h), FA Cup first round, 13 November 2004.
Last appearance:	v Carlisle United (a), Conference National Play-off semi-final second leg, 6 May 2005.
Appearances:	31
Goals:	1

Playing career:
Luton Town (youth), Slough Town (December 1995), Harrow Borough (February 1997), Harrow Borough (January 1999), St Albans City (March 2000), Yeading (August 2000), Wealdstone (October 2000), Yeading (December 2000), Aylesbury United (February 2001), Chesham United (August 2002), Harrow Borough (March 2003), Lewes (June 2003), Crystal Palace (trial, November 2003), Sheffield United (trial, October 2004), Aldershot Town (November 2004), Lewes (trial, June 2005), Canvey Island (August 2005), Maidenhead United (June 2006), Chelmsford City (December 2006), Maidenhead United (trial, July 2007), Staines Town (August 2007), Horsham (March 2008). Carshalton Athletic (June 2008)

Club honours:
Isthmian League Division One South (Lewes 2003–04), Isthmian League Play-off Final (Lewes 2004).

A match-winner on his day, Dwain possesses pace, vision and the ability to score goals. He began as a youth player at Luton Town and went on to play for Slough Town and Harrow Borough. However, in the summer of 1997 he decided to take a break from the game for personal reasons and did not play again until January 1999, when he re-signed for Harrow.

He signed for St Albans City in March 2000 and then had short spells elsewhere before signing for Aylesbury United in February 2001. His all-round play helped the Ducks gain promotion from Isthmian League Division One the following season, but he departed in the summer for Chesham United and then former club Harrow before signing for Lewes in June 2004. His form at the Dripping Pan that season helped the club win the Isthmian League Division One South title and one of the two subsequent Play-off Finals, thus gaining promotion to the Conference South.

Dwain started the 2004–05 season in the same form as he had finished the previous one, which led to him trialling at Sheffield United before joining Aldershot Town in November 2004. His Shots form was erratic, but that did not stop him endearing himself to the fans by scoring in a 4–0 televised drubbing of local rivals Woking and being part of the Shots side that lost to Carlisle United in the Conference National Play-off semi-final.

During the summer of 2005, Dwain trialled at former club Lewes before signing for Canvey Island and then joining Maidenhead United the following summer. He moved on to Chelmsford City a few months later and helped attain a third-place finish in the Isthmian League Premier Division before having a trial at another former club, Maidenhead United, in the summer of 2007 and then signing for Isthmian League Premier Division Staines Town. He was instrumental in helping the Swans reach the FA Cup third round in 2007–08 before being beaten by League Two side Peterborough United. As part of that run, Staines beat Conference Premier side Woking and League Two's Stockport County.

In March 2008, with Staines sitting in fourth place, Dwain moved to divisional rivals Horsham (who were sitting fifth) but the move was not overly fruitful, as the Swans qualified for the end-of-season Play-offs whereas the Hornets finished in 11th spot. Financial constraints saw Dwain depart Queen Street in June 2008 and sign for Carshalton Athletic.

Tony Cleeve — Right-back/Midfielder

Born: 24 December 1974, Frimley.

Aldershot Town FC record:

Debut:	v Malden Vale (h), Isthmian League Associate Members' Trophy second round, 25 January 1994.
Last appearance:	as substitute v Thame United (a), Isthmian League Division One, 25 April 1998.
Appearances:	128 + 12
Goals:	19

Playing career:
Southampton (colts and youth), Cove (October 1993), Aldershot Town (January 1994), Basingstoke Town (June 1994), Aldershot Town (July 1995), Millwall (trial, September 1995), Basingstoke Town (July 1998), Hampton (1ML, October 1999), Bognor Regis Town (1ML, January 2000).

Club honours:
Isthmian League Division One (Aldershot Town 1997–98).

Tony was a competitive defender who could also play in midfield. In fact, much of his early career was spent as an attacking midfielder. He began at Southampton at the age of 11 and worked his way up through the colts and youth teams. He moved to Cove in October 1993 but was on the move again three months later when he joined Aldershot Town. He was a bit-player as the club gained promotion from Isthmian League Division Two that season, so it was no surprise that he went in search of regular first-team football at local rivals Basingstoke Town in June 1994.

Tony returned to the Rec the following summer for a fee of £3,500, but his performances soon brought him to the attention of Millwall, who invited him for a trial in the September. A transfer looked to be on the cards; however, he got injured shortly after his trial ended, and all hopes of a move had disappeared by the time he returned to fitness in the new year.

Tony settled into the right-back spot for the Shots and was a key member of the side that won the Isthmian League Division One title the following season, having missed just one League game in 1996–97. That summer, the club recouped £3,000 of their outlay when Tony returned to the Camrose, from where he made later loan moves to Hampton and Bognor Regis Town before retiring in the summer of 2000 to concentrate on running his own landscaping business.

Les Cleevely — Goalkeeper

Born: 23 September 1965, Clapham.

Aldershot Town FC record:

Debut: v Brading Town (h), Hampshire Senior Cup second round, 1 November 2001.
Last appearance: Croydon (h), Isthmian League Cup first round, 11 December 2001.
Appearances: 2

Playing career:
Southampton (from apprentice, December 1982), Notts County (summer 1983), Brentford (February 1984), Crystal Palace (October 1984), Kungsbaka (Sweden, March 1985), Wealdstone (October 1985), Farnborough Town (December 1985), Epsom and Ewell (March 1987), Carshalton Athletic (July 1987), Welling United (August 1994), Enfield (November 1994), Yeovil Town (February 1995), Carshalton Athletic (July 1995; player-goalkeeping coach from October 1995), Sutton United (player-goalkeeping coach October 1996), Dulwich Hamlet (July 1998; player-manager from November 2000), Croydon (March 2001), Aldershot Town (NC, player-assistant goalkeeping coach, September 2001), Tooting and Mitcham United (November 2003).

Representative honours:
England Youth.

Club honours:
Hampshire Senior Cup (Farnborough Town 1986), Surrey Senior Cup (Carshalton Athletic 1990, 1992), London Challenge Cup (Carshalton Athletic 1991, Dulwich Hamlet 1999), Isthmian League Cup (Sutton United 1998).

Post-playing coaching/management career:
Assistant manager (to Jimmy Bolton) of Carshalton Athletic after Billy Smith left (January 2005 to September 2005), assistant manager of Walton and Hersham (November 2006), manager of Walton and Hersham (March 2007).

Les was a seasoned 'keeper (as well as being one of non-League football's 'characters') who made more than 1,100 appearances during his career. He started as an apprentice at Southampton and signed full professional forms in December 1982. Moves to Notts County, Brentford and Crystal Palace then followed, but he never made the first team at any of those clubs.

In March 1985 Les went to Sweden to play for Kungsbaka before returning to the UK and, after a brief stint at Wealdstone, signing for Farnborough Town in December 1985. Fifteen months and a Hampshire Cup-winners' medal later, he joined Epsom and Ewell and saw out the 1986–87 season there.

In July 1987 he began his affiliation with Carshalton Athletic – a club for whom he made more than 500 appearances (in two spells) and where he was voted Player of the Year no less than three times. He also won the Surrey Senior Cup twice and the London Challenge Cup once, as well as helping them attain a top-10 finish in the Isthmian League Premier Division in each of his seven seasons at Colston Avenue. Les left Carshalton in July 1994 but returned the following summer after brief stints elsewhere.

In October 1995 Les took up the role of player-goalkeeping coach at the club before departing for the same role at fellow Isthmian League Premier Division side Sutton United a year later, helping them achieve successive third-place finishes in the Isthmian League Premier Division.

Les joined Dulwich Hamlet in July 1998 and was part of the side that reached the first round of that season's FA Cup (where they lost to Southport), as well as being voted Player of the Year in 1999 and again in 2000. He assumed the role of player-manager at Champion Hill in November 2000, following Dave Garland's departure. But, unable to prevent the club sliding down the table, Les resigned his position and joined Croydon in March 2001.

In September he came to Aldershot Town and (in addition to being a player) assisted Paul Priddy with the coaching of the 'keepers, and he made two first-team appearances before retiring around the start of 2002.

However, he came out of retirement in November 2003 to help out Tooting and Mitcham United before retiring from playing for good in the summer of 2004.

Les returned to Carshalton in January 2005 as assistant to newly appointed boss Jimmy Bolton, and the duo helped secure the club's place in the Conference South with a win at Eastbourne Borough on the last day of the 2004–05 season before departing Colston Avenue a month into the following season. Les then became Bobby Paterson's assistant at Walton and Hersham in November 2006 and took up the mantle of manager after Paterson's resignation the following March. A piece of role reversal then came into play when he appointed Jimmy Bolton as his assistant.

Les runs his own goalkeeping academy and, at various points in his career, has also coached at Millwall, Fulham, Crystal Palace, Tottenham Hotspur and Chelsea (where he currently works with Stuart Searle). He resigned from the manager's position at Stompond Lane at the end of the 2007–08 season, citing his workload at his academy and at Chelsea as the determining factors.

Sam Cobbett — Midfielder

Born: 21 October 1980, Aldershot.

Aldershot Town FC record:

Debut: as substitute v Berkhamsted Town (a), Isthmian League Cup third round, 5 January 1999.
Last appearance: as substitute v Enfield (h), Isthmian League Premier Division, 1 May 1999.
Appearances: 4 + 10

Playing career:
Mytchett Athletic (youth), Aldershot Town (from youth, December 1998), Bracknell Town (summer 1999), Hartley Wintney (summer 2000), Kirkham and Wesham (summer 2003), Hartley Wintney (summer 2004).

Club honours:
Isthmian League Cup (Aldershot Town 1999 [unused substitute]), Basingstoke Senior Cup (Hartley Wintney 2003), West Lancashire League (Kirkham and Wesham 2003–04).

Sam is the elder brother of Camberley Town midfielder Ben Cobbett and began as a youth player at Mytchett Athletic. He then joined the Aldershot Town youth team and signed full contract forms in December 1998.

After leaving the Shots, Sam played for Bracknell Town and Hartley Wintney before moving up North in the summer of 2003 and playing for West Lancashire League side Kirkham and Wesham. Having won the League title in 2003–04, Sam returned South and rejoined Hartley Wintney, where he experienced relegation from the Combined Counties Premier Division in 2004–05. The next three seasons in Division One brought a mixture of fortune as fifth, 16th and third-place finishes were achieved.

Omari Coleman — Forward

Born: 23 November 1981, Birmingham.

Aldershot Town FC record:

Debut: v Dagenham and Redbridge (a), Conference National, 9 October 2005.
Last appearance: v Burnham (a), FA Cup first round, 5 November 2005.
Appearances: 7
Goals: 1

Playing career:
Millwall (youth), Croydon (October 1999), Dulwich Hamlet (January 2002), Watford (July 2004), Lincoln City (July 2005), Aldershot Town (1ML, October 2005), Gravesend and Northfleet (1ML, November 2005), Crawley Town (January 2006), Carshalton Athletic (August 2006), Dulwich Hamlet (December 2006), Fisher Athletic (London, DR, December 2006), Worthing (February 2007), Welling United (August 2007), Bromley (March 2008).

Club honours:
London Senior Cup (Dulwich Hamlet 2004).

Omari is the younger brother of ex-Croydon striker Levi Coleman, and he came to the Rec on loan during the 2005–06 season. However, like several other loanees around that time, he failed to produce. He was a youth player with Millwall before joining Croydon in October 1999, playing in the reserves. When he did eventually force his way into the side the following season, he tended to be used as a winger rather than a forward.

Omari moved to Dulwich Hamlet in January 2002 and was the club's top scorer in 2002–03 (25 goals) and 2003–04 (28 goals), with his goals in the latter season contributing greatly to them reaching the Isthmian League Division One South Play-off Final, which they lost on penalties to Wealdstone. That same season, he scored both goals in Hamlet's 2–0 victory over Tooting and Mitcham United in the London Senior Cup Final. That was to be the last act of his time at Champion Hill, as he left in July to join Watford for a fee of £2,750, but injury hampered his attempts to break into the first team.

Several moves followed, including a month's loan at Aldershot Town in October 2005, but Omari found it hard to establish himself. He joined Worthing in February 2007, with his signing reportedly ending a six-month long chase by Rebels boss Danny Bloor. Following his arrival at Woodside Road, Omari put in several good performances but could not prevent relegation from the Isthmian League Premier Division.

In August 2007 he signed for Welling United and made a scoring debut against Bognor Regis Town on the opening day of the Conference South season. By the following March, the club were hovering dangerously above the drop zone, so personnel changes were implemented and Omari was one of those who left. He signed for Bromley and, in an ironic twist of fate, scored twice on his debut against Welling before the Lillywhites eventually finished the season in 11th place

Owen Coll — Utility defender

Born: 9 April 1976, Donegal.

Aldershot Town FC record:

Debut:	v Chertsey Town (a), Isthmian League Cup second round, 24 November 1998.
Last appearance:	v Havant and Waterlooville (at Southampton FC), Hampshire Senior Cup Final, 1 May 2002.
Appearances:	185 + 5 (seventh in all-time top 10)
Goals:	18

Playing career:
Enfield Rangers (youth, August 1993), Tottenham Hotspur (from trainee, July 1994), Yeovil Town (1ML, February 1995), AFC Bournemouth (March 1996), Barnet (trial, July 1998), Yeovil Town (August 1998), Oxford United (trial, August 1998), Northampton Town (trial, September 1998), Stevenage Borough (October 1998), Aldershot Town (November 1998), Scunthorpe United (trial, July 1999), Grays Athletic (May 2002), Hitchin Town (August 2003), Cheshunt (January 2004).
Owen has made 24 Football League appearances.

Representative honours:
Republic of Ireland Juniors, Republic of Ireland Under-21s (three caps).

Club honours:
Isthmian League Cup (Aldershot Town 1999), Hampshire Senior Cup (Aldershot Town 1999, 2000, 2002), Isthmian League Charity Shield (Aldershot Town 1999).

Owen is one of a select few Aldershot Town players to have played in a European club competition – he played in three of Tottenham Hotspur's four Intertoto Cup games in the summer of 1995. Having started out at his local youth side Enfield Rangers, he moved to Spurs and signed full professional forms in July 1994. He played two FA Trophy games (both against Stevenage Borough) on loan at Yeovil Town in February 1995 and was capped at Under-21 level by the Republic of Ireland before leaving White Hart Lane in March 1996 to join AFC Bournemouth. He made his Football League debut for the Cherries against Bristol Rovers in March 1996 and drifted in and out of the side over the next two years.

Trials at Barnet, Oxford United and Northampton Town, a brief return to Huish Park and a short spell at Stevenage Borough preceded Owen's arrival at the Rec in November 1998. He made an immediate impact by scoring on his debut, and he progressed sufficiently in his first season with the Shots to be offered a trial at Scunthorpe United in July 1999.

Owen matured into a committed defender and was part of the Shots sides that triumphed in some minor Cups and regularly pushed for promotion from the Isthmian League Premier Division. He left the Rec in May 2002 and joined fellow Premier Division side Grays Athletic, but he had a wretched time there, with a knee injury eventually forcing his release in December 2002.

Following exploratory surgery and his subsequent recuperation, he joined Hitchin Town in August 2003 but never recaptured the form that he had produced with the Shots. He retired in the summer of 2004 and currently works for a company involved in the underpinning of buildings.

Danny Colley — Right-back

Born: 31 July 1981, Bracknell.

Aldershot Town FC record:

Debut: v Basingstoke Town (h), Isthmian League Premier Division, 5 April 1999.
Last appearance: v Heybridge Swifts (a), Isthmian League Premier Division, 27 April 1999.
Appearances: 6

Playing career:

Wycombe Wanderers (youth), Aldershot Town (youth, July 1998), Chertsey Town (1ML, January 2000), Flackwell Heath (1ML, February 2000), Windsor and Eton (August 2000), Wokingham Town (October 2000), Sandhurst Town (October 2003), Cove (summer 2005).

Danny was a young right-back who had previously been part of the youth set-up at Wycombe Wanderers. Although he was at the Rec for approximately two years, his six first-team appearances all came in a three-week period at the end of the 1998–99 season. He was loaned to Chertsey Town and Flackwell Heath the following season before joining Windsor and Eton in August 2000.

Danny later played for Wokingham Town (where he experienced relegation from Isthmian League Division Two at the end of his first season), Sandhurst Town and Cove before giving up playing in the summer of 2006. He currently works as a gas engineer.

Steve Collis — Goalkeeper

Born: 18 March 1981, Harrow.

Aldershot Town FC record:

Debut: v Grays Athletic (a), Isthmian League Cup quarter-final, 5 March 2002.
Last appearance: v Heybridge Swifts (h), Isthmian League Premier Division, 30 March 2002.
Appearances: 6

Playing career:

Watford (trainee, July 1997), Barnet (NC, August 1999), Chesham United (1999–2000 season), Nottingham Forest (July 2000), Bristol Rovers (trial, July 2001), Yeovil Town (August 2001), Aldershot Town (1ML, March 2002), Tiverton Town (3ML, August 2002), Southend United (June 2006).
Steve has made 65 Football League appearances.

Steve began his career at the Watford Academy, where he was managed by Gary Johnson (his future boss at Yeovil Town). He joined Barnet on an 'emergency' non-contract basis in August 1999 to act as cover for the injured Lee Harrison, but he did not make an appearance. He did, however, make a solitary appearance for Chesham United before joining Nottingham Forest in July 2000. The following summer, he was released and trialled at Bristol Rovers before signing for Yeovil, where he vied for the number-one jersey with ex-Aldershot FC 'keeper Jon Sheffield.

Steve arrived at the Rec on a one-month loan in March 2002 but returned to Huish Park to make one appearance as the Glovers finished third in the Conference. It was a similar story the following season when he was loaned out to Tiverton Town for the first three months of the season before returning to Yeovil and waiting until the penultimate game of the Conference-winning campaign to make an appearance.

Steve's first appearance for Yeovil as a League club was in a Football League Trophy match against AFC Bournemouth in October 2003, but he had to wait until March 2004 to get a League outing, playing the last 11 games of the season as the club narrowly missed out on promotion (on goal difference). He started the first two games of the following season but did not play again until the following March.

Steve played in approximately half of the club's games in 2005–06 before departing for Southend United in the summer, making just one substitute appearance in the 2006–07 season as the Shrimpers were relegated out of the Championship.

The following season, he played in just under half of Southend's League games but did not figure after the New Year's Day defeat to Bristol Rovers. The Shrimpers finished the season in sixth place, and Steve was an unused substitute for both legs of their aggregate defeat to Doncaster Rovers in the Play-off semi-finals. A few days after the aforementioned Play-off defeat, Steve was released by the Roots Hall side and is currently without a club.

Brett Cooper — Right-back/Midfielder

Born: 27 March 1985, Portsmouth.

Aldershot Town FC record:

Debut: as substitute v Bedford Town (a), Isthmian League Premier Division, 24 September 2002.
Last appearance: v Eastleigh (h), Hampshire Senior Cup quarter-final, 27 January 2004.
Appearances: 7 + 6

Playing career:
Aldershot Town (from youth, August 2002), Uxbridge (1ML, March 2003), Chertsey Town (SLL, August 2003), Frimley Green (STL, March 2004), Basingstoke Town (July 2004), Ashford Town (July 2005), Ashford Town (November 2007).

Representative honours:
Aldershot and Farnborough District Schoolboys, Hampshire Schools, Isthmian League XI.

Brett was part of the Aldershot Town youth set-up and his versatility at right-back and right midfield contributed to him being offered a full contract in August 2002. However, he never quite managed to establish himself at the Rec so he joined Basingstoke Town in July 2004, following a one-month loan at Uxbridge, a season-long loan at Chertsey Town and a very brief spell at Frimley Green.

The following summer, Brett joined Mark Butler's Ashford Town (Middlesex) and was part of the side that finished the season as runners-up to Clevedon Town in the Southern League Division One West. At the end of the 2006–07 season, he took a break from playing and went out to the States to work as a coach in the New York Red Bulls' soccer school. Brett returned to Short Lane in November 2007, and Ashford eventually finished sixth that season, narrowly missing out on the Play-offs.

Grant Cornock — Forward

Born: 2 February 1980, Watford.

Aldershot Town FC record:

Debut: as substitute v Harrow Borough (h), Isthmian League Premier Division, 5 September 1999.
Last appearance: as substitute v Aylesbury United (a), Isthmian League Premier Division, 7 September 1999.
Appearances: 0 + 2

Playing career:
Watford (from trainee, July 1998), Yeading (August 1999), Aldershot Town (NC, September 1999), Hemel Hempstead Town (January 2000), Harrow Borough (March 2000).

Grant was another of those players who failed to impress at the Rec. His scoring record in Watford's youth team facilitated his signing in July 1998, but he never made a first-team appearance. Following his release from Watford in the summer of 1999, he played briefly for Yeading before joining Aldershot Town in the September. Two non-descript performances meant he soon departed to play for Hemel Hempstead Town and Harrow Borough, leaving the latter club in May 2000.

Grant then plied his trade in the local Hertfordshire leagues, with the 'This Is Local London' website reporting in September 2001 that 'the former professional forward showed he has lost none of his goalscoring instinct by smashing nine goals in the Duke of York's 16–0 demolition of Met Police Bushey B'. Any Shots fans reading would have wished he could have done that in the Isthmian League rather than saving it for a West Hertfordshire League Division Three match.

By 2006 Grant had attained a BA and is believed to be working as a physical education teacher at a school in Hemel Hempstead.

Jason Cousins — Centre-back

Born: 14 October 1970, Hayes.

Aldershot Town FC record:

Debut: v Hitchin Town (a), Isthmian League Premier Division, 17 August 2002.
Last appearance: v Bashley (at Southampton FC), Hampshire Senior Cup Final, 8 May 2003.
Appearances: 36 + 7
Goals: 1

Playing career:
Brentford (from trainee, July 1989), Wycombe Wanderers (July 1991), Aldershot Town (June 2002), Windsor and Eton (June 2003), Maidenhead United (summer 2005).

Representative honours:
Isthmian League XI.

Club honours:
Championship Shield (Wycombe Wanderers 1991), Bob Lord Trophy (Wycombe Wanderers 1992), Conference (Wycombe Wanderers 1992–93), FA Trophy (Wycombe Wanderers 1993), Division Three Play-off Final (Wycombe Wanderers 1994), Isthmian League Premier Division (Aldershot Town 2002–03), Hampshire Senior Cup (Aldershot Town 2003).
Jason has made 317 Football League appearances, scoring six goals.

Jason is a legendary figure at Wycombe Wanderers, but he began his career as a trainee at Brentford. His debut for the Bees (against Bury in January 1989) came while he was still a trainee, and he signed full professional forms that summer.

In 1990–91 he was a member of the Brentford side that lost to Birmingham City in the Southern Area Final of the Associate Members' Cup before beginning an 11-year association with Wycombe in July 1991. He was a central figure in the Chairboys winning several pieces of silverware, the most prestigious of which (in non-League terms) was the Conference and FA Trophy double in 1992–93, with Jason scoring in the trophy victory against Runcorn. He also appeared in Wycombe's first-ever Football League match in August 1993 and was a member of the side (along with Dave Carroll and Matt Crossley) that beat Preston North End in that season's Division Three Play-off Final.

Jason was voted the club's Player of the Year in 1995 and 1999 before helping them come to national prominence by reaching the 2000–01 FA Cup semi-final, where they lost to Liverpool by the odd goal in three.

After making 473 appearances for the Chairboys, he joined Aldershot Town in June 2002 and helped the club win the Isthmian League Premier Division title. The Shots played at Canvey Island in the run-up to the title, and this game is considered by many to be Jason's best game for the Shots by far, as (having come on as a substitute for the injured Ray Warburton) he almost single-handedly kept the opposing attack at bay.

In the summer of 2003 Jason left the Rec and joined Windsor and Eton, whom he helped to promotion from the Isthmian League Division One South in his first season. After a couple of seasons at Stag Meadow, Jason made two appearances for Maidenhead United before retiring in September 2005.

Bertrand Cozic — Midfielder

Born: 18 May 1975, Quimper, France.

Aldershot Town FC record:

Debut: v Halifax Town (a), Conference National, 20 August 2005.
Last appearance: v Altrincham (h), Conference National, 27 August 2005.
Appearances: 2

Playing career:

CFC Quimper (France), En Avant Guingamp (France), Union Sportive Quevilly (France), Bihorel (France), Bath City (trial, July 2002), Team Bath (July 2002), Cheltenham Town (August 2003), St Patrick's Athletic (August 2003), Notts County (trial, February 2004), Hereford United (March 2004), Northampton Town (August 2004), Kidderminster Harriers (January 2005), Aldershot Town (NC, August 2005), Team Bath (September 2005), Exeter City (July 2006).
Bertrand has made 36 Football League appearances, scoring one goal.

Club Honours:

Conference Premier Play-Off Final (Exeter City 2008 [unused substitute]).

Bertrand spent the early part of his career playing in his homeland. In July 2002 he trialled at Bath City and then signed for close neighbours Team Bath, where he was part of the side that progressed to the FA Cup first round in 2002–03 before losing to Mansfield Town.

In August 2003 Bertrand moved to Cheltenham Town, making his debut as a substitute in a League Cup tie against Queen's Park Rangers that same month. He did not stay long at Whaddon Road (a common trend in his career until he arrived at Exeter City) and moved to Irish side St Patrick's Athletic before trialling at Notts County and then joining Hereford United in March 2004.

Bertrand was released at the end of the season, joined Northampton Town in the August and then moved on to Kidderminster Harriers the following January. Unfortunately, the Harriers were relegated from the Football League at the end of the season, which resulted in his departure. He arrived at the Rec in August 2005 but returned to Team Bath after making just two appearances.

The following July, he trialled at Exeter City and impressed sufficiently to be offered a contract. Although Exeter finished the season as runners-up to Morecambe in the Conference National Play-Off Final, Bertrand played no part in those end-of-season games.

Injury restricted him to just 18 appearances in the 2007–08 season as the Grecians finished fourth in the Conference Premier. He was then an unused substitute as they beat Cambridge United in the Play-off Final, thus ensuring their return to the Football League after a five-year absence.

Adam Crittenden — Forward

Born: 6 January 1981, Bracknell.

Aldershot Town FC record:

Debut:	v Fareham Town (h), Hampshire Senior Cup second round, 2 November 2004.
Last appearance:	as substitute v Canvey Island (a), Conference National, 7 December 2004.
Appearances:	2 + 2
Goals:	2

Playing career:

Wycombe Wanderers (youth), Windsor and Eton (youth), Bracknell Town (March 1999), Windsor and Eton (August 2000), Bracknell Town (August 2001), Aldershot Town (NC, November 2004), Windsor and Eton (December 2004), Bracknell Town (trial, July 2005), Cove (July 2005), Ash United (August 2006), Bracknell Town (trial, July 2007), Camberley Town (August 2007), Bracknell Town (November 2007).

Adam is a forward who does not seem to have had a consistent run in any first team; however, when he does play, he seems to score. He is the younger brother of fellow Shot Nick Crittenden and was part of the youth set-ups at both Wycombe Wanderers and Windsor and Eton before moving to Bracknell Town in March 1999. He returned to Stag Meadow in August 2000 before going back to Bracknell a year later.

During his second spell at Larges Lane, he was part of the side that was promoted to Isthmian League Division One South following League restructuring in the summer of 2002, as well as being the club's top scorer in 2003–04 (27 goals), an achievement that paved the way for a move to Aldershot Town in November 2004.

Although Adam's stay at the Rec was brief, he twice entered the record books (along with his brother) – his debut was the only instance of brothers playing in the same game for the Shots, and the Crittendens followed this by being the only brothers to score for the club in the same season.

Adam rejoined Windsor and Eton the following month and then had spells with Cove, Ash United, Bracknell Town and Camberley Town. In November 2007 he was one of a number of new signings who were brought in to

Bracknell Town (again) to try to halt the club's slide down the Southern League Division One South and West, but they struggled for the whole season and avoided relegation by just one place and two points.

Nick Crittenden — Midfielder/Winger

Born: 11 November 1978, Ascot.

Aldershot Town FC record:

Debut:	v York City (h), Conference National, 14 August 2004.
Last appearance:	as substitute v Southport (a), Conference National, 29 April 2006.
Appearances:	83 + 18
Goals:	15

Playing career:
Chelsea (from trainee, July 1997), Plymouth Argyle (1ML, October 1998), Yeovil Town (August 2000), Aldershot Town (June 2004), Weymouth (May 2006), Dorchester Town (June2008).
Nick has made 33 FA Premier League and Football League appearances, scoring two goals.

Representative honours:
England Semi-Professional XI (one cap, one goal).

Club honours:
FA Trophy (Yeovil Town 2002), Conference (Yeovil Town 2002–03).

Nick started out as a trainee at Chelsea, where he won the Young Player of the Year award in 1997, which acted as a springboard to him signing full professional forms in July of that year. He made his senior debut against Southampton in a League Cup tie in November 1997 and another two senior appearances followed that season.

A one-month loan to Plymouth Argyle came in October 1998 before he was released from Stamford Bridge at the end of the 1999–2000 season. He signed for Yeovil Town in August 2000 and played a pivotal role in the Glovers finishing as runners-up to Rushden and Diamonds in the Conference that season. He won one of the supporters' Player of the Year awards, as well as being voted into the 2001 Conference Team of the Year. His performances not only helped the club finish third in the Conference and win the FA Trophy (by beating Stevenage Borough) but they also led to him making his sole appearance for the England Semi-Professional XI – he was a scoring substitute against the USA in March 2002.

The 2002–03 season saw Nick help Yeovil finally achieve Football League status when they won the Conference at a canter, finishing 17 points clear of Morecambe. He then appeared in the club's first-ever Football League match against Rochdale in August 2003 and was regularly involved as they went on to attain a creditable eighth-place finish in their first season as a League club.

In June 2004 Nick signed for Aldershot Town and was part of the side that lost to Carlisle United in the Conference National Play-off semi-final. Just about the only bright spot of that tie for him was that his goal gave the Shots a 1–0 home victory in the first leg. He stayed at the Rec for one more season before signing for Conference National outfit Weymouth in May 2006, helping them to a mid-table finish in 2006–07.

However, the Terras had a worse time in 2007–08 as they finished in 18th place, with the point gained in a goalless draw against the Shots in the penultimate game of the season guaranteeing their Conference Premier safety. Nick made 39 appearances for the Terras in all competitions that season, scoring four goals before leaving shortly after the end of the campaign and dropping down a division to join Conference South side Dorchester Town.

Ryan Crockford — Midfielder

Born: 3 December 1986, Reading.

Aldershot Town FC record:

Debut:	as substitute v Gravesend and Northfleet (a), Conference National, 1 April 2006.
Last appearance:	v Southport (a), Conference National, 29 April 2006.
Appearances:	3 + 3

Playing career:
Reading (from academy, July 2005), Aldershot Town (2ML, March 2006), Sutton United (July 2006), Thatcham Town (November 2006), Didcot Town (summer 2007), Reading Town (December 2007).

Representative honours:
Wales Under-17s.

Ryan is a central-midfielder who was disappointing during a spell on loan from Reading. He graduated from the Royals' academy, where his performances had earned him a call-up to the Wales Under-17s and led to him signing full professional forms in July 2005.

Ryan came to the Rec on a two-month loan deal in March 2006 but failed to make an impression in his six appearances. Having failed to make the first team at the Madejski Stadium, he dropped down the leagues, signing firstly for Sutton United and then Thatcham Town before joining Didcot Town in the summer of 2007. However, he only played in the Railwaymen's reserve side before leaving after being arrested and charged with grievous bodily harm with intent in November 2007, following an incident in Reading town centre. Ryan joined Reading Town the following month, but his season ended in April 2008 when he was found guilty of the aforementioned charge and given a four-year custodial sentence. For the record, Reading Town finished the season in 13th spot in the Combined Counties League Premier Division.

Matt Crossley — Defender

Born: 18 March 1968, Basingstoke.

Aldershot Town FC record:

Debut:	v Sutton United (h), Isthmian League Premier Division, 19 August 2000.
Last appearance:	v Gravesend and Northfleet (a), Isthmian League Premier Division, 31 March 2001.
Appearances:	31 + 1

Playing career:
Newbury Town (April 1984), Aldershot FC (YTS, August 1984), Basingstoke Town (March 1986), Overton United (August 1986), Wycombe Wanderers (August 1987), Kingstonian (June 1997), Aldershot Town (June 2000), Woking (trial, May 2001), Andover (player-coach, August 2001).
Matt has made 96 Football League appearances, scoring three goals.

Representative honours:
Hampshire Youth, Isthmian League XI, FA XI.

Club honours:
Berks and Bucks Senior Cup (Wycombe Wanderers 1990), FA Trophy (Wycombe Wanderers 1991, 1993; Kingstonian 1999, 2000), Conference (Wycombe Wanderers 1992–93), Division Three Play-off Final (Wycombe Wanderers 1994), Isthmian League Premier Division (Kingstonian 1997–98), Team Talk Challenge Trophy (Kingstonian 1999), Wessex League (Andover 2001–02).

Post-playing coaching/management career:
Assistant manager of Woking (November 2002).

Matt was a steady centre-back and is the son of ex-Shots commercial manager Ian Crossley. He played a few games at Newbury Town while still at school, before joining Aldershot FC on the Manpower Services Work Scheme (along with Mark Frampton) and signing YTS forms in August 1984. He tasted life in the senior squad that November when appearing as a substitute in a testimonial for the club's legendary skipper Joe Jopling against Aston Villa.

Matt had a brief spell at Basingstoke Town before moving to Overton United and then signing for Wycombe Wanderers in August 1987. He enjoyed great success in his 10 years with Wycombe – he was an FA Trophy winner twice and a member of the Chairboys side that won the Conference in 1992–93. He appeared in the club's first-ever Football League match against Carlisle United in August 1993 and was a member of the side that beat Preston North End in that season's Division Three Play-off Final.

Matt moved to Kingstonian in June 1997 and continued to be a winner. He was a member of the Ks side that won the Isthmian League Premier Division in 1997–98 and experienced personal glory by winning the Player of the Year that season. He also won the FA Trophy twice more, captaining the Ks to their 1999 and 2000 triumphs when they beat Forest Green Rovers and Kettering Town respectively.

In June 2000 Matt joined Aldershot Town in exchange for a £2,500 fee and performed consistently in a season that would see the Shots finish fourth in the Isthmian League Premier Division. He was released at the end of the season and, having trialled at Woking, joined Andover in the role of player-coach in August 2001, helping the club win that season's Wessex League title before retiring in the summer of 2002. In November of that year, he became assistant to Glenn Cockerill at the Shots' local Conference rivals Woking, where the duo's first season in charge nearly ended in disaster, as the Cards avoided relegation by virtue of a win against Telford United on the last day of the season.

The club finished in the top half of the table in the next three seasons and also lost to Grays Athletic in the 2006 FA Trophy Final, but a run of poor results saw the pair sacked in March 2007. Matt is not currently involved in football and works as a trader in stocks and shares.

Jimmy Dack — Midfielder

Born: 2 June 1972, Roehampton.

Aldershot Town FC record:

Debut: v Chesham United (a), Isthmian League Premier Division, 1 September 1998.
Last appearance: as substitute v Heybridge Swifts (h), Isthmian League Premier Division, 9 December 1998.
Appearances: 18 + 3

Playing career:
Brentford (youth), Epsom and Ewell (summer 1989), Wimbledon (trial, summer 1990), Sutton United (August 1990), Dorking (3ML, February 1993), Crawley Town (August 1993), Carshalton Athletic (November 1994), Sutton United (June 1995), Kingstonian (trial, July 1998), Aldershot Town (August 1998), Sutton United (January 1999), Farnborough Town (August 2000), Crawley Town (August 2001), Tooting and Mitcham United (July 2002), Carshalton Athletic (player-coach, June 2003).

Representative honours:
Isthmian League XI.

Club honours:
Bob Lord Trophy (Sutton United 1991), Isthmian League Full Members' Cup (Sutton United 1996), Isthmian League Cup (Sutton United 1998), Isthmian League Premier Division (Sutton United 1998–99, Farnborough Town 2000–01), Surrey Senior Cup (Sutton United 1999).

Post-playing coaching/management career:
Assistant manager-coach of Stevenage Borough (May 2004), youth-team coach/first-team coach of Woking (July 2005), assistant manager of Fisher Athletic (London, summer 2006), assistant manager of Grays Athletic (January 2007), caretaker manager of Sutton United (March 2008), assistant manager at Welling United (May 2008).

Jimmy was an energetic wide midfielder who was not averse to scoring goals. He started out as a youth player at Brentford before going on to play for Epsom and Ewell and then trialling at Wimbledon.

In August 1990 he signed for Conference side Sutton United but suffered relegation at the end of the season. Having been loaned out to Dorking at the end of the 1992–93 season, he signed for Southern League Premier Division side Crawley Town in August 1993 and helped the club to a top-five finish that season.

In November 1994 he joined Carshalton Athletic before returning to Gander Green Lane the following June. He helped the club win some minor silverware and attain successive top-three finishes in the Isthmian League Premier Division (1996–97 and 1997–98), then signed for Aldershot Town in August 1998 after a trial at Kingstonian.

His goalscoring touch deserted him at the Rec, so people were not surprised when he returned to Sutton (in exchange for £2,000) for a third spell in January 1999. It proved to be the right move, as the season ended with him being part of the side that won the Isthmian League Premier Division title and the Surrey Senior Cup. Unfortunately, the following season turned out be a case of déjà vu for Jimmy, as he experienced relegation with the Us for a second time.

In August 2000 Jimmy joined Farnborough Town and contributed greatly to the club winning that season's Isthmian League Premier Division title. Surprisingly, he left Cherrywood Road and rejoined Crawley in August 2001 before moving on to Tooting and Mitcham United and then returning to Carshalton as player-coach in June 2003.

Jimmy retired from playing in the summer of 2004 and made a move into coaching, joining the staff at Stevenage Borough. From there, he became youth-team coach and then first-team coach at Woking before working as Justin Edinburgh's assistant at both Fisher Athletic (London) and Grays Athletic.

Jimmy left Grays in October 2007 and was out of football until the following March, when he took over as caretaker manager of Sutton United following the departure of Ernie Howe. Unfortunately, despite Jimmy's best efforts in the five games for which he was in charge, the Us were relegated out of Conference South by virtue of a rock-bottom finish.

Midway through May 2008 it was announced that he would not be taking on the role permanently, reportedly due to a failure to reach an agreement regarding the playing budget. Shortly after that announcement, Jimmy became assistant manager to Andy Ford at Welling United. Away from football, Jimmy works as a taxi driver.

Scott Davies — Midfielder

Born: 10 March 1988, Aylesbury.

Aldershot Town FC record:

Debut:	v Kidderminster Harriers (a), Conference Premier, 11 August 2007.
Last appearance:	v Stafford Rangers (a), Conference Premier, 29 March 2008.
Appearances:	35 + 7
Goals:	11

Playing career:
Watford (schoolboy), Wycombe Wanderers (youth), Reading (from academy, summer 2006), Yeading (1ML, September 2006), Aldershot Town (SLL, July 2007).

Representative honours:
Republic of Ireland Under-17s, Republic of Ireland Under-19s.

Club honours:
Conference Premier (Aldershot Town 2007–08).

Scott is an attacking midfielder and the son of ex-Aylesbury United defender Kevin Davies. He started his career as a schoolboy at Watford and became a youth player at Wycombe Wanderers before moving to the Reading academy in October 2002. His consistent performances made him the natural choice to captain the Royals' youth side (which he has done on several occasions), as well as leading to him signing full professional forms in the summer of 2006.

Scott joined Yeading on a one-month loan deal in September 2006 but left after just five appearances to play for the Republic of Ireland in the UEFA Under-19 Championships. He joined the Shots on a season-long loan in July 2007 after impressing in a pre-season friendly against Crystal Palace, and he scored with a thunderous shot on his debut at Kidderminster Harriers on the opening day of the season.

As the season progressed, Scott improved and contributed some spectacular long-range goals, both from open play and from set-pieces. In fact, Scott was so good that many Shots fans support the notion that he is the best-ever Shots loanee. He won many rave reviews during a season that saw the Shots reach the FA Trophy semi-finals and win the Conference Premier title; one of his most memorable contributions was the 94th-minute winner at title-chasing rivals Torquay United at the start of March. That goal was later deemed to be the Goal of the Season at the annual Conference awards. Unfortunately, Scott missed the run-in to the title due to serving a six-match suspension (to which his three red cards over the course of the season contributed) and undergoing an ankle operation.

Jamie Davis — Midfielder

Born: 23 September 1981, Guildford.

Aldershot Town FC record:

Debut:	v Newport (Isle of Wight, A), Hampshire Senior Cup, 15 November 2000.
Appearances:	1

Playing career:
Kingstonian (youth), Aldershot Town (youth), Sandhurst Town, Ash United (November 2002).

Jamie's career began when he was a youth player at Kingstonian before joining the Shots, for whom his sole appearance came as part of a very young Shots side that were thrashed 5–0 in a County Cup match. He went on to play for Sandhurst Town and Ash United, leaving the latter in May 2005. Details of his subsequent career and current whereabouts are unknown.

Rhys Day — Centre-back

Born: 31 August 1982, Bridgend.

Aldershot Town FC record:
Debut: v Gravesend and Northfleet (h), Conference National, 12 August 2006.
Appearances: 85 + 8
Goals: 9

Playing career:
Manchester City (from trainee, September 1999), Blackpool (3ML, December 2001), Mansfield Town (November 2002), Aldershot Town (July 2006).
Rhys has made 112 Football League appearances, scoring 12 goals.

Representative honours:
Wales Youth, Wales Under-21s (11 caps).

Club honours:
Conference Premier (Aldershot Town 2007–08).

Rhys is an ex-Wales Under-21 international and the younger brother of professional snooker player Ryan Day. He began as a trainee at Manchester City and signed full contract forms in September 1999, joining Blackpool on a three-month loan in December 2001 and making his senior debut against Stoke City on New Year's Day 2002.

Rhys joined Mansfield Town on a two-month loan in November 2002 and impressed sufficiently for the move to become permanent. He soon gained a reputation as a good man-marker and was hailed as one of the most talented players outside the top flight, with that perception being all the more remarkable as the Stags were relegated from Division Two that season.

Despite the relegation, Rhys maintained a good level of performance and was in the side that lost the 2004 Division Three Play-off Final (on penalties) to Huddersfield Town. He subsequently missed significant parts of the 2004–05 and 2005–06 seasons due to various injuries and was eventually released.

Rhys joined the Shots in July 2006 and was a member of the side that achieved a club-best FA Cup progression when beaten by Blackpool in the third round in January 2007. He was given the Shots captaincy for the 2007–08 season but suffered a slight dip in form in mid-season. However, he was still a vital part of the side that lost to Ebbsfleet United in the FA Trophy semi-finals, with that defeat denying the club and its fans a day out at Wembley. Yet that disappointment was more than compensated for as Rhys led the club to the 'promised land' of the Football League by winning the Conference Premier title. At the end of May 2008, Rhys signed a one-year extension to his contract at the Rec.

Richard Dean — Midfielder

Born: 9 September 1974, Aldershot.

Aldershot Town FC record:
Debut: as substitute v Dorking (h), Isthmian League Division One, 19 November 1994.
Last appearance: v Eastleigh (a), Hampshire Senior Cup second round, 3 January 1996.
Appearances: 1 + 7

Playing career:
Aldershot FC (apprentice, August 1991), Queen's Park Rangers (trial, July 1992), Aldershot Town (trial, July 1992), Swindon Town (trial, July 1992), Reading (apprentice, August 1992), Wokingham Town (November 1993), Hampton (February 1994), Aldershot Town (November 1994), Bracknell Town (January 1997).

Richard was a midfielder whose career was blighted by back and ankle injuries. He started his career as a striker and a winger before settling into the centre of midfield. His father (Alan Dean) played for the Shots in the mid-1960s, and Richard signed for the 'old' club as an apprentice in the summer of 1991.

Following the demise of the club, he had trials at Queen's Park Rangers, the newly formed Aldershot Town and Swindon Town before being offered the chance to continue his apprenticeship at Reading in August 1992. Unfortunately, he was not offered a professional contract at Elm Park and so left in November 1993 to sign for local side Wokingham Town.

Three months later, he joined Hampton before coming back to the Rec in November 1994, but his injury problems persisted and he made just eight appearances in little over a year. A back injury was the main cause of Richard missing the next 12 months, so it was with some relief that he joined Bracknell Town in January 1997. He played sporadically until the summer of 1999, when he had to give in to his injuries and retire. Richard currently works as a glazier with his father.

Ahmed Deen — Winger/Wing-back

Born: 30 June 1985, Goderich, Sierra Leone.

Aldershot Town FC record:

Debut: v Tamworth (h), Conference National, 13 August 2005.
Last appearance: v Fleet Town (h), Hampshire Senior Cup third round, 10 January 2006.
Appearances: 12 + 6
Goals: 2

Playing career:

West Ham United (youth), Leicester City (scholar, July 2001), Peterborough United (August 2004), Hornchurch (3ML, November 2004), Aldershot Town (August 2005), Fisher Athletic (London, January 2006), St Albans City (February 2007), Bury (trial, July 2007), Leyton Orient (trial, September 2007), Brentford (trial, October 2007), Bishop's Stortford (November 2007), Macclesfield Town (June 2008).
Ahmed has made five Football League appearances.

Representative honours:

Sierra Leone full international (four caps).

Club honours:

Isthmian League Cup (Fisher Athletic [London] 2006), London Senior Cup (Fisher Athletic [London] 2006).

Ahmed is a Sierra Leonean international who can play as either a winger or wing-back. Having been unsuccessful in breaking into the first team at West Ham United and Leicester City, he joined Peterborough United on trial in August 2004 and was offered a full professional contract shortly afterwards.

In November 2004 he was loaned to Hornchurch before returning to London Road and making his Posh debut as a substitute against Torquay United in February 2005. He was released by Peterborough that summer and came to the Rec as a trialist, playing under a pseudonym so as not to alert other clubs of his availability. He won himself a contract but subsequently showed only occasional flashes of his pre-season form. This resulted in him leaving in January 2006 to join Fisher Athletic (London), where he helped the club to complete the Isthmian League Cup and London Senior Cup double that season. Ahmed then moved to St Albans City in February 2007 but was released at the end of the season.

In June 2007 he made his debut for Sierra Leone in an African Cup of Nations qualifier against Togo, and then he tried to get back into the Football League by trialling at Bury, Leyton Orient and Brentford. He signed for Bishop's Stortford in November 2007 and scored twice on his debut against Maidenhead United.

Ahmed scored 11 goals in all competitions in 2007–08 as the Bishops finished 10th in the Conference South, which resulted in him being called up by Sierra Leone for their World Cup qualifying matches in the summer. In June 2008 Ahmed got another stab at the Football League when he joined League Two side Macclesfield Town.

Ricky Denny — Midfielder/Forward

Born: 1968, London.

Aldershot Town FC record:

Debut: v Croydon (h), Isthmian League Division One, 1 March 1997.

Last appearance:	as substitute v Chertsey Town (h), Isthmian League Division One, 16 August 1997.
Appearances:	7 + 4
Goals:	1

Playing career:
Maidenhead United, Brook House, Hanwell Town (summer 1993), Farnborough Town (summer 1994), Wokingham Town (1ML, January 1995), Aldershot Town (February 1997), Harrow Borough (September 1997).

Club honours:
Southern League Premier Division (Farnborough Town 1993–94).

Ricky was a midfielder-cum-forward who began playing in the reserves at Maidenhead United. He then moved to Brook House before joining fellow Spartan League side Hanwell Town, where his scoring rate in his first 1993–94 season was phenomenal – 45 goals in 54 appearances. Unsurprisingly, this brought him to the attention of many clubs, with Farnborough Town winning the race for his signature in the summer of 1994.

Ricky made a scoring debut against Stevenage Borough in the August and ended up netting seven goals in his first seven games. By the start of November his goals had started to dry up, and he was loaned to Wokingham Town for a month in January 1995. On his return to Boro, he recaptured his form slightly, scoring six goals in nine games; however, the next couple of seasons were rather barren (three goals in 1995–96 and just one in 1996–97), which resulted in him joining the Shots in February 1997.

Ricky made a scoring debut yet again but then failed to score in his next 10 appearances, the last of which was as a substitute on the opening day of the 1997–98 season. He joined Harrow Borough in September 1997 and stayed at the Earlsmead Stadium until the following March. Details of his subsequent career are virtually unknown, but he reportedly retired in the summer of 2001.

Jon Denton **Defender**

Born: 26 February 1966, Perivale.

Aldershot Town FC record:

Debut:	as substitute v Leyton Pennant (h), Isthmian League Division One, 7 February 1998.
Last appearance:	v Newport (Isle of Wight, at Eastleigh FC), Hampshire Senior Cup semi-final, 12 March 1998.
Appearances:	1 + 3

Playing career:
Hillingdon Borough, Harefield United, Hounslow (summer 1986), Yeading (August 1989), Chertsey Town (September 1994), Hayes (August 1995), Chertsey Town (January 1996), Aldershot Town (February 1998), Billericay Town (August 1998), Yeading (player-coach, September 1998), Chertsey Town (March 2001).

Club honours:
FA Vase (Yeading 1990), Isthmian League Division Two South (Yeading 1989–90), Isthmian League Premier Division (Hayes 1995–96).

Post-playing coaching/management career:
Joint assistant manager of Yeading (1998–99 season).

Jon was an experienced defender who was approaching the end of his career by the time he joined Aldershot Town. Having spent the early part of his career at Hillingdon Borough and Harefield United, Jon signed for Hounslow in the summer of 1986 and was part of the side that finished as runners-up to Abingdon Town in the Hellenic League Premier Division in 1986–87, as well as being voted their Player of the Year in 1989. He moved to Yeading that summer and was captain for most of his time at the club.

In 1989–90 Jon was part of the Isthmian League Division Two South and FA Vase double-winning side, with the latter being achieved after a replay (Jon played in the drawn game at Wembley but missed the 'decider' due to suspension). His season was then finished off nicely by being named the Dings' Player of the Year.

In September 1994 Jon left the Warren and signed for Chertsey Town, where he was part of the side that pipped the Shots for promotion from Isthmian League Division One on the last day of the 1994–95 season. He joined Hayes the following summer and started the season as a regular in the side that went on to win the Isthmian League Premier Division, thus gaining Conference status for the first time in the club's history. However, Jon did not see the title won, as he had returned to Alwyns Lane in the January.

Chertsey were relegated in Jon's last full season with the club, before he played for Aldershot Town near the end of the 1997–98 season. Jon started the 1998–99 season at Billericay Town and then rejoined Yeading as player-coach before retiring and making the step up to joint assistant manager later that season. It is not known when he left that role, but it is known that he came out of retirement in March 2001 to re-sign for Chertsey, and it is believed that he retired for good that summer.

Jonny Dixon — Forward

Born: 16 January 1984, Murcia, Spain.

Aldershot Town FC record:

Debut: v Morecambe (h), Conference National, 6 November 2004.
Last Appearance: v York City (a), Conference Premier, 26 January 2008.
Appearances: 67 + 7
Goals: 32

Playing career:

Wycombe Wanderers (from scholar, February 2003), Crawley Town (1ML, December 2003), Aldershot Town (3ML, November 2004), Aldershot Town (3ML, January 2006), Aldershot Town (January 2007), Brighton & Hove Albion (January 2008).
Jonny has made 77 Football League appearances, scoring seven goals.

Club honours:

Hampshire Senior Cup (Aldershot Town 2007), Conference Premier (Aldershot Town 2007–08).

Jonny started out as a schoolboy striker at Wycombe Wanderers, occasionally playing as a midfielder. He signed as a scholar in August 2001, made his senior debut in a League game against Northampton Town the following August and signed full professional forms in February 2003.

Jonny had an unproductive loan spell at Crawley Town before signing for Aldershot Town on a three-month loan deal in November 2004. He quickly became the fans' favourite, scoring nine goals in 13 appearances and becoming the only loan player to score a hat-trick, doing so in the final game of his loan spell against Gravesend and Northfleet in January 2005. He returned to the Rec for another three-month loan period in January 2006, and this spell yielded four goals from 10 games.

Jonny's last game for Wycombe was as a substitute in their 1–1 draw with Chelsea in the League Cup semi-final first leg in January 2007. The following day, Shots manager Terry Brown finally ended his two-year chase for Jonny by paying Wycombe a fee of £6,000, which was partially funded by a trust that had been set up by the fans.

In January 2008 Jonny became the Shots' record sale (since superseded) when a whirlwind deal took him to League One side Brighton & Hove Albion for £56,000. Unfortunately, he picked up an ankle injury in training a couple of days after arriving, which meant that he did not make his debut until the beginning of March. The Seagulls eventually finished the season in seventh place, missing the Play-offs by one place.

Scott Donnelly — Midfielder/Forward

Born: 25 December 1987, Hammersmith.

Aldershot Town FC record:

Debut: v Christchurch (h), Hampshire Senior Cup second round, 27 November 2007.
Appearances: 9 + 7
Goals: 5

Playing career:

Queen's Park Rangers (from scholar, February 2006), Leyton Orient (trial, January 2007), Wealdstone (January 2007), Aldershot Town (trial, summer 2007), Aldershot Town (NC, November 2007).
Scott has made 13 Football League appearances.

Representative honours:
England Under-17s.

Club honours:
Setanta Shield (Aldershot Town 2008), Conference Premier (Aldershot Town 2007–08).

Scott is primarily a central-midfielder but can also play on the wing, and his shooting skills also allow him to play as an emergency forward. He came through the youth set-up at Queen's Park Rangers (the manager of whom was future Shots boss Gary Waddock) and made his senior debut as a 16-year-old substitute against Preston North End in October 2004, earning him fourth spot in the list of QPR's youngest-ever first-team players. However, injury limited him to just two appearances that season.

In February 2006 Scott signed full professional forms, with his main responsibility when he played being set-pieces. Unfortunately, within 12 months he was released and subsequently joined Southern League Premier Division side Wealdstone. Having seen the season out with the Stones, Scott was released and his only post-Wealdstone football has been with Aldershot Town.

Scott trialled at the Rec in the summer of 2007 and went on to play regularly for the reserve side. In November 2007 he signed for the Shots on a non-contract basis in order to play in the Hampshire Cup second-round tie against Christchurch. It was originally intended that he would only play in minor Cup games, but his performances, application and ability to score spectacular goals changed the plan, and he signed permanently in March 2008.

Scott was a member of the Shots side that reached that season's FA Trophy semi-finals, as well as being a goalscorer in the Setanta Shield Final victory over Rushden and Diamonds. However, he ensured his legendary status by scoring the Shots' goal in the 1–1 draw at Exeter City that secured the 2007–08 Conference Premier title and, with it, promotion to the Football League.

Simon Downer — Right-back/Centre-back/Midfielder

Born: 19 October 1981, Romford.

Aldershot Town FC record:

Debut:	v Gravesend and Northfleet (h), Conference, 6 March 2004.
Last appearance:	v Shrewsbury Town (at Stoke City FC), Conference Play-off Final, 16 May 2004.
Appearances:	13

Playing career:
Leyton Orient (from trainee, October 1999), Newcastle United (trial, February 2001), Aldershot Town (2ML, March 2004), Hornchurch (November 2004), Redbridge (August 2005), Weymouth (August 2005), Grays Athletic (January 2007).
Simon has made 79 Football League appearances.

Club honours:
Conference South (Weymouth 2005–06).

Simon can play in a variety of positions and began as a trainee at Leyton Orient. He made his senior debut in a Football League Trophy game against Peterborough United in December 1998 and signed full professional forms at Brisbane Road in October 1999. His talents caught the eye of West Ham United and Tottenham Hotspur before he was offered a trial at Newcastle United, during which he impressed sufficiently to be offered a chance to return to St James' Park for a second trial. However, Os' progression through to the 2001 Division Three Play-off Final (which they lost to Blackpool) prevented him taking up that offer.

By September 2001 Simon was suffering constant pain in one of his knees, with his problem eventually being diagnosed as tendonitis. This resulted in him having two operations and being out of action for 17 months. His injury jinx struck again in September 2003 when he picked up a groin injury, and he did not play again until the following March, when he arrived at the Rec on a two-month loan.

Simon fitted in well and was a member of the side that lost to Hednesford Town in the FA Trophy semi-finals and the side that suffered the heartbreak of losing the Conference Play-off Final to Shrewsbury Town. That summer, Simon retired and went to work as a labourer but soon realised that he wanted to play again, so signed for Hornchurch in November 2004.

Simon made his debut in an FA Cup first-round tie at Boston United, suffering the double disappointment of being sent off and seeing the Urchins lose. Fate dealt him another blow shortly afterwards, as he injured his other knee and decided to retire again!

In August 2005 Simon came out of retirement for a second time and signed for Isthmian Premier League Redbridge, but he made just two appearances before moving to Weymouth later that month. The move turned out to be a fruitful one, as the Terras finished the season as Conference South champions. However, in January 2007 Simon was forced to leave the Wessex Stadium as part of cost-cutting measures and was duly snapped up by fellow Conference side Grays Athletic. Simon played in just over half of Grays' League games in the 2007–08 season as a 10th-place finish was attained in the Conference Premier.

Roscoe D'Sane — Forward

Born: 16 October 1980, Epsom.

Aldershot Town FC record:

Debut:	v Enfield (a), Isthmian League Premier Division, 4 September 2002.
Last appearance:	as substitute v Scarborough (a), Conference National, 9 October 2004.
Appearances:	102 + 8
Goals:	48 (joint-seventh in all-time top 10)

Playing career:

Crystal Palace (from trainee, June 1999), Brentford (trial, summer 2000), Plymouth Argyle (trial, July 2001), Woking (trial, July 2001), Slough Town (August 2001), Southend United (November 2001), Woking (December 2001), Aldershot Town (May 2002), Wealdstone (March 2006), Lewes (March 2006), AFC Wimbledon (July 2006), Accrington Stanley (June 2007), Torquay United (January 2008).

Roscoe has made 24 Football League appearances, scoring seven goals.

Representative honours:

Isthmian League XI, England National Game XI (seven caps, four goals).

Club honours:

Isthmian League Premier Division (Aldershot Town 2002–03), Hampshire Senior Cup (Aldershot Town 2003).

Roscoe is a striker who possesses pace and excellent balance. He was a trainee at Crystal Palace and signed a full pro contract in June 1999 but never made a first-team appearance. After various trials, a Slough Town spell and a brief stay at Southend United, he joined Woking in December 2001 and managed five goals in 16 games.

That summer, he signed for Aldershot Town, where his performances led to him making his England National Game XI debut as a substitute against Belgium in February 2003. He scored regularly for the Shots, and his 18 goals that season (which made him the club's top scorer) helped the club win the Isthmian League Premier Division title (Roscoe scored in the 1–1 Easter Monday draw at Sutton United, which secured the title) and the Hampshire Senior Cup.

In May 2003 he became the first Shots player to score for the National Game XI when netting against the Republic of Ireland in the Four Nations Tournament. That goal also contributed to him being England's top scorer as they won the tournament.

Roscoe played (and scored) in the Shots' first-ever Conference game against Accrington Stanley in August 2003, and he followed that up in November when he became the first Shots player to captain his country, donning the armband against Belgium. This also made him the first-ever black player to captain the National Game XI. Later that season, he was the lone goalscorer in the 3–1 aggregate defeat by Hednesford Town in the FA Trophy semi-finals. He was also a member of the side that lost to Shrewsbury Town (after extra-time) in the Conference Play-off Final.

Roscoe again finished the season as the club's top scorer (27 goals) but was beset by bad luck the following season, when he injured both knees in a League game at Scarborough in the October. This would later be diagnosed as tendonitis. He worked tremendously hard to try to regain his fitness, but after 17 months he had to resign himself to the fact that a return to part-time football was on the cards, and he never pulled on a red-and-blue shirt again.

Roscoe had spells with Wealdstone and Lewes before joining ex-Shots boss Terry Brown at AFC Wimbledon in July 2006, where he finished the season as top scorer (21 goals) and helped the club reach the Isthmian League Premier Division Play-off semi-final, which they lost to Bromley.

In June 2007 he fulfilled his dream of returning to the Football League when League Two side Accrington Stanley reportedly beat Torquay United to his signature. However, Torquay did not give up and an undisclosed fee took Roscoe to Plainmoor in January 2008. At the time of his leaving, Roscoe had scored seven goals in 22 League Two games for Stanley.

The move to the West Country reunited Roscoe with his ex-Shots teammates Paul Buckle (the Gulls' boss) and former strike partner Tim Sills, and he immediately delivered by scoring on his debut against AFC Wimbledon in an FA Trophy third-round tie. Roscoe scored just two more goals during the 2007–08 season as the Gulls finished third in the Conference Premier, lost the Play-off semi-final to local rivals Exeter City and lost to fellow Conference Premier side Ebbsfleet United in the FA Trophy Final.

Koo Dumbuya — Midfielder/Winger

Born: 10 July 1971, Freetown, Sierra Leone.

Aldershot Town FC record:

Debut: as substitute v Petersfield United (a), Isthmian League Division Three, 28 December 1992.
Last appearance: as substitute v Thame United (a), Isthmian League Division Two, 4 April 1994.
Appearances: 3 + 14

Playing career:
Brentford (schoolboy), Aldershot FC (from apprentice, July 1989), Wokingham Town (January 1990), Bracknell Town (February 1990), Chertsey Town (summer 1991), Aldershot FC (January 1992), Wokingham Town (March 1992), Staines Town (March 1992), Basingstoke Town (trial, July 1992), Aldershot Town (August 1992), Dorking (July 1994), Burnham (March 1995), Fleet Town (December 1995), Sandhurst Town (January 1996), Burnham (November 1996), Fleet Town (January 1998), Witney Town (October 1999), Wokingham Town (January 2000), Cove (summer 2000), Fleet Town (summer 2001), Hampton and Richmond Borough (trial, summer 2002), Chertsey Town (August 2002), Wokingham Town (March 2003), Cove (summer 2003; player-manager from summer 2004), Camberley Town (player-manager, July 2005), Godalming Town (summer 2006).

Club honours:
Isthmian League Division Three (Aldershot Town 1992–93), Combined Counties League (Cove 2000–01), Combined Counties League Cup (Cove 2001), Southern Counties Floodlit Cup (Fleet Town 2002).

Post-playing coaching/management career:
Manager of Cove (July 2007).

Koo played as either a right-sided midfielder or winger and was one of those players who never really seemed to settle at any of his clubs. He was a schoolboy and an apprentice at Brentford, but he left Griffin Park in the summer of 1988 and signed on as a second-year apprentice with Aldershot FC. He signed full professional forms in July 1989, but he never made a competitive appearance in either of his two spells at the club.

Koo joined a number of clubs, including Aldershot FC again, before returning to the Rec to sign for the newly formed Shots. He was an unused substitute (and wore the number-12 shirt) in the club's first-ever League game against Clapton, before eventually making his debut at the end of the year, with his appearance in the League game at Petersfield United qualifying him as the first black player to play for the club.

Koo left the Rec in July 1994 and joined Dorking before moving on to Burnham, Fleet Town and Sandhurst Town. He rejoined Burnham in November 1996 but sustained a knee injury that led to him leaving in the summer of 1997. Following an operation to address his injury, he re-signed for Fleet Town in January 1998 and stayed until October 1999, when he left to play for Witney Town and Wokingham Town (for a third time) before signing for Cove.

Koo was a member of the side that completed the Combined Counties League and Cup double in 2000–01 before returning to Fleet in the summer of 2001, where he was involved in winning promotion from the Wessex League to the Southern League Eastern Division.

After a couple of club spells, he re-signed for Cove in the summer of 2003 and took up the role of player-manager a year later. This was followed by a period the player-manager's role at near neighbours Camberley Town before he joined Godalming Town, playing mainly in the reserves.

Koo retired from playing at the end of the 2006–07 season and returned to Cove as manager in July 2007, and a solid season saw them finish in fourth spot in the Combined Counties League Premier Division that season. Earlier in his career, Koo coached at Reading's academy (from 1997 to 2000) and managed Farnborough Town's youth team (from 2000 to 2002). Away from football, he works as a personal trainer and sports coach.

Adam Dunsby — Goalkeeper

Born: 19 November 1982, Isleworth.

Aldershot Town FC record:

Debut:	v Newport, Isle of Wight, (a), Hampshire Senior Cup second round, 15 November 2000.
Appearances:	1

Playing career:
Brentford (schoolboy and youth), Chelsea (youth trial), Mytchett Athletic (youth), Aldershot Town (youth), Burnham (September 2001), Hampton and Richmond Borough (December 2001),Yeading (1ML, January 2002), Wokingham Town (February 2002), Hartley Wintney (August 2002).

Adam was one of several players who came into the Shots' youth team from local side Mytchett Athletic. Aside from that, he was previously at Brentford and had a youth trial at Chelsea.

Details of his post-Shots career are sketchy, but it is known that he played for Burnham (for whom he appeared twice), Hampton and Richmond Borough (played once), a loan at Yeading (appeared twice), Wokingham Town and Hartley Wintney.

Adam left Hartley Wintney in the summer of 2004 and had a shoulder operation a little while later. He has been unable to play since and works as an engineer.

Andy Edwards — Defender

Born: 17 September 1971, Epping.

Aldershot Town FC record:

Debut:	v Dagenham and Redbridge (h), Conference National, 26 August 2006.
Last appearance:	as substitute v Crawley Town (h), Conference National, 13 January 2007.
Appearances:	18 + 2

Playing career:
West Ham United (trainee, summer 1987), Southend United (from trainee, December 1989), Birmingham City (July 1995), Peterborough United (November 1996), Leyton Orient (trial, March 2003), Rushden and Diamonds (March 2003), Southend United (May 2004), Grays Athletic (1ML, January 2006), Aldershot Town (July 2006). Andy has made 526 Football League appearances, scoring 21 goals.

Club honours:
Division Three Play-off Final (Peterborough United 2000, Southend United 2005), Division Three (Rushden and Diamonds 2002–03), League One (Southend United 2005–06).

Post-playing coaching/management career:
Coach at St Albans City (January 2008).

Andy began as a trainee at West Ham United. He then joined Southend United on the same basis and made his debut for the Essex side against Wigan Athletic in December 1988, a full 12 months before signing full professional forms. It was not until the 1992–93 season that Andy established himself as an important first-team regular at Roots Hall, missing only 11 League games over the next three seasons.

In July 1995 newly promoted Birmingham City (the previous season's Division Two champions) paid £350,000 for Andy's services, but he only stayed at St Andrews for 16 months before dropping down a division to join Peterborough in an exchange deal that took Martyn O'Connor in the opposite direction. The season would end with Peterborough being relegated, but they nearly bounced straight back the following season when Andy was ever present in the side that missed the Play-offs by three points. Andy continued to play consistently well, and Colchester United (and ex-Shots) boss Steve Wignall tried to sign Andy in November 1998 but Posh boss Barry Fry turned down the reported five-figure offer.

Andy's consistency continued right up to his last game for the Posh against Port Vale. Unfortunately for Andy, his last contribution for the club in that game was to be red-carded. He later signed for Rushden and Diamonds in March 2003, playing in the club's last 12 games of a season that ended with them winning the Division Three title. The following season, however, was not as joyous, as he played in just over half the games as the Diamonds went straight back down.

Andy left Nene Park that summer, re-signed for Southend United and enjoyed two successive promotions as Lincoln City were disposed of in the 2005 Division Three Play-off Final, and the League One title was secured the following season.

Andy came to the Rec in July 2006 and was a member of the Shots side that reached the FA Cup third round in 2006–07 before losing at Blackpool. His Shots career was ended by a broken leg sustained in a tackle with Crawley Town forward (and ex-Shot) Scott Rendell in January 2007. He eventually recovered and was taken on as a coach at St Albans City, managed by his ex-Birmingham City teammate Steve Castle. By the end of 2007–08, Andy's reported hopes of making a return to playing had not come to fruition and it is believed that he officially retired.

Tommy Ellis — Midfielder/Forward

Born: 21 February 1983, Farnborough, Kent.

Aldershot Town FC record:

Debut: as substitute v Brading Town (h), Hampshire Senior Cup second round, 1 November 2001.
Appearances: 0 + 1

Playing career:

Chelsea (schoolboy), Fulham (schoolboy), Carshalton Athletic (youth), West Ham United (trial), Aldershot Town (July 2001), Dorking (November 2001), Farnborough Town (June 2002), Bromley (1ML, August 2002), Egham Town (November 2002), Carshalton Athletic (November 2002), Croydon Athletic (February 2003), Bromley (summer 2003), Egham Town (August 2003), Tooting and Mitcham United (October 2003), Banstead Athletic (July 2004), Dorking (July 2005), Tooting and Mitcham United (July 2006), Banstead Athletic (October 2007).

Tommy can play as an attacking midfielder or as a forward, and he played at Chelsea and Fulham as a schoolboy before joining Carshalton Athletic's youth set-up. A trial at West Ham United followed before he joined Aldershot Town in July 2001.

Shortly after making his sole appearance (in November 2001), he joined Dorking on a four-month loan and made the move to Meadowbank permanent in March 2002. He joined Farnborough Town that summer, but was soon loaned to Bromley before joining Egham Town in the November. However, his stay at Tempest Road was fleeting, as he left almost immediately to rejoin divisional rivals Carshalton.

In February 2003, with the Robins on course for the Isthmian League Division One South title, Tommy left and had spells at Croydon Athletic, Bromley, Egham (again) then Tooting and Mitcham United in October 2003. He left nine months later and played for Banstead Athletic and Dorking before rejoining the Terrors in July 2006, leaving a month into the season.

Tommy's whereabouts for the next year or so are unknown, but he did rejoin Banstead Athletic a couple of months into the 2007–08 season (scoring on his debut against Chertsey Town), and the club finished the season in 17th place in the Combined Counties League Premier Division.

Gary Elphick — Defender

Born: 17 October 1985, Brighton.

Aldershot Town FC record:

Debut: v Canvey Island (h), Conference National, 24 January 2006.
Last appearance: as substitute v York City (a), Conference National, 12 February 2006.
Appearances: 2 + 1

Playing career:
Brighton & Hove Albion (from academy, May 2005), Bognor Regis Town (1ML, August 2003), Lewes (1ML, February 2004), Eastbourne Borough (1ML, September 2004), St Albans City (4ML, December 2004), Aldershot Town (trial, July 2005), Aldershot Town (2ML, January 2006), St Albans City (March 2006), Havant and Waterlooville (December 2007).
Gary has made two Football League appearances.

Club honours:
Hertfordshire Senior Cup (St Albans City 2005), Conference South Play-off Final (St Albans City 2006).

Gary is the son of ex-Stoke City player Gary Elphick Snr and older brother of Brighton & Hove Albion midfielder Tommy. He started as an academy player with Brighton and was loaned out to neighbouring sides Bognor Regis Town, Lewes and Eastbourne Borough plus Conference South side St Albans City, signing full professional forms with the Seagulls in May 2005.

Gary trialled with the Shots during the 2005–06 pre-season before making his senior debut for Brighton as a substitute against Sheffield United in September 2005. Unfortunately, he was sent off in his only other game (and his only start) for the Sussex side, against Reading in December 2005.

The following month Gary joined Aldershot Town on a two-month loan but played just three games before his parent club accepted an offer from St Albans for their ex-loanee. It was to prove a good move for him, as the Hertfordshire side gained promotion to the Conference National via a Play-off Final victory over Histon, and he earned a personal honour the following season when he was voted Player of the Year.

At the start of the 2007–08 season, reports began to circulate that Gary was finding the travelling involved in playing for St Albans too much, so it was no surprise when he signed for fellow Conference South side Havant and Waterlooville in December. Unfortunately for Gary, he missed Hawks' famous FA Cup run that season as a result of having played for St Albans earlier in the competition, but he still played his part in the club finishing in seventh place in the League, missing the Play-offs by just two points.

Rob Elvins — Forward

Born: 17 September 1986, Alvechurch.

Aldershot Town FC record:

Debut:	v Kidderminster Harriers (a), Conference Premier, 11 August 2007.
Appearances:	39 + 10
Goals:	11

Playing career:
West Bromwich Albion (from scholar, July 2005), Cheltenham Town (1ML, September 2006), York City (2ML, January 2007), Oxford United (trial, March 2007), Aldershot Town (June 2007).
Rob has made five Football League appearances.

Club honours:
Conference Premier (Aldershot Town 2007–08).

Rob joined West Bromwich Albion as a 10-year-old and progressed through various levels, top-scoring for the reserve side in 2004–05 and being rewarded with a full contract in July 2005, but he never made a first-team appearance while at The Hawthorns – the closest he came was as an unused substitute in an FA Cup third-round replay at Reading in January 2006.

Rob moved to Cheltenham Town on loan in September 2006 and made his Football League debut as a substitute against Huddersfield Town. He went on to make four more substitute appearances for the Robins before returning to The Hawthorns. He was then loaned out to the Shots' Conference rivals York City in January 2007 but failed to score in nine appearances. With his exit from The Hawthorns looking likely, Rob trialled at Oxford United in March 2007 before being released by the Baggies at the end of the 2006–07 season.

Rob joined Aldershot Town in June 2007, citing the vocal support offered by the Shots fans as one of the main reasons for his decision. He displayed a tireless work rate, often unnoticed, throughout the season, and his 11 goals in 49 games contributed to the Shots reaching the FA Trophy semi-finals and winning the Conference Premier title that season.

Lee Endersby — Winger

Born: 22 July 1973, London.

Aldershot Town FC record:

Debut: as substitute v Leatherhead (a), Isthmian League Division One, 28 February 1998.
Last appearance: v Grays Athletic (a), FA Cup third qualifying round, 31 October 1998.
Appearances: 16 + 8
Goals: 5

Playing career:
Arsenal (youth), Brimsdown Rovers (December 1991), Wembley (January 1993), Harrow Borough (February 1994), Stevenage Borough (October 1996), Enfield (January 1997), Aldershot Town (February 1998), Slough Town (October 1998), Farnborough Town (July 1999), Carshalton Athletic (1ML, November 2000), Yeading (January 2001), Bishop's Stortford (February 2001), Wisbech Town (May 2001), Hitchin Town (August 2001), Dulwich Hamlet (September 2001), Tooting and Mitcham United (September 2002), Hendon (January 2003), Enfield (August 2003), Fisher Athletic (London, January 2004).

Representative honours:
Isthmian League XI, England Semi-Professional XI (one cap).

Club honours:
Isthmian League Division One (Aldershot Town 1997–98), Isthmian League Cup (Farnborough Town 2000).

Lee was a tricky winger who was a bit of an enigma while at the Rec, but he could be creative enough to mesmerise opposing defenders. He started as a youth player at Arsenal and then moved on to Brimsdown Rovers and Wembley before signing for Harrow Borough in February 1994.

Season-on-season, Lee's game improved to the point where he made his sole appearance for the England Semi-Professional XI against Holland in April 1996. A brief spell at Stevenage Borough preceded a £15,000 move to Enfield in January 1997, and Lee was a major factor in the Es finishing as runners-up to Yeovil Town in that season's Isthmian League Premier Division.

Like several others, Lee followed his Enfield boss George Borg to the Rec, signing for a fee of £1,500 in February 1998. Unfortunately, the Rec faithful only saw fleeting glimpses of his talents in a season in which the Shots win the Isthmian League Division One title. Eight months later, he moved on to Slough Town for a fee of £5,000, which equalled the Shots' record sale at the time.

A move to Farnborough Town followed in July 1999, and he was part of the side that won the Isthmian League Cup, but his career seemingly tailed off from then on, and he reportedly retired in the summer of 2004. Lee's current whereabouts are unknown.

Chukki Eribenne — Forward

Born: 2 November 1980, Westminster.

Aldershot Town FC record:

Debut: v Dagenham and Redbridge (a), Conference National, 11 December 2004.
Last appearance: Forest Green Rovers (a), Conference National, 26 December 2004.
Appearances: 1 + 2

Playing career:
Coventry City (from trainee, January 1998), Helsingborg (Sweden, 1ML, January 2000), AFC Bournemouth (June 2000), Hereford United (1ML, October 2002), Northampton Town (trial, May 2003), Havant and Waterlooville (August 2003), Weymouth (July 2004), Aldershot Town (1ML, December 2004), Farnborough Town (2ML, January 2005), Grays Athletic (January 2007), Gravesend and Northfleet (2ML, March 2007), Ebbsfleet United (May 2007). Chukki has made 47 Football League appearances, scoring one goal.

Club honours:
Russell Cotes Cup (Havant and Waterlooville 2004), Conference South (Weymouth 2005–06), FA Trophy (Ebbsfleet United 2008 [unused substitute]).

Like many others, Chukwunyeaka (to give him his proper name) had a non-productive loan spell at the Rec. He began as a trainee at Coventry City, and a loan spell at Swedish side Helsingborg preceded a move to AFC Bournemouth for whom he debuted on the opening day of the 2000–01 season against Bristol Rovers. He scored the Cherries' goal in a 1–1 draw that day, but this was to be the only time he scored for them in 55 appearances.

A one-month loan at Hereford United and a trial at Northampton Town followed before he dropped out of the Football League to join Havant and Waterlooville in August 2003. This move helped Chukki discover his scoring touch, and he finished the season as Hawks' top scorer (19 goals), as well as being voted Player of the Year. That prompted Weymouth, who were newly promoted to the Conference South, to sign him in July 2004, but he struggled to continue his form of the previous season and so came to the Rec on loan in the December.

Chukki was loaned to Farnborough Town in January and made a scoring debut against Crawley Town before returning to Weymouth. The following season, his 13 goals (which made him joint-top scorer along with Raphael Nade) helped fire the Terras to the Conference South title.

Unfortunately, Chukki struggled to find the net in 2006–07, scoring just four times in 24 appearances before signing for Grays Athletic in January 2007. Two months later, he joined Gravesend and Northfleet on a two-month loan and then returned to Stonebridge Road in the summer on a permanent basis, by which time the club had changed their name to Ebbsfleet United. Chukki proceeded to score nine goals as the club finished in 11th in the Conference Premier. He was also an unused substitute in their FA Trophy Final victory against Torquay United before being released shortly after the season's end. At the time of writing, it is understood that Chukki is still without a club.

Solomon Eriemo — Defender/Midfielder

Born: 26 January 1967, London.

Aldershot Town FC record:

Debut:	v Rothwell Town (h), FA Trophy third qualifying round, 26 November 1994.
Last appearance:	v Waterlooville (a), Hampshire Senior Cup quarter-final, 23 January 1996.
Appearances:	39 + 7
Goals:	3

Playing career:
Leytonstone and Ilford, Walthamstow Avenue (August 1986), Leyton Wingate, Wealdstone (1988–89 season), Kingstonian (January 1991), Hayes (1ML, October 1994), Aldershot Town (November 1994), Carshalton Athletic (February 1996), Hendon (September 1996), Crawley Town (January 1997), Croydon (July 1998), St Leonards (August 2000).

Club honours:
Isthmian League Division One (Croydon 1999–2000), Isthmian League Cup (Croydon 2000).

Solomon was a tall defender and midfielder who was immediately the centre of controversy when he joined Aldershot Town in 1994, after a relatively quiet start to his career. His Shots debut came in an FA Trophy tie against Rothwell Town, but the club were thrown out of the tournament days later as a result of his former club, Kingstonian, failing to cancel his registration prior to him playing in the tie.

For the next 14 months, he performed consistently in the Shots sides that were challenging for promotion, but he left to join Carshalton Athletic in February 1996 and had spells with Hendon, Crawley Town and Croydon, whom he helped win the Isthmian League Division One and Isthmian League Cup double before leaving to join St Leonards in August 2000. Details of Solomon's subsequent career are unknown.

Gavin Evans — Midfielder

Born: 19 September 1982, Frimley.

Aldershot Town FC record:

Debut:	as substitute v Walton and Hersham (a), Isthmian League Cup first round, 12 September 2000.
Appearances:	0 + 1

Playing career:
Crystal Palace (youth), Mytchett Athletic (youth), Aldershot Town (youth), Hartley Wintney (September 2001), Ash United (August 2004).

Representative honours:
Surrey Youth.

Club honours:
Basingstoke Senior Cup (Hartley Wintney 2003).

Gavin was another youngster to make a sole appearance for the Shots. He was a youth player at Crystal Palace before playing for local side Mytchett Athletic and then the Shots. He later played for Combined Counties sides Hartley Wintney and Ash United, helping the latter attain successive top-four finishes in the Combined Counties League Premier Division in 2005–06 and 2006–07.

The 2007–08 season was a different story for Ash United, as they finished 15th, with Gavin missing just one game in the League campaign, top scoring with 23 goals in all competitions and winning the Player of the Year award.

Nathan Fealey — Midfielder

Born: 12 March 1973, Aldershot.

Aldershot Town FC record:

Debut:	as substitute v East Thurrock United (a), Isthmian League Division Three, 3 October 1992.
Last appearance:	v Maidenhead United (h), Isthmian League Division One, 28 January 1995.
Appearances:	41 + 3
Goals:	3

Playing career:
Southampton (youth), Reading (from trainee, July 1991), Woking (trial, summer 1992), Aldershot Town (August 1992), Fleet Town (summer 1995), Egham Town (summer 1996), Fleet Town (March 1997), Cove (summer 2000), Fleet Town (summer 2001), Badshot Lea (December 2004; player-assistant manager from summer 2005). Nathan has made one Football League appearance.

Representative honours:
Aldershot and District Schoolboys (captain), North East Hampshire Youth, Hampshire Youth (captain).

Club honours:
Isthmian League Division Three (Aldershot Town 1992–93), Russell Cotes Cup (Fleet Town 1998).

Before he got into the professional game, Nathan was part of the Southampton-based Wellington Sports side that won the Gothia Cup (best described as a junior World Cup) in Sweden in 1986. Having been a youth player at Southampton, he joined Reading as a trainee and signed full professional forms in July 1991, making just one appearance against Peterborough United in February 1992 before he was released that summer.

Having trialled at Woking, Nathan joined Aldershot Town and played in around a third of their games as they won the Isthmian League Division Three title. The following season, he was part of the side that gained a second successive promotion, but then he hardly featured in the 1994–95 season due to work commitments.

After moves to Fleet Town and Egham Town, he returned to Fleet in March 1997 and spent part of his time co-managing their reserve side with Neil Roberts. In the summer of 2000 (and following Fleet's relegation back to the Wessex League), he joined Cove but left less than six months later and took a break from the game.

The summer of 2001 saw Nathan assume the role of joint player-manager of Fleet Town's reserves (again with Neil Roberts). In December 2004 he joined Badshot Lea, taking on the role of player-assistant manager the following summer. He retired from playing in the summer of 2006 and currently works as an IT manager.

James Field — Midfielder

Born: 11 April 1987, Frimley.

Aldershot Town FC record:

Debut:	as substitute v Fareham Town (h), Hampshire Senior Cup, 2 November 2004.
Last appearance:	as substitute v Forest Green Rovers (a), Conference Challenge Cup Southern Section quarter-final, 15 February 2005.

Appearances: 2 + 4
Goals: 1

Playing career:
Aldershot Town (youth), Fleet Town (SLL, August 2005), Fleet Town (July 2006).

Representative honours:
Hampshire Youth.

Club Honours:
Russell Cotes Cup (Fleet Town 2007, 2008), Basingstoke Senior Cup (Fleet Town 2008), Aldershot Senior Cup (Fleet Town 2008).

James is the younger brother of ex-Fleet Town midfielder Lewis Field and was a steady performer for the Shots' youth side, making all of his first-team appearances (while a youth-team member) during the 2004–05 season. He was loaned to neighbours Fleet Town for the whole of the following season and performed so well that it came as no surprise when he was signed permanently following his release from the Rec in the summer of 2006.

James made 55 appearances for Fleet in the 2007–08 season and top scored with 30 goals, which contributed to them finishing as runners-up to Farnborough in Southern League Division One South and West. Unfortunately, they lost to Uxbridge in the resultant Play-off semi-final. The Blues later beat New Milton Town to retain the Russell Cotes Cup, defeated Alresford Town to claim the Basingstoke Senior Cup (a game in which James was a goalscorer) and overcame Badshot Lea in a bad-tempered Aldershot Senior Cup Final. Fleet's only Final defeat of the season came against Tadley Calleva in the North Hants Cup. An added bonus for James came at the end of the season, when he was voted Player of the Year. To date, he has made nearly 160 appearances and scored 52 goals for Fleet – not bad for a midfielder!

Colin Fielder — Midfielder

Born: 5 January 1964, Winchester.

Aldershot Town FC record:
Debut: v Purfleet (a), Isthmian League Premier Division, 22 August 1998.
Last appearance: v Farnborough Town (a), Isthmian League Premier Division, 26 December 2000.
Appearances: 102 + 16
Goals: 8

Playing career:
Aldershot FC (from apprentice, January 1982), Karelian Pallo Ry (Finland, 3ML, May 1982), Leatherhead (1ML, 1983–84 season), Waterlooville (1ML, 1984–85 season), Wimbledon (trial, 1984–85 season), Farnborough Town (July 1987), Slough Town (August 1991), Woking (August 1992), Yeovil Town (player-coach, December 1996), Aldershot Town (July 1998; player-coach from summer 1999), Chertsey Town (August 2001), Staines Town (September 2001), Alton Town (March 2002).

Representative honours:
FA Colts, FA XI, Middlesex Wanderers.

Club honours:
Division Four Play-off Final (Aldershot FC 1987), Hampshire Senior Cup (Farnborough Town 1991, Aldershot Town 1999, 2000), Southern League Premier Division (Farnborough Town 1990–91), Isthmian League Premier Division (Yeovil Town 1996–97), Isthmian League Charity Shield (Woking 1992, Aldershot Town 1999), Surrey Senior Cup (Woking 1994, 1996), FA Trophy (Woking 1994, 1995), Somerset Premier Cup (Yeovil Town 1997, 1998), Isthmian League Cup (Aldershot Town 1999).
Colin has made 68 Football League appearances, scoring eight goals.

Colin was very popular among fans and fellow players and started out as an apprentice at Aldershot FC. He signed full contract forms in January 1982 and made his senior debut against Torquay United in the final away game of the 1981–82 season.

That summer, he was loaned to Finnish Second Division side Karelian Pallo Ry, where he played nine games and just missed out on the promotion Play-offs. Further loans elsewhere helped Colin mature and gain valuable experience for his future career.

In 1987 he was a member of the Aldershot FC side (together with future Aldershot Town Manager Steve Wignall) that won the Division Four Play-off Final against Wolverhampton Wanderers, thus earning them the distinction of being the first-ever team promoted via the Play-offs.

That summer, he joined Farnborough Town and enjoyed some minor Cup success. He was also involved in some history-making in 1988–89 when the club finished as runners-up to Leytonstone and Ilford in the Isthmian League Premier Division. However, the Essex side were refused promotion due to their ground being unsatisfactory, so Boro were promoted in their place, thus entering the Conference for the first time in their history. Colin was named as captain for 1989–90, but the season ended with the club being relegated to the Southern League Premier Division.

During his career, Colin had a knack of scoring important goals and one such instance came in May 1991, when he set a captain's example by scoring the winning goal in the 2–1 victory over Atherstone, which ensured Boro's return to the Conference.

In August 1991 Slough Town broke their transfer record by paying £18,000 for Colin – a record that still stands today. Despite his best efforts, the club finished in the bottom three, and he was allowed to join Woking (newly promoted to the Conference) in a swap deal with George Friel.

Colin's influence was evident throughout his time at Kingfield, with the Cards finishing their first-ever season in the Conference in a respectable eighth place and following that up with a third-place finish and two successive runners-up finishes (behind Macclesfield Town in 1994–95 and Stevenage Borough in 1995–96). Colin also captained Woking to their FA Trophy Final wins in 1994 (over Runcorn) and 1995 (against Kidderminster Harriers), scoring in the last minute of extra-time to win the latter Final.

In December 1996 Colin joined Yeovil Town as player-coach and helped them win that season's Isthmian League Premier Division title. He went on to score on his Aldershot Town debut in July 1998 and missed just one League game that season, as well as being involved in winning the Isthmian League Cup and Hampshire Senior Cup double.

In the summer, he was appointed as player-coach at the Rec and continued to perform consistently as the club pushed for promotion. With his appearances being limited to just 10 in the 2000–01 season, he left the Shots in January 2001 and took a short break from football. In August of that year, he signed for Chertsey Town but moved on to Staines then Alton Town, helping them gain promotion from the Hampshire League into the Wessex League.

Colin retired in the summer of 2002 and currently runs a boys' football team in Alton, as well as working as a sales representative for a carpet manufacturer.

Neil Finn — Goalkeeper

Born: 29 December 1978, Rainham.

Aldershot Town FC record:

Debut: v Moneyfields (h), Hampshire Senior Cup second round, 10 November 1998.
Last appearance: v Chertsey Town (a), Isthmian League Cup second round, 24 November 1998.
Appearances: 3

Playing career:

West Ham United (from trainee, July 1997), Dorchester Town (1ML, March 1998), Barnet (July 1998), Aldershot Town (NC, November 1998), Harrow Borough (March 1999), Romford (August 2004).
Neil has made one FA Premier League appearance.

Neil was originally a trainee with West Ham United and, as a result of an injury crisis at Upton Park, made an unexpected debut in the FA Premier League game against Manchester City on New Year's Day 1996. This gave him a place in the record books as the Hammers' youngest-ever post-war player (aged 17 years and 3 days) – a record he was to hold for nearly eight years.

Neil signed full professional forms in July 1997 but never made another first-team appearance. After a loan at Dorchester Town and then signing for Barnet, he arrived at the Rec in November 1998 but left in December. What he did next is unknown, but it is known that he signed for Harrow Borough in March 1999, leaving in the summer. He then took some time out of the game before signing for Essex Senior League side Romford in August 2004.

Neil quickly established himself as first-choice at Rush Green Road and won the manager's Player of the Year trophy in his first season. Another solid season in 2005–06 saw him win the supporters' Player of the Year trophy, as well as being named captain, and he was a major influence in securing the runners'-up spot (to Brentwood Town) in the Essex Senior League in 2006–07.

The following season, Romford finished in fifth spot in the League, but Neil played just three times in the campaign and made just nine appearances in all competitions. To date, he has made over 120 appearances for the club.

Steve Flinn — Midfielder

Born: 15 October 1980, Raynes Park.

Aldershot Town FC record:

Debut: as substitute v AFC Totton (h), Hampshire Senior Cup quarter-final, 29 February 2000.
Appearances: 0 + 1

Playing career:

Wimbledon (July 1999), Aldershot Town (NC, February 2000), Croydon Athletic (July 2000), Metropolitan Police (August 2003).

Club honours:

Isthmian League Division Three (Croydon Athletic 2001–02).

Steve is another of those players who seemed to disappear as quickly as they arrived at the Rec. Having played for Wimbledon, he signed for Aldershot Town in February 2000 but departed in the summer for Croydon Athletic.

Steve was part of the Athletic side that won the Isthmian League Division Three title in 2001–02 before later moving to Metropolitan Police, where he played mostly in their reserves. In 2007–08 Met Police finished fourth in the Isthmian League Division One South, but lost the resultant Play-off semi-final to Cray Wanderers.

Scott Forrester — Forward

Born: 7 May 1982, Wandsworth.

Aldershot Town FC record:

Debut: as substitute v Basingstoke Town (h), Isthmian League Premier Division, 28 April 2001.
Last appearance: v Braintree Town (a), Isthmian League Premier Division, 18 April 2002.
Appearances: 14 + 31
Goals: 9

Playing career:

Millwall (youth), Crystal Palace (youth), Sutton United (from youth, September 1999), Reading (trial), Luton Town (trial, April 2000), Dulwich Hamlet (November 2000), Aldershot Town (March 2001), Billericay Town (June 2002), Boreham Wood (September 2002), Hayes (July 2003), Sutton United (August 2004), AFC Wimbledon (trial, July 2005), Worthing (2006–07 season), Leatherhead (August 2007).

Scott began his career as a youth player at Millwall and Crystal Palace before moving into the Conference with Sutton United, for whom he signed a full contract in September 1999. While at Gander Green Lane, he trialled at Reading and Luton Town and was reportedly on the verge of a £135,000 move to the latter club, but the sacking of Hatters boss Lennie Lawrence put paid to that.

Scott joined Dulwich Hamlet on a one-month loan in November 2000 and signed permanently at the end of the period. His performances there brought him to the attention of Shots boss George Borg, which resulted in him moving to the Rec the following March, but he never really lived up to the billing that had accompanied his arrival and departed for Billericay Town (managed by Borg by then) in June 2002. However, his stay there was short, as he joined Boreham Wood three months later and was part of the side that was relegated from the Isthmian League Premier Division at the end of the 2002–03 season. He then moved on to Hayes before returning to Sutton in August 2004, being released the following January.

Having reportedly become increasingly disillusioned with football, Scott decided to take a break from the game to concentrate on an acting career and subsequently appeared in Sky One's football drama *Dream Team* plus the films *Goal, Goal 2, Starship Dave* and *Dhan Dhan Dhan Goal*. He was also the body double for Liverpool and Spain forward Fernando Torres in a series of TV adverts for a well-known sportswear brand.

Scott made an official return to the game in August 2007 when he signed for Leatherhead, who were managed by his former Sutton teammate, David Harlow. Unfortunately, the Tanners had a fairly mediocre 2007–08 season (during which Scott scored eight times in all competitions) and finished in 17th place in Isthmian Division One South.

Mark Frampton — Forward

Born: 14 May 1968, Frimley.

Aldershot Town FC record:

Debut: as substitute v Egham Town (h), Isthmian League Division Two, 21 August 1993.
Last appearance: as substitute v Thame United (a), Isthmian League Division Two, 4 April 1994.
Appearances: 15 + 12
Goals: 6

Playing career:
Aldershot FC (YTS, August 1984), Farnborough Town (March 1986), Fleet Town (August 1990), Aldershot Town (July 1993), Wokingham Town (1ML, December 1993), Fleet Town (June 1994), Molesey (October 2003).

Representative honours:
Hampshire Youth.

Club honours:
Wessex League (Fleet Town 1994–95), Southern Counties Floodlit Cup (Fleet Town 2002).

Mark was at Aldershot FC on the Manpower Services Work Scheme and signed YTS forms for the club in August 1984. He joined Farnborough Town in March 1986 but did not become a fixture in the side until the 1988–89 season, when he was a member of the side that reached the Conference for the first time in the club's history. He scored 18 goals in 53 appearances for Farnborough before joining Fleet Town in August 1990 for a club record fee of £2,000. His goals helped the club attain 10th, 11th and eighth spots in the Wessex League in his first three seasons before he returned to the Rec (albeit to the 'new' club) in July 1993.

Mark was a bit-part player up until December when he joined Wokingham Town on a month's loan. Following his return, he scored a last-minute winner to help the Shots reach that season's FA Vase quarter-final and be promoted from Isthmian League Division Two.

In June 1994 Mark rejoined Fleet Town for a fee of £400 and was part of the side that won the Wessex League that season, as well as being the club's top scorer in 1998–99 (18 goals), 1999–2000 (16 goals) and 2000–01 (34 goals). He formed a formidable partnership with Ian Mancey during the 2001–02 season, with the pair scoring 68 goals between them in all competitions, and Mark's 27 League goals that season helped the club gain promotion from the Wessex League to the Southern League Eastern Division.

Over the course of his two spells at Fleet, Mark has become a dual record holder – he is their record appearance-maker (520 games) and their record goalscorer (302 goals).

In October 2003 Mark joined his ex-Fleet manager, Steve Beeks, at Molesey, but his time at Walton Road was ruined by injury and subsequent club struggles. He retired due to injury in January 2005 and currently works in property and project management. He also plays for the Fleet Town veterans' side along with fellow ex-Shots Nathan Fealey, Neil Musgrove and Jon Richards.

Luke Garrard — Goalkeeper

Born: 17 March 1979, Brentford.

Aldershot Town FC record:

Debut: v Dulwich Hamlet (a), Isthmian League Premier Division, 4 March 1999.
Appearances: 1

Playing career:
Hampton (youth), Tooting and Mitcham (August 1998), Harrow Borough (August 1998), Walton Casuals (September 1998), Bracknell Town (November 1998), Aldershot Town (NC, March 1999), Walton Casuals (July

1999), Leatherhead (March 2000), Walton and Hersham (December 2000), Molesey (July 2004), Croydon Athletic (May 2005), Kingstonian (June 2006).

Luke began as a youth player at Hampton and had brief spells elsewhere before joining Aldershot Town in March 1999. However, he was unlucky to concede four goals in his only appearance. That summer, he returned to Walton Casuals before joining Leatherhead and Walton and Hersham.

In November 2002 Luke suffered a very bad knee injury that kept him out of the game for nearly two years – he did not play again until he signed for Molesey in July 2004. The following summer, he signed for Croydon Athletic and helped the Rams to a club-best eighth-place finish in Isthmian League Division One.

In June 2006 Luke joined Kingstonian and proceeded to be sent off midway through the first half of his debut against Ashford Town. The Ks finished the 2007–08 season in seventh place in Isthmian League Division One South, missing the Play-offs by three points.

Mark Garvey — Midfielder

Born: 12 June 1982.

Aldershot Town FC record:

Debut:	as substitute v Worthing (a), Isthmian League Full Members' Cup second round, 2 February 1999.
Last appearance:	v Walton and Hersham (a), Isthmian League Cup first round, 12 September 2000.
Appearances:	1 + 1

Playing career:

Portsmouth (youth), Aldershot Town (youth).

Mark was a youth player at Portsmouth and with the Shots, but nothing else is known about his career or his current whereabouts.

Marcus Gayle — Centre-back/Forward

Born: 27 September 1970, Hammersmith.

Aldershot Town FC record:

Debut:	v Gravesend and Northfleet (h), Conference National, 12 August 2006.
Last appearance:	v Fleet Town (at AFC Bournemouth), Hampshire Senior Cup Final, 5 May 2007.
Appearances:	24 + 6
Goals:	7

Playing career:

Brentford (from trainee, July 1989), Kuopion Palloseura (Finland, 6ML, May 1990), Wimbledon (March 1994), Glasgow Rangers (March 2001), Watford (August 2001), Brentford (March 2005), Aldershot Town (July 2006), AFC Wimbledon (May 2007).

Marcus has made 528 Football League, FA Premier League and Scottish Premier League appearances, scoring 66 goals.

Representative honours:

England Youth, Jamaica full international (14 caps, three goals).

Club honours:

Division Three (Brentford 1991–92), Hampshire Senior Cup (Aldershot Town 2007), Isthmian League Premier Division Play-off Final (AFC Wimbledon 2008).

Marcus is a 6ft 3in giant who can play as a centre-back or a centre-forward and whose appearances in the latter stages of his career have been limited by knee injuries. He started out as a trainee at Brentford and made his senior debut as a substitute against Preston North End in October 1988. He signed full professional forms in July 1989 and then had a six-month loan spell with Finnish side Kuopion Palloseura in May 1990 to gain experience, scoring 13 goals in 28 games and finishing as top scorer that season.

After a relatively successful couple of seasons back at Brentford, a £250,000 fee took Marcus to Wimbledon in March 1994, thus giving him his first taste of FA Premier League football. The move also meant that he became the third member of his family to play for the Dons – his cousins Brian and John had already done so.

At the end of the 1994–95 season, he played in the Intertoto Cup and was also part of the Dons side that reached the semi-finals of both the 1996–97 FA and League Cups, where they lost to Chelsea and Leicester City respectively. Perhaps Marcus' most memorable contribution in a Dons shirt was his bullet header that secured a 1–0 victory over holders Manchester United in the fourth-round replay of that aforementioned FA Cup run.

In February 1998 Marcus made his debut for Jamaica against Brazil and then appeared on the world stage when he played in the final stages of that year's World Cup in France.

After Wimbledon were relegated in 1999–2000, Marcus joined Glasgow Rangers in March 2001 for a fee of £900,000. He managed to play just four matches for the Ibrox club before the same fee took him to Watford in August of that year. The club reached the 2002–03 FA Cup semi-finals, where Marcus scored the Hornets' goal in the 2–1 defeat by Southampton. That was the season that first saw him play as a centre-back, and his successful adaptation to the role was rewarded by him winning the 2003 Player of the Year award.

Marcus had an injury-ravaged 2004–05 season and made just three substitute appearances before he rejoined Brentford in March 2005 and was part of the side beaten in the League One Play-off semi-finals by Sheffield Wednesday. He was also involved in the Play-offs the following season before being released and joining Aldershot Town in July 2006.

Marcus 'double achieved' against Kidderminster Harriers in a League match in the October – he became the first-ever Shots substitute to score a hat-trick, as well as scoring his three goals in record time (nine minutes and 39 seconds had elapsed between his first and third strikes). Remarkably, this was also the first hat-trick of his career.

Later that season, he played in the FA Cup third-round defeat at Blackpool (the furthest the club had ever gone in the competition). Having been in and out of the side all season, Marcus left the Rec that summer and became ex-Shots boss Terry Brown's first signing as AFC Wimbledon manager. When he made his debut (as a substitute) against Harrow Borough at the start of the September, he became only the second player to play competitively for both Wimbledon and AFC Wimbledon (Jermaine Darlington was the first). Marcus then claimed a 'Wimbledon first' when scoring against Maidenhead United in an FA Trophy first-round game in December 2007, thus becoming the first-ever player to score competitively for both Wimbledon clubs.

Marcus scored three goals in 29 appearances in all competitions in 2007–08 as third place in the Isthmian League Premier Division was attained (the Dons' highest-ever finish in the pyramid), with this being followed by a win over Staines Town in the Play-off Final to gain promotion to the Conference South. That Final was Marcus's last game, as he announced his retirement shortly afterwards, and it has been reported that he will be concentrating on obtaining some coaching qualifications.

Matt Gearing — Midfielder/Winger/Forward

Born: 11 September 1986, Northampton.

Aldershot Town FC record:

Debut:	as substitute v Crawley Town (h), Conference National, 5 September 2005.
Last appearance:	as substitute v Grays Athletic (a), FA Trophy first-round replay, 20 December 2005.
Appearances:	1 + 7

Playing career:

Northampton Town (academy, July 2003), Aldershot Town (SLL, August 2005), Bedford Town (1ML, February 2006), Rugby Town (1ML, March 2006), Corby Town (trial, July 2006), Stamford (trial, July 2006), Rugby Town (July 2006), Hemel Hempstead Town (September 2007).

Matt joined Aldershot Town on a season-long loan in August 2005 but only played eight times, departing by Christmas. He was an academy player at Northampton Town before arriving at the Rec and operating as a forward, but he can also play in midfield or down either flank.

Unable to stake a claim for a first-team place at Sixfields, he was loaned out before making a permanent move to Rugby in the summer of 2006. He left Hutlin Road to join their Southern League Premier Division rivals Hemel Hempstead Town in September 2007.

Matt made 27 appearances in all competitions but failed to score as the Tudors finished in seventh place, missing the Play-offs by a solitary point and two places.

Luke Gedling — Midfield

Born: 29 August 1980, Brighton.

Aldershot Town FC record:

Debut: as substitute v Accrington Stanley (h), Conference, 10 August 2003.
Last appearance: as substitute v Leigh RMI (h), Conference, 21 February 2004.
Appearances: 4 + 6

Playing career:
Southampton (schoolboy and youth), Horsham (summer 1997), Worthing (November 1998), Lewes (August 1999), Ringmer (March 2000), Redhill (August 2000), Horsham (August 2001), Lewes (July 2002), Gravesend and Northfleet (December 2002), Aldershot Town (August 2003), Carlisle United (trial, November 2003), Horsham (March 2004), Rayo Vallecano (Spain, trial, summer 2004), Worthing (September 2004), Ringmer (September 2004), Folkestone Invicta (November 2004), Rayo Vallecano (Spain, trial, December 2004), Ringmer (January 2005), Burgess Hill Town (July 2005), Ringmer (September 2006).

Club honours:
Sussex Floodlight Cup (Horsham 2002), Isthmian League Charity Shield (Aldershot Town 2003).

Luke is a creative, attacking midfielder who can use both feet and who has spent a great deal of his career in and around Sussex. Having played schoolboy and youth football at Southampton, he got his non-League start at Horsham before going on to Worthing (where he only played in the reserves) and Lewes.

Luke went to Ringmer in March 2000 and saved them from relegation before following manager Russell Mason to Redhill, then returning to Horsham for 2001–2002. Having helped the Hornets win the Sussex Floodlight Cup and secure the runners'-up spot behind Lewes in Isthmian League Division Two, Luke rejoined the Rooks and then moved on to Gravesend and Northfleet in December 2002.

Luke successfully trialled with Aldershot Town in the 2003–04 pre-season and signed a contract in the August. He came on as a substitute in the club's first-ever Conference game against Accrington Stanley but was never a first-team regular at the Rec.

In March 2004 he returned to Horsham before embarking on a European adventure that summer. As a result of a connection that Russell Mason (his manager at Ringmer and Redhill) had in Spain, Luke was invited for a trial at Second Division side Rayo Vallecano. He spent a couple of months at the Teresa Rivero Stadium and made a good impression on the management. Unfortunately, injuries dictated that the club needed to sign players other than midfielders, so he returned home.

Luke had various club spells, including another trial back at Rayo Vallecano, before a move to Burgess Hill Town in the summer of 2005. He was appointed captain and finished the 2005–06 season as Hillians' top scorer (10 goals). Popular with the supporters, there was more than a little surprise when he left in October 2006 to return to Ringmer for a fourth spell.

Luke scored 10 goals in 49 appearances in all competitions in 2007–08 as the Blues finished 10th in the Sussex County League Division One. They also lost the John O'Hara League Cup Final 10–9 on penalties (after a goalless draw) to Shoreham.

Richard Gell — Midfield

Born: 8 December 1975, Park Royal.

Aldershot Town FC record:

Debut: v Hendon (a), Isthmian League Premier Division, 14 August 1999.
Last appearance: as substitute v Grays Athletic (a), Isthmian League Premier Division, 11 January 2003.
Appearances: 114 + 46 (10th in all-time top 10)
Goals: 9

Playing career:
Chelsea (youth), Wycombe Wanderers (youth), Yeading (January 1995), Chesham United (June 1998), Aldershot Town (June 1999), Aylesbury United (February 2003), Staines Town (May 2003), Northwood (August 2005), North Greenford United (2006–07 season).

Club honours:
Isthmian League Charity Shield (Aldershot Town 1999), Hampshire Senior Cup (Aldershot Town 2000 and 2002), Isthmian League Premier Division (Aldershot Town 2002–03).

Richard was an attacking midfielder and is the twin brother of ex-Northwood defender (and record appearance-holder) Chris Gell. He was a youth player at Chelsea and Wycombe Wanderers before signing for Yeading in January 1995. Although they were relegated in the 1997–98 season, a string of steady performances had brought him to the attention of several clubs, and his signing for Chesham United ensured at least another season in the division.

Richard joined Aldershot Town in June 1999 and always gave 100 per cent as the club continually pushed for promotion to the Conference. One of his finest moments at the Rec came in Aldershot Town's 10-year celebration match against a full-strength Chelsea side in August 2002 when he scored past Blues 'keeper Ed de Goey from a distance, in what many people described as 'the best goal of the six seen on the night'.

Having already made a significant contribution to the club winning that season's Isthmian League Premier Division title, Richard left the Rec in February 2003 to join Aylesbury United. He followed Ducks boss Steve Cordery to Staines Town that summer and was appointed captain. A knee injury prevented appearances, and he eventually left in August 2005 to sign for newly promoted Northwood. Richard departed after only two months, and it is not known what he did immediately afterwards. A stint at North Greenford United followed, but details of his recent career and current whereabouts are unknown.

Rob Gier — Defender

Born: 6 January 1980, Ascot.

Aldershot Town FC record:

Debut:	v Torquay United (h), Conference Premier, 15 August 2007.
Last appearance:	v Rushden and Diamonds (a), Conference Premier, 26 April 2008.
Appearances:	45 + 1

Playing career:
Wimbledon (from apprentice, June 2000), Rushden and Diamonds (July 2004), Aldershot Town (trial, August 2006), Cambridge United (NC, August 2006), Woking (January 2007), Welling United (trial, July 2007), Aldershot Town (August 2007), Grays Athletic (May 2008).
Rob has made 138 Football League appearances, scoring two goals.

Club honours:
Setanta Shield (Aldershot Town 2008), Conference Premier (Aldershot Town 2007–08).

Rob is a very useful player, because he can play at either full-back or in the centre of defence. He started as an apprentice at Wimbledon, signing full professional forms in June 2000 and making his debut as a substitute against Crewe Alexandra in October of that year.

Rob signed for Rushden and Diamonds in July 2004, following Wimbledon's relegation. However, his time at Nene Park was not very fruitful. The club finished 22nd in League Two at the end of his first season and rock bottom of the Football League at the end of the 2005–06 season. He was released by Rushden that summer and turned out for the Shots in a reserve game against Crystal Place in the August, before signing for Cambridge United later that month.

In January 2007 Rob joined fellow Conference side Woking, trialling with Welling United (who were managed by his ex-Woking teammate Neil Smith) in the summer before coming to the Rec on the same basis and impressing sufficiently to be given a full contract at the start of August.

That season, Rob was a regular member of the sides that reached the FA Trophy semi-finals, won the Setanta Shield and finished 15 points clear of second-placed Cambridge United to win the Conference Premier title. Rob was surprisingly released at the end of the 2007–08 season and signed for Grays Athletic shortly afterwards.

Chris Giles — Centre-back/Forward

Born: 16 April 1982, Milborne Port.

Aldershot Town FC record:

Debut:	as substitute v Scarborough (h), Conference, 20 March 2004.

Last appearance:	as substitute v Carlisle United (a), Conference National Play-off semi-final second leg, 6 May 2005.
Appearances:	44 + 7
Goals:	2

Playing career:
Sherborne, Yeovil Town (from youth, June 2000), Weston-Super-Mare (2ML, March 2002), Weymouth (1ML, August 2002), Gravesend and Northfleet (3ML, December 2002), Stevenage Borough (trial, 2003–04 season), Woking (1ML, February 2004), Aldershot Town (March 2004), Crawley Town (July 2005), Stevenage Borough (trial, October 2006), Forest Green Rovers (November 2006), Crawley Town (May 2008).
Chris has made one Football League appearance.

Representative honours:
Wales Non-League XI (three caps, two goals).

Club honours:
FA Trophy (Yeovil Town 2002).

Chris is a quick and agile player who is equally comfortable playing as a centre-back or a centre-forward. He joined Yeovil Town as a youth player and, having won the 1999–2000 youth team Player of the Year award, signed full contract forms that summer and made his debut in a 5–0 defeat in the Conference Trophy semi-final against Kingstonian in April 2001.

A two-month loan move to Weston-Super-Mare then preceded his appearance as a substitute for Yeovil in the club's FA Trophy Final victory over Stevenage Borough in 2002. He played just six times during Glovers' 2002–03 Conference-winning season – in fact, he played more games on loan at Weymouth and Gravesend and Northfleet that season than he did at Huish Park. His sole Football League appearance for Yeovil came in January 2004 (as a substitute against Macclesfield Town) before a trial at Stevenage, a one-month loan at Woking and a move to Aldershot Town in the March.

Chris was part of the Shots side that lost to Hednesford Town in that season's FA Trophy semi-finals, as well as playing against Shrewsbury Town in the 2004 Conference Play-off Final. That summer, Chris gained his first international honours when he was part of the Wales non-League XI that won the Four Nations Tournament and, in doing so, became the first Shots player to play for Wales at that level.

He experienced Play-off heartache again the following season, when he appeared in the second leg of the semi-final defeat against Carlisle United. Chris left the Rec that summer and signed for Crawley Town, but the club struggled all season, finished in the bottom half of the Conference National and went into administration after the season's end.

In July 2006 he was due to sign a contract with Forest Green Rovers but sustained a thigh injury in training. Thankfully, he recovered from the injury and eventually signed on at the New Lawn in November 2006. He was part of the Forest Green side that reached the second round of the FA Cup in 2007–08, where they were defeated by Swindon Town.

Chris scored four goals in 36 appearances in all competitions that season and played no small part in attaining a club-best eighth-place finish in the Conference Premier. Chris was released by Forest Green at the end of the 2007–08 season and rejoined Crawley Town shortly afterwards.

Andy Glasspool — Goalkeeper

Born: 30 January 1973, Portsmouth.

Aldershot Town FC record:

Debut:	v Thurrock (a), FA Trophy third round, 16 January 2005.
Last appearance:	v Forest Green Rovers (a), Conference Challenge Cup quarter-final, 15 February 2005.
Appearances:	3

Playing career:
Aldershot FC (apprentice, September 1989), Liss Athletic, Aldershot Town (NC, October 2004), Kingstonian (March 2006), Liss Athletic (July 2007).

Andy began his career as an apprentice at Aldershot FC in September 1989 but left the following February.

Details of his subsequent career are relatively unknown, although it is believed that he played for Liss Athletic for a considerable time prior to coming to Aldershot Town in October 2004.

Andy arrived at the Rec primarily to assist goalkeeping coach Paul Priddy. However, with reserve 'keeper Richard Barnard having departed and young 'keeper Ben Lauder-Dykes breaking his nose, Andy signed on a non-contract basis as cover for Nikki Bull. He stayed long enough to be an unused substitute in both legs of that season's Play-off semi-final against Carlisle United and, during the summer of 2005, agreed to stay on for another season. However, a shoulder injury put paid to that and he was released.

In March 2006 he made one appearance for Kingstonian before returning to Liss in July 2007. Andy made 23 League appearances in the 2007–08 season as the club finished in 16th position in Wessex League Division One.

When he's not playing football, Andy works as a leisure services manager for a company with close links to the MoD, and is heavily involved in activities pertaining to Aldershot's selection as the base for the British team in the 2012 Olympic Games.

Michael Gordon — Midfielder

Born: 11 October 1984, Tooting.

Aldershot Town FC record:

Debut: as substitute v Tamworth (h), Conference National, 13 August 2005.
Appearances: 0 + 1

Playing career:

Arsenal (trainee), Wimbledon (February 2003), Swindon Town (August 2004), Havant and Waterlooville (October 2004), Aldershot Town (NC, July 2005), Crawley Town (August 2005), Sutton United (December 2005), Worthing (September 2006), AFC Wimbledon (November 2006), Walton and Hersham (January 2007), Harrow Borough (summer 2007), Hemel Hempstead Town (DR, October 2007), Northwood (December 2007).
Michael has made 20 Football League appearances.

Representative honours:

England Schoolboys.

Michael started out as a trainee at Arsenal before being loaned to Wimbledon in February 2003, becoming permanent a month later. He made his debut for the Dons as a substitute against Derby County in April 2003 and was part of the squad that was relegated from Division One at the end of the following season. Following that relegation, he was released and had a three-month spell at Swindon Town before signing for Havant and Waterlooville in October 2004.

Michael left Westleigh Park in June 2005 and joined the Shots as a non-contract player the following month, but his career in the red and blue solely comprised the second half of the opening League game of 2005–06 against Tamworth.

A short spell at Crawley Town was followed by him participating in Sutton United's mid-table Conference South finish in 2005–06. Michael then briefly joined Worthing in September 2006 but was released and played a solitary game for AFC Wimbledon's reserves. Spells at Walton and Hersham (where he experienced relegation from the Isthmian League Premier Division) and Harrow Borough followed before he dual registered at Hemel Hempstead Town and signed for Northwood at the end of the year. Michael scored twice in 24 appearances in 2007–08 as the Woods finished in 10th place in Isthmian League Division One North.

Phillip Gordon — Midfielder

Born 7 November 1987, Jamaica.

Aldershot Town FC record:

Debut: v Fleet Town (h), Hampshire Senior Cup third round, 10 January 2006.
Appearances: 1

Playing career:

Aldershot Town (youth).

Representative honours:
British Army Youth (captain).

Phillip was a youth-team midfielder who was also a serving soldier. He captained the army's youth team in 2005–06 and made his only senior appearance for the Shots midway through that same season. His appearances were limited by his army service, but he still managed to score 10 goals in seven youth-team games that season, as well as netting once in two reserve-team appearances.

Work commitments forced Phillip to leave the Rec in February 2006 and nothing else is known about his subsequent career.

Jamie Gosling — Midfielder/Forward

Born: 21 March 1982, Bristol.

Aldershot Town FC record:

Debut:	as substitute v Scarborough (h), Conference, 20 March 2004.
Last appearance:	v Shrewsbury Town (at Stoke City FC), Conference Play-off Final, 16 May 2004.
Appearances:	12 + 1
Goals:	1

Playing career:
Bristol Rovers (schoolboy), Team Bath (August 2000), Bath City (November 2000), Cheltenham Town (trial, April 2003), Yeovil Town (July 2003), Aldershot Town (2ML, March 2004), Chester City (trial, summer 2004), Boston United (trial, summer 2004), Hereford United (trial, summer 2004), Team Bath (August 2004), Weymouth (November 2004), Torquay United (M, December 2004), Woking (February 2005), Forest Green Rovers (NC, August 2005), Basingstoke Town (March 2006), Hungerford Town (May 2006), Bath City (June 2008).
Jamie has made 19 Football League appearances, scoring two goals.

Club honours:
Hellenic League Challenge Cup (Hungerford Town 2007, 2008).

Jamie can play as an attacking midfielder or as a forward. He was a schoolboy at Bristol Rovers before joining Team Bath in August 2000, and his 18 goals in his first 14 games soon brought him to the attention of neighbours Bath City.

Jamie moved to Twerton Park three months into the 2000–01 season, but still managed to finish top scorer. He quickly adapted to the higher level of football, and consistently stood out in what was primarily a lower to mid-table side.

Towards the end of the 2002–03 season, he trialled at Cheltenham Town before becoming the first signing made by Yeovil Town as a Football League side in July 2003. He only played a dozen more League games after his debut before joining Aldershot Town on a two-month loan in March 2004.

During that spell, he was a member of the Shots side that lost to Hednesford Town in the FA Trophy semi-finals and the side that lost to Shrewsbury Town in the 2004 Conference Play-off Final. That summer, Jamie was released by Yeovil and trialled at several clubs before opting for a return to Team Bath. However, his return to the Scholars was punctuated by injury, and he eventually left to join Conference South side Weymouth.

Having played in an FA Trophy second-round match against Redbridge, Jamie made a surprise return to the League with Torquay United, albeit on a month-to-month contract. He then saw out the season with the Shots' Conference National rivals Woking. A three-month spell at Forest Green Rovers, trials at Boston United and Chester City and a groin operation then followed before he joined Basingstoke Town in March 2006.

Jamie signed for Hellenic League Premier Division side Hungerford Town in May 2006, and there was concern for his health the following March when he suffered a collapsed lung in a League match against Shortwood United. Thankfully, he recovered and played well enough for the rest of the season as the club won the League Challenge Cup, and he was offered a contract extension that summer.

The 2007–08 season saw Jamie score 31 goals in all competitions as Hungerford finished third in the Hellenic League Premier Division and beat Almondsbury Town to retain the Hellenic League Challenge Cup. In June 2008 Jamie made a return to the conference South when he re-signed for Bath City.

Lee Gosling **Midfielder/Winger**

Born: 5 March 1970, Basingstoke.

Aldershot Town FC record:

Debut:	v Heybridge Swifts (h), Isthmian League Division One, 12 August 1995.
Last appearance:	v Pagham (h), FA Cup first qualifying round, 9 September 1995.
Appearances:	5 + 2

Playing career:

Portsmouth (from trainee, July 1988), Gosport Borough (August 1991), Bognor Regis Town (August 1992), Aldershot Town (August 1995).

Lee was a midfielder and winger who began as a trainee at Portsmouth before signing full professional forms in July 1988. Following his release from Fratton Park, he experienced relegation twice when he played for local sides Gosport Borough and Bognor Regis Town before signing for Aldershot Town in August 1995. Unfortunately, Lee's Shots career was short-lived, as he was forced to retire due to injury in November 1995, a few months short of his 26th birthday. Details of his subsequent career and current whereabouts are unknown.

Andrew Grace **Defender**

Born: 26 October 1983, Frimley.

Aldershot Town FC record:

Debut:	v Newport (Isle of Wight, a), Hampshire Senior Cup second round, 15 November 2000.
Last appearance:	v Brading Town (h), Hampshire Senior Cup second round, 1 November 2001.
Appearances:	2

Playing career:

Aldershot Town (youth), Metropolitan Police (January 2002), Frimley Green (summer 2003).

Andrew is the nephew of ex-Frimley Green midfielder Russell Grace and was a member of the Shots' youth side when he made his two first-team appearances. His debut provided a club first, as it is the only instance of an uncle and nephew playing in the same game for the Shots. He left the Rec and signed for Metropolitan Police in January 2002, staying at Imber Court until the summer of 2003, when he joined Frimley Green. The 2007–08 season saw Frimley Green finish in fifth place in the Combined Counties League Division One.

Russell Grace **Midfielder**

Born: 5 October 1963, Isleworth.

Aldershot Town FC record:

Debut:	v Newport (Isle of Wight, a), Hampshire Senior Cup second round, 15 November 2000.
Appearances:	1

Playing career:

Frimley Green, Aldershot Town (STL, November 2000).

Very little is known about Russell other than that he is the uncle of Andrew Grace. He was playing for local side Frimley Green at the time of a one-match loan at the Rec in November 2000, and he currently works as a financial adviser.

Mark Graham **Midfielder/Winger**

Born: 24 October 1974, Newry.

Aldershot Town FC record:

Debut:	v Gravesend and Northfleet (h), Isthmian League Premier Division, 21 October 2000.

Last appearance: v Billericay Town (a), Isthmian League Premier Division, 2 March 2002.
Appearances: 72 + 3
Goals: 2

Playing career:
Queen's Park Rangers (from trainee, May 1993), Cambridge United (trial, April 1999), Cambridge United (July 1999), Glenavon (November 1999), Stevenage Borough (NC, August 2000), Barry Town (NC, September 2000), Aldershot Town (October 2000), Billericay Town (March 2002), Canvey Island (March 2003), St Albans City (June 2003), Hornchurch (October 2003), Bishop's Stortford (3ML, August 2004), Braintree Town (November 2004), St Albans City (July 2005), Maidenhead United (February 2006), Cambridge City (W, August 2006).
Mark has made 19 FA Premier League and Football League appearances.

Representative honours:
Northern Ireland Schoolboys, Northern Ireland Youth, Northern Ireland B (four caps).

Mark is the older brother of ex-Barnet midfielder Richard Graham and started out as a trainee right-back at Queen's Park Rangers. He signed full professional forms in May 1993 and made his QPR debut as a substitute against Swindon Town in September 1996. Although he did not make many club appearances, he still performed well enough to earn international honours at various levels for Northern Ireland.

In April 1999 Mark trialled at Cambridge United before signing permanently three months later (following his release from Loftus Road). In November 1999 he signed for Irish League side Glenavon before having brief spells at Stevenage Borough and League of Wales side Barry Town.

Mark joined Aldershot Town in October 2000 and performed consistently well for the Shots as they achieved top-four finishes in the Isthmian League Premier Division in his near two seasons at the club. His Shots career came to a sad end in March 2002 when he and teammate Ollie Adedeji were sacked for fighting with each other during a League game at Billericay Town.

Ironically, Mark signed for Billericay the following month but could not play until the following season, as he had been signed after the transfer deadline. He then had short spells elsewhere before joining Hornchurch, with whom he reached the FA Cup second round in 2003–04 (where they lost to Tranmere Rovers). He joined Bishop's Stortford on a three-month loan in August 2004 and was unfortunate to be central to the club being thrown out of the Conference Cup, as they had fielded him when he was ineligible.

In November 2004 he signed for Braintree on a three-month loan and made the move permanent the following February. He rejoined St Albans City that summer, with his trickery and performances having already played an important part in putting them on course to eventually finish as runners-up to Conference South champions Weymouth by the time he left to join Maidenhead United in February 2006. He then played briefly for Cambridge City but subsequently retired and currently works as a delivery driver.

Joel Grant — Forward/Winger

Born: 26 August 1987, Hammersmith.

Aldershot Town FC record:
Debut: as substitute v Halifax Town (h), Conference National, 2 September 2006.
Appearances: 40 + 21
Goals: 10

Playing career:
Arsenal (academy), Watford (from academy, March 2006), Aldershot Town (3ML, August 2006), Luton Town (trial, July 2007), Aldershot Town (August 2007), Crewe Alexandra (June 2008).
Joel has made seven Football League appearances.

Representative honours:
Jamaica Under-20s (four caps), Jamaica Under-21s (nine caps), Jamaica Under-23s.

Club honours:
Setanta Shield (Aldershot Town 2008), Conference Premier (Aldershot Town 2007–08).

Joel is a tricky player with quick feet who can play as a striker or as a winger. He is the cousin of former Shots teammate Nathan Koo-Boothe and started out at Arsenal's academy before moving to Watford, making his debut as a substitute in a League Cup tie against Notts County in August 2005. He then made seven Football League appearances for the Hornets before signing full professional forms in March 2006, but he never appeared for the first team again.

Joel joined Aldershot Town on a three-month loan in August 2006 but was (by his own admission) disappointing during that spell. While at the Rec, he represented Jamaica in a two-leg CONCACAF Under-20s World Championships Play-off in November 2006, scoring twice in the first leg.

Joel was released by Watford in the summer of 2007 and trialled at Luton Town before returning to the Rec as a trialist and signing non-contract forms in the August. In December 2007 he signed a contract that kept him at the club for the remainder of the season and then proceeded to mesmerise opposing defenders (being christened 'the non-League [Cristiano] Ronaldo' by the Setanta Sports television channel) as the Shots reached the FA Trophy semi-finals and won the Setanta Shield, plus the 2007–08 Conference Premier title. Joel signed a year's extension to his Shots contract at the start of May 2008. However, he surprisingly left the Rec at the end of the following month when he took the fast-track route to League One by signing for Crewe Alexandra for a Shots record fee of £130,000.

John Grant — Forward

Born: 9 August 1981, Manchester.

Aldershot Town FC record:

Debut: v Gravesend and Northfleet (h), Conference National, 12 August 2006.
Appearances: 83 + 7
Goals: 48 (joint-seventh in all-time top 10)

Playing career:

Crewe Alexandra (from trainee, July 1999), Hyde United (1ML, March 2001), Rushden and Diamonds (1ML, November 2001), Northwich Victoria (2ML, February 2002), Hereford United (June 2002), Telford United (July 2003), Shrewsbury Town (July 2004), Halifax Town (March 2005), Aldershot Town (July 2006).
John has made 26 Football League appearances, scoring two goals.

Representative honours:

England National game XI (4 caps, 1 goal).

Club honours:

Hampshire Senior Cup (Aldershot Town 2007), Setanta Shield (Aldershot Town 2008), Conference Premier (Aldershot Town 2007–08).

John signed as a professional for Crewe Alexandra in July 1999 and made his debut on the opening day of the 1999–2000 season against Crystal Palace. He managed just seven League games for the Alex and was loaned out to several teams before moving to Hereford United in June 2002. He scored just three League goals in a season that saw the Bulls fall away towards the end of the campaign and finish sixth in the Conference.

John then played for divisional rivals Telford United before joining Shrewsbury Town in July 2004, scoring twice in 19 appearances before moving to Halifax Town, for whom he was a scoring substitute in an extra-time defeat to his former club Hereford in the 2006 Conference National Play-off Final. John also finished the season as the club's top scorer with 13 goals, which led to a move to Aldershot Town in July 2006.

He settled very quickly, scoring twice on his debut against Gravesend and Northfleet on the opening day of the 2006–07 season. He also played and scored in the defeat by Blackpool as the Shots made a club-best progression to the FA Cup third round in January 2007. The season ended well for John, with him being top scorer (23 goals) and Player of the Year, and making his England National Game XI debut as a substitute against the Republic of Ireland in May 2007. He was also part of the national squad that won that year's Four Nations Tournament.

The 2007–08 season brought a mixture of fortunes for John – he missed a portion of the season due to tendonitis, scored his first-ever senior hat-trick (in a televised game against Salisbury City in the December) and signed a contract extension in February 2008 that committed him to the club until the end of the 2009–10 season. However, shortly after signing that extension, he sustained a stress fracture of his leg in an FA Trophy game at Tamworth and was expected to miss the remainder of the season, but he battled through and made a comeback at the end of March.

John ended the season as top scorer (25 goals), with those goals helping the club win the Setanta Shield and achieve the dream of promotion to the Football League as Conference Premier champions. John's final contribution of the season was to score the Shots' last non-League goal (a penalty) as they drew 1–1 at Rushden and Diamonds on the final day of the season. At the League's annual end-of-season awards ceremony, John was one of five Shots players named in the Conference Premier Team of the Year.

Leroy Griffiths — Forward

Born 30 December 1976, Lambeth.

Aldershot Town FC record:

Debut:	v Halifax Town (h), Conference National, 21 January 2006.
Last appearance:	v Grays Athletic (h), Conference National, 17 April 2006.
Appearances:	15 + 2
Goals:	6

Playing career:

Banstead Athletic, Corinthian-Casuals (August 1998), Hampton and Richmond Borough (February 2000), Norwich City (trial, July 2000), Queen's Park Rangers (May 2001), Farnborough Town (1ML, August 2002), Margate (1ML, November 2002), Farnborough Town (August 2003), Grays Athletic (September 2003), Fisher Athletic (London, May 2005), Aldershot Town (3ML, January 2006), Grays Athletic (3ML, February 2007), Havant and Waterlooville (July 2007), Corinthian-Casuals (October 2007), Lewes (DR, October 2007), Gillingham (November 2007).
Leroy has made 61 Football League appearances, scoring five goals.

Club honours:

Conference South (Grays Athletic 2004–05), Isthmian League Premier Division Play-off Final (Fisher Athletic [London] 2006).

Leroy is an energetic striker who began playing for Banstead Athletic's reserves before tasting first-team football at Corinthian-Casuals. After spells elsewhere, he eventually realised his dream of becoming a professional when Queen's Park Rangers paid £40,000 for him in May 2001. He played fairly regularly that season but contributed just three goals to the cause as the club finished a respectable eighth in Division Two.

The following season, Leroy made only six appearances in all competitions for QPR and had loan spells at Farnborough Town and Margate before being released from Loftus Road in the summer. He made a brief return to Farnborough before signing for Grays Athletic in September 2003. Leroy's 10 goals contributed to that season's sixth-place finish in the Isthmian League Premier Division, which ensured that the club would be part of the newly formed Conference South the following season.

During the 2004–05 season, Leroy contributed to the Blues attaining success – he scored 26 goals as the inaugural Conference South title was won and was also a goalscorer against Burton Albion in the FA Trophy semi-finals. However, he was controversially left out of the side that beat Hucknall Town in the Final, due to a reported falling out with teammate Vill Powell on a pre-Final trip to Spain.

Despite his part in that season's successes, Leroy left to join Fisher Athletic (London) and was playing his part in the club's push towards the Play-offs when he joined Aldershot Town on a three-month loan in January 2006. He immediately endeared himself to the fans by scoring twice on his debut, enhancing this by playing with a passion that is often missing from loanees.

A permanent move did not materialise, so Leroy returned to Fisher and helped defeat his former club Hampton and Richmond Borough in the Isthmian League Premier Division Play-off Final to gain promotion to the Conference South. He also finished the season having scored 16 goals in 29 games.

Leroy returned to Grays on a three-month loan in February 2007 but still managed to finish the season as Fisher's top scorer (16 goals). Surprisingly, he was allowed to leave Fisher at the end of the season and joined Havant and Waterlooville on trial before signing permanently later in July (on the same day as ex-Shot Jamie Slabber).

Unfortunately, his time at Westleigh Park was short, as a reported falling out with Hawks boss Ian Baird led to him rejoining Corinthian-Casuals. Leroy also signed for Conference South side Lewes on a dual-registration basis that month, but that agreement lasted but a month before he got another chance of playing in the Football League, joining Gillingham on a two-month loan. This allowed him to team up with his ex-Grays boss Mark Stimson, and the move was made permanent in the January transfer window.

Leroy finished the season having scored twice in 24 appearances for the Gills as they finished 22nd in League One, which resulted in their relegation. Shortly after the season, Leroy was one of eight players released from Priestfield. At the time of writing, it is believed that he has not yet signed for another club.

Matt Griffiths **Midfielder**

Born: 26 April 1986, Frimley.

Aldershot Town FC record:

Debut: as substitute v Brockenhurst (h), Hampshire Senior Cup second round, 21 October 2003.
Appearances: 0 + 1

Playing career:
Aldershot Town (youth), Chertsey Town (1ML, August 2004), Camberley Town (2004–05 season), Badshot Lea (January 2006).

Matt is a central-midfielder and another one-game player for the Shots. He was loaned to Chertsey Town at the start of the 2004–05 season before joining Camberley Town and then Badshot Lea in January 2006. His talent for scoring goals played a significant part in the club gaining promotion to the Hellenic League Premier Division in 2006–07. Matt's game improved significantly, and he became a highly influential member of the side, being appointed captain for the 2007–08 season and subsequently leading the club to an 11th-place League finish and to the Aldershot Senior Cup Final, which they lost to Fleet Town. Matt's efforts throughout the season were suitably rewarded when he was voted the supporters' Player of the Year.

Andy Guppy **Midfielder**

Born: 21 August 1972, Winchester.

Aldershot Town FC record:

Debut: as substitute v Barton Rovers (h), Isthmian League Division One, 2 November 1996.
Last appearance: v Basingstoke Town (a), Isthmian League Division One, 26 December 1996.
Appearances: 2 + 3

Playing career:
Pirelli General (July 1992), Farnborough Town (July 1994), Port Vale (trial, July 1995), Stafford Rangers (September 1995), Newcastle Town (November 1995), Leek Town (February 1996), Aldershot Town (October 1996).

Andy is the younger brother of ex-Wycombe Wanderers and England winger Steve Guppy. He started out at his local club Pirelli General, who were reigning Hampshire League champions at the time, and moved to Farnborough Town in July 1994 but only appeared in the reserves before moving up to Staffordshire.

Andy gave up his job as a commercial heating engineer and spent some time training with his brother at Division One side Port Vale to try to make it as a professional. During his time there, he played a few games in the reserves but decided that he would have to leave Vale Park to further his career. That decision led him to Stafford Rangers, Newcastle Town and Leek Town before moving back down South and signing for Aldershot Town in October 1996.

Within a couple of months, Andy's off-field activities were impinging on his time, so he gave up football at the start of 1997 to concentrate on several business interests, one of which was the management and development of his brother's career.

Leon Gutzmore **Forward**

Born: 30 October 1976, Camden Town.

Aldershot Town FC record:

Debut: v Dulwich Hamlet (h), Isthmian League Premier Division, 2 January 1999.
Last appearance: as substitute v Whitchurch United (h), Hampshire Senior Cup second round, 2 November 1999.
Appearances: 30 + 9
Goals: 10

Playing career:
Cambridge United (trainee), Saffron Walden Town (August 1995), Cambridge United (NC, September 1995), Billericay Town (November 1995), Leyton Orient (trial, July 1998), Southend United (trial, July 1998), Aldershot

Town (December 1998), Bedford Town (November 1999), Braintree Town (March 2000), Cambridge City (December 2001), Boreham Wood (trial, July 2003), Arlesey Town (August 2003), Aylesbury United (July 2004), Hemel Hempstead Town (February 2005), Histon (March 2005), Aylesbury United (February 2006), Brackley Town (June 2006), Histon (September 2006), Aylesbury United (September 2006), Barton Rovers (July 2007), AFC Kempston Rovers (September 2007), Arlesey Town (February 2008).
Leon has made two Football League appearances.

Representative honours:
Isthmian League XI.

Club honours:
Hampshire Senior Cup (Aldershot Town 1999), Cambridgeshire Invitation Cup (Histon 2005), Southern League Premier Division (Histon 2004–05).

Leon could be deadly in and around the box on his day. He began as a trainee at Cambridge United, returning in September 1995 after playing for Saffron Walden Town. He signed dual-registration forms with Isthmian League Division One side Billericay Town and left Cambridge in March 1996 to concentrate on his New Lodge career, where he was top scorer for three seasons with 28, 26 and 51 goals respectively. The last of these campaigns fired the club to a second-place finish (behind the Shots) and promotion from Isthmian League Division One. He also won Player of the Year in the first and last of these seasons.

Leon had a couple of trials before a club record fee of £11,000 brought him to the Rec in December 1998, with Joe Nartey moving to New Lodge on loan in return. In total, Leon had scored 118 goals in 155 games for Billericay. He scored on his Shots debut but managed just six goals that season, one of which was a 35-yard belter against Harrow Borough at the Rec near the end of the season.

By November 1999 he had failed to reproduce the goalscoring flair that he had shown at Billericay (reportedly due to off-the-field problems) and was sold to fellow Isthmian League Division One side Bedford Town for a club record £6,000. He moved to Braintree Town in March 2000, and his 21 goals in 2000–01 helped the club gain promotion to the Isthmian League Premier Division before he joined Cambridge City in December 2001. Unfortunately, his goals then dried up, but he rediscovered his scoring touch after joining Arlesey Town in August 2003, top-scoring with 30 goals in 45 games in the 2003–04 season.

Leon went on to play for Aylesbury United, Hemel Hempstead Town, Histon and Brackley Town. He left Aylesbury for the third and last time in the summer of 2007, having scored 33 goals in 81 games across his three spells. He played briefly for Brackley Town again before joining AFC Kempston Rovers in September 2007.

Leon then took a break from the game before rejoining Arlesey later in the season, with his three goals helping the Blues finish the 2007–08 campaign in 15th position in the Isthmian League Division One North.

Scott Guyett — Centre-back

Born: 20 January 1976, Ascot.

Aldershot Town FC record:

Debut:	v Tamworth (h), Conference National, 13 August 2005.
Last appearance:	v Kidderminster Harriers (h), Conference National, 15 October 2005.
Appearances:	13
Goals:	1

Playing career:
Taringa Rovers (Australia), Brisbane City (Australia), Gresley Rovers (August 1995), Southport (July 1998), Oxford United (June 2001), Chester City (August 2002), Yeovil Town (July 2004), Aldershot Town (2ML, August 2005).
Scott has made 123 Football League appearances, scoring two goals.

Representative honours:
FA XI, England Semi-Professional XI/England National Game XI (five caps).

Club honours:
Southern League Premier Division (Gresley Rovers 1996–97), Derbyshire Senior Cup (Gresley Rovers 1996, 1997), Conference (Chester City 2003–04), League Two (Yeovil Town 2004–05).

Scott is a strong centre-back and the older brother of ex-Taringa Rovers centre-back Dean Guyett. He was born in Ascot but grew up in Australia and spent the early part of his career playing for Taringa Rovers and Brisbane City in his adoptive homeland.

In August 1995 he joined Gresley Rovers, with the club attaining a club-best progression to the FA Trophy quarter-finals (where they lost to Macclesfield Town) in his first season there. He was an integral part of the side that won the Southern League Premier Division and County Cup double the following season. Unfortunately, the club were denied promotion due to their ground grading, and this resulted in many players leaving the club. To his credit, Scott stayed and tried to help the club recover but his efforts were in vain, as the club finished the following season in the bottom six.

However, Scott played well enough to earn himself a move to Conference side Southport, where he was central to the club dragging itself up from the bottom five in the table to a top-10 finish in 1999–2000 and a top-four place in 2000–01. He excelled in the latter season to the point where he made his England Semi-Professional XI debut against Holland in March 2001, later captaining the side and being voted into the Conference Team of the Year.

That summer, Scott tasted life in the Football League when he followed manager Mark Wright to Oxford United, but the club struggled and finished the campaign in 21st place. August 2002 saw him join Chester City, where Wright had also moved the previous November. Scott was part of the side that won the Conference, was voted into the Conference Team of the Year for a second time and won the club's Player of the Year award. He was also involved in the England National Game XI winning the 2003 Four Nations Tournament.

In July 2004 Scott signed for Yeovil Town and made 18 appearances that season as the League Two title was won, although he did not appear after February. He joined Aldershot Town on a two-month loan in August 2005, but the fans' opinions on him during that time were split. He continued to perform consistently once back at Huish Park and was a member of the side that lost the 2007 League One Play-off Final to Blackpool. Scott appeared in 34 of Yeovil's 2007–08 League games as a disappointing 18th-place finish was attained in League One.

Phil Hadland — Midfielder

Born: 20 October 1980, Warrington.

Aldershot Town FC record:

Debut:	as substitute v Boreham Wood (a), Isthmian League Premier Division, 18 December 1999.
Last appearance:	as substitute v Staines Town (h), FA Trophy third round, 15 January 2000.
Appearances:	1 + 5

Playing career:
Reading (from trainee, June 1999), Aldershot Town (1ML, December 1999), York City (trial, August 2000), Rochdale (August 2000), Leyton Orient (July 2001), Carlisle United (1ML, November 2001), Brighton & Hove Albion (March 2002), Darlington (August 2002), Chester City (October 2002), Gillingham (trial, November 2002), Leek Town (March 2003), Colchester United (NC, July 2003), Leek Town (September 2003), Northwich Victoria (July 2004), Leek Town (1ML, November 2004), Stalybridge Celtic (December 2004), Leek Town (1ML, March 2005), Bradford Park Avenue (August 2005), Hednesford Town (June 2006), Kidsgrove Athletic (July 2007), Colwyn Bay (June 2008).
Phil has made 50 Football League appearances, scoring four goals.

Phil is an attacking midfielder who seems to have performed steadily but quietly throughout his career. He made his sole appearance for Reading in a League Cup tie against Barnsley in September 1998 while still a trainee and signed full professional forms the following June. He came to the Rec on loan six months later but did not particularly stand out in any of his half-dozen appearances.

Phil was released by Reading in the summer of 2000 and went on to play for a number of clubs, most recently Kidsgrove Athletic in 2007–08, who finished 17th in the Northern Premier League Division One South, thus avoiding relegation by just one place. In June 2008, he was one of a number of signings made by Northern Premier League Division One side Colwyn Bay.

Jesse Hall — Defender/Midfielder

Born: 16 July 1977, Hammersmith.

Aldershot Town FC record:

Debut: v Billericay Town (h), Isthmian League Premier Division, 6 March 1999.
Last appearance: as substitute v Enfield (h), Isthmian League Premier Division, 1 May 1999.
Appearances: 13 + 2

Playing career:

Wembley (August 1997), Hendon (trial, July 1998), Hampton (November 1998), Aldershot Town (March 1999), Wealdstone (August 1999), Hendon (November 1999), Southall (March 2000), Harrow Borough (August 2000), Yeading (August 2001), Hampton and Richmond Borough (December 2002).

Club honours:

Hampshire Senior Cup (Aldershot Town 1999 [unused substitute]).

Jesse was a battling young left-sided midfielder who played for Wembley, Hendon (on trial) and Hampton before joining the Shots in March 1999. Unfortunately, he failed to make an impact at the Rec and was released that summer. He went on to play for several clubs, including Southall in 2000, who finished the season 20 points adrift at the bottom of Isthmian League Division Three; Harrow Borough, who fared only slightly better by avoiding relegation from the Isthmian League Premier Division by two points; and Hampton and Richmond again in December 2002. He was released two months later, but nothing is known of his subsequent career or current whereabouts.

Lewis Hamilton — Right-back

Born: 21 November 1984, Derby.

Aldershot Town FC record:

Debut: v Tamworth (h), Conference National, 13 August 2005.
Last appearance: v Woking (h), Conference National, 22 April 2006.
Appearances: 29 + 3

Playing career:

Derby County (academy), Queen's Park Rangers (August 2004), Kingstonian (1ML, December 2004), AFC Wimbledon (1ML, March 2005), Aldershot Town (August 2005), Lewes (July 2006), Worthing (1ML, September 2006).

Lewis has made one Football League appearance.

Club honours:
Conference South (Lewes 2007–08).

Lewis is a speedy right-back who was an academy player at Derby County before being released at the end of the 2003–04 season and joining Queen's Park Rangers, making a sole appearance in April 2005 after loan spells.

Lewis came to the Rec as a trialist and impressed sufficiently to be offered a contract in August 2005 but seemingly struggled to adapt to the standard of football in the Conference National and so left to join Lewes the following summer.

Again, Lewis struggled to perform consistently but a loan spell at Worthing did some good, as he looked a different player when he returned to the Dripping Pan. He played an active part in the Rooks attaining a top-10 finish in that season's Conference South and in equalling the club-best progression to the FA Cup first round, where they lost to Darlington. Lewis made 26 appearances in all competitions in 2007–08 as the Rooks were crowned Conference South champions.

Dean Hammond — Midfielder

Born: 7 March 1983, Hastings.

Aldershot Town FC record:

Debut:	v Shrewsbury Town (h), Conference, 13 September 2003.
Last appearance:	v Halifax Town (h), Conference, 11 October 2003.
Appearances:	7

Playing career:
Brighton & Hove Albion (from scholar, June 2002), Aldershot Town (1ML, September 2003), Leyton Orient (1ML, October 2003), Colchester United (January 2008).
Dean has made 171 Football League appearances, scoring 25 goals.

Dean is a ball-winning midfielder who made his debut as a substitute for Brighton & Hove Albion in a Football League Trophy tie against Cardiff City in December 2000, signing full professional forms in June 2002.

In order to gain some experience, Dean was loaned out to Aldershot Town in September 2003 then Leyton Orient the following month, and it was obvious that he was good enough to hold down a regular place in a higher league side. He was a regular for Albion in 2004–05 as they avoided relegation from the Championship by a point, only to finish rock bottom the following season.

Dean was named as Brighton captain midway through the 2006–07 season but Championship side Colchester United paid £250,000 to take Dean to Layer Road in January 2008. The season was to end in disappointment for club and player, as the Us were relegated by virtue of their rock-bottom finish.

Mark Hammond — Midfielder/Winger/Forward

Born: 3 October 1978, Sidcup.

Aldershot Town FC record:

Debut:	as substitute v Maidenhead United (h), Isthmian League Premier Division, 4 March 2003.
Last appearance:	as substitute v Bashley, Hampshire Senior Cup Final (at Southampton FC), 8 May 2003.
Appearances:	4 + 4
Goals:	1

Playing career:
Millwall (youth), Welling United (August 1997), Dover Athletic (July 1998), Cray Wanderers (February 1999), Millwall (trial, April 2000), Millwall (September 2000), Cray Wanderers (November 2000), Grimsby Town (trial, summer 2001), Aldershot Town (March 2003), Lewes (August 2003), Bromley (September 2003), Cray Wanderers (August 2004), Maidstone United (September 2004), Erith and Belvedere (February 2005), Cray Wanderers (trial, July 2005), Whyteleafe (August 2005), Croydon Athletic (July 2006), Cray Wanderers (November 2006), Collaroy Cromer Strikers (Australia, April 2007), Sutton United (September 2007), Leatherhead (October 2007), Erith Town (November 2007), Sittingbourne (November 2007), Erith and Belvedere (January 2008), Cray Wanderers (March 2008).

Representative honours:
North Kent Youth.

Club honours:
Kent League (Cray Wanderers 2002–03), Hampshire Senior Cup (Aldershot Town 2003).

Mark is a strong, creative midfielder who can also play as a winger or a forward. He has spent the majority of his career in and around Kent and has also worked as an actor. Originally a youth player at Millwall, he was set to sign a contract after playing for several clubs elsewhere, but illness and injury kept him out of the game for a few months. He eventually signed for the Lions in September 2000 before signing with former club Cray a couple of months later.

Mark joined Aldershot Town in February 2003 for £1,000, having already made enough appearances for Cray to guarantee himself a medal as part of the squad that eventually won the Kent League Championship. He ended the season for the Shots as a County Cup winner, as well as getting his debut TV role in Sky One's *Dream Team* for the upcoming 2003–04 season (he also appeared in the 2004–05 series).

Mark joined Lewes in the summer of 2003 but took a break from playing in October 2005 as his acting career gained momentum – he appeared in the film *Green Street* and the E4 reality series *Five Go Dating*. He also coached Cray's reserve side from January to May 2006. Returning to playing in July 2006, he joined Croydon Athletic but left the following April to go to Australia, where he signed for Manly Warringah Premier League side Collaroy Cromer Strikers.

Having scored twice in eight appearances 'down under', Mark returned to the UK in October 2007 and had a number of brief club spells, as well as working with movie director Guy Ritchie on an advert for a well-known sportswear brand at the beginning of 2008. Meanwhile, he re-signed for Erith and Belvedere but was restricted to a single appearance due to a bout of meningitis. Once recovered, he returned to Cray in March but did not play again that season as a result of suffering from Gilmore's Groin.

Ben Harding — Midfielder

Born: 6 September 1984, Carshalton.

Aldershot Town FC record:

Debut:	v Halifax Town (h), Conference National, 2 September 2006.
Appearances:	65 + 12
Goals:	6

Playing career:
Wimbledon/Milton Keynes Dons (from scholar, October 2001), Forest Green Rovers (2ML, November 2005), Aldershot Town (4ML, August 2006), Grays Athletic (4ML, January 2007), Aldershot Town (July 2007).
Ben has made 51 Football League appearances, scoring six goals.

Representative honours:
England Under-15s, England Under-16s, England C (three caps).

Club honours:
Setanta Shield (Aldershot Town 2008), Conference Premier (Aldershot Town 2007–08).

Ben is a creative midfielder who can play on the left or in the centre of the park. He began as a scholar at Wimbledon, making his debut against Rotherham United in November 2003. He played the last 25 minutes of that match in goal after the starting goalkeeper (Paul Heald) was injured and his replacement (Lee Worgan) sent off! To his credit, Ben did not concede a goal and went on to play 15 League games that season as the Dons were relegated after finishing bottom of Division One.

In November 2005 Ben was loaned to Forest Green Rovers and made nine appearances, scoring one goal. Relegation came again for the Dons at the end of that season as injuries restricted him to just 10 appearances. He spent a discouraging four months on loan with the Shots in 2006 and was released in the summer.

However, Ben returned to the Rec as a trialist and immediately looked a completely different player to the one that had disappointed during his loan spell. His metamorphosis was such that, following rave reviews from fans and reporters alike, he signed a contract in August 2007, performed magnificently during the season and was one of the main contenders for the Player of the Year trophy (finishing runner-up to Nikki Bull). His performances also resulted in him making his England C debut against Wales in February 2008, as well as helping the Shots reach that season's FA Trophy semi-finals and win the Setanta Shield.

Ben was an ever present in the 2007–08 League campaign and played no small part in the winning of the Conference Premier title. It was no surprise, therefore, that he signed a new two-year contract just days after the season ended. The following month, Ben was part of the England C squad that won a second successive Four Nations Tournament, as well as being named in the Conference Premier Team of the Year.

George Hardy — Centre-back

Born: 7 September 1988, Aldershot.

Aldershot Town FC record:

Debut:	v Christchurch (h), Hampshire Senior Cup second round, 27 November 2007.
Appearances:	2 + 1

Playing career:
Aldershot Town (NC, from youth, summer 2007), Fleet Town (DR, August 2007), Ashford Town (DR, October 2007).

George is a young centre-back who progressed from the youth team to signing as a non-contract player in the summer of 2007. He also played at Fleet Town and Ashford Town (Middlesex) on a dual-registration basis during the 2007–08 season. George's three appearances for the Shots that season all came in the Hampshire Senior Cup.

Paul Harford — Midfielder

Born: 21 October 1974, Chelmsford.

Aldershot Town FC record:

Debut:	v Enfield (h), Isthmian League Premier Division, 18 August 2001.
Last appearance:	as substitute v Boreham Wood (a), Isthmian League Premier Division, 27 April 2002.
Appearances:	28 + 5
Goals:	4

Playing career:
Arsenal (trainee, July 1991), Blackburn Rovers (August 1993), Wigan Athletic (1ML, September 1994), Shrewsbury Town (1ML, December 1994), Farnborough Town (summer 1996), Sacramento Knights (US, L, May 1998), Welling United (October 1998), Sutton United (October 1998), Aldershot Town (May 2001), Bracknell Town (player-coach, May 2002), Leatherhead (player-assistant manager, December 2002; joint player-manager from summer 2003; player-manager from February 2004).
Paul has made nine Football League appearances.

Representative honours:
Surrey Schoolboys, Isthmian League XI.

Club honours:
Isthmian League Premier Division (Sutton United 1998–99), Surrey Senior Cup (Sutton United 1999).

Post-playing coaching/management career:
Academy coach at Fulham (July 2005), assistant manager of Sutton United (March 2006).

Paul is the son of the late ex-Blackburn Rovers manager Ray Harford and was primarily a tall, ball-winning midfielder, although he did play in defence and as a forward at various points in his career. He was a trainee at Arsenal and a full-time professional at Blackburn Rovers but had to wait until joining Wigan athletic on loan to make his senior debut (against Barnet in September 1994). A further loan at Shrewsbury Town followed before he joined the Shots' local rivals Farnborough Town in the summer of 1996.

Ben helped the club finish seventh in the Conference and then picked up the Player of the Year award the following 1997–98 season. He spent the summer months playing in the US Indoor Soccer League for Sacramento Knights before deciding against a return to League football with Gillingham in October 1998. He opted instead to sign for fellow Conference side Welling United, playing just one game, then Sutton United, where he was a mainstay of the midfield that won the Isthmian League Premier Division title and county Cup double.

A £4,000 fee brought Paul to Aldershot Town in May 2001, but his debut in the opening game of the season against Enfield was soured by a medial ligament injury. From then on, he never had a settled run in the side and an ankle ligament injury picked up later in the season signalled the end of his time at the Rec.

After successful coaching and managing spells, Paul retired in November 2004. He returned in July 2005 to work as a coach at Fulham's academy before becoming assistant manager at his former club, Sutton, the following March, helping the club to attain two mid-table finishes before leaving in the summer of 2007. Paul currently works as a taxi driver and runs a mortgage consultancy.

Mo Harkin — Midfielder

Born: 16 August 1979, Londonderry.

Aldershot Town FC record:

Debut:	v Chesham United (a), Isthmian League Premier Division, 3 November 2001.
Last appearance:	v Boreham Wood (h), Isthmian League Premier Division, 10 November 2001.
Appearances:	2

Playing career:
Wycombe Wanderers (from trainee, February 1997), Carlisle United (August 2001), Aldershot Town (NC, November 2001), Nuneaton Borough (January 2002), Crawley Town (June 2002), Forest Green Rovers (March 2005), Lewes (May 2005), Havant and Waterlooville (May 2006), Eastbourne Borough (June 2008).
Mo has made 77 Football League appearances, scoring two goals.

Representative honours:
Northern Ireland Youth, Northern Ireland Under-21s (nine caps).

Club Honours:
Southern League Cup (Crawley Town 2003), Sussex Senior Cup (Crawley Town 2003), Southern League Championship Trophy (Crawley Town 2003, 2004), Southern League Premier Division (Crawley Town 2003–04).

Mo is a midfield playmaker and the younger brother of ex-Manchester City player Joe Harkin. He was the first-ever player to progress to senior level from the Wycombe Wanderers youth scheme, doing so in February 1997. Mo's early career went well, and he gained Northern Ireland Youth and Under-21 honours, scoring on his debut for the latter against Malta in March 2000. Unfortunately, he did not perform consistently for the Wycombe first team and spent more time on the bench than on the pitch, and rumours circulated of a reported £800,000 move to Aston Villa.

In 2000–01 Mo played in the early part of the club's FA Cup run but missed out on the chance to play Liverpool at Villa Park in the semi-final after a reported falling-out with boss Lawrie Sanchez. Five appearances at Carlisle United followed before he joined Aldershot Town in November 2001.

After a spell at Nuneaton Borough, he joined Crawley Town and was an integral part of the squad that won the Southern League Cup and Sussex Senior Cup double in 2003 before winning the Southern League Premier Division the following season, thus gaining their first-ever promotion to the Conference National.

Mo joined Forest Green Rovers then Lewes, but the 2005–06 season was to end in joy then immediate despair for both club and player: the Rooks qualified for the Play-offs by virtue of achieving a fourth-place finish in the Conference South but were then denied their right to take part by the Conference's decision to exclude them due to ground development issues.

Mo went on to have a successful time with Havant and Waterlooville, with one of the highlights coming in 2007–08 when they reached the fourth round of the FA Cup. Amazingly, in the match against Liverpool, the Hawks led twice at Anfield before eventually losing 5–2 to the Merseyside giants. Mo scored twice in 32 games in all competitions during the 2007–08 season as the Hawks finished in seventh place in the Conference South, missing the Play-offs by just two points and two places. In June 2008, Mo took a step up by signing for Conference Premier new boys Eastbourne Borough.

Mark Harper — Centre-back

Born: 23 July 1969, Wolverhampton.

Aldershot Town FC record:

Debut:	v Maidenhead United (a), Isthmian League Division One, 1 November 1997.
Last appearance:	v Bromley (h), FA Trophy second round, 21 November 1998.
Appearances:	48 + 4
Goals:	3

Playing career:

Wolverhampton Wanderers (youth), Bedfont (summer 1989), Egham Town (summer 1992), Hampton (November 1992), Chertsey Town (August 1994), Kingstonian (July 1997), Aldershot Town (November 1997), Sutton United (December 1998), Farnborough Town (August 1999), Metropolitan Police (July 2002; player-assistant manager from summer 2003), Leatherhead (July 2004; player-coach from summer 2005; player-assistant manager from summer 2006), Horsley (December 2007).

Representative honours:

Staffordshire Youth, Middlesex FA XI.

Club honours:

Isthmian League Premier Division (Kingstonian 1997–98, Sutton United 1998–99, Farnborough Town 2000–01), Isthmian League Division One (Aldershot Town 1997–98), Surrey County Intermediate League Western Premier Division (Horsley 2007–08).

Mark was a commanding centre-back who started out as a youth player with his local side Wolverhampton Wanderers. His early clubs included Bedfont, Egham Town, Hampton, Chertsey Town and Kingstonian before he signed for the Shots in November 1997. Oddly, Mark ended the season with two Championship-winners' medals, as the Shots won the Isthmian League Division One title and he had already played enough games at the Ks to qualify him for a medal, as they won the Isthmian League Premier Division that season.

For the second successive season, Mark was a title winner after joining Sutton United in December 1998, but he left that summer as his work commitments meant that he would not be able to dedicate enough time to Conference football.

Mark later joined the Shots' local rivals, Farnborough Town, and was a mainstay of the defence that helped secure the Isthmian League Premier Division title in 2000–01. In July 2002 he joined Metropolitan Police (where he was one of the first non-Police personnel to play) but suffered the cruel blow of breaking his leg in a pre-season game and missed the entire season. He became player-assistant manager at Imber Court in the summer of 2003 before moving to near neighbours Leatherhead (solely as a player) in July 2004.

In the summer of 2005 Mark became player-coach and a year later he was appointed player-assistant manager to Dave Harlow. He left Fetcham Grove in October 2007 when new manager Ian Hazel decided that he did not figure in his plans. Mark joined Surrey County Intermediate League Western Premier Division side Horsley in December 2007, where he finished the season as a League winner.

Michael Harper — Forward

Born: 4 February 1985, Guildford.

Aldershot Town FC record:

Debut:	v Braintree Town (h), Isthmian League Premier Division, 24 August 2002.
Last appearance:	as substitute v Hednesford Town (h), FA Trophy semi-final first leg, 27 March 2004.
Appearances:	9 + 24
Goals:	8

Playing career:

Aldershot Town (from youth, August 2002), Bognor Regis Town (1ML, January 2003), Aylesbury United (1ML, March 2004), Staines Town (initially on SLL, July 2004), Windsor and Eton (1ML, October 2004), Chertsey Town (January 2005), Badshot Lea (summer 2006).

Club honours:

Isthmian League Premier Division (Aldershot Town 2002–03), Isthmian League Charity Shield (Aldershot Town 2003).

Michael is a strong hard-working forward who graduated from the Shots' youth team. He signed full contract forms in August 2002 and scored twice on his debut against Braintree Town later that month. A further nine League games in that season's Isthmian League Premier Division-winning campaign followed, but his only other goal came in a Hampshire Cup tie against Andover.

A one-month loan at Bognor Regis Town in January 2003 served to give Michael some valuable experience before he was a playing substitute in the Shots' first-ever Conference game against Accrington Stanley in August 2003. He played in the first leg of the club's FA Trophy semi-final against Hednesford Town in March 2004, before moving to Aylesbury United on loan at the end of the month.

Unfortunately, his loan spell at Buckingham Road was cut short by a broken arm sustained in a League match against Chesham United the following month. He signed at Staines Town after a loan, but things did not quite work out for Michael and he was loaned to Windsor and Eton before leaving to join Chertsey Town in January 2005. The move seemed to be just what Michael needed, as he finished the season as the Curfews' top scorer (12 goals).

He joined a plethora of ex-Shots youth-team players when he moved to Hellenic League Division One East side Badshot Lea in the summer of 2006, and he soon developed other areas of his game in addition to his goalscoring. He was a vital part of the side that gained promotion to the Premier Division at the end of that season and that finished the 2007–08 season in 11th spot in the League and as losing finalist to Fleet Town in the Aldershot Senior Cup Final.

Steve Harris — Centre-back

Born: 9 February 1966, Farnham.

Aldershot Town FC record:

Debut:	v Horsham (h), Isthmian League Division Three, 29 August 1992.
Last appearance:	v Chertsey Town (h), 7 May 1994.
Appearances:	104
Goals:	9

Playing career:
Farnham Town (August 1984), Aldershot FC (trial, September and October 1989), Aldershot Town (August 1992), Basingstoke Town (£2,000, July 1994).

Representative honours:
Combined Counties League XI.

Club honours:
Combined Counties League (Farnham Town 1990–91, 1991–92), Dan Air Elite Cup (Farnham Town 1992), Combined Counties Premier Challenge Cup (Farnham Town 1992), Isthmian League Division Three (Aldershot Town 1992–93), Hampshire Senior Cup (Basingstoke Town 1996, 1997).

Steve was a very dependable and strong defender who signed for Farnham Town in the summer of 1984. Early on in his time at the Memorial Ground, he was invited for a trial at Aldershot FC and played two reserve games but nothing materialised. He matured into a consistent player and captained Farnham to back-to-back Combined Counties League titles in 1990–91 and 1991–92. The second of these formed part of a Combined Counties treble (League title, Dan Air Elite Cup and Premier Challenge Cup) that the club achieved – the first time any club had performed that feat.

Steve joined the Shots in the summer of 1992 as a result of the unfortunate demise of Farnham Town. He missed the season's opener against Clapton due to a knee injury but played in all the remaining League games as the Shots eased to the Isthmian League Division Three title (winning it by 18 points). He was a member of the Shots side that reached the FA Vase quarter-final and the side that was promoted from Isthmian League Division Two the following season – a season in which he was also the joint winner of the Player of the Year award with Keith Baker.

In July 1994 Steve rather surprisingly left the Rec to join Basingstoke Town. The £2,000 that was paid, as part of the deal that saw Paul Chambers move the other way, made him the first player to leave the Rec for a fee. Unsurprisingly, he went on to win the Player of the Year award three times, and he was a major factor in the Stoke gaining promotion to the Isthmian League Premier Division at the end of the 1996–97 season, by virtue of finishing as runners-up to Chesham United.

Steve missed a large proportion of the 1998–99 season through injury and then retired from football in the summer of 2000 – some would say too early – to concentrate on his decorating business.

Wes Harrison — Utility

Born: 11 December 1980, Munster, Germany.

Aldershot Town FC record:

Debut:	as substitute v Brading Town (h), Hampshire Senior Cup second round, 1 November 2001.
Appearances:	0 + 1

Playing career:
Walton and Hersham (youth), Aldershot Town (summer 2001), Leatherhead (October 2002), Sutton United (March 2006), Kingstonian (July 2006), Uxbridge (October 2006), Godalming Town (November 2006), Walton and Hersham (summer 2007), Guildford City (DR, September 2007), Walton Casuals (February 2008).

Wes is a utility player who is comfortable in defence, midfield or up front, but he is probably best known for his role as a winger. He started out as a youth player at Walton and Hersham and made his Swans debut in February 2000. He left in the summer of 2001 and joined the Shots but made just one appearance.

Wes then moved on to Leatherhead before joining Sutton United in March 2006, reuniting with Paul Harford (his player-manager at Leatherhead), who had just been appointed as assistant manager at Gander Green Lane. Spells elsewhere followed before he joined Walton Casuals, who finished the 2007–08 season in 16th place in Isthmian Division One South.

Stuart Harte — Right-back

Born: 12 December 1977, Basingstoke.

Aldershot Town FC record:

Debut: v Aylesbury United (a), Isthmian League Premier Division, 7 September 1999.
Last appearance: v Harrow Borough (a), Isthmian League Premier Division, 4 December 1999.
Appearances: 8

Playing career:

Bristol Rovers (from trainee, July 1996), Bath City (1ML, March 1997), Farnborough Town (October 1997), Aldershot Town (June 1999), Staines Town (December 1999), Bracknell Town (August 2001), Hampton and Richmond Borough (March 2003), Metropolitan Police (July 2003), Margate (July 2007), Carshalton Athletic (February 2008).

Stuart is an assured and capable right-back who began as a trainee at Bristol Rovers before signing full professional forms in July 1996. A one-month loan spell at neighbours Bath City at the tail end of the 1996–97 season preceded a move to Farnborough Town. Unfortunately, Stuart and the club endured a wretched time during his near two seasons there, narrowly avoiding relegation from the Conference in 1997–98 and finishing rock bottom the following season.

Stuart stood out in a bad side in that latter season, which prompted Aldershot Town to pay their neighbours £1,000 for his services in June 1999. Oddly, he made just eight appearances for the Shots before being allowed to join Staines Town at the end of the year.

Stuart moved on to Bracknell Town in August 2001 and was influential in the Robins finishing in fourth spot in Isthmian League Division Three that season. Stuart later signed for Hampton then Metropolitan Police. The club finished in the bottom five of Isthmian League Division One South in his first season, but he played a big part in the next three seasons' improvements – in both 2004–05 and 2005–06 the club reached the Isthmian League Division One Play-off semi-finals (beaten by Bromley and Dover Athletic respectively), and they finished six points and one place outside the Play-offs in 2006–07.

Stuart was joint Player of the Year with Stuart MacKenzie in 2006 before leaving to join Margate. He started the 2007–08 season very well, but his work commitments started to impinge on his game. This resulted in his contract at Hartsdown Park being cancelled by mutual consent in February 2008 and him joining fellow Isthmian League Premier Division side Carshalton Athletic. He played 12 games for the Robins towards the end of the 2007–08 season as they finished 18th in the League, avoiding relegation on goal difference.

Michael 'Junior' Harvey — Defender/Midfielder

Born: 1 May 1979, Plymouth.

Aldershot Town FC record:

Debut: as substitute v Dulwich Hamlet (h), Isthmian League Premier Division, 11 December 1999.
Last appearance: as substitute v Andover (at Basingstoke Town FC), Hampshire Senior Cup Final, 8 May 2000.
Appearances: 11 + 13
Goals: 2

Playing career:

Chelsea (schoolboy), Barnet (trainee), Woking (trial, July 1997), Kingstonian (August 1997), Slough Town (January 1998), Hampton (March 1998), Leatherhead (August 1998), Chertsey Town (February 1999), Harrow Borough (September 1999), Aldershot Town (December 1999), Billericay Town (July 2000), Slough Town (September 2000), Dagenham and Redbridge (trial, August 2003), Ford United (August 2003), AFC Wimbledon (September 2003), Lewes (February 2004), AFC Wimbledon (September 2005), Chesham United (February 2006), St Albans City (June 2007).

Club honours:
Hampshire Senior Cup (Aldershot Town 2000), Isthmian League Division One South (Lewes 2003–04), Isthmian League Play-off Final (Lewes 2004).

'Junior' is the son of ex-TV Gladiator Mike 'Bullitt' Harvey and is actually better known in the entertainment world than in the football world. He can play as either a defender or midfielder and can be a handful when adopting the latter role.

Junior began as a schoolboy at Chelsea and then became a trainee at Barnet, but an ankle injury at the age of 19 ended his professional ambitions. He played for a number of Isthmian League sides before signing for Aldershot Town in December 1999. His last contribution in a Shots shirt was to score the final goal (after coming on as a substitute) in the 9–1 thrashing of Andover in the 2000 Hampshire Senior Cup Final. He then had a brief spell at Billericay Town before signing for Slough Town in September 2000 and getting sent off on his debut against Hendon.

Following Slough's relegation from the Isthmian League Premier Division at the end of that season, he signed for Ford United, having impressed while playing against them for Dagenham and Redbridge in a pre-season friendly. A month later, he joined AFC Wimbledon before moving to Lewes the following February and helping the club win the Isthmian League Division One South title and one of the subsequent Play-off Finals against Kingstonian for entry into the newly formed Conference South.

The following season, Junior's work commitments meant he did not appear for the Rooks until after the new year when he helped the club's push for the Play-offs – a set of games that they qualified for but were denied due to ground development issues.

In September 2005 he returned to AFC Wimbledon but left the following February to become one of Luther Blissett's first signings for Chesham United. That summer, he took a break from football and did not return to playing until June 2007 when he signed for St Albans City. However, his return was brief, as he left Clarence Park a couple of months later, and it is not known what he did playing-wise after that.

Amid his football career, Junior became a member of the successful garage band So Solid Crew, using the stage name MC Harvey, latterly dropping the 'MC'. He later left the group to develop his TV career, with stints on Channel 4 and Sky One. He also appeared in the 2003 crime thriller video release *Out For A Kill,* was part of the original cast of the stage musical *Daddy Cool* and voices the commentary on the sports video game *FIFA Street*. With regard to his personal life, Junior is separated from pop singer and *Strictly Come Dancing* winner Alesha Dixon.

Ian Hathaway — Winger

Born: 22 August 1968, Wordsley.

Aldershot Town FC record:

Debut:	as substitute v Billericay Town (a), Isthmian League Premier Division, 26 September 1998.
Last appearance:	v Heybridge Swifts (a), Isthmian League Premier Division, 5 May 2001.
Appearances:	88 + 31
Goals:	12

Playing career:
West Bromwich Albion (apprentice), Wolverhampton Wanderers (W, February 1986), Dudley Town (August 1986), Stourbridge (October 1986), Bedworth United, Mansfield Town (February 1989), Rotherham United (March 1991), Torquay United (July 1993), Chesterfield (1ML, March 1996), Colchester United (June 1997), Aldershot Town (September 1998), Woking (trial, May 2001), Staines Town (trial, July 2001), Andover (October 2001), Ludgershall Sports (summer 2002), Mottisfont (July 2006).
Ian has made 209 Football League appearances, scoring 17 goals.

Club honours:
Isthmian League Charity Shield (Aldershot Town 1999), Isthmian League Cup (Aldershot Town 1999), Hampshire Senior Cup (Aldershot Town 1999 and 2000).

Post-playing coaching/management career:
Manager of Broughton (December 2001).

Ian was a quick, powerful little winger who possessed the most accurate left foot that one is ever likely to see. He started as an apprentice at West Bromwich Albion but never made a first-team appearance. Spells at Midlands sides followed before he joined Division Three side Mansfield Town in February 1989, with the £8,000 fee being a then record sale for the Greenbacks.

Ian made his Stags debut as a substitute against Preston North End the following month, and his trickery and nippy wing play contributed greatly to the club narrowly avoiding relegation that season. The unsuccessful 1990–91 season saw Ian join Rotherham United, who went down with the Stags at the end of the season, in March 1991 in a swap deal that saw Steve Spooner move in the opposite direction.

Ian played just eight games during the 1991–92 season and missed the whole of the following season after contracting pneumonia. In July 1993 he joined Torquay United and was part of the squad that reached the Division Three Play-off semi-finals. Torquay later endured a terrible 1995–96 campaign as the Gulls finished bottom of Division Three. However, they were reprieved from relegation when Conference winners Stevenage Borough were denied promotion due to their 'unfit' ground.

Ian was loaned out then released and joined Colchester United in June 1997, where he was part of the side that reached the 1998 Division Three Play-offs. He joined Aldershot Town on a one-month loan in September 1998 and fitted in so well that the move became permanent at the end of the spell. Although he caused havoc down the flanks, he was publicly berated more than once by Shots manager George Borg for being overweight. However, that did not stop him becoming a crowd favourite at the Rec, memorably supplying the cross from which Gary Abbott scored an injury-time winner against Basingstoke Town in the 1999 Hampshire Senior Cup Final.

With the Shots having won minor silverware during his time at the Rec, Ian departed in the summer of 2001 and joined Andover in October. However, he made just one appearance before retiring two months later and becoming manager of Hampshire League Division Two side Broughton, as well as working as a postman. He led the club to a mid-table finish in 2001–02 and then left in the summer, resuming his playing career at divisional rivals Ludgershall Sports. He stayed there until just after the start of the 2005–06 season, and it is not known what he did immediately after that. However, he signed for Mottisfont in July 2006 and left at the end of the season. Details of his subsequent career and current whereabouts are unknown.

Asa Head — Midfielder

Born: 13 October 1969, Aldershot.

Aldershot Town FC record:

Debut:	v Chertsey Town (h), Isthmian League Division One, 25 February 1995.
Last appearance:	v Wokingham Town (h), Isthmian League Division One, 26 April 1997.
Appearances:	35 + 30
Goals:	8

Playing career:

Southampton (trainee), Ash United (August 1993), Aldershot Town (February 1995), Havant Town (July 1997), Molesey (July 1998).

Asa was a creative midfielder who had been a trainee at Southampton before signing for Ash United in August 1993. He made the step up to Isthmian League football when he joined the Shots in February 1995 and, although not a regular, put in many solid performances and scored a few important goals as the club challenged strongly for promotion from Division One.

In July 1997 he left, signed for Havant Town and played in the club's last-ever season before their merger with Waterlooville. Asa signed for Molesey in July 1998 but left four months later, and details of his subsequent career are unknown. It is believed that Asa currently lives in America.

Greg Heald — Centre-back

Born: 26 September 1971, Enfield.

Aldershot Town FC record:

Debut:	v Crawley Town (h), Conference National, 5 September 2005.
Last appearance:	v Scarborough (h), Conference National, 25 March 2006.
Appearances:	37
Goals:	4

Playing career:
Norwich City (youth), Watford House Wanderers, Enfield (summer 1990), Peterborough United (July 1994), Barnet (August 1997), Leyton Orient (March 2003), Rochdale (March 2004), York City (trial, August 2005), Burton Albion (NC, August 2005), Ashton United (August 2005), Aldershot Town (August 2005), Thurrock (June 2006), Enfield Town (NC, January 2008).
Greg has made 294 Football League appearances, scoring 23 goals.

Representative honours:
England Schoolboys, Middlesex Youth, England Under-18s, FA XI, England Semi-Professional XI (one cap).

Club honours:
Middlesex Senior Cup (Enfield 1991).

Post-playing coaching/management career:
Youth-team coach at Wycombe Wanderers (July 2007).

Greg was a dominant centre-back who had a penchant for scoring headers from set-pieces. He started out as a youth player at Norwich City before dropping into non-League football with a successful stint at Watford House Wanderers and Enfield.

In July 1994 he joined Peterborough United for a fee of £35,000 and made his debut against Bristol Rovers on the opening day of the 1994–95 season. His third season there ended in relegation from the Second Division, and he subsequently joined his former Posh boss, John Still, at Barnet for a fee of £130,000 (still a Bees record). Greg was an integral part of the side that reached the Division Three Play-off semi-finals (where they lost to Colchester United) in his first season at Underhill.

After another successful season, the Bees had a complete about-turn in fortune the following season and were relegated out of the Football League. Every player at Underhill was subsequently transfer-listed but Greg gallantly remained with the club for the next two seasons (being named as captain for the 2002–03 season) as they battled to reclaim their place in the Football League.

During that time, he made his one and only appearance for the England Semi-Professional XI against Holland in April 2002 and was voted into the 2001–02 Conference Team of the Year. With the Bees all set for a mid-table finish in the Conference, monetary problems forced the sale of Greg and teammate Wayne Purser to Leyton Orient in March 2003 for a combined fee of £18,000.

Twelve months later and unable to claim a regular place at Brisbane Road, he moved to Rochdale and the club narrowly avoided relegation that season. Following his release from Spotland, Greg joined Burton Albion then Ashton United briefly before joining Aldershot Town in August 2005. He performed steadily for the Shots but left in March 2006 due to a combination of not being able to commit to full-time football and reportedly considering a possible career as a teacher or firefighter.

After a spell with Thurrock, Greg retired at the end of the 2006–07 season before being appointed youth-team coach at Wycombe Wanderers. However, he left his post at Adams Park in December 2007 to become a teacher and resumed his playing career at Isthmian League Division One North side Enfield Town the following month, retiring in March 2008.

Simon Higgins — Right-back

Born: 14 August 1982, Reading.

Aldershot Town FC record:

Debut:	v Walton and Hersham (a), Isthmian League Cup first round, 12 September 2000.
Last appearance:	as substitute v Newport (Isle of Wight, a), Hampshire Senior Cup second round, 15 November 2000.
Appearances:	2 + 1

Playing career:
Staines Town (youth), Aldershot Town (youth), Hartley Wintney (2002–03 season), Ash United (2004–05 season).

Simon was a youth-team right-back and is the son of ex-Farnborough Town director Ron Higgins. His three appearances for the Shots came in a two-month period as part of the club's policy of blooding youth-team players in minor competitions, after which he went on to play for Hartley Wintney and Ash United. Simon made 10 appearances for Ash in the 2007–08 season as they finished in 15th spot in the Combined Counties Premier Division.

James Hinchin — Forward

Born: 20 October 1986, Ascot.

Aldershot Town FC record:

Debut: as substitute v Andover (a), Hampshire Senior Cup quarter-final, 1 February 2005.
Last appearance: as substitute v Forest Green Rovers (a), Conference Cup fourth round, 15 February 2005.
Appearances: 0 + 3

Playing career:
Aldershot Town (youth), Marlow (1ML, August 2004), Cove (1ML, 2004–05 season), Badshot Lea (1ML, 2004–05 season), Bracknell Town (1ML, October 2004), Badshot Lea (March 2005).

Club honours:
Hellenic League Supplementary Cup (Badshot Lea 2006).

'Jumbo', as he is affectionately known, began his career as a member of the Shots' youth team before being loaned elsewhere. He joined Badshot Lea permanently in March 2005 and helped the club win the Hellenic League Supplementary Cup in 2006, gain promotion to the Hellenic League Premier Division in 2006–07 and finish 11th in said division in 2007–08. Badshot Lea were also beaten by Fleet Town in that season's Aldershot Senior Cup Final.

Johnson Hippolyte — Forward

Born 9 June 1967, Willesden.

Aldershot Town FC record:

Debut: as substitute v Whyteleafe (a), Isthmian League Division One, 11 October 1997.
Last appearance: v Berkhamsted Town (h), Isthmian League Division One, 2 May 1998.
Appearances: 26 + 2
Goals: 12

Playing career:
Hounslow (summer 1988), Uxbridge (summer 1989), Chalfont St Peter (summer 1990), Wealdstone (summer 1991), Yeading (July 1993), Chertsey Town (July 1995), Chesham United (summer 1996), Dulwich Hamlet (July 1997), Aldershot Town (October 1997), Hampton (August 1998), Chesham United (player-coach, March 1999), Yeading (player-coach, August 2000; joint player-manager [with Naz Bashir] from March 2001, taking sole charge in December 2001).

Club honours:
Isthmian League Division One (Chesham United 1996–97, Aldershot Town 1997–98).

Post-playing coaching/management career:
Manager of Maidenhead United (October 2006).

Managerial honours:
Isthmian League Cup (Yeading 2003), Isthmian League Division One North (Yeading 2003–04), Isthmian League Division One North Manager of the Year (2004), Isthmian League Premier Division (Yeading 2004–05), Middlesex Charity Cup (Yeading 2005), Middlesex Senior Cup (Yeading 2005).

Johnson is affectionately known as 'Drax' and has a wealth of experience in the non-League game. He spent the early years of his career at clubs including Uxbridge, Yeading (where he was a member of the side that reached the FA Cup first round for the first time in the club's history in 1993–94) and Chertsey Town.

Greg joined Chesham United in the summer of 1996, and his goals helped the Generals to win the 1996–97 Isthmian League Division One title. After a brief spell at Dulwich Hamlet, Drax signed for Aldershot Town and his 12 goals contributed greatly to him being part of the Division One title-winning side for the second successive season in 1997–98.

August 1998 saw him move to Hampton, who proceeded to have a dismal 1998–99 season, finishing in the bottom five. Notwithstanding the fact that he left in March 1999 to rejoin Chesham United (as player-coach), he still managed to finish the season a Beavers' top scorer, albeit with just six goals.

In 1999–2000 Greg combined his playing duties with that of manager of Chesham's reserve side and helped the club to a creditable third-place finish in the Isthmian League Premier Division. He left the Meadow to become player-coach at Yeading in August 2000 and took on the role of joint player-manager with Naz Bashir towards the end of the 2000–01 season, eventually taking sole charge in December 2001.

Each of his first three seasons at the Warren ended in bottom-half-of-the-table finishes, but he did lead them to victory in the Isthmian League Cup in 2003. However, the next two League campaigns would be triumphal, as he led the Ding to back-to-back Championships. In 2003–04 they won the Isthmian League Division One North title (for which Greg was given the divisional 'Manager of the Year' award), and followed that up in 2004–05 by winning the Premier Division, thus gaining promotion to the Conference South. This was the highest up the non-League pyramid that the club had ever gone, and they combined this with winning the Middlesex Cup double (Senior Cup and Charity Cup) in the latter season. However, Drax's finest achievement as Yeading boss was surely leading them to the FA Cup third round in January 2005 where they were beaten, but by no means disgraced, 2–0 by Premier Division Newcastle United.

Johnson left to take over as boss of Maidenhead United in October 2006. He proceeded to lead them to the FA Cup first round for the first time in 25 years and repeated the feat in 2007–08. Although Drax effectively retired from playing in the summer of 2004, he has always remained registered as a player in case of emergencies and has made a handful of appearances due to player shortages and injuries. When he is not overseeing team affairs at York Road, Drax works as a building manager for the Royal Borough of Kensington and Chelsea.

Chris Hollins — Midfielder

Born: 20 March 1974, Bickley.

Aldershot Town FC record:

Debut:	as substitute v Heybridge Swifts (h), Isthmian League Division One, 5 November 1994.
Last appearance:	as substitute v Ruislip Manor (h), Isthmian League Division One, 8 April 1995.
Appearances:	12 + 6
Goals:	1

Playing career:

Queen's Park Rangers (youth), Charlton Athletic, Oxford University, Aldershot Town (November 1994).

Chris is the son of ex-Chelsea midfielder John Hollins and the nephew of ex-Aldershot FC 'keeper Dave Hollins. He was a youth player at Queen's Park Rangers and played for Charlton Athletic reserves before studying at Oxford University. He scored in Oxford's 5–0 victory over Cambridge in the 1994 Varsity Match at Craven Cottage and was also a 'cricket blue', who, while in his university side, joined the elite band of cricketers who have scored a century at Lords.

In November 1994 Chris joined Aldershot Town and immediately stood out as a player who could possibly play at a higher level. This view was enhanced by him scoring a spectacular goal against Bognor Regis Town shortly after his arrival. Prior to joining the Shots, Chris had begun working for Sky TV and his increasing work commitments caused him to be released from the Rec in April 1995. It is believed that he never played competitive football again.

Chris later worked for Channel One, GMTV, Meridian TV, Channel 5, BBC Sport (during which time he presented *Grandstand* and *Football Focus*) and BBC News 24. He has also appeared in the Sky One reality series *The Match*, on BBC1's *Breakfast Show* and had a cameo role in the 2007 film *Run, Fatboy, Run*.

Gary Holloway — Midfielder

Born: 19 March 1979, Kingston-upon-Thames.

Aldershot Town FC record:

Debut:	v Morecambe (a), Conference National, 8 March 2005.

Last appearance: v Southport (a), Conference National, 29 April 2006.
Appearances: 44 + 4
Goals: 4

Playing career:
Walton and Hersham (from youth, August 1996), Hampton and Richmond Borough (summer 2000), Farnborough Town (October 2001), Stevenage Borough (February 2003), Farnborough Town (July 2004), Aldershot Town (March 2005), Lewes (July 2006), Havant and Waterlooville (May 2008).

Representative honours:
FA XI.

Club honours:
Conference South (Lewes 2007–08).

Gary is a skilful midfielder who began as a youth player at Walton and Hersham, making his senior debut for the Swans towards the end of the 1995–96 season and signing full contract forms in August 1996. He was on the fringes of the side that was promoted to the Isthmian League Premier Division at the end of the 1996–97 season, as well as being in the side that made the return journey three years later. However, he had stood out, and a summer move to near neighbours Hampton and Richmond Borough enabled him to stay in the Premier Division.

Gary continued to mature and command rave reviews during the 2000–01 season, and this led to him getting his first taste of Conference football with newly promoted Farnborough Town in October 2001. He adapted to the Conference very quickly, never looking overawed, and played in just under half of Boro's League games in a season that culminated in a seventh-place finish. He was later part of the Boro side that achieved a club-best FA Cup progression when losing to FA Premier League high-flyers Arsenal in a fourth-round tie at Highbury in January 2003.

Gary left for Stevenage Borough then returned, only to leave again to join Aldershot Town in March 2005. He was part of the Shots side that lost to Carlisle United in the Play-off semi-finals at the end of the season. He returned to part-time football with Lewes, and his consistent and influential performances throughout that season won him the 2007 Player of the Year award at the Dripping Pan.

The following season got better for the Rooks, as Gary made 33 League appearances and scored four times to help win the Conference South title, thus gaining Conference Premier status for the first time in the club's history. However, Gary did not stay long following that triumph, as an undisclosed fee took him to Havant and Waterlooville shortly after the season's end.

Danny Holmes — Midfielder/Winger

Born: 13 June 1972, Luton.

Aldershot Town FC record:
Debut: as substitute v Metropolitan Police (h), Isthmian League Division Two, 4 September 1993.
Last appearance: as substitute v Billericay Town (a), Isthmian League Division One, 14 October 1997.
Appearances: 185 + 9 (sixth in all-time top 10)
Goals: 14

Playing career:
Middlesbrough (from trainee, January 1990), AFC Bournemouth (July 1991), Farnborough Town (SLL, August 1991), Farnborough Town (December 1992), Aldershot Town (August 1993), Salisbury City (November 1997), Bognor Regis Town (August 1999), Andover (October 1999), Poole Town (November 2000), Lymington and New Milton (November 2000), Bournemouth Poppies (June 2001), Holt United (Dorset, October 2003).
Danny has made one Football League appearance.

Representative honours:
Bedfordshire Schools, Bedfordshire Youth.

Post-playing coaching/management career:
Under-11s Manager of AFC Bournemouth (summer 2006).

Danny is the younger brother of ex-Blackburn Rovers midfielder Matty Holmes, the nephew of ex-Everton and Scotland midfielder Bruce Rioch and the cousin of ex-Hull City left-back Gregor Rioch. He was a tricky little midfielder who could also play as a winger, and he was renowned for his ability to run at and beat opposing defenders, with his crosses setting up many a goal.

Having had youth trials at the FA's Centre of Excellence at Lilleshall, Danny appeared in the 1990 FA Youth Cup Final for Middlesbrough (managed by his uncle at the time) before joining AFC Bournemouth in July 1991. The following month, he joined Farnborough Town on a season-long loan deal and was a member of the side that lost to First Division West Ham United in an FA Cup third-round replay in January 1992.

Danny left Dean Court, returning to Farnborough on a permanent basis in December 1992. That season, he was a member of the Boro side that experienced the high of reaching the FA Trophy quarter-finals, where they lost to Witton Albion, and the low of being relegated from the Conference.

In August 1993 Danny joined Aldershot Town, and his mazy runs and acrobatic goal celebrations were a staple part of the Shots reaching the FA Vase quarter-finals (before being beaten by Atherton Laburnum Rovers) and being promoted from Isthmian League Division Two in 1993–94, by virtue of a third-place finish.

Danny won the Player of the Year award at the Rec in 1996 but then suffered a knee injury that needed an operation and caused him to miss virtually all of the first three months of the 1996–97 season. He left the Rec in November 1997 and signed for Salisbury City before going on to play for Bognor Regis Town and Andover, where he was a member of the side that were thumped 9–1 by the Shots in the 2000 Hampshire Senior Cup Final.

He later joined Poole Town, Lymington and New Milton, Bournemouth Poppies and Holt United before retiring in the summer of 2005. He is currently working on his coaching badges and manages the Under-11s team at AFC Bournemouth. Away from football, Danny works as a window cleaner.

Lee Holsgrove — Midfielder

Born: 13 December 1979, Aylesbury.

Aldershot Town FC record:

Debut:	v Enfield (a), Isthmian League Premier Division, 28 November 1998.
Last appearance:	v Bashley (at Southampton FC), Hampshire Senior Cup Final, 8 May 2003.
Appearances:	102 + 15
Goals:	12

Playing career:
Millwall (from apprentice, July 1996), Wycombe Wanderers (March 1998), Aldershot Town (2ML, November 1998), Aldershot Town (May 2000), Boreham Wood (1ML, January 2001), Hayes (1ML, January 2002), Hayes (July 2003), Windsor and Eton (January 2005).
Lee has made 10 Football League appearances.

Representative honours:
Isthmian League XI.

Club honours:
Hampshire Senior Cup (Aldershot Town 2002, 2003), Isthmian League Premier Division (Aldershot Town 2002–03).

Lee is the son of ex-Wolverhampton Wanderers centre-back John Holsgrove and the brother of fellow ex-players Peter and Paul. He started his footballing life as an apprentice at Millwall and signed full professional forms in July 1996. In March 1998 a £7,500 fee took him to Wycombe Wanderers, but he had to wait until May 1999 to make his senior debut (as a substitute against Wigan Athletic).

In November 1998 he joined Aldershot Town on a two-month loan deal and performed exceedingly well, with his 'speciality' being runs from deep that often ended with him unleashing a shot from distance. Indeed, he signed off his loan spell at the Rec by scoring a spectacular long-range goal following a run from deep against Sylvans Sports in a Hampshire Senior Cup quarter-final tie. Lee never got the chance to command a regular first-team place with Wycombe and was released in the summer of 2000, returning to the Rec on a permanent basis.

Strangely, he was seemingly singled out for criticism by George Borg on more than one occasion, the first instance of which resulted in him joining Boreham Wood on loan in January 2001, where he got himself sent off on his debut. The same fate befell him 12 months later on his loan debut for Hayes against Dover. The Holsgrove trio all played in that match – the first time three brothers had played in the same Hayes team since 1924.

In March 2002 Terry Brown (Hayes' manager during the aforementioned loan spell) took over from Borg at the Rec, and Lee was given a new lease of life. His game improved noticeably, and he played a major role in the club achieving a top-three finish that season. The club and Lee excelled themselves the following season, as the Hampshire Cup and Isthmian League Premier Division title were won, with the latter resulting in promotion to the Conference for the first time in the club's history.

With business commitments preventing Lee playing for the Shots in the Conference, he rejoined Hayes permanently and helped the club to a top-half finish in the Isthmian League Premier Division in 2003–04, which granted them access to the newly formed Conference South.

In January 2005 Lee joined his brothers at Windsor and Eton and all three Holsgroves wrote themselves into the post-war history books later that month when they scored in the Isthmian League Premier Division match against Heybridge Swifts. Lee retired at the end of the 2005–06 season following the Royalists' relegation from the Isthmian League Premier Division and currently works for a data protection company in London.

Photograph courtesy of Eric Marsh.

Dave Hooker — Forward

Born: 20 November 1968, Aldershot.

Aldershot Town FC record:

Debut:	as substitute v Bournemouth Poppies (h), Hampshire Senior Cup second round, 25 October 1994.
Last appearance:	v Maidenhead United (h), Isthmian League Division One, 28 January 1995.
Appearances:	9 + 7
Goals:	4

Playing career:

Ash United (August 1991), Aldershot Town (October 1994), Ash United (March 1995), Ash United (August 1999), Badshot Lea (2000–01 season).

Dave was a striker who spent his entire career playing within a few miles of Aldershot. Details of his early career are unknown, but it is known that he signed for Ash United in August 1991 and finished the season as the top goalscorer in the entire Combined Counties League (31 goals). He was also the club's top scorer the following season (19 goals) before leaving in the summer of 1993. What he did immediately after that is unknown, but he came to the Rec in October 1994 and was in and out of the side over the next five months, after which he rejoined Ash and later Badshot Lea during the 2000–01 season. No further information is known about Dave's career, but it is known that he currently works for a local motor factory.

Dean Hooper — Right-back/Midfielder

Born: 13 April 1971, Harefield.

Aldershot Town FC record:

Debut:	v Hitchin Town (a), Isthmian League Premier Division, 17 August 2002.
Last appearance:	as substitute v Shrewsbury Town (at Stoke City FC), Conference Play-off Final, 16 May 2004.
Appearances:	77 + 1
Goals:	1

Playing career:

Brentford (youth), Marlow (summer 1991), Yeading (August 1992), Chalfont St Peter (August 1993), Hayes (April 1994), Swindon Town (March 1995), Peterborough United (1ML, December 1995), Hayes (summer 1996), Stevenage Borough (November 1996), Leyton Orient (trial, March 1997), Kingstonian (July 1997), Peterborough United (August 1998), Dagenham and Redbridge (3ML, February 2002), Aldershot Town (May 2002), Weymouth (July 2004), St Albans City (August 2004), Lewes (May 2005), Cambridge United (January 2007).
Dean has made 121 Football League appearances, scoring two goals.

Representative honours:
Isthmian League XI, England Semi-Professional XI (one cap).

Club honours:
Isthmian League Premier Division (Kingstonian 1997–98), Isthmian League Premier Division (Aldershot Town 2002–03), Hampshire Senior Cup (Aldershot Town 2003).

Dean originally started out as a midfielder but is best known as a hard-tackling and committed right-back, with his commitment often getting him into trouble with referees! Nonetheless, he was very popular among the Shots faithful.

Dean was originally a youth player at Brentford before signing for Marlow, for whom he was a playing substitute in an FA Cup first-round tie against West Bromwich Albion in November 1991. He then played for Yeading and Chalfont St Peter, where he experienced relegation from Isthmian League Division One before joining Hayes at the tail end of the 1993–94 season.

The following season, he performed consistently for the Missioners to the point where the club were well on the way to a third-place finish in the Isthmian League Premier Division, but Division One Swindon Town paid £15,000 to take him to the County Ground in March 1995. He made his debut as a substitute against Grimsby Town later that month, but the season ended in disappointment as the club was relegated.

The following season was a completely different story as the Robins won the Division Two title, but he played no part in that campaign and was released in the summer. He rejoined Conference new boys Hayes but departed in the November to join fellow Conference side Stevenage Borough and was an active member in the latter part of the 1996–97 season as the club finished third in the Conference and reached the FA Trophy semi-finals (where they lost to Woking).

Having trialled at Leyton Orient, Dean joined Kingstonian in July 1997 and his performances at Kingsmeadow led to his sole appearance for the England Semi-Professional XI against Holland in March 1998, with his season culminating in the Ks winning the Isthmian League Premier Division title. He looked all set to play in the club's first-ever season in the Conference but rejoined Peterborough on a permanent basis in August 1998, and the club achieved a top-10 finish in his first season.

Having fallen out of favour at London Road, Dean joined Dagenham and Redbridge on a three-month loan in February 2002. He came to the Rec that summer and was a valuable member of the side that won the Isthmian League Premier Division in 2002–03. He played in Aldershot Town's first-ever Conference game against Accrington Stanley and helped the club reach that season's Conference Play-off Final, in which he was a playing substitute.

Dean left the Rec that summer and had a couple of club spells before joining Lewes. The 2005–06 season ended with the Rooks qualifying for the Conference South Play-offs, but the Conference excluded them due to ground development issues.

In January 2007 he joined Conference National side Cambridge United but injury restricted him to just three appearances before he retired in the summer of 2007, after which he is believed to have continued working as a builder, painter and decorator.

Jon Horsted — Midfielder

Born: 26 October 1980, Ascot.

Aldershot Town FC record:

Debut:	as substitute v Berkhamsted Town (a), Isthmian League Cup third round, 5 January 1999.
Last appearance:	v Worthing (a), Isthmian League Full Members' Cup second round, 2 February 1999.
Appearances:	1 + 1

Playing career:
Aldershot Town (youth), Plymouth Argyle (trial), Queen's Park Rangers (trial), Farnham Town (August 1999), Wokingham Town (September 2000), Burnham (August 2003).

Representative honours:
Hampshire Schools.

Jon was a midfielder in the Shots' youth team when he made his two senior appearances. He went on to spend a season at Farnham Town before winning Player of the Year after signing for Wokingham Town. However, the joy of that award was tainted by the fact that the club were relegated from Isthmian League Division Two.

Jon joined Burnham in August 2003 and again won a Player of the Year award in his first season. In December 2005 Jon sustained a horrendous knee injury and spent the best part of a year trying to get back to playing, before being forced to retire in November 2006. Jon currently works as a storeman for an oil company.

Jamie Horton — Midfielder

Born: 20 April 1963, Aldershot.

Aldershot Town FC record:

Debut: v Basingstoke Town (h), Isthmian League Division One, 26 December 1995.
Last appearance: v Kingstonian (at Aldershot Town FC), Isthmian League Cup Final, 6 May 1996.
Appearances: 32
Goals: 9

Playing career:

Godalming Town (summer 1981), Ash United (September 1983), Camberley Town (DR, September 1986), Farnborough Town (August 1987), Aldershot Town (December 1995), Fleet Town (August 1996), Hampton (January 1997), Ash United (player-manager, July 1997; player-manager until May 2000 then reverted to player; player-manager from October 2001; player-assistant manager from March 2003).

Representative honours:

FA XI, Southern League XI.

Club honours:

Combined Counties Premier Challenge Cup (Godalming Town 1983, Ash United 1998), Hampshire Senior Cup (Farnborough Town 1991), Southern League Premier Division (Farnborough Town 1990–91, 1993–94), Combined Counties League (Ash United 1986–87, 1998–99), Aldershot Senior Cup (Ash United 1999, 2002).

Jamie was a midfielder who could quickly turn defence into attack. It could be said that he was destined to eventually play for the Shots due to the fact that his grandfather Sonny (an outside-right) and uncle Billy (a centre-forward) both played for Aldershot FC.

Jamie spent the early part of his career at Godalming Town, Ash United and Camberley Town before starting an eight-year association with Farnborough Town in August 1987. The following season, he was part of the squad that reached the Conference for the first time in the club's history, due to Leytonstone and Ilford being refused promotion. Unfortunately, that season ended with the club being relegated to the Southern League Premier Division.

The 1992–93 season presented Jamie with a second Southern League Premier Division winners' medal, but history repeated itself and the club dropped down again at the end of the following season. Over the years, Farnborough have had some good runs in the FA Cup and Jamie was involved when they took First Division West Ham United to a third-round replay (which the Hammers won 1–0) in January 1992.

Jamie eventually left Cherrywood Road in December 1995, having made over 350 appearances for the club, and moved across the county to Aldershot Town. At the time, the fierce rivalry between the two clubs meant that many Shots fans were not overly enamoured with his arrival. However, his pleasant off-field persona combined with the fact that he gave as much in the Shots' red and blue as he had in the yellow of Farnborough soon won the dissenters over.

Having helped the club finish fifth in Isthmian League Division One, Jamie left and played for Fleet Town and Hampton before returning to Ash United as player-manager in July 1997. Ash had struggled for the previous three seasons but, in the first five years of Jamie's time there, they were never outside the top three and had various other successes, including runners'-up spot in the Combined Counties League and victory in the 2002 Aldershot Senior Cup Final. He eventually progressed to the player-assistant manager role, which he stayed in until retiring in the summer of 2006. Jamie currently works as a builder and is also a member of the groundstaff at Ash.

Terry Howard — Centre-back

Born: 26 February 1966, Stepney.

Aldershot Town FC record:

Debut: v Barton Rovers (a), Isthmian League Division One, 21 March 1998.

Last appearance: v Aylesbury United (a), Isthmian League Premier Division, 24 April 1999.
Appearances: 60
Goals: 6

Playing career:
Chelsea (from apprentice, February 1984), Crystal Palace (1ML, January 1986), Chester City (1ML, January 1987), Orient/Leyton Orient (March 1987), Wycombe Wanderers (February 1995), Woking (July 1996), Yeovil Town (December 1997), Aldershot Town (March 1998), Gravesend and Northfleet (trial, summer 1999), Boreham Wood (July 1999), Braintree Town (August 2000), Great Wakering Rovers (July 2002; player-assistant manager from January 2004).
Terry has made 399 Football League appearances, scoring 33 goals.

Representative honours:
England Youth.

Club honours:
Division Four Play-off Final (Leyton Orient 1989), FA Trophy (Woking 1997).

Terry was a commanding centre-back who started out as an apprentice at Chelsea. He signed full professional forms in February 1984 and made his Football League debut against Aston Villa in April 1985. Following loans at Crystal Palace and Chester City, he joined Orient in March 1987 for a fee of £10,000.

During his first two full seasons at Brisbane Road, he twice played in games where the club equalled their record victory (8–0) – against Rochdale in October 1987 and Colchester United in October 1988. He was later part of the side that won the 1989 Division Four Play-off Final against Wrexham and the side that finished rock bottom of Division Two in 1994–95. However, Terry was not around to see the latter, as he was famously sacked by caretaker manager John Sitton at half-time in a League game against Blackpool in February 1995 – an event that has subsequently been shown many times on TV.

Terry then had just over a season with Wycombe Wanderers before signing for Woking in July 1996, where he was a member of the side that beat Dagenham and Redbridge in the 1997 FA Trophy Final. He joined Yeovil Town but left three months later to join Aldershot Town, scoring on his debut in a season that would see the Shots win the Isthmian League Division One title, although Terry did not play enough games to be awarded a medal.

Terry went on to play with Boreham Wood, Braintree Town and Great Wakering Rovers, where he became player-assistant manager in January 2004 following the appointment of his ex-Leyton Orient teammate, Alan Hull, as manager. When Hull was sacked in February 2005, Terry resigned and subsequently retired from playing. He currently works as a fishmonger and has reportedly qualified as a sports physician recently.

Gareth Howells — Goalkeeper

Born: 13 June 1970, Guildford.

Aldershot Town FC record:

Debut: v Enfield (h), Isthmian League Premier Division, 18 August 2001.
Last appearance: v Purfleet (a), Isthmian League Premier Division, 3 May 2003.
Appearances: 63 + 3

Playing career:

Fulham (youth), Sutton United (1ML, 1986–87 season), Enfield (1ML, August 1987), Malmö FF (Sweden, 1ML, September 1987), Tottenham Hotspur (from trainee, July 1988), Farnborough Town (SLL, August 1988), Swindon Town (2ML, January 1990), Leyton Orient (1ML, March 1990), Torquay United (August 1990), Farnborough Town (summer 1992), Stockport County (September 1992), Kettering Town (November 1992), Hellenic (South Africa, January 1993), Dorking (December 1993), St Albans City (July 1994), Sutton United (July 1998), Aldershot Town (July 2001), Havant and Waterlooville (July 2003; player-goalkeeping coach from August 2006), Eastleigh (player-goalkeeping coach, October 2007).
Gareth has made 83 Football League appearances.

Representative honours:

Isthmian League XI, Surrey FA XI.

Club honours:

Division Four Play-off Final (Torquay United 1991), London Challenge Cup (St Albans City 1995), Hertfordshire Charity Cup (St Albans City 1998), Isthmian League Premier Division (Sutton United 1998–99), Surrey Senior Cup (Sutton United 1999), Hampshire Senior Cup (Aldershot Town 2002, 2003 [unused substitute]).

Gareth is a very accomplished 'keeper whose performances have contributed to the winning of many games and honours. He is the younger brother of ex-Tottenham Hotspur midfielder David Howells and began his career in Fulham's youth team. He had spells elsewhere before joining Tottenham Hotspur, signing full professional forms in July 1988. Almost immediately he was sent on a season-long loan to Farnborough Town, where his game improved quickly, thus establishing him as a very able stopper, and his season culminated in Boro reaching the Conference for the first time in their history.

Further loans at Swindon Town and Leyton Orient preceded an initially temporary then permanent move to Torquay United in August 1990. The Gulls' season gathered pace, and they ended it by winning the Division Four Play-off Final (beating Blackpool on penalties), with Gareth keeping his nerve to score the decisive spot-kick.

A brief return to Farnborough was followed by other club spells, and he joined St Albans City in July 1994. During his four seasons there, they regularly finished in the top half of the table. He was voted Player of the Year in 1996 and helped the club progress to the FA Cup second round in 1996–97 before losing to Bristol City.

In July 1998, having played over 200 games, Gareth left Clarence Park to join Sutton United, where his first two seasons were a mixture of joy and disappointment, winning the Surrey Senior Cup and Isthmian League Premier Division double in 1998–99 but suffering relegation the following season.

In July 2001 Gareth joined Aldershot Town and played a major role in them finishing the season in third place in the Isthmian League Premier Division. The following season was not as good for Gareth, as injury and the arrival of Nikki Bull limited him to just five League games in the Shots' title-winning season.

Gareth moved to Havant and Waterlooville in 2003, missing out on the Conference South Play-offs in 2005–06 by a solitary point. That, in itself, was frustrating enough, but their cause had not been helped by a three-point deduction pertaining to Tony Taggart's transfer from Weymouth.

In August 2006 Gareth took on the role of player-goalkeeping coach with the Hawks but followed manager Ian Baird out of Westleigh Park to Eastleigh in October 2007, where he again carried out the role of player-goalkeeping coach. He made seven appearances in the 2007–08 season as the Spitfires finished in sixth position in the Conference South, missing the Play-offs by two points and one place.

Gareth did enjoy some success in 2007–08, albeit in Sunday league football. He was player-joint manager of Crown and Anchor Nomads (a Woking-based pub side playing in the Second Division of the Surrey and Hants

Border League) and was part of the side that achieved a unique treble. They beat Goldsworth Park Rangers to win the Twyford-Pollard Cup, thus becoming the first team from outside the league's top division to do so. They also won their division and beat Stoughton Villa 6–4 in extra-time to win the Guildford Hospital Cup.

Kirk Hudson — Midfielder/Forward

Born: 12 December 1986, Rochford.

Aldershot Town FC record:

Debut: v Basingstoke Town (a), Hampshire Senior Cup quarter-final, 14 January 2006.
Appearances: 51 + 43
Goals: 27

Playing career:

Ipswich Town (schoolboy and youth), Southampton (youth trial), Glasgow Celtic (youth), AFC Bournemouth (August 2005), Southend United (trial, November 2005), Thurrock (1ML, November 2005), Aldershot Town (January 2006), Ashford Town (1ML, September 2006).
Kirk has made one Football League appearance.

Representative honours:

England Schoolboys.

Club honours:

Scottish Premier Under-19 League (Glasgow Celtic 2004–05), Scottish FA Youth Cup (Glasgow Celtic 2005), Hampshire Senior Cup (Aldershot Town 2007), Setanta Shield (Aldershot Town 2008), Conference Premier (Aldershot Town 2007–08).

Kirk is a pacy impact player who scares the living daylights out of defences when he runs at them. He played schoolboy and youth football before moving North of the border to join Glasgow Celtic. This turned out to be a pivotal point in Kirk's career, as he gained a reputation as a regular goalscorer.

Kirk was surprisingly released by Celtic in the summer of 2005 and trialled at AFC Bournemouth, where he impressed sufficiently to sign a short-term contract, making his sole Football League appearance as a substitute against Swindon Town in the September. He had a couple of spells elsewhere before appearing at Aldershot Town in January 2006 as a trialist and scoring twice on his debut against Basingstoke Town in the Hampshire Senior Cup quarter-final, thus becoming the only trialist to score on his debut.

Kirk was signed on full contract forms in July 2006 and was sent on a one-month loan to Ashford Town (Middlesex) a couple of months later. A hungrier Kirk returned but he still didn't quite seem the 'finished article'. Whatever was missing appeared by the bucketload in the 2007–08 season, and he earned rave reviews from fans and pundits alike. Those plaudits proved to be wholly warranted when Kirk signed a contract extension (until the end of the 2009–10 season) in March 2008, after which he played his part in reaching the FA Trophy semi-finals and followed that up by being one of the goalscorers as the Setanta Shield was won. Kirk's season then culminated in him being one of 24 Shots players that can describe themselves as Conference Premier title winners. He also reaped individual glory when he was named as the Conference Premier Young Player of the Year.

Josh Huggins — Midfielder

Born: 3 November 1990, Frimley.

Aldershot Town FC record:

Debut: as substitute v Christchurch (h), Hampshire Senior Cup second round, 27 November 2007.
Appearances: 0 + 3

Playing career:

Aldershot Town (youth).

During the 2007–08 season, Josh progressed from the Shots' Under-16 side and played for the first team in minor Cup competitions while still a member of the youth team.

John Humphrey — Forward

Born: 2 July 1969, Godalming.

Aldershot Town FC record:

Debut:	as substitute v Banstead Athletic (h), Isthmian League Division Two, 7 April 1994.
Last appearance:	v Hitchin Town (a), Isthmian League Cup first round, 8 September 1998.
Appearances:	51 + 23
Goals:	18

Playing career:

Godalming Town (youth), Molesey (youth), Leatherhead (summer 1986), Bristol Rovers (trial), Cambridge United (trial), Tottenham Hotspur (trial), Millwall (February 1991), Exeter City (1ML, December 1991), Aldershot Town (March 1994), Uxbridge (1ML, August 1998), Leatherhead (November 1998).
John has made two Football League appearances.

John was a very talented forward but was one of those players unfortunate enough to be dubbed as 'injury-prone'. He started his career as a youth player at Godalming Town and Molesey before moving to Leatherhead in the summer of 1986. He played a fair amount of reserve-team football while working at becoming an automatic inclusion in the Tanners' first team. During that time, he had trials at a number of professional clubs until his performances and goals led to him joining Division Two side Millwall for a fee of £20,000 in February 1991.

Despite his departure from Fetcham Grove, he still managed to finish that season as the club's top scorer. Unfortunately, he sustained a cruciate ligament injury in his second game on loan with Exeter at St James Park, which kept him out of action for 18 months and eventually brought his professional career to a premature end.

John's luck did not improve much after he arrived at the Rec, as he missed several games through injury. However, he will be remembered for scoring one of the goals in the 3–0 home victory over Hampton in April 1994 which clinched promotion to Isthmian League Division One, and for a spectacular long-range goal at Hitchin Town in the Isthmian League Cup semi-final first leg in February 1996.

Unfortunately, he missed most of the 1996–97 season through injury and then had a loan spell at Uxbridge before returning to Leatherhead in November 1998. He retired in the summer of 1999 and currently works in the administrations department for an educational examination board.

Richard Hurst — Goalkeeper

Born: 23 December 1976, Hammersmith.

Aldershot Town FC record:

Debut:	v Billericay Town (h), Isthmian League Premier Division, 9 November 2002.
Last appearance:	v Bournemouth Poppies (h), Hampshire Senior Cup third round, 3 December 2002.
Appearances:	4 + 1

Playing career:

Queen's Park Rangers (from trainee, April 1995), Aylesbury United (1ML, March 1999), Kingstonian (July 1999), St Albans City (October 2000), Chelmsford City (July 2001), Aldershot Town (NC, November 2002), Chesham United (December 2002).

Representative honours:

Isthmian League XI.

Club honours:

FA Trophy (Kingstonian 2000 [unused substitute]).

Richard started his career as a trainee at Queen's Park Rangers and signed a full professional contract in April 1995. He played for Aylesbury United, Kingstonian, St Albans City and Chelmsford City before having a brief spell at the Rec.

In December 2002 he joined Chesham United but left the following March and subsequently retired, with nothing being known of his current whereabouts.

Otis Hutchings **Midfielder**

Born: 18 February 1971, Hammersmith.

Aldershot Town FC record:

Debut:	v Barton Rovers (h), Isthmian League Division One, 25 October 1997.
Last appearance:	v Carshalton Athletic (a), Isthmian League Premier Division, 6 May 2000.
Appearances:	54 + 2
Goals:	9

Playing career:
Gillingham (youth), Watford (youth), Chelsea (trainee), Walton and Hersham (August 1995), Tooting and Mitcham (August 1996), Molesey (February 1997), Dulwich Hamlet (March 1997), Aldershot Town (October 1997), Hendon (trial, August 1998), Hampton (August 1998), Chesham United (December 1998), Boreham Wood (November 1999), Aldershot Town (December 1999), Boreham Wood (July 2000), Chesham United (trial, July 2001), Yeading (August 2001).

Club honours:
Isthmian League Division One (Aldershot Town 1997–98; Boreham Wood 2000–01).

Otis was a tall, strong midfielder and is the older brother of ex-Farnborough Town midfielder Carl Hutchings. He played youth football at Gillingham and Watford and was a trainee at Chelsea before embarking on spells with a few Isthmian League sides.

Otis arrived for his first spell at Aldershot Town in October 1997, and his strength in the tackle coupled with his aerial ability played a major part in the club winning the Isthmian League Division One title. That was not his only reward that season, as he was also voted Player of the Year.

Otis left the Rec that summer, trialled at Hendon and then played for Hampton and Chesham United before signing for Boreham Wood in November 1999. However, he was back at the Rec a month later and carried on where he left off performance-wise, helping the club finish the season as runners-up in the Isthmian League Premier Division and reach the Hampshire Senior Cup Final. He rejoined newly relegated Boreham Wood in July 2000, and his dominance of the midfield enabled them to go straight back up by virtue of winning the Division One title.

As with his title win in the same division with the Shots three years previously, a personal accolade accompanied Otis's League-winners' medal – he was voted as Wood's Most Improved Player for the season. He then trialled briefly back at Chesham and spent two seasons at Yeading before retiring in summer 2003. Otis currently works as a bricklayer.

Danny Hylton **Forward**

Born: 25 February 1989, Camden Town.

Aldershot Town FC record:

Debut:	as substitute v Fleet Town (h), Hampshire Senior Cup third round, 10 January 2006.
Appearances:	24 + 22
Goals:	11

Playing career:
Aldershot Town (from youth, May 2007), Harlow Town (1ML, March 2007).

Representative honours:
Hampshire Under-18s.

Club honours:
Hampshire Senior Cup (Aldershot Town 2007), Setanta Shield (Aldershot Town 2008), Conference Premier (Aldershot Town 2007–08).

Danny is a young forward whose endless running makes him a handful for defences. His 34 goals in 39 appearances for the Shots' youth team resulted in him making his senior debut in January 2006 and winning that season's youth team Player of the Year award.

In March 2007 he went on loan to Harlow Town but played just once (against Ware) before the agreement was cut short by injury. His promise was recognised when he signed full contract forms for the Shots in May 2007, and the significant improvement he made during the 2007–08 season was rewarded in February 2008 with a contract extension, which committed him to the club until the end of the 2009–10 season.

Danny was part of the Shots squad that attained a club-best-equalling progression to the FA Trophy semi-finals and the side that won the Setanta Shield that season. He also made 23 appearances, including nine starts, and scored five goals in a League campaign that culminated in promotion to the Football League as Conference Premier champions.

Mikhael Jaimez-Ruiz — Goalkeeper

Born: 12 July 1984, Merida, Venezuela.

Aldershot Town FC record:

Debut: v Christchurch (h), Hampshire Senior Cup second round, 27 November 2007.
Appearances: 11 + 1

Playing career:

Graceland University (US), St Gregory University (US), Olimpia Gherla (Romania, January 2004), CFR Cluj Napoca (Romania, July 2004), Ariesul Turda (Romania, 3ML, March 2005), West Ham United (trial, February 2006), Tottenham Hotspur (trial, January 2006), Brentford (trial, summer 2006), Barnet (NC, October 2006), Northwood (February 2007), Wycombe Wanderers (trial, March 2007), Aldershot Town (NC, April 2007), Aldershot Town (July 2007).

Representative honours:

Venezuela Under-17s (one cap), Venezuela Under-20s (one cap), Venezuela Under-23s (one cap), Venezuela full international (one cap).

Club honours:

Hertfordshire Senior Cup (Barnet 2007), Setanta Shield (Aldershot Town 2008), Conference Premier (Aldershot Town 2007–08).

Mikhael is unsurprisingly the only Venezuelan ever to play for Aldershot Town. Having finished his secondary education in his homeland, he went to America to study and played university football there. He came to Europe in 2004 and played for Romanian sides, where he was an unused substitute for CFR Cluj as they lost one of the 2005 Intertoto Cup Finals to French Ligue One side Lens. He also played his sole full international that year – a friendly against Guatemala.

Mikhael trialled at a number of English clubs in 2006 and was a member of Barnet's Hertfordshire Senior Cup-winning side in 2007. He played briefly for Northwood and trialled at Wycombe Wanderers before joining Aldershot

Town as a trialist towards the end of the 2006–07 season. He subsequently joined on a non-contract basis in the April and was the substitute goalkeeper in the last two League games of the season.

Mikhael returned to the Rec in the summer of 2007 and was rewarded with a full contract in the July but found his appearances limited mainly to Cup competitions. He was an unused substitute in both legs of the FA Trophy semi-final against Ebbsfleet United and was the hero of the Setanta Shield Final victory over Rushden and Diamonds – he saved a penalty in extra-time and made the trophy-winning save in the penalty shoot-out. He also made three League appearances (including one as a substitute) near the end of a season that saw the Shots crowned as Conference Premier champions.

Mikhael was one of several Shots players to sign new contracts in the summer of 2008, with his stay at the Rec being extended by a further 12 months.

Nigel James — Centre-back

Born: 21 January 1977, Kennington.

Aldershot Town FC record:

Debut: v Carshalton Athletic (a), Isthmian League Full Members' Cup second round, 22 December 1997.
Last appearance: as substitute v Harrow Borough (h), Isthmian League Premier Division, 17 April 1999.
Appearances: 2 + 3

Playing career:

Luton Town (scholar), Woking, Horsham, Aldershot Town (NC, December 1997), Horsham, Molesey, Aldershot Town (NC, April 1999), Sandhurst Town, Crawley Town, Kingstonian.

Nigel was a young centre-back who made a handful of appearances in a central-midfield role, to which he was unaccustomed, in two spells with the Shots. He is the cousin of ex-Shots loanee Ben Abbey and began his footballing life as a scholar at Luton Town. He also played for a number of clubs but details of his time at those clubs are virtually unknown. He currently works as assistant manager and scout at Fulham's academy, as well as running his own soccer school.

Nick Jansen — Forward

Born: 22 September 1976, Reading.

Aldershot Town FC record:

Debut: as substitute v Selsey (h), FA Cup preliminary qualifying round, 26 August 1995.
Last appearance: as substitute v Ruislip Manor (h), Isthmian League Division One, 29 August 1995.
Appearances: 0 + 2
Goals: 1

Playing career:

Southampton (trainee, July 1993), Aldershot Town (August 1995), Farnborough Town (September 1995), Staines Town (July 1999).

Nick was a forward who arrived at Aldershot Town in the summer of 1995 having been released by Southampton, where he had been a trainee. Both his appearances came in a three-day period in August 1995, during which he became the first-ever Shots substitute to score on his debut.

The following month, he moved to neighbouring Farnborough Town but sustained a stomach injury in only his fourth game for the club (against Bath City in December 1996) – an injury that hampered his time there and from which he never really recovered.

Nick joined Staines Town in the summer of 1999; however, he was still troubled by his earlier injury and retired at the end of that season. Nick is currently a partner in a recruitment consultancy serving the construction industry.

Tobi Jinadu — Centre-back/Left-back

Born: 14 July 1984, Lagos, Nigeria.

Aldershot Town FC record:

Debut: as substitute v Tamworth (a), Conference National, 2 October 2004.

Last appearance: v Dagenham and Redbridge (h), Conference National, 11 March 2006.
Appearances: 23 + 11
Goals: 2

Playing career:
Woodford Town (2000–01 season), Mullingar Town (2001–02 season), Clapton, Harrow Borough (October 2002), Wembley (January 2003), Bristol Rovers (trial, March 2003), Cambridge City (August 2003), Welling United (September 2003), Croydon (October 2003), Sutton United (November 2003), Aldershot Town (July 2004), Lewes (2ML, March 2005), Queen's Park Rangers (trial, July 2006), Sutton United (trial, July 2006), Hayes (August 2006), Thurrock (September 2006), Bromley (January 2007), Hampton and Richmond Borough (March 2007), Dagenham and Redbridge (trial, July 2007), Heybridge Swifts (August 2007).

Tobi started his footballing life as a forward, playing for Woodford Town in the Essex Senior League as a 16-year-old. He then followed this with a handful of spells, mainly for Isthmian League sides, before signing for Bristol Rovers as a non-contract player in March 2003. Month-long spells led to him signing for Sutton United in November 2003, and it was here that Tobi's career seemed to pick up.

He was a regular towards the end of the season as the Us finished as runners-up to Canvey Island in the Isthmian League Premier Division. He joined Aldershot Town that summer, but his debut was delayed for three months due to a foot injury. His initial performances in the red-and-blue shirt were a little disappointing, but his game did improve as a result of playing alongside the vastly experienced Ray Warburton.

Unable to command a regular place, Tobi was loaned to Lewes in March 2005 and scored on his debut against Bognor Regis Town before eventually leaving the Rec at the end of the 2005–06 season. He played against the Shots (in a friendly) as a trialist for Queen's Park Rangers in the July and later signed for Hayes, Thurrock and then Bromley.

Tobi joined Hampton and Richmond Borough at the tail end of the 2006–07 season, just in time to play a handful of games as they won the Isthmian League Premier Division and earned promotion to the Conference South. He then signed for Heybridge Swifts in August 2007; however, he was released in February 2008, and it is not known if he signed for another club before the end of the season.

Leyton Johns — Midfielder
Born: 14 October 1976, Alton.

Aldershot Town FC record:
Debut: as substitute v Wokingham Town (a), Isthmian League Division One, 4 May 1996.
Last appearance: as substitute v Abingdon Town (a), Isthmian League Division One, 23 August 1997.
Appearances: 0 + 3

Playing career:
Aldershot Town (youth).

Leyton was a youth-team midfielder who made three substitute appearances for the Shots in as many seasons. He left in January 1998 to join the Royal Marines, and no other information pertaining to him is known.

Brett Johnson — Defender
Born: 15 August 1985, Hammersmith.

Aldershot Town FC record:
Debut: as substitute v Barnet (h), Conference, 6 February 2004.
Last appearance: v Carlisle United (a), Conference National Play-off semi-final second leg, 6 May 2005.
Appearances: 33 + 10
Goals: 2

Playing career:
Ashford Town (August 2002), Aldershot Town (February 2004), Reading (trial), Northampton Town (June 2005), Gravesend and Northfleet (1ML, November 2005), Grays Athletic (4ML, January 2006), Luton Town (trial, March 2008).
Brett has made 30 Football League appearances.

Representative honours:
Middlesex Under-18s, Middlesex Under-19s, Surrey County Combined Colleges Under-19s.

Brett can play anywhere in defence and was not the first player to make a marked improvement playing alongside 'super' Ray Warburton at the centre of Aldershot's back four.

He joined Ashford Town (Middlesex) in August 2002 and quickly came to the attention of other clubs. This resulted in a move to Aldershot Town in February 2004, and he played a handful of games before the season's end. The following season, he was a fairly regular inclusion in the side that reached the Play-offs for a second successive season before being beaten by Carlisle United.

During his time at the Rec, Brett was tracked by several Football League sides and trialled at Reading. In June 2005 a fee of £30,000 took him to League Two side Northampton Town, and he made his debut against Lincoln City on the opening day of the 2005–06 season. However, he was never really given a chance to establish himself in his first two seasons at Sixfields, making just 10 League appearances in total. He was loaned out, and while it was rumoured that he would return to the Rec on loan that never happened.

Brett played slightly more of a part in Northampton's 2007–08 campaign but spent some time trialling at Luton Town, after being told he would be released at the end of the season. At the time of writing it is believed that Brett is without a club.

Miles Jones — Midfielder

Born: 17 December 1987, Kingston-upon-Thames.

Aldershot Town FC record:

Debut:	v Christchurch (h), Hampshire Senior Cup second round, 27 November 2007.
Appearances:	1
Goals:	1

Playing career:
Brentford (youth), Woking (youth), Hayes/Hayes and Yeading United (summer 2006), Corinthian-Casuals (1ML, December 2006), Aldershot Town (trial, March 2007), Aldershot Town (trial, summer 2007), Aldershot Town (NC, November 2007), LA Galaxy (US, trial, December 2007), Waltham Forest (December 2007).

Representative honours:
Barbados Under-23s (three caps).

Miles was a youth player at Brentford before joining Woking, where his displays for the youth and reserve teams were rewarded when he made his sole first-team appearance against Stevenage Borough in March 2005.

While at Kingfield, he took part in the Sky One TV reality show *Football Icon* and reached the last 20 contestants. He joined Hayes in the summer of 2006 and won several Man of the Match awards early on. He also spent some time that season on loan at Corinthian-Casuals (again getting rave reviews) and played as a trialist for Aldershot Town in reserve games.

International honours came Miles's way in September 2007 when he won Under-23s caps for Barbados, scoring on his debut against Aruba in an Olympic Qualifier. He returned to the Rec as a trialist in the summer of 2007 before being released by what is now Hayes and Yeading United in November 2007. He signed as a non-contract player with the Shots a few days later and scored on his debut, which resulted in the Shots fans being treated to his trademark acrobatic goal celebrations.

The following month, Miles went out to the States and trialled with LA Galaxy, doing well enough to be invited back for training. He signed for Isthmian League Division One North outfit Waltham Forest in December 2007 and was selected by Barbados for the CONCACAF region qualifiers for the 2010 World Cup shortly afterwards.

A reorganisation behind the scenes at the Stags led to Miles being one of a number of players to leave in March 2008, and he then played out the season in the Shots' reserve side.

Ian Jopling — Forward

Born: 5 January 1974, Leicester.

Aldershot Town FC record:

Debut:	as substitute v Hungerford Town (a), Isthmian League Division Two, 23 October 1993.

Last appearance: as substitute v Basingstoke Town (h), Isthmian League Division One, 17 April 1995.
Appearances: 0 + 12
Goals: 1

Playing career:
Heath End (January 1991), Cove (summer 1991), Aldershot Town (October 1993), Hungerford Town (1ML, November 1994), Egham Town (1ML, January 1995), Egham Town (January 1996), Camberley Town (March 1996), Camberley Town (summer 1997), Aldershot Town reserves (1998–99 season), Molesey (DR, February 1999), Ash United (August 1999), Farnborough North End (DR, summer 2000), Camberley Town (December 2001), Ash United (July 2002), Camberley Town (DR, November 2002), Farnborough North End (summer 2004).

Representative honours:
Hampshire FA XI.

Club honours:
Aldershot Senior Cup (Camberley Town 1998), Hampshire League Division Two (Farnborough North End 2000–01), Hampshire Intermediate Cup (Farnborough North End 2005).

Ian is the son of ex-Aldershot FC captain Joe Jopling and has a reputation locally as a powerful and consistent goalscorer, both in Saturday and Sunday football.

Having played as a centre-back for Heath End and then playing for Cove, Ian moved to Aldershot Town a couple of months into the 1993–94 season. He set the record for the fastest goal scored by a Shots substitute when he scored just 20 seconds after coming on against Lewes in the penultimate away game. The following season, during which he scored regularly for the reserves but made just five substitute appearances for the Shots' first team, he had loan spells then joined Egham Town and later Camberley Town.

Having taken a break from the game for the whole of the 1996–97 season, Ian rejoined Camberley Town, where he was joint-top scorer with Tim Sills in 1997–98 (both scored 23 goals). The following season, he helped the club reach the FA Cup first round for the first time and the FA Vase fifth round.

Ian played a handful of games for the Shots' reserve side before joining Molesey then Ash United, and his goals assisted in the attainment of the runners'-up spot behind Ashford Town (Middlesex) in that season's Combined Counties League. He dual registered at Hampshire League Division Two side Farnborough North End and helped Ash to a third-place finish in the Combined Counties League.

In December 2001 Ian left Ash to rejoin neighbouring Camberley, but he could not prevent relegation from Isthmian League Division Two. A return to Ash came in July 2002, with the now customary re-signing with Camberley (on a dual-registration basis) following in the November.

Ian returned to the Rec in Ash's colours in November 2003 for a local Cup tie against a Shots reserve side, and it was no surprise that he scored. However, in doing so, he caught his studs in the turf and was subsequently stretchered off with a broken leg! He left Ash the following summer to rejoin Farnborough North End, and the season finished with them winning the Hampshire Intermediate Cup.

Ian then retired and currently runs his own building and fencing company. He also has another string to his sporting bow, as he regularly participates in events organised by the PDC (Professional Darts Corporation). He is currently ranked 236th in the world and is the training partner of Aldershot's James Wade, who is the reigning PDC World Grand Prix champion.

Dominic Joyce — Goalkeeper

Born: 23 January 1970, Canterbury.

Aldershot Town FC record:
Debut: v Oxford City (a), Isthmian League Full Members' Cup first round, 17 December 1996.
Appearances: 1

Playing career:
Fleet Town (summer 1995), Aldershot Town (December 1996), Bracknell Town (1997–98 season), Newport (Isle of Wight, 1998–99 season).

Details of Dominic's early career are unknown, but it is known that he signed for Fleet Town in the summer of 1995 and left the following February. It is not known what he did immediately after that, but he joined Aldershot Town in December 1996 and made his sole appearance that month. He later played elsewhere, but no information is known about his current whereabouts.

Sheikh Kamara — Midfielder

Born: 6 March 1982, Freetown, Sierra Leone.

Aldershot Town FC record:

Debut: v Slough Town (a), Isthmian League Full Members' Cup first round, 24 October 2000.
Last appearance: v Newport (Isle of Wight, a), Hampshire Senior Cup second round, 15 November 2000.
Appearances: 2

Playing career:

Cambridge United (trainee, September 1998), Aldershot Town (from youth, October 2000), Kingstonian (August 2001), Egham Town (October 2002), Windsor and Eton (October 2002), Aldershot Town (trial, July 2004).

Sheikh was a speedy midfielder who signed as a trainee at Cambridge United in September 1998. His release from the Abbey Stadium resulted in him coming to Aldershot Town, initially playing in the youth team and then signing full contract forms in September 2000. He later played for Kingstonian, Egham Town and Windsor and Eton before briefly reappearing at the Rec as a pre-season trialist in July 2004. No further details pertaining to Sheikh are known.

Darren Keown — Forward

Born: 5 May 1978, Chertsey.

Aldershot Town FC record:

Debut: v Worthing (a), Isthmian League Division One, 19 August 1997.
Last appearance: v Carshalton Athletic (a), Isthmian League Full Members' Cup second round, 22 December 1997.
Appearances: 14 + 10
Goals: 5

Playing career:
Aldershot Town (youth), Millwall (from trainee, October 1995), Harrow Borough (1ML, January 1997), Ashford Town (1ML, March 1997), Aldershot Town (August 1997), Newport (Isle of Wight, February 1998), Westfield (summer 1999).

Club honours:
Isthmian League Division One (Aldershot Town 1997–98).

Darren was a stocky forward who actually played for Aldershot Town's Under-15s in the early 1990s. He went on to become a trainee at Millwall and signed full professional forms in October 1995. Loan spells preceded his summer 1997 release, after which he signed for the Shots. He scored three League goals as the Shots won the Isthmian League Division One in 1997–98 but had left to join Newport (Isle of Wight) by the time the title was secured.

Newport had signed Darren in the hope that his goals would get them promoted from the Southern League Southern Division, but despite him scoring from the halfway line on his debut against Margate, it was not to be, and they finished in fourth place. He left St George's Park in the summer of 1998 and took a year out of the game before signing for Combined Counties League side Westfield, where he stayed for two seasons. Darren retired in the summer of 2001 and currently works as a scaffolder.

Adam King — Midfielder

Born: 4 October 1969, Hillingdon.

Aldershot Town FC record:

Debut:	as substitute v Epsom and Ewell (h), Isthmian League Associate Members' Trophy third round, 1 March 1994.
Last appearance:	as substitute v Abingdon Town (h), Isthmian League Division One, 4 October 1994.
Appearances:	7 + 6

Playing career:
West Ham United (from trainee, June 1988), Plymouth Argyle (March 1990), Bristol Rovers (1ML, November 1990), Brentford (December 1991), Hendon (March 1992), Woking (trial, February 1993), Slough Town, Aldershot Town (February 1994), Kunton (Hong Kong, October 1994), Uxbridge (January 1995), Maidenhead United (July 1996).
Adam has made 16 Football League appearances.

Representative honours:
England Youth.

Adam began his career as a trainee at West Ham United and signed full professional forms in June 1998. A £25,000 fee took him to Plymouth Argyle in March 1990. Two bottom-eight finishes and a one-month loan at Bristol Rovers followed before he moved to Brentford in December 1991.

Adam then moved on to various clubs before joining Aldershot Town in February 1994. He made just two appearances that season, with his debut (strangely) coming as a substitute for injured goalkeeper Phil Burns. Adam left the Rec in October 1994 and spent a few months out in Hong Kong before returning to the UK and playing for Uxbridge and Maidenhead United. He left the latter club in September 1996 and nothing is known about his career from that point.

Ryan Kirby — Defender/Midfielder

Born: 6 September 1974, Wanstead.

Aldershot Town FC record:

Debut:	v St Albans City (h), Isthmian League Premier Division, 27 January 2001.
Last appearance:	v Havant and Waterlooville (at Southampton FC), Hampshire Senior Cup Final, 1 May 2002.
Appearances:	79 + 1
Goals:	3

Playing career:
Ridgeway Rovers (youth), Brimsdown Rovers (youth), Arsenal (from trainee, July 1991), Doncaster Rovers (July 1994), Crewe Alexandra (NC, August 1996), Preston North End (trial, August 1996), Wigan Athletic (August 1996), Northampton Town (September 1996), Stevenage Borough (November 1996), Aldershot Town (1ML, January 2001), Aldershot Town (March 2001), Harlow Town (July 2002), Thurrock (August 2004), Fisher Athletic (London, March 2005), Harlow Town (player-coach, February 2006; player-manager from November 2006).
Ryan has made 85 Football League appearances.

Representative honours:
Essex Schools, London Schools, Isthmian League XI, Middlesex Wanderers.

Club honours:
Hampshire Senior Cup (Aldershot Town 2002), Isthmian League Cup (Thurrock 2004 [held over from previous season]), Isthmian League Charity Shield (Thurrock 2004), Southern League Eastern Division (Fisher Athletic [London] 2004–05), London Senior Cup (Fisher Athletic [London] 2005), East Anglian Cup (Harlow Town 2006), Isthmian League Division One North Play-off Final (Harlow Town 2007).

Ryan is primarily a centre-back but has often played in midfield. In his younger years, he played at Ridgeway Rovers with David Beckham before eventually signing as a professional at Arsenal in July 1991.

Ryan joined Doncaster Rovers in July 1994 and had two seasons there (during which the club steadily declined due to off-the-field problems) and brief spells elsewhere before joining Stevenage Borough in November 1996. Ryan's calmness on the ball enabled him to fit in seamlessly, and he played a major part in Boro's successes, including reaching the FA Trophy semi-finals (where they lost to Woking) and finishing third in the Conference that season.

In total, Ryan made over 200 appearances for the Hertfordshire side before joining Aldershot Town on a one-month loan deal in January 2001, signing on a permanent basis in March 2001. He then played in every game as the Shots achieved a third-place finish in the Isthmian Premier Division in 2001–02 before departing that summer and playing for Harlow Town, Thurrock and Fisher Athletic (London) in March 2005.

In February 2006 Ryan left high-flying Fisher to rejoin Harlow Town as player-coach, stepping up to the post of player-manager in the November. His influence on and off the park saw the Hawks enter the Play-offs, where they received a slice of luck – their designated semi-final opponents (Maldon Town) had opted out of being involved in any potential promotion, so Harlow received a 'bye' into the Final, where they beat AFC Sudbury on penalties to gain promotion to the Isthmian League Premier Division.

A mediocre 2007–08 campaign saw Harlow finish two points outside the relegation zone in 15th place. The only bright spot of the season for Ryan was that he was selected for the Middlesex Wanderers representative side.

Paul Kitson — Forward

Born: 9 January 1971, Peterlee.

Aldershot Town FC record:
Debut: as substitute v Canvey Island (a), Conference National, 16 August 2005.
Appearances: 0 + 1

Playing career:
Leicester City (from trainee, December 1988), VS Rugby (1ML, March 1988), Derby County (March 1992), Newcastle United (September 1994), West Ham United (February 1997), Charlton Athletic (2ML, March 2000), Crystal Palace (1ML, September 2000), Brighton & Hove Albion (August 2002), Rushden and Diamonds (August 2003), St Albans City (trial, summer 2004), Aldershot Town (NC, August 2005), Rushden and Diamonds (player-coach, January 2006).
Paul has made 302 FA Premier League and Football League appearances, scoring 78 goals.

Representative honours:
England Under-21s (seven caps, two goals).

Paul was a forward whose career was plagued by injury but still managed to command close to £6 million in transfer fees. He began his footballing life as a trainee at Leicester City and, having had a loan spell at Southern League Premier Division side VS Rugby, signed professional forms in December 1988.

In March 1992 a fee of £1.3 million took Paul to Midlands rivals Derby County, where he scored 36 goals in 105 League appearances but endured disappointment on three occasions – he was part of the sides that reached the Division Two Play-off semi-final in 1991–92 (losing to Blackburn Rovers), that lost the 1993 Anglo-Italian Cup Final to Cremonese and that lost the 1994 Division One Play-off Final to his former side Leicester.

In September 1994 Newcastle United paid £2.25 million for him. Sadly, injury restricted him to 36 appearances, during which he scored 10 goals in just over two years at St James' Park.

Paul joined West Ham United for £2.3 million in February 1997 and scored on his Hammers debut against Tottenham Hotspur, finishing the season as the club's leading League scorer (eight goals). He played in all but one of the games that saw the Hammers beat French side Metz in the Intertoto Cup Final in 1999, thus qualifying for the UEFA Cup, where their progress was ended by Steaua Bucharest in the second round. Loans followed before Paul left Upton Park to sign for Brighton & Hove Albion in August 2002. Unfortunately, his injury curse struck again, causing him to miss the majority of the season.

In the summer of 2003 it was widely believed that Paul would have to retire due to injury. However, he trialled with Second Division Rushden and Diamonds and was offered a contract. Unfortunately, the Diamonds were relegated and, following an unsuccessful pre-season trial at St Albans City, Paul retired.

In August 2005 he came out of retirement to join Aldershot Town but picked up an injury in his only appearance and was released. He spent four months recuperating from the injury before rejoining Rushden and Diamonds (as player-coach) in January 2006, but he did not make any appearances for Rushden that season. The club were relegated, and he subsequently retired (again) that summer. Apart from the fact that he plays 'masters' football, no further information pertaining to Paul is known.

Marc Kleboe — Centre-back

Born: 15 May 1984, Chertsey.

Aldershot Town FC record:

Debut: v Brading Town (h), Hampshire Senior Cup second round, 1 November 2001.
Last appearance: as substitute v Braintree Town (a), Isthmian League Premier Division, 18 April 2002.
Appearances: 1 + 1

Playing career:
Staines Town (youth), Aldershot Town (from youth, summer 2002), Metropolitan Police (2ML, October 2002), Chesham United (2ML, March 2003), Yeading (1ML, August 2003), Frimley Green (February 2004), Yeading (summer 2004), Bisley (summer 2005), Guildford City (summer 2007).

Representative honours:
Surrey Youth.

Club honours:
Isthmian League Premier Division (Yeading 2004–05).

Marc is a commanding centre-back who was originally a youth player at Staines Town. He moved over to the youth set-up at Aldershot Town and broke into the first team during the 2001–02 season while still a member of the youth team. At the time, he was also working with the club's Football in the Community scheme.

Marc's performances in the reserves and youth team led to him signing full contract forms in the summer of 2002, and it was shortly after this that he took up a role within a community football scheme in Feltham. In order to gain first-team experience, Marc was loaned out but, unfortunately, he got injured on his debut for Yeading and missed a large part of the 2003–04 season before leaving the Rec and signing for Frimley Green in February 2004.

Marc returned to Yeading in the summer of 2004, and his presence at the centre of defence was instrumental in the winning of that season's Isthmian League Premier Division. Following an injury-blighted stint at Bisley, he joined Guildford City in the summer of 2007 and they finished runners-up to Merstham in the Combined Counties League Premier Division.

In April 2008 Marc gave up his job as a PE teacher to take on the role of full-time community football officer at Farnborough.

Nathan Koo-Boothe — Centre-back/Midfielder

Born: 18 July 1985, Westminster.

Aldershot Town FC record:

Debut: as substitute v Christchurch (h), Hampshire Senior Cup second round, 27 November 2007.
Last appearance: v Basingstoke Town (h), Hampshire Senior Cup quarter-final, 19 February 2008.
Appearances: 3 + 1

Playing career:

Watford (from trainee, summer 2002), Milton Keynes Dons (summer 2004), Grays Athletic (1ML, November 2005), Kettering Town (February 2006), Coventry City (trial, summer 2007), Barnet (trial, summer 2007), Dundee (trial, September 2007), Aldershot Town (October 2007).
Nathan has made one Football League appearance.

Representative honours:

Jamaica Under-21s, Jamacia Under-23s (five caps).

Nathan is a giant 6ft 4in centre-back who can also play in the centre of midfield. He is the cousin of Shots forward Joel Grant and began as a trainee at Watford, where he signed full professional forms in the summer of 2002. However, he had to wait until he signed for Milton Keynes Dons to make his senior debut, which came in a League Cup tie against Peterborough United in August 2004, with his sole Football League appearance (against Oldham Athletic) coming four days later.

Nathan was loaned out and then played for Jamaica's Under-21 side in the Central American and Caribbean Games in July 2006. He was released by the Dons in February 2006 and signed for Conference North side Kettering Town but was unfortunate enough to break his leg against Stalybridge Celtic that October and never played for the club again. He controversially left Rockingham Road in the summer of 2007, following a wrangle with the club over an alleged breach of club rules concerning his recuperation from his broken leg.

Nathan trialled at several clubs before joining Aldershot Town on a non-contract basis in October 2007. He committed himself to the club for the remainder of the season a month later but could not force his way into the side and was released in February 2008, having made four appearances in Cup competitions. Details of his subsequent career are unknown.

Martin Kuhl — Midfielder

Born: 10 January 1965, Frimley.

Aldershot Town FC record:

Debut: v St Albans City (h), Isthmian League Premier Division, 27 January 2001.
Last appearance: v Yeading (h), Isthmian League Charity Shield, 19 August 2003.
Appearances: 8 + 7
Goals: 1

Playing career:

Chelsea (schoolboy), Birmingham City (from apprentice, January 1983), Sheffield United (March 1987), Watford (February 1988), Portsmouth (September 1988), Derby County (September 1992), Notts County (1ML, September 1994), Bristol City (December 1994), Leyton Orient (trial, July 1997), Happy Valley (Hong Kong, July 1997), Farnborough Town (August 1999), Carshalton Athletic (August 2000), Aldershot Town (NC, January 2001).
Martin has made 474 Football League appearances, scoring 44 goals.

Representative honours:

Hong Kong League XI.

Club honours:

Hong Kong Senior Shield (Happy Valley 1997–98), Hong Kong First Division (Happy Valley 1998–99), Isthmian League Charity Shield (Aldershot Town 2003).

Post-playing coaching/management career:

Community officer at Aldershot Town (January 2001), youth/reserve-team coach at Aldershot Town (summer

2001), first-team coach at Aldershot Town (summer 2003), assistant manager of Aldershot Town (November 2004), caretaker manager of Aldershot Town (March–May 2007), assistant manager and first-team coach at Aldershot Town (May 2007).

Martin's reputation as a hard, tough-tackling midfielder often detracted from his vision and passing ability. He started as a schoolboy at Chelsea before becoming an apprentice at Birmingham City, signing full professional forms in January 1983.

During his time at St Andrews, the club endured a bit of a yo-yo existence – they were relegated from the First Division in 1983–84, promoted back up in 1984–85 and relegated again in 1985–86. The last of these seasons also saw the Blues become victims of an FA Cup giant-killing when they lost 2–1 at home to Alliance Premier League side Altrincham.

With the club heading for a bottom-four finish in 1986–87, Martin moved on to Sheffield United and then Watford (in February 1988), who suffered relegation from Division One before a £125,000 fee took him to a struggling Portsmouth. He had his most productive goalscoring season in 1990–91 (13 goals) and was instrumental in the club finishing ninth in Division Two and reaching the FA Cup semi-final, which they lost on penalties to eventual winners Liverpool.

In September 1992 Derby County paid £650,000 for Martin's services, and he played in the Rams' Anglo-Italian Cup Final defeat to Cremonese that season. His dominance of the midfield also contributed greatly to top-eight finishes in 1992–93 and 1993–94.

Martin went on to play for Notts County, Bristol City, Leyton Orient and Hong Kong side Happy Valley. While out in the (then) UK colony, the club won the Hong Kong Senior Shield in 1997–98 and the First Division title in 1998–99. He also helped them reach the quarter-finals of the Asian Cup-Winners' Cup in the latter season, with his battling qualities making him an obvious choice for the League's representative side.

In August 1999 Martin signed for Farnborough Town, and the Shots fans got a glimpse of what he was capable of when he scored a spectacular long-range goal for Boro at the Rec in an Isthmian League Cup tie in the December. He joined Carshalton Athletic the following summer and came to Aldershot Town in January 2001, making six appearances that season, as well as being the club's football in the community officer, before retiring and joining the youth and reserve-team coaching staff.

Over the years, Martin has become a well-respected coach. He holds a UEFA A qualification and has worked with (among others) the youth players at Reading. His last appearance for the Shots was in the 2003 Isthmian League Charity Shield victory over Yeading.

Martin became Terry Brown's assistant in November 2004 after Stuart Cash's departure, and he took over as caretaker manager and applied for the job on a full-time basis following Brown's resignation as Shots manager in March 2007. He made the interviewee shortlist and was beaten to the job by Gary Waddock, but (to his credit) stayed on at the Rec as assistant. The management duo succeeded in winning the 2008 Setanta Shield before cementing their places in Aldershot Town history and the hearts of the fans by masterminding the winning of the ultimate prize – the 2007–08 Conference Premier title and promotion to the Football League! Clarification of Martin's importance to the club came at the end of June 2008 when, along with boss Gary Waddock, he signed a new three-year contract at the Rec. Away from this duties at the Rec, Martin is a regular participant in 'masters' football tournaments.

Matt Langston — Defender

Born: 2 April 1981, Brighton.

Aldershot Town FC record:

Debut:	v Purfleet (h), Isthmian League Premier Division, 7 December 2002.
Last appearance:	v Braintree Town (a), Isthmian League Premier Division, 28 December 2002.
Appearances:	5
Goals:	1

Club honours:

Conference South (Histon 2006–07).

Playing career:

Watford (from trainee, October 1998), Aldershot Town (1ML, December 2002), Barnet (2ML, March 2003), Barnet (trial, summer 2003), Stevenage Borough (August 2003), Cambridge City (November 2003), Histon (June 2006).

Matt is a commanding centre-back who has a habit of causing havoc at attacking set-pieces. He signed full professional forms at Watford in October 1998, but a combination of injuries and the continued good form of players ahead of him in the Vicarage Road pecking order meant that his chances of getting into the senior squad were always limited.

Matt came to the Rec on a one-month loan deal in December 2002 and scored on his debut against Purfleet. He later played for Barnet, Stevenage Borough and Cambridge City, where he won Player of the Year in 2004 and was named as captain for the 2004–05 season. Under his captaincy, the Lilywhites achieved three club bests that season – they reached the FA Cup second round and the FA Trophy fifth round, as well as finishing runners-up to Grays Athletic in the Conference South.

In June 2006 Matt joined local and divisional rivals Histon and was a major influence in them winning the 2006–07 Conference South title. The 2007–08 season was another rewarding one League-wise, as Matt made 24 appearances and scored four goals to help the Stutes to a club-best seventh-place finish in the Conference Premier.

Dean Larkham — Right-back/Midfield

Born: 19 April 1976, Frimley.

Aldershot Town FC record:

Debut: v Worthing (a), Isthmian League Full Members' Cup, 2 February 1999.
Appearances: 1

Playing career:
Aldershot FC (schoolboy and youth), AFC Bournemouth (youth trial, April 1992), Southampton (youth trial, April 1992), Aldershot Town (youth), Bracknell Town (summer 1994), Cove (November 1994), Fleet Town (1994–95 season), Westfield (1994–95 season), Farnborough Town (1994–95 season), Chertsey Town (1994–95 season), Bracknell Town (summer 1995), Westfield, Aldershot Town (NC, January 1999), Fleet Town (October 2000), Cove (August 2002), Hartley Wintney (December 2002), Godalming Town (2004–05 season).

Dean is the son of ex-Aldershot Town scout Eddie Larkham and the brother-in-law of ex-Farnborough Town midfielder Ian Savage. He played schoolboy and youth-team football for Aldershot FC and, when they went bust in 1992, had youth trials at AFC Bournemouth and Southampton.

Dean returned to the Rec to join the youth team at the 'new' club before joining Bracknell Town in the summer of 1994. During that season, Dean played for a number of other clubs before re-signing for Aldershot Town on a non-contract basis in January 1999 and making his sole appearance the following month. He then went on to play for four more clubs before retiring in the summer of 2005 and currently runs his own printing business.

Ben Lauder-Dykes — Goalkeeper

Born: 2 May 1985, Aldershot.

Aldershot Town FC record:

Debut: v Fareham Town (h), Hampshire Senior Cup second round, 2 November 2004.
Last appearance: v Winchester City (at AFC Bournemouth), Hampshire Senior Cup Final, 2 April 2005.
Appearances: 4 + 1

Playing career:
Aldershot Town (youth), Chertsey Town (STL, March 2004), Farnham Town (1ML, April 2005), Farnham Town (summer 2005), Badshot Lea (November 2005), Ash United (trial, August 2006), Ashford Town (August 2006).

Representative honours:
Hampshire Youth, Hampshire Under-21s, Isthmian League XI.

Club honours:
Isthmian League Cup (Ashford Town [unused substitute] 2007).

Ben was one of the youth-team goalkeepers when he made his appearances for the Shots' first team. Prior to making his senior debut in November 2005, he had a short-term loan at Chertsey Town and was then unfortunate to break his nose near the start of the season.

Ben was loaned to Farnham Town in April 2005, with the move becoming permanent that summer, but he left after a few months and joined Hellenic League Division One East side Badshot Lea, where he saw out the season. The following August, he trialled at Ash United and then signed for Ashford Town, where he was mainly an unused substitute. He left Short Lane in the summer of 2007 and is currently taking a break from the game.

Jayson Lay — Defender/Midfielder

Born: 10 January 1982, Aldershot.

Aldershot Town FC record:

Debut:	as substitute v Walton and Hersham (a), Isthmian League Cup first round, 12 September 2000.
Last appearance:	as substitute v Slough Town (a), Isthmian League Full Members' Cup first round, 24 October 2000.
Appearances:	0 + 2

Playing career:
Kingstonian (youth), Aldershot Town (youth), Ash United (August 2001), Hampton and Richmond Borough (DR, July 2002), Metropolitan Police (DR, October 2002), AFC Guildford (summer 2004), Tongham (October 2004), Milford and Witley (summer 2006), Ash United (February 2008).

Representative honours:
Surrey Schools.

Club honours:
Aldershot Senior Cup (Ash United 2002), Surrey County Intermediate League Western Premier Division (Tongham 2004–05), Surrey Intermediate League Western Premier Division Cup (Tongham 2005).

Jayson is a youngster who can play as a midfielder or a defender and who had played youth football for Kingstonian before joining the same set-up at Aldershot Town.

Having made his two Shots appearances in minor Cup competitions during the 2000–01 season, he joined Ash United in August 2001 and was on the periphery of the side that finished as runners-up to AFC Wallingford in the Combined Counties League in 2001–02. He also played in the Ash side that won the Aldershot Senior Cup that season.

Photograph courtesy of Eric Marsh.

Jayson had short-term dual-registration spells elsewhere before leaving Ash in January 2003 and taking a break from the game. He returned in the summer of 2004 when he signed for AFC Guildford, but he moved on to Surrey County Intermediate League Western Premier Division side Tongham a few months later. His first season at Poyle Road culminated in winning the League title and the Premier Division Cup.

Following a respectable sixth-place finish in 2005–06, Jayson left Tongham and dropped back down to the Western Premier Division with Milford and Witley, remaining there until February 2008, when he returned to Ash.

Dave Lee — Midfielder

Born: 28 March 1980, Basildon.

Aldershot Town FC record:

Debut:	as substitute v Barnet (a), Conference National, 26 February 2005.
Last appearance:	v Burton Albion (h), Conference National, 27 January 2007.
Appearances:	29 + 7
Goals:	1

Playing career:

Tottenham Hotspur (from trainee, July 1998), Luton Town (trial, January 2000), Gillingham (February 2000), Southend United (August 2000), Hull City (June 2001), Brighton & Hove Albion (January 2002), Bristol Rovers (1ML, October 2002), Yeovil Town (trial, February 2003), Cambridge United (trial, April 2003), Thurrock (1ML, October 2003), Oldham Athletic (October 2004), Thurrock (NC, December 2004), Kidderminster Harriers (trial, January 2005), Stevenage Borough (February 2005), Aldershot Town (February 2005), Harlow Town (January 2007), Cambridge United (trial, February 2007), Braintree Town (March 2007), AFC Hornchurch (August 2007), Harlow Town (October 2007), East Thurrock United (March 2008).

Dave has made 71 Football League appearances, scoring nine goals.

Club honours:

Isthmian League Charity Shield (Thurrock 2004).

Dave began his career as a trainee at Tottenham Hotspur and signed full professional forms in July 1998 but did not make any first-team appearances. He had spells at Gillingham, Southend United – where he was joint-top

League goalscorer – Hull City and Brighton & Hove Albion. Despite scoring regularly for Brighton's reserves, he was continually overlooked for the first team and had to look elsewhere to get games.

Having had a couple of trials, a loan spell and just six League appearances for Brighton, Dave was released in September 2004 and signed for Oldham Athletic but returned to former club Thurrock three months later. He made just one appearance and scored one goal during his second spell at Ship Lane – a 1–0 FA Trophy third-round victory against the Shots!

Dave made a sole appearance for Stevenage a week before signing for Aldershot Town in February 2005. His ability to pass the ball accurately from midfield helped the Shots reach the Conference National Play-off semi-finals that season before he suffered a horrendous leg break in a League game at Canvey Island in August 2005. He made his comeback in December 2006 and was a member of the Shots side that lost in the FA Cup third round to Blackpool the following month. However, some would say that he never fully recovered from his leg break, so maybe it was no great surprise that he was released shortly after that FA Cup tie.

Dave later played for Harlow Town, Braintree Town and AFC Hornchurch, making his debut in a nine-goal thriller against Ashford Town on the opening day of the 2007–08 season. The Urchins won 5–4, and the victory was made even sweeter for Dave due to the fact that he opened the scoring.

Two months later, Dave rejoined Harlow Town, where he stayed for five months before leaving to join struggling East Thurrock United. Unsurprisingly, Dave arrived too late to prevent the Rocks finishing 20th and being relegated by virtue of their inferior goal difference.

Dwane Lee — Midfielder

Born: 26 November 1979, Hillingdon.

Aldershot Town FC record:

Debut: v Billericay Town (h), Isthmian League Premier Division, 9 November 2002.
Last appearance: v Kingstonian (h), Isthmian League Premier Division, 26 November 2002.
Appearances: 3

Playing career:

Yeading (from youth, October 1998), Aldershot Town (1ML, November 2002), Exeter City (July 2003), Stoke City (trial, July 2004), Barnet (August 2004), Yeading (trial, August 2006), Grays Athletic (trial, August 2006), Kidderminster Harriers (August 2006), Stevenage Borough (August 2006), Maidenhead United (November 2006), Kettering Town (May 2008).

Dwayne has made 27 Football League appearances, scoring four goals.

Representative honours:

Grenada full international.

Club honours:

Isthmian League Cup (Yeading 2003), Conference National (Barnet 2004–05), Southern League Premier Division Play-off Final (Maidenhead United 2007).

Dwane is a tricky midfielder and an expert at set-pieces. He began as a youth player at Yeading and was given a full contract in October 1998. He performed steadily for the Ding before arriving at the Rec on a one-month loan in November 2002, but he did not really impress.

Having won the Isthmian League Cup with Yeading, Dwane trialled at Exeter City in the summer of 2003 and played well enough to earn himself a contract. However, confusion surrounded his arrival as it was thought that his signing may have breached the terms of a transfer embargo that had been imposed on the Grecians, but the signing was later proved to have been perfectly 'legal'. He played in around half of Exeter's games as they finished the 2003–04 season in sixth place, missing the Play-offs by a solitary point.

Dwane's performances that season led to him making his international debut for Grenada in a World Cup qualifier against Guyana. He then trialled at Stoke City before joining Barnet in August 2004, and his mazy runs plus the occasional goal helped the Bees win the 2004–05 Conference National title. He made his Football League debut on the opening day of the 2005–06 season, but a reported dressing room incident involving another player led to him leaving Underhill.

Following a couple of trials and brief spells at other clubs, he signed for Maidenhead United in November 2006. He helped the Magpies to a fourth-place finish in that season's Southern League Premier Division and played in the Play-offs, which resulted in promotion to the Conference South. He was part of the Maidenhead side that equalled a club-best progression to the FA Cup first round in 2007–08 (where they were surprisingly defeated by Horsham), and also in the team that just avoided relegation from the Conference South by finishing in 17th spot.

Dwane left York Road in May 2008, when he became the first summer signing for Conference Premier new boys Kettering Town.

David Lewis — Midfielder

Born: 21 October 1976, Frimley.

Aldershot Town FC record:

Debut: v Wokingham Town (a), Isthmian League Division One, 4 May 1996.
Appearances: 1

Playing career:

Portsmouth (youth), Fleet Town (youth, summer 1994), Cove (from youth), Aldershot Town (summer 1995), Fleet Town (October 1999).

Club honours:

Wessex League (Fleet Town 1994–95), Aldershot Senior Cup (Fleet Town 1995).

David played youth football at Portsmouth before joining Fleet Town in the summer of 1994, and he was a member of the side that won the Wessex League and Aldershot Senior Cup double in 1994–95.

That summer, David joined Aldershot Town but had to wait until the final League game of the season at Wokingham Town to make his sole appearance. He left the club shortly afterwards, and what he did next is unknown. However, it is known that he took a couple of years out of the game before re-signing for Fleet in October 1999, making a solitary appearance that month. Details of David's subsequent career are unknown.

Jon Lloyd — Defender/Midfielder

Born: 30 December 1982, Frimley.

Aldershot Town FC record:

Debut: v Walton and Hersham, Isthmian League Cup first round, 12 September 2000.
Last appearance: v Newport (Isle of Wight, a), Hampshire Senior Cup second round, 15 November 2000.
Appearances: 3
Goals: 1

Playing career:

Mytchett Athletic (youth), Aldershot Town (from youth, August 2000), Camberley Town (August 2001), Leatherhead (July 2002), Camberley Town (July 2004), Sandhurst Town (December 2004), Bisley (June 2007).

Club honours:

Aldershot Senior Cup (Sandhurst Town 2006).

Jon was a teenage defender-cum-midfielder who graduated from the Shots' youth team, having joined from local side Mytchett Athletic. He signed full contract forms in August 2000 and made a scoring debut the following month, before signing for Camberley Town in August 2001.

Jon moved to Leatherhead in July 2002 and spent two seasons there before re-signing for Camberley in July 2004. However, his return to Krooner Park lasted just six months, as he moved to Sandhurst Town and then on to Bisley, who finished eighth in the Hellenic League Division One East in 2007–08.

Adam Logie — Defender/Midfielder

Born: 30 April 1984, Ascot.

Aldershot Town FC record:

Debut: as substitute v Locksheath (h), Hampshire Senior Cup third round, 2 December 2003.
Appearances: 0 + 1

Playing career:
Brentford (youth), Kingstonian (youth), Aldershot Town (from youth, August 2003), Hartley Wintney (1ML, November 2003), Burnham (1ML, December 2003), Burnham (July 2004), Hayes (July 2006), Ashford Town (June 2007).

Adam's versatility allows him to play in defence or midfield. He played as a youth at Brentford and Kingstonian before joining Aldershot Town's youth team, and he impressed sufficiently to be rewarded with a full contract in August 2003. His sole first-team appearance (in December 2003) was sandwiched between loan moves to Hartley Wintney and Burnham.

In July 2004 he signed permanently for Burnham and was a member of the side that reached the FA Cup first round in 2005–06, where they lost to the Shots. With his game improving all the time, Adam joined Conference South side Hayes in July 2006 and was appointed captain for the coming season. Unfortunately, he had joined a club that would struggle for a second successive season, and a bottom-three finish combined with uncertainty about the club's future led to him joining Ashford Town in June 2007.

Adam scored seven goals in all competitions in the 2007–08 season as the Tangerines finished just outside the Isthmian League Premier Division Play-offs in a highly commendable sixth place.

Jay Lovett — Right-back

Born: 22 January 1978, Plymouth.

Aldershot Town FC record:

Debut:	v Halifax Town (a), Conference, 24 February 2004.
Appearances:	1

Playing career:
Plymouth Argyle (trainee, July 1994), Saltdean United (August 1996), Crawley Town (July 1999), Brentford (August 2000), Crawley Town (6ML, October 2001), Lincoln City (trial, November 2002), Hereford United (2ML, January 2003), Gravesend and Northfleet (2ML, March 2003), Farnborough Town (June 2003), Lewes (October 2003), Aldershot Town (STL, February 2004), Eastbourne Borough (June 2006).

Club honours:
Isthmian League Division One South (Lewes 2003–04), Conference South Play-off Final (Eastbourne Borough 2008).
Jay has made 28 Football League appearances.

Jay was originally a trainee at his local side Plymouth Argyle before moving to Sussex League Division One side Saltdean United in August 1996. During his three seasons there, the club did not finish outside the top six, and his final season culminated in a runners'-up spot behind Burgess Hill Town.

Jay's gradual improvement brought him to the attention of several higher League sides, and in July 1999 he moved to neighbouring Crawley Town and later Brentford for £75,000 – a record for a player leaving the Broadfield Stadium. He made his debut for the Bees against Port Vale in October 2000 and eventually played in 25 of the club's League games that season. However, he made just two appearances in 2001–02, as well as having a six-month loan spell back at Crawley.

Jay had stints at various clubs before joining Lewes on a two-month loan in October 2003, with the move becoming permanent at the end of the term. In February 2004 he played his solitary game for Aldershot Town – on a cold evening in Halifax – before finishing the season as a title winner, when the Rooks won Isthmian League Division One South and then beat Kingstonian in one of the resultant Play-off Finals to secure promotion to the Conference South. Jay was then part of the Lewes side that endured the double heartache of being denied their right to participate in the 2004–05 and 2005–06 Play-offs, due to issues over the development and grading of the Dripping Pan.

Jay later won Player of the Year at Eastbourne Borough and was part of the side that equalled the club's best performance in the FA Cup by reaching the first round before losing to Weymouth in 2007–08. He also helped Borough finish the season as runners-up to Lewes in the Conference South and then beat Hampton and Richmond Borough in the Play-off Final to secure promotion to the Conference Premier for the first time in the club's history.

Brian Lucas — Midfielder

Born: 31 January 1961, Farnborough, Hampshire.

Aldershot Town FC record:

Debut: v Clapton (h), Isthmian League Division Three, 22 August 1992.
Last appearance: v Tring Town (a), Isthmian League Division Three, 27 March 1993.
Appearances: 28 + 7
Goals: 8

Playing career:
Aldershot FC (from apprentice, July 1978), Farnborough Town (July 1984), Basingstoke Town (August 1985), Wokingham Town (August 1988), Basingstoke Town (August 1990), Aldershot Town (August 1992).
Brian has made 125 Football League appearances, scoring 19 goals.

Representative honours:
Aldershot and Farnborough Schools, Hampshire Schools, Hampshire Youth.

Club honours:
Isthmian League Division One (Farnborough Town 1984–85), Isthmian League Division Three (Aldershot Town 1992–93).

Brian was a skilful midfielder who was initially an apprentice at Aldershot FC. He signed full contract forms in July 1978 and made his debut against Walsall in February 1980. The club had a couple of relatively successful League seasons during Brian's time there – he made 31 appearances during the 1980–81 season (when they finished sixth in Division Four) and played 23 times in 1983–84 (as they finished fifth). Brian left the Rec in the summer of 1984 and moved to Farnborough Town (who were in Isthmian League Division One at the time). He made a scoring debut against Hampton on the opening day of the 1984–85 season and contributed 13 goals (in all competitions) to a season that saw the League title won.

In August 1985 Brian joined Basingstoke Town and spent three seasons at the Camrose, the last of which ended with the club being relegated from the Isthmian League Premier Division. He managed to stay in the division by joining Wokingham Town in August 1988 and then rejoined Basingstoke before returning to the Rec in August 1992. He wore the number-seven shirt in Aldershot Town's first-ever competitive game, against Clapton, and he and Chris Tomlinson became the first players to play first-team football for both Aldershot FC and Aldershot Town.

Brian grabbed a piece of history for himself when netting against Thame United in November 1992, thus becoming the first Shots substitute to score a goal. He also played a pivotal role in the club finishing its inaugural season as League champions, although his last appearance was a month or so before the season's end. Brian retired shortly afterwards and currently runs his own sportswear supply company.

Russell Lucas — Defender

Born: 15 April 1986, Frimley.

Aldershot Town FC record:

Debut: v Brockenhurst (h), Hampshire Senior Cup second round, 21 October 2003.
Last appearance: v Locksheath (h), Hampshire Senior Cup third round, 2 December 2003.
Appearances: 2

Playing career:
Reading (youth), Molesey (youth), Aldershot Town (youth), Bracknell Town (July 2005).

Representative honours:
Wales Under-15s, Wales-Under 16s, Wales Under-17s, Hampshire Youth.

Russell is capable of playing in either full-back position and joined the Shots' youth team having played at the same level for both Reading and Molesey. During his time at Reading, he represented Wales at various youth levels. His last known club was Bracknell Town, whom he joined in July 2005, but no further information relating to Russell's career is known.

Hugh McAuley — Midfielder/Forward

Born: 13 May 1976, Plymouth.

Aldershot Town FC record:

Debut: v York City (h), Conference National, 14 August 2004.
Last appearance: v York City (a), Conference National, 6 February 2005.
Appearances: 28 + 4

Playing career:

Aston Villa (trainee, summer 1993), Liverpool (trainee, October 1993), Southport (August 1994), Burscough (January 1995), Northwich Victoria (July 1995), Barrow (January 1996), Conwy United (February 1996), Stockport County (trial, summer 1997), Leek Town (August 1997), Portsmouth (trial, July 1998), Crystal Palace (trial, August 1998), Cheltenham Town (July 1999), Southend United (trial, March 2002), Kidderminster Harriers (March 2003), Burscough (August 2003), Stalybridge Celtic (September 2003), Northwich Victoria (October 2003), Vauxhall Motors (November 2003), Forest Green Rovers (January 2004), Aldershot Town (June 2004), Forest Green Rovers (February 2005), Northwich Victoria (June 2005), Tamworth (July 2005), Kettering Town (October 2005), Hucknall Town (March 2006), Leigh RMI (September 2006).
Hugh has made 104 Football League appearances, scoring nine goals.

Representative honours:

Sefton Schools.

Hugh was a well-travelled attacking midfielder/forward with a goalscoring reputation and is the son of ex-Liverpool winger and backroom staff member Hughie McAuley. He was a trainee at Aston Villa and Liverpool and played for a number of clubs following his release from Anfield in the summer of 1994.

In 1996 Hugh got a taste of European competition when he played in the Intertoto Cup for Conwy United. He scored against Austrian side Marco Polo Ried later in the tournament and, in doing so, gained the accolade of being the first League of Wales player to score in the competition.

After several trials and signing for Leek Town, the 1998–99 season was to have a bittersweet ending for Hugh – he finished the season as Leek's top scorer (19 goals) and was voted into the *Mail on Sunday* Team of the Year, but the club were relegated. In July 1999 Hugh's goals finally brought the reward of a move into the Football League, as reigning Conference champions Cheltenham Town paid £20,000 to bring him to Whaddon Road. He made his debut as a substitute in their first-ever Football League game against Rochdale on the opening day of the 1999–2000 season, but his 39 appearances that campaign yielded just four goals. The following season he scored just three times in 35 appearances, although both seasons did end in very creditable top-nine finishes for the club.

Hugh left Cheltenham in March 2003 and a few club stints preceded his signing for Forest Green Rovers in January 2004, and he contributed some solid performances to help the club avoid relegation. That summer, Hugh joined Aldershot Town and put in some wonderful performances to help push the club towards the Play-offs for the second successive season. He returned briefly to Forest Green in the February before rejoining Northwich Victoria in June 2005. However, he joined Tamworth shortly afterwards following Victoria's expulsion from the Conference National due to administration irregularities.

Hugh finished his career off with spells at Kettering Town, Hucknall Town and Leigh RMI before retiring in the summer of 2007. He currently runs his own luxury vehicle sourcing company.

Barry McCoy — Defender

Born: 12 October 1980, Ascot.

Aldershot Town FC record:

Debut: as substitute v Braintree Town (h), FA Trophy second round, 27 November 1999.
Last appearance: v Carshalton Athletic (a), Isthmian League Premier Division, 6 May 2000.
Appearances: 3 + 2

Playing career:

Wycombe Wanderers (trainee, July 1996), Reading (trainee, January 1998), Aldershot Town (from youth, October 1999), Fleet Town (2ML, January 2000), Wokingham Town (June 2000), Binfield (summer 2002), Windsor and

Eton (October 2002), Wokingham Town (December 2002), Egham Town (December 2002), Binfield (April 2003), Wokingham Town/Wokingham and Emmbrook (July 2003), Bisley (July 2006), Flackwell Heath (August 2006), Farnborough (July 2007), Bisley (1MDRL, August 2007), Guildford City (August 2007).

Representative honours:
Hellenic League Division One East XI.

Club honours:
Isthmian League Charity Shield (Aldershot Town 1999), Hellenic League Division One East (Bisley 2006–07).

Barry began as a forward in Wycombe Wanderers' youth team before converting to defence and becoming a regular in the reserves. He moved on to become a trainee at Reading and then came to the Rec and captained the Shots' youth team. His performances in that team led to him signing a full contract in October 1999, and he made his senior debut the following month.

Barry left the Rec that summer and had spells with Wokingham Town, Binfield, Windsor and Eton and Egham Town. After re-signing for Wokingham Town in July 2003 the club merged with Emmbrook Sports the following summer, and Barry was appointed as captain for the 2004–05 season. In April 2005 he had what can be best described as an 'eventful week' – he was sent off three times in the space of seven days, with his first offence of the three – an alleged headbutt – earning him a massive 112-day ban!

Barry eventually returned to playing in February 2006 and left that summer to join divisional rivals Bisley, where he formed a solid partnership with (fellow ex-Shot) Paul Andrews. By the end of the 2006–07 season, the pair had contributed to the winning of the Hellenic League Division One East title, after which Barry signed for the newly formed Farnborough FC. He later signed for Guildford City in the (reported) hope that he would play regular first-team football. The move nearly ended with Barry being a League winner, but City finished the season in the runners'-up spot behind Merstham in the Combined Counties League Premier Division.

Steve McGrath — Centre-back/Right-back

Born: 25 January 1969, Park Royal.

Aldershot Town FC record:

Debut:	v Leatherhead (a), Isthmian League Cup quarter-final, 9 February 1999.
Last appearance:	v Aylesbury United (a), Isthmian League Premier Division, 7 September 1999.
Appearances:	21
Goals:	5

Playing career:
Shamrock, Yeading (August 1994), Enfield (October 1996), Yeovil Town (September 1998), Old Actonians, Aldershot Town (February 1999), Yeading (September 1999), Brook House (March 2001), Aylesbury United (June 2002), Staines Town (July 2003), Brook House (February 2004), Hendon (February 2005).

Club honours:
Middlesex Senior Cup (Enfield 1998), Isthmian League Cup (Aldershot Town 1999), Hampshire Senior Cup (Aldershot Town 1999).

Post-playing coaching/management career:
Reserve-team manager of Hounslow Borough.

Steve was a tall, brave centre-back who could also play at right-back and whose height often caused problems for opposing defenders at set-pieces. Details of Steve's early career are unknown, although he reportedly played for Shamrock FC prior to joining Yeading in August 1994. He joined George Borg's Enfield in October 1996 for a reported four-figure fee, and his strength and power were instrumental in the club finishing as runners-up to Yeovil Town in the Isthmian League Premier Division that season. They also went some way to earning Steve the 1997 Player of the Year award.

Steve joined Yeovil Town briefly and then Old Actonians before linking up again with Borg in February 1999, when he signed for Aldershot Town and played in the side that won the Isthmian League Cup and Hampshire Senior Cup double that season. He later rejoined Yeading and played for various other clubs including Hendon, where he was instrumental in turning a side languishing at the bottom of the Isthmian League Premier Division into one that would finish the 2004–05 season in a respectable mid-table position. Steve left Claremont Road in September 2005 and, apart from a reported spell as reserve-team manager at Hounslow Borough, nothing else is known of his career or whereabouts from thereafter.

Aaron McLean — Forward

Born: 25 May 1983, Hammersmith.

Aldershot Town FC record:

Debut:	v Hayes (a), Isthmian League Premier Division, 29 March 2003.
Last appearance:	as substitute v York City (a), Conference National, 6 February 2005.
Appearances:	68 + 26
Goals:	26

Playing career:
Leyton Orient (from trainee, July 2001), Grays Athletic (2ML, September 2002), Colchester United (trial, March 2003), Aldershot Town (March 2003), Grays Athletic (February 2005), Peterborough United (October 2006). Aaron has made 101 Football League appearances, scoring 38 goals.

Representative honours:
England National Game XI (5 caps).

Club honours:
Isthmian League Premier Division (Aldershot Town 2002–03), Hampshire Senior Cup (Aldershot Town 2003), Conference South (Grays Athletic 2004–05), FA Trophy (Grays Athletic 2006).

Aaron is an energetic and tireless forward who started as a trainee at Leyton Orient. He made his debut as a substitute against Reading in a Football League Trophy tie in December 1999 and signed full professional forms in July 2001.

The 2002–03 season saw him have a two-month loan spell at Grays Athletic (scoring three goals in six games) and a trial at Colchester United before joining Aldershot Town in the March. In total, he had made 45 appearances for Leyton Orient in all competitions (39 as a substitute) but scored just three goals.

The Rec faithful soon witnessed his pace and recognised his amazing aerial ability by affectionately dubbing him 'Springs', with his character being epitomised by the fact that he is often described as 'playing with a smile on his face'. He ended the 2002–03 season having helped the club win the Isthmian League Premier Division and the Hampshire Senior Cup – he scored both goals in the 2–1 victory over Bashley. He also played in the club's first-ever Conference game against Accrington Stanley in August 2003, and his continued improvement throughout the season led to him making his England National Game XI debut against Belgium two months later. He played in the defeat to Hednesford Town in that season's FA Trophy semi-finals and was the Shots' goalscorer when they drew 1–1 with Shrewsbury Town (after extra-time) in the 2004 Conference Play-off Final, before losing a penalty shoot-out.

The 2004–05 season saw Aaron struggle to score – he managed just two strikes in 25 League games. It was also reported that he was looking for a move to a club nearer his home, so it was no surprise when he was allowed to leave the Rec in February 2005 to join Grays Athletic for a fee of £5,000. However, the season ended happily for Aaron as the club won the Conference South title, as well as the FA Trophy later.

Aaron began the 2006–07 season with Grays, and his 13 goals in 17 games paved the way for him to join Peterborough United on loan in the October. He scored on his debut against Accrington Stanley, and his four goals in his first eight games persuaded the club to sign him permanently for a fee of £150,000 (a record for Grays) at the turn of the year. Despite leaving, he still finished as Grays' top scorer that season. He went on to score seven goals in 16 games for the Posh before injury ended his season in February, but he had made such an impact that he still won that season's Player of the Year award.

Aaron returned from injury at the start of the 2007–08 season and played as if he had never been away, scoring on the opening day of the season and then going on to set a club record of scoring in seven consecutive League games. Both club and player had a successful campaign, as the Posh were promoted by virtue of finishing runners-up to Milton Keynes Dons in League Two. In addition to this, he scored 33 goals in 53 appearances in all competitions, with 29 of those goals not only giving him the League Two Golden Boot but making him the top scorer in the entire Football League. Aaron's performances throughout the season saw him voted into the League Two Team of the Year, as well as winning him the Player of the Year award at London Road.

Chris McPhee — Forward/Midfielder/Right-back

Born: 20 March 1983, Eastbourne.

Aldershot Town FC record:

Debut:	v Tamworth (h), Conference National, 13 August 2005.
Last appearance:	as substitute v Kidderminster Harriers (h), Conference National, 15 October 2005.
Appearances:	12 + 2
Goals:	2

Playing career:

Brighton & Hove Albion (from trainee, June 2002), Aldershot Town (2ML, August 2005), Swindon Town (2ML, March 2006), Torquay United (July 2006), Ebbsfleet United (August 2007), Weymouth (June 2008).

Chris has made 105 Football League appearances, scoring four goals.

Representative Honours:

England C (two caps).

Club honours:

FA Trophy (Ebbsfleet United 2008).

Chris is best known as a forward and began as a trainee at Brighton & Hove Albion, for whom he made his debut as a 16-year-old substitute against Swansea City in December 1999, signing full professional forms in June 2002. He came to the Rec on a two-month loan deal at the start of the 2005–06 season but disappointed.

Chris was unable to get more than a handful of games for Brighton that season and so joined Swindon Town on loan in the March and then Torquay United. Unfortunately, he endured a frustrating 2006–07 season, during which he played 43 games in all competitions and scored just one (FA Cup) goal. To make matters worse, Swindon were promoted and Torquay dropped out of the Football League!

Chris left Plainmoor and trialled at newly renamed Conference Premier side Ebbsfleet United before signing permanently in August 2007, with his versatility enabling him to play ably in midfield and as a very competent right-back when required. Chris scored three goals in the FA Trophy, including two in the first leg of the semi-

final against the Shots. He then endured an eventful end to the first half of the Final against Torquay United, as he missed a 41st-minute penalty before scoring the only goal of the game four minutes later! Chris's season was rounded off by being part of the England C squad that won the Four Nations Tournament, with him making his debut in the competition opener against Gibraltar. At the time of writing, Chris then rejected the offer of a new contract at Stonebridge Road and, as a result of him reportedly looking for a club nearer to his West Country home, signed for Weymouth.

Fiston Manuella — Midfielder

Born: 11 February 1981, Angola.

Aldershot Town FC record:

Debut:	v Margate (a), Conference, 12 August 2003.
Last appearance:	v Barnet (a), Conference, 20 September 2003.
Appearances:	9
Goals:	1

Playing career:
Crystal Palace (youth), Brentford (trainee, July 1998), Hampton and Richmond Borough (summer 1999), Chertsey Town (1ML, December 1999), Aylesbury United (June 2002), Aldershot Town (1ML, August 2003), Farnborough Town (October 2003), Crawley Town (March 2004), Staines Town (October 2004), Chelmsford City (September 2006), Wycombe Wanderers (trial, July 2007), Lincoln City (trial, July 2007), Boreham Wood (August 2007), Bromley (December 2007), Boreham Wood (March 2008).

Representative honours:
Isthmian League XI, England Semi-Professional XI (one cap).

Club honours:
Isthmian League Charity Shield (Aldershot Town 2003), Southern League Cup (Crawley Town 2004), Southern League Championship Trophy (Crawley Town 2004 [unused substitute]), Southern League Premier Division (Crawley Town 2003–04), Hertfordshire Senior Cup (Boreham Wood 2008 [unused substitute]).

Fiston is a tough-tackling central-midfielder who has been a regular entry into the notebooks of referees throughout his career. He came to the UK from Angola and was known as 'Fiston Mputu' in his early years here but later adopted his mother's maiden name (Manuella) for personal reasons.

Having played youth-team football at Crystal Palace, Fiston joined Hampton and Richmond Borough in the summer of 1999 and was loaned to Chertsey later that season to gain some valuable experience. He was part of the Borough side that was knocked out of the FA Cup by Barnet at the first round stage in 2000–01, and his battling qualities made him the natural candidate for the Beavers captaincy in 2001–02 – a season during which a club-best progression to the FA Trophy fourth round was made.

In June 2002 he joined Aylesbury United, where his continued good form was rewarded by him winning his only England National XI cap against Belgium in February 2003. In August of that year, Fiston joined Aldershot Town on a one-month loan and played well enough for a permanent move to be discussed, although it didn't to fruition.

Shortly after he returned to Buckingham Road, Fiston reportedly refused to play in an FA Cup second-qualifying-round tie against Braintree Town because he did not want to be Cup-tied. As a consequence, he was sold to Farnborough Town for £3,000. Five months later, Boro recouped £2,000 of their outlay when he was sold to Crawley Town, where he played in the run-in as the club won the Southern League Premier Division, as well as playing in the first leg of the League Cup Final against Moor Green.

Fiston joined Staines Town in October 2004 and helped the club to successive top-10 finishes in 2004–05 and 2005–06. In August 2006 he gained national notoriety when he served a two-month prison sentence after pleading guilty to headbutting Dunstable Town's Marc Kefford during a game in September 2005.

On his release from jail, he played for Chelmsford City, Boreham Wood and Bromley, returning to the former after a three-month break from the game. Fiston's season initially ended in disappointment, as the Wood were relegated from the Isthmian League Premier Division (on goal difference), having finished 19th. However, Halifax Town's subsequent expulsion from the Conference Premier caused a 'knock on' through the pyramid, and the Wood were reprieved. However, Fiston's joy was short-lived, as he was released from Meadow Park in June 2008 and, at the time of writing, is still without a club.

James Mariner **Midfielder**

Born: 4 December 1980, Guildford.

Aldershot Town FC record:

Debut: v Worthing (a), Isthmian League Full Members' Cup second round, 2 February 1999.
Appearances: 1

Playing career:
Aldershot Town (youth), Raunds Town (October 1999), Godalming and Guildford/Godalming Town (summer 2002).

Representative honours:
Surrey Youth.

Club honours:
Combined Counties League (Godalming Town 2005–06), Combined Counties Premier Challenge Cup (Godalming Town 2006).

James is a midfielder and was a member of the Shots' youth team when making his sole senior appearance. He left the Rec in the summer of 1999 and studied at Northampton University, playing for Raunds Town in the Southern League Eastern Division during that time. After graduating, he joined Godalming and Guildford in the summer of 2002 and won the Player of the Year award in his first season.

James has held the position of vice-captain at Godalming and Guildford and was a central figure in the club completing the Combined Counties League and Premier Challenge Cup double in 2006. The 2007–08 season saw the club attain a 12th-place finish in the Southern League Division One South and West. To date, James has made over 250 appearances for the Gs.

Kyle Matthews **Midfielder/Forward**

Born: 18 October 1987, Park Royal.

Aldershot Town FC record:

Debut: as substitute v Kidderminster Harriers (a), Conference National, 18 March 2006.
Last appearance: as substitute v Woking (h), Conference National, 22 April 2006.
Appearances: 2 + 5
Goals: 1

Playing career:
Chelsea (youth), Watford (academy, July 2004), Aldershot Town (1ML, March 2006), Northwood (July 2006), Harrow Borough (December 2006), Northwood (September 2007), Harrow Borough (October 2007), Hayes and Yeading United (January 2008).

Club honours:
Middlesex Charity Cup (Harrow Borough 2007).

Kyle was a pacy right-sided midfielder-cum-forward who started out playing in Chelsea's youth team before joining Watford's academy. He joined Aldershot Town on a month's loan in March 2006 but returned to Vicarage Road, having been disappointing. He was released by Watford that summer and joined Southern League Premier side Northwood, but within six months he had moved to Harrow Borough.

Within a month of the 2007–08 season starting, Kyle returned to Northwood but failed to claim a regular spot in the side so rejoined Harrow the following month and moved on to Hayes and Yeading United three months later. Following his arrival at Church Road, he made eight appearances as United finished the 2007–08 season in 13th spot in the Conference South.

Shaun May **Midfielder**

Born: 29 September 1964, Aldershot.

Aldershot Town FC record:

Debut: v Clapton (h), Isthmian League Division Three, 22 August 1992.

Last appearance: v Collier Row (h), Isthmian League Division Two, 12 March 1994.
Appearances: 40 + 17
Goals: 8

Playing career:
Crystal Palace (schoolboy), Aldershot FC (youth), Churt, Wrecclesham, Farnham Town (summer 1987), Aldershot Town (summer 1992), Cove (1ML, October 1993), Basingstoke Town (summer 1994), Farnham Town (summer 1995).

Representative honours:
Combined Counties League XI.

Club honours:
Combined Counties League (Farnham Town 1990–91, 1991–92), Dan Air Elite Cup (Farnham Town 1992), Combined Counties Premier Challenge Cup (Farnham Town 1992, 1996), Isthmian League Division Three (Aldershot Town 1992–93).

Shaun was a midfielder with a talent for the accurate delivery of free-kicks. He started out as a schoolboy at Crystal Palace before signing on as a youth player with Aldershot FC in the 1981–82 season, appearing occasionally in the reserves. He played local football before signing for Farnham Town in the summer of 1987, and it was at the Memorial Ground that his career really took off. He was part of the Farnham side that won the Combined Counties League in 1990–91 but the following season got even better, as he was a key member of the side that was the first to complete the Combined Counties treble (League title, Dan Air Elite Cup and Premier Challenge Cup).

Shaun joined Aldershot Town in the summer of 1992 and wore the number-10 shirt in the club's first-ever game against Clapton. His pin-point passing and composure on the ball greatly contributed to the Shots strolling to the Isthmian League Division Three title that season. He injured his ankle in the summer of 1993 and missed the start of the season. Once recovered, he played mostly for the reserves but made a handful of first-team appearances in a campaign that saw the club promoted for a second successive season.

In October 1993 he was loaned to Cove before returning to play for the Shots in the latter stages of their run to the FA Vase quarter-finals, where they were beaten by Atherton Laburnum Rovers. In the summer of 1994, Shaun signed for Basingstoke Town before making a return to Farnham, where his first three seasons saw the club achieve top-six finishes in the Combined Counties League, with the Challenge Cup being won in 1996. Shaun retired at end of the 2000–01 season and currently works as an operations manager for a CCTV company.

Ivan Mballa — Forward

Born: 26 September 1974, Amiens, France.

Aldershot Town FC record:

Debut: as substitute v Braintree Town (h), Isthmian League Premier Division, 1 September 2001.
Appearances: 0 + 1

Playing career:

ASFC Vindelle (France), AJ Auxerre (France), Raith Rovers (August 2000), Aldershot Town (NC, August 2001), Cumnock Juniors (March 2007).
Ivan has made 31 Scottish League appearances, scoring eight goals.

Ivan was a dual French/Ivory Coast national forward. Details of his pre-UK career are sketchy, but it is known that he played for French sides ASFC Vindelle and AJ Auxerre before coming to these shores. He was recommended to Raith Rovers by his cousin (ex-Celtic defender Oliver Tebily) and made a scoring debut after coming on as a substitute against Alloa Athletic on the opening day of the 2000–01 season.

Ivan reportedly had several disciplinary problems that ultimately led to him being released at the end of the season. He came to the Rec in August 2001 but disappointed greatly during the 18 minutes that he played as a substitute against Braintree Town. He departed the Rec almost immediately and reportedly returned to France before eventually coming back to Scotland and joining Junior West Premier Division side Cumnock Juniors in March 2007. Ivan was released that summer, and nothing else is known about his career or current whereabouts.

Junior Mendes — Forward

Born: 15 September 1976, Balham.

Aldershot Town FC record:

Debut: as substitute v Kidderminster Harriers (h), Conference Premier, 1 March 2008.
Appearances: 6 + 4
Goals: 4

Playing career:

Chelsea (from trainee, July 1995), St Mirren (April 1996), Oxford United (trial, July 1998), Carlisle United (1ML, November 1998), Dunfermline Athletic (July 2000), Wolverhampton Wanderers (trial, November 2000), Rushden and Diamonds (trial, November 2001), St Mirren (June 2002), Mansfield Town (January 2003), Huddersfield Town (July 2004), Northampton Town (3ML, October 2005), Grimsby Town (3ML, January 2006), Notts County (July 2006), Lincoln City (2ML, March 2007), FC Mika (Armenia, trial, November 2007), Aldershot Town (February 2008).
Junior has made 261 Football League, Scottish Premier League and Scottish League appearances, scoring 52 goals.

Representative honours:

Montserrat full international (two caps, one goal).

Club honours:

Scottish League Division One (St Mirren 1999–2000), Setanta Shield (Aldershot Town 2008), Conference Premier (Aldershot Town 2007–08).

Junior is a pacy and powerful forward who is very adept at holding the ball up while waiting for support. He is the cousin of Leyton Orient forward Wayne Gray and was originally a trainee at Chelsea, where he signed full professional forms in July 1995 but never broke into the first team. He was released from Stamford Bridge in April 1996 and moved North of the border to sign for Scottish First Division outfit St Mirren. Although he played in every League game that season, he scored just three goals. The following season, he was St Mirren's top scorer (nine goals), and that summer he tried his luck back in England with a trial at Oxford United.

Junior became a winner when his five goals assisted the Saints in winning the Division One title in 1999–2000. He left Love Street that summer and joined fellow Premier League side Dunfermline Athletic for a fee of £20,000, a move that led to him being publicly slated by St Mirren boss Tom Hendrie. Things didn't really work out for

Junior at Dunfermline, and he left East End Park at the end of the season and trialled at Rushden and Diamonds but then did not play for the rest of the 2001–02 season.

Strangely, Hendrie brought Junior back to St Mirren in June 2002, but Junior left to join Mansfield Town and then Huddersfield. He made a scoring debut for Montserrat against Antigua and Barbuda in a CONCACAF Cup match in November 2004 and, later that season, was part of the Huddersfield side that put together a nine-game unbeaten run that saw them miss out on the League One Play-offs by a solitary point.

During the 2005–06 season Junior had a couple of loan spells before signing for Notts County, but he reportedly fell out with boss Steve Thompson. He was loaned out to Lincoln City in March 2007 and helped the Imps into the League Two Play-off semi-finals before returning to Meadow Lane. Junior's former club, St Mirren, were rumoured to be interested in re-signing him in July 2007, but a move never materialised. The following month, he was released by County and went out to Armenia in November 2007 to train with FC Mika. The club were on the verge of qualifying for the UEFA Cup, but any hope that Junior may have had of participating in the club's last five games of the season were ended when he picked up a medial ligament injury.

Junior returned to the UK and joined Aldershot Town as a trialist in February 2008 (having been recommended by ex-Mansfield teammate Rhys Day) and impressed sufficiently to be signed on a contract until the end of the season. He was a lively addition to the side and scored both goals in the 4–2 aggregate defeat by Ebbsfleet United in that season's FA Trophy semi-final. He then endeared himself to the fans by setting up Scott Davies's injury-time winner at title rivals Torquay United in March 2008 and followed that up by being one of the goalscorers in the Setanta Shield Final. In total, Junior made six League appearances in a campaign that saw the Conference Premier title won. His efforts were rewarded a few weeks after the season finished when he signed a deal to keep him at the Rec until the end of 2008.

Gavin Mernagh — Forward

Born: 11 June 1978, Slough.

Aldershot Town FC record:

Debut:	v Staines Town (a), Isthmian League Division One, 15 November 1997.
Last appearance:	v Newport (Isle of Wight, at Eastleigh FC), Hampshire Senior Cup semi-final, 12 March 1998.
Appearances:	7 + 6
Goals:	2

Playing career:

Queen's Park Rangers (trainee, July 1994), Chesham United (January 1996), Slough Town (August 1996), Enfield (August 1997), Aldershot Town (November 1997), Chertsey Town (March 1998), Maidenhead United (August 1998), Yeading (February 1999), Beaconsfield SYCOB (August 1999), Chertsey Town (November 1999), Enfield (August 2000), Windsor and Eton (October 2000), Egham Town (August 2001), Flackwell Heath (January 2002), Marlow (September 2003), Wokingham Town (September 2003), Flackwell Heath (October 2003), Marlow (November 2003), Burnham (March 2004), Egham Town (August 2004), Beaconsfield SYCOB (September 2005), Bisley (September 2005), Camberley Town (October 2006), Burnham (September 2007).

Club honours:

Isthmian League Division One (Aldershot Town 1997–98).

Having been a trainee at Queen's Park Rangers, Gavin dropped into non-League football with Isthmian League Division One side Chesham United in January 1996. He made the step up into the Conference with Slough Town that summer but never commanded a regular place – hardly surprising, as one of the players he was trying to oust was future Shots legend Gary Abbott!

Gavin joined Enfield in August 1997 but left soon after when ex-Es boss George Borg took him to Aldershot Town in the hope that he could fire the club to promotion from Isthmian League Division One. Despite scoring on his debut, Gavin (again) could not make one of the forward's positions his own and so, having made enough appearances to qualify for a League-winners' medal, joined Chertsey Town in March 1998.

Gavin went on to play for a number of clubs, including a season and a half at Wilks Park, which turned out to be a mixture of fortunes. In 2001–02 the club finished in the bottom three of Isthmian League Division Three. However, the following season they finished third in the (reorganised) Division Two and reached the

FA Cup fourth qualifying round for the first time in their history before being beaten by Crawley Town. Gavin also finished as the club's top scorer that season.

In September 2007 Gavin returned to Burnham for a second spell and later took on the role of player-assistant manager of the reserve side. However, a back injury prevented him from playing much in a season that saw the club finish in 10th place in the Southern League Division One South and West, and it is believed that the injury forced him to retire in the summer of 2008.

Adam Miller — Midfielder

Born: 19 February 1982, Hemel Hempstead.

Aldershot Town FC record:

Debut:	v Forest Green Rovers (a), FA Cup fourth qualifying round, 25 October 2003.
Last appearance:	v Morecambe (h), Conference National, 6 November 2004.
Appearances:	51 + 2
Goals:	12

Playing career:

Ipswich Town (scholar, July 1998), Southend United (trial, September 2000), Canvey Island (October 2000), Grays Athletic (August 2002), Gravesend and Northfleet (September 2003), Aldershot Town (October 2003), Queen's Park Rangers (November 2004), Peterborough United (1ML, September 2005), Oxford United (trial, January 2006), Stevenage Borough (January 2006), Gillingham (November 2007).
Adam has made 46 Football League appearances, scoring three goals.

Representative honours:

England National Game XI (one cap).

Club honours:

FA Trophy (Canvey Island 2001, Stevenage Borough 2007).

Adam is a vastly talented player who started at Ipswich Town's academy. He trialled at Southend United in September 2000 and was offered a contract by manager Alan Little; however, fate intervened when David Webb came in to replace Little and the offer was withdrawn. The following month, he joined Canvey Island and the season ended with him having played a vital part in taking the runners'-up spot to Farnborough Town in the Isthmian League Premier Division and beating Forest Green Rovers to win the FA Trophy.

The Gulls' success (and Adam's improvement) continued the following season, as they achieved a club-best FA Cup third-round progression and again finished as Premier Division runners-up, this time to Gravesend and Northfleet. Adam played in a more attacking role that season and scored 12 goals in all competitions.

Adam had spells with Grays Athletic and Gravesend and Northfleet before signing for Aldershot Town in October 2003. His ability to turn defence into attack from the centre of the park and his eight goals that season were a contributing factor to the club reaching the FA Trophy semi-finals and the Conference Play-off Final. Personal glory accompanied those achievements, as Adam made his only appearance for the England National Game XI (against Italy in the February) and then won the non-League Young Player of the Year award.

Adam's performances for the Shots had drawn many admirers from higher up the pyramid, and in November 2004 he became the first Aldershot Town player to be transferred to a Football League club for a fee, when Queen's Park Rangers paid £30,000 plus an additional £10,000 when he had made 10 first-team appearances, which he duly did. He made his QPR debut against Nottingham Forest the following month but seemingly struggled to perform consistently.

During the 2005–06 season, Adam joined Stevenage Borough in the January. He played a deeper midfield role than he had done at the Rec, and his signing nearly paid dividends, as the club narrowly missed getting into the Play-offs. The 2006–07 season did bring success, as Stevenage beat Kidderminster Harriers to win the FA Trophy in what was the first-ever Final held at the new Wembley Stadium. Adam got a second chance at playing in the Football League when he signed for Gillingham on a month's loan in November 2007. This move became permanent in the January transfer window, with a reported £65,000 joint fee being paid for Adam and his Stevenage teammate John Nutter. Adam went on to make 28 appearances and score three goals for the Gills that season, but that could not prevent the club from finishing 22nd in League One and being relegated.

Jason Milletti — Left-back/Midfielder

Born: 18 September 1987, Guildford.

Aldershot Town FC record:

Debut: as substitute v Fareham Town (h), Hampshire Senior Cup second round, 2 November 2004.

Appearances: 10 + 2

Playing career:

Reading (schoolboy and youth), Aldershot Town (from youth, August 2007), Fleet Town (1ML, August 2005), Camberley Town (1ML, January 2006 season), Chesham United (1ML, March 2006), Camberley Town (1ML, April 2006), Oxford City (1ML, August 2006), Godalming Town (1ML, October 2006), Camberley Town (6ML, November 2006), Fleet Town (SLL, August 2007), Cove (SLL, August 2007), Ashford Town (5ML, October 2007), Fleet Town (3ML, February 2008).

Representative honours:

Hampshire Under-18s (captain).

Club honours:

Hampshire Senior Cup (Aldershot Town 2007 [unused substitute]), Aldershot Senior Cup (Camberley Town 2007).

Jason is a versatile player who is equally competent as a left-back or a left-sided midfielder. He started out playing schoolboy and youth-team football at Reading before joining Aldershot Town, for whom he has been a reserve-team regular. His senior debut for the Shots came in the 2004–05 season when he was still a member of the youth team.

During the 2005–06 season, Jason was loaned out while continuing to play for the Shots' youth and reserve sides, garnering regular praise for his performances. The majority of his 2006–07 season was again spent on loan, although he did appear for the Shots' first team in the Hampshire Senior Cup-winning run.

In August 2007 Jason's potential was rewarded by him signing full contract forms at the Rec. In order to give him first-team football, he signed for Fleet Town on a season-long loan later that month, but he was unfortunate to get injured playing for the Shots' reserves shortly afterwards. By the time he had recovered, Fleet were in the throes of FA Cup and FA Trophy games (for which he was ineligible), plus they had signed another left-back so the loan was cut short. Jason then signed for Ashford Town (Middlesex) on loan before rejoining Fleet on the same basis in February 2008 and playing for Cove the following month (having registered with them at the start of the season). He was on the bench several times for the Shots during their 2007–08 Conference Premier title-winning season, but his five appearances that season all came in minor Cup competitions.

Stewart Mitchell — Right-back/Wing-back

Born: 4 March 1961, South Shields.

Aldershot Town FC record:

Debut: v AFC Lymington (h), Hampshire Senior Cup first round, 27 September 1994.
Last appearance: v Wembley (h), Isthmian League Division One, 1 April 1995.
Appearances: 19 + 2

Playing career:

Gateshead, Northwood, Hayes (1982–83 season), Hampton (February 1983), Hendon (August 1983), Burnham, Slough Town (December 1984), Maidenhead United (summer 1985), Windsor and Eton (summer 1986), Woking (June 1989), Basingstoke Town (August 1992), Marlow (August 1993), Aldershot Town (August 1994), Aylesbury United (August 1995), Barton Rovers (October 1995).

Representative honours:

FA XI, Isthmian League XI.

Club honours:

Isthmian League Cup (Woking 1991), Surrey Senior Cup (Woking 1991), Isthmian League Premier Division (Woking 1991–92), Isthmian League Charity Shield (Woking 1991), Berks and Bucks Senior Cup (Marlow 1994).

Stewart was a dependable right-back/wing-back who began his footballing career in his native North East with Gateshead. He came down South and played for several clubs before signing for Woking in June 1989. Stewart went on to have a successful time at Woking, winning the Isthmian League Cup and Surrey Senior Cup double, as well as the Isthmian League Premier Division title and promotion to the Conference for the first time in the club's history. He also won a Player of the Year award.

Stewart left Kingfield and played for Basingstoke Town and Marlow, with whom he won the Berks and Bucks Cup, before being recruited by Aldershot Town in August 1994. He played in around half of the games that season as the Shots finished fourth in Isthmian League Division One, missing promotion on goal difference. He then played for Aylesbury United and Barton Rovers before retiring in the summer of 1996, but nothing is known about him after that date.

Mark Molesley — Midfielder

Born: 11 March 1981, Hillingdon.

Aldershot Town FC record:

Debut: v Gravesend and Northfleet (h), Conference National, 12 August 2006.
Last appearance: v Altrincham (a), Conference National, 28 April 2007.
Appearances: 40 + 2
Goals: 1

Playing career:

Hayes (from youth, May 2000), Cambridge City (June 2005), Aldershot Town (May 2006), Stevenage Borough (May 2007), Grays Athletic (May 2008).

Representative honours:

Great Britain Colleges (captain), England National Game XI (four caps).

Mark is an energetic, ball-winning central-midfielder who began his career at Hayes under future Shots boss Terry Brown. He was the first player to progress through the club's FEDO youth scheme into the first team, signing full contract forms in May 2000 and making his senior debut in the final League game of the season against Nuneaton Borough. He continued to gain experience in Hayes' first team and was unfortunate to be a member of the side that was relegated out of the Conference in 2001–02. He was also a regular member of the side that earned top-eight finishes in the Isthmian League Premier Division in 2002–03 and 2003–04.

Having played over 200 games for the Missioners, Mark moved to Cambridge City in the summer of 2005, and his seven goals from 34 starts brought him to the attention of several Conference clubs. In May 2006 he joined Aldershot Town and was a regular in the side that reached the FA Cup third round for the first time in the club's history and achieved a ninth-place finish in the Conference National.

Mark made his England National Game XI debut against the Republic of Ireland in May 2007 and was part of the squad that went on to win that year's Four Nations Tournament. After just one season at the Rec, Mark signed for Stevenage Borough, where he was unfortunate to miss four months of the season (primarily due to a thigh injury). Mark's disappointment was compounded by the fact that he was released at the end of the season, but he soon found a new club as he was snapped up by Grays Athletic.

Paul Moody — Forward

Born: 13 June 1967, Portsmouth.

Aldershot Town FC record:

Debut:	v Hitchin Town (a), Isthmian League Premier Division, 17 August 2002.
Last appearance:	v Eastleigh (h), Hampshire Senior Cup quarter-final, 28 January 2003.
Appearances:	23 + 3
Goals:	10

Playing career:

Challengers, Fareham Town, Waterlooville (August 1989), Southampton (July 1991), Reading (1ML, December 1992), Oxford United (February 1994), Fulham (July 1997), Millwall (July 1999), Oxford United (September 2001), Aldershot Town (July 2002), Gosport Borough (June 2003).

Paul has made 288 FA Premier League and Football League appearances, scoring 106 goals.

Representative honours:

Isthmian League XI.

Club honours:

Division Two (Millwall 2000–01), Isthmian League Premier Division (Aldershot Town 2002–03).

Paul was a big, 6ft 3in centre-forward who was a handful for opposing defenders. Having played for local league sides, he joined Waterlooville in August 1989 for a fee of £4,000 and proceeded to finish as the top scorer in two seasons (28 goals in 1989–90 and 25 goals in 1990–91) and win successive Player of the Year awards.

In July 1991 Fareham made a tidy profit when Paul made a £50,000 leap into Division One with Southampton, but the move never really worked out – in his near three seasons at The Dell, he made just 14 appearances in all competitions and failed to score.

In February 1994 Paul joined Oxford United for £60,000 and proceeded to score eight goals in 15 games, which gave him the top scorer's trophy, but he could not prevent the club from being relegated out of Division One. By the summer of 1997 Paul's goalscoring ability had increased his value, and Fulham parted with a then record £200,000 to bring him to Craven Cottage. It proved money well-spent, as he found the back of the net 15 times that season as the West Londoners reached the Division Two Play-off semi-finals.

Although Fulham were to be crowned Division Two champions in 1998–99, the season brought early heartache for Paul, as he sustained a broken leg against Stoke City in the September. This kept him out of action until the last week of the season, but he ended the campaign on a high, coming on as a second-half substitute and scoring a hat-trick in 13 minutes to secure a 3–0 victory over Preston North End! That was Paul's last contribution at Craven Cottage, as he was allowed to join Millwall for £140,000 that summer.

He scored 11 goals in the 1999–2000 season as the Lions reached the Division Two Play-off semi-finals before losing out to Wigan Athletic. The 2000–01 season was more successful, as his 13 goals helped steer the club to the Division Two title.

Paul returned to Oxford (now in Division Three) before joining Aldershot Town in July 2002, but he failed to live up to the expectations that his excellent pre-Shots career had generated. Injury caused him to struggle to perform consistently, and his only notable achievement while with the Shots was scoring the club's fastest-ever penalty (55 seconds against Grays Athletic in the September).

Having made enough appearances to qualify for an Isthmian League Premier Division-winners' medal, Paul left the Rec in February 2003. Shortly afterwards, he was the subject of an unsuccessful approach by Winchester City, but he had decided he was going to retire. He reversed this decision in June 2003 and signed for Gosport Borough, but he picked up a calf injury in pre-season training and then broke two ribs on his debut in the August, which forced him to wait nearly four months to play his second game. He played sporadically during the remainder of the season before finally retiring in the summer of 2004. Paul is now a qualified interior designer and makes his living buying and renovating properties, as well as running his own tanning, fitness and holistic studio.

Andy Mumford — Midfielder

Born: 18 June 1981, Neath.

Aldershot Town FC record:

Debut: v Dagenham and Redbridge (a), Conference, 26 December 2003.
Last appearance: v Barnet (h), Conference, 6 February 2004.
Appearances: 6
Goals: 1

Playing career:
Llanelli (March 1999), Swansea City (June 2000), Llanelli (1ML, 2000–01 season), Haverfordwest County (1ML, November 2000), Port Talbot Athletic (3ML, February 2001), Merthyr Tydfil (6ML, November 2001), Oxford United (trial, July 2003), Newport County (3ML, September 2003), Aldershot Town (2ML, December 2003), Aldershot Town (trial, July 2004), Grimsby Town (trial, July 2004), Port Talbot Town (August 2004), Aberystwyth Town (October 2004), Port Talbot Town (July 2006), Llanelli (January 2007).
Andy has made 62 Football League appearances, scoring six goals.

Representative honours:
English and Welsh Colleges, Wales Schoolboys, Wales Youth, Wales Under-21s (four caps).

Club honours:
Welsh Premier League (Llanelli 2007–08), Welsh League Cup (Llanelli 2008).

Andy is an accomplished ball-winning central-midfielder who overcame diabetes in order to achieve his ambition of being a professional footballer. Following a brief spell at Llanelli as a 17-year-old, he joined Swansea City and spent his early years there, being loaned back to Llanelli as well as having temporary spells elsewhere. On his return to the Vetch Field, his passing ability and usefulness at free-kicks earned him a place in the first team, and he grabbed his opportunity with both hands and played 24 games for the Swans the following season, as well as appearing for the Welsh Under-21s and winning the Player of the Year award.

Andy trialled at Oxford United and was loaned to Newport County before joining Aldershot Town on the same basis in December 2003. He made a scoring debut against Dagenham and Redbridge, and his competitiveness enabled him to fit effortlessly into the Shots' midfield. He was released by Swansea in the summer of 2004 and returned to the Rec for a trial but looked a shadow of the previous season's loanee and was not offered a deal. He had stints at a number of clubs before beginning his third spell at Llanelli in January 2007 and helping the club gain a third-place finish in that season's Welsh Premier League. He later scored in the 6–6 aggregate draw against Lithuanian side FK Vetra Vilnius in the 2007 Intertoto Cup – a result that saw the Reds eliminated on the away goals rule.

The 2007–08 season proved to a busy one for both club and player, as his 10 goals in 38 appearances helped Llanelli win the Welsh Premier League title. The Reds also won the Welsh League Cup for the first time in their history (beating Rhyl in the Final) but lost to Newport County in the FAW Premier League Cup Final and were beaten by Bangor City in an ill-tempered Welsh Cup Final.

Neil Musgrove — Forward

Born: 13 April 1977, Farnham.

Aldershot Town FC record:

Debut: as substitute v Leyton Pennant (h), Isthmian League Division One, 30 September 1995.
Last appearance: v Thame United (h), Isthmian League Division One, 11 February 1997.
Appearances: 6 + 5
Goals: 1

Playing career:
AFC Bournemouth (schoolboy), Farnham Town (youth), Torquay United (youth trial), Shrewsbury Town (youth

trial), Aldershot Town (youth trial), Northampton Town (trainee, July 1993), Aldershot Town (September 1995), Fleet Town (2ML, March 1997), Fleet Town (summer 1997), Molesey (February 1998), Fleet Town (July 2001), Sandhurst Town (August 2002), Hartley Wintney (summer 2003), Ash United (October 2003), Wrecclesham (summer 2004).

Representative honours:
Aldershot, Farnborough and District Schoolboys.

Club honours:
Aldershot and District League Senior Division (Wrecclesham 2007–08), Aldershot and District League Cup (Wrecclesham 2008 [unused substitute]).

Neil played schoolboy football for AFC Bournemouth and youth football for local side Farnham Town. He then had various youth trials before signing on as a trainee with Northampton Town in July 1993. Unfortunately, he was never offered the chance to turn full professional by the Cobblers and was released in the summer of 1995.

He joined the Shots in the September but made less than a dozen appearances in nearly two seasons at the Rec. He saw out the tail end of the 1996–97 season on loan at Fleet Town before joining permanently that summer. He joined Molesey in February 1998 but rejoined Fleet in July 2001 and was a member of the side that gained promotion from the Wessex League to the Southern League Eastern Division that season.

Neil later played elsewhere before joining Aldershot and District League side Wrecclesham in the summer of 2004. He contributed three goals as Wrecclesham won the Senior Division and League Cup double in 2007–08, beating Sandhurst Devels to win the latter competition.

Tarkan Mustafa — Right-back/Midfielder

Born: 28 August 1973, Islington.

Aldershot Town FC record:

Debut:	v Hereford United (h), Conference National, 30 January 2005.
Last appearance:	v Basingstoke Town (a), Hampshire Senior Cup quarter-final, 14 January 2006.
Appearances:	22 + 6

Playing career:
Norwich City (youth), Leyton (October 1993), Clapton, Wimbledon (trial, March 1995), Kettering Town (July 1995), Barnet (August 1997), Kingstonian (August 1998), Leyton Orient (trial, May 2000), Rushden and Diamonds (June 2000), Coventry City (trial, December 2002), Doncaster Rovers (1ML, December 2002), Dagenham and Redbridge (February 2003), Hornchurch (May 2004), Peterborough United (trial, December 2004), Aldershot Town (January 2005), Billericay Town (1ML, October 2005), Lewes (January 2006), Worthing (February 2006), Thurrock (September 2006), Eastleigh (November 2006), Worthing (August 2007), East Thurrock United (October 2007), Braintree Town (November 2007), Redbridge (January 2008).
Tarkan has made 45 Football League appearances, scoring one goal.

Representative honours:
FA XI, England Semi-Professional XI (two caps).

Club honours:
FA Trophy (Kingstonian 1999, 2000), Conference (Rushden and Diamonds 2000–01), Division Three (Rushden and Diamonds 2002–03).

Tarkan is primarily a right-back, but he can also play as a right-sided midfielder and has even been known to play as a winger. He played youth-team football at Norwich City before tasting senior football and then having a couple of seasons in the Conference with Kettering Town, where his ability to defend and embark on attacking runs led to a move into the Football League with Barnet.

Tarkan made his debut for the Bees as a substitute against Exeter City in August 1997 but played less than a dozen games over the season. In August 1998 he joined Conference new boys Kingstonian, where he was an FA Trophy-winner twice – he scored the only goal of the game in the Wembley victory against Forest Green Rovers in 1999 and also played in the victory over Kettering the following year. That latter season also saw him voted into the Conference Team of the Year. He left Kingsmeadow shortly after, trialling at Leyton Orient before signing for Rushden and Diamonds.

Tarkan made his England Semi-Professional XI debut against Wales in February 2001. Furthermore, he missed just one league game as the Diamonds won the Conference title, thus securing promotion into the Football League for the first time in their history. He was voted into the Conference Team of the Year for the second successive season, and he started Rushden's first-ever game in Division Three against York City. He went on to play in just over half of the club's games that season as they attained a highly commendable sixth-place finish before losing the Play-off Final to Cheltenham Town.

Tarkan left Nene Park in February 2003, dropping back down into the Conference with Dagenham and Redbridge. At the end of that season, he was part of history, having played in the inaugural Conference Play-off Final against Doncaster Rovers at Stoke City's Britannia Stadium. Tarkan had scored an equaliser to take the game into extra-time, but the Daggers lost 3–2, unfortunately. That Final is also unique in British footballing terms, as it is the only instance of a club being promoted by virtue of a 'golden goal'.

In May 2004 Tarkan followed Daggers boss Garry Hill to Hornchurch; however, by the November, the club were in serious financial trouble following the collapse of their main sponsor (Carthium Limited), and Tarkan was one of several players who were released. A trial at Peterborough United preceded him joining Aldershot Town in January 2005, and he played in all but three of the Shots' remaining games as they reached that season's Play-off semi-finals.

Tarkan's form dipped the following season, and he struggled to command a regular place so was loaned out before leaving for spells elsewhere, including Eastleigh, Worthing, East Thurrock United, Braintree Town and Redbridge. Despite being docked a point for fielding an ineligible player, Redbridge still managed to finish the season in third place in Isthmian League Division One North. They lost the subsequent Play-off Final to Canvey Island by way of a penalty shoot-out.

Joe Nartey — Forward

Born: 28 May 1976, Accra, Ghana.

Aldershot Town FC record:

Debut:	v Billericay Town (h), Isthmian League Division One, 28 March 1998.
Last appearance:	v Sutton United (h), Isthmian League Charity Shield, 6 December 1999.
Appearances:	41 + 35
Goals:	27

Playing career:

Hillingdon Borough, Hayes (August 1994), Harrow Borough (summer 1996), Chertsey Town (November 1996), Aldershot Town (March 1998), Billericay Town (1ML, December 1998), Chesham United (December 1999), Sutton United (July 2000), Boreham Wood (October 2000), Maidenhead United (November 2000), Dulwich Hamlet (February 2001), St Albans City (trial, July 2001), Enfield (July 2001), Hendon (November 2001), Hemel Hempstead Town (January 2002), Hornchurch (January 2003), Barking and East Ham United (March 2003), Maidenhead United (March 2003), Leyton (July 2003), Waltham Forest (September 2003), Erith and Belvedere (August 2004), Hendon (January 2005), Windsor and Eton (February 2005).

Club honours:

Middlesex Senior Cup (Hayes 1996), Isthmian League Charity Shield (Aldershot Town 1999), Hampshire Senior Cup (Aldershot Town 1999).

Post-playing coaching/management career:

Reserve-team manager of Waltham Forest (August 2007).

Joe was a striker with bags of pace, who spent the early part of his career with Hillingdon Borough, Hayes and Harrow Borough. He signed for Chertsey Town in November 1996 and was a member of the side that was relegated from the Isthmian League Premier Division that season. Both club and player improved the following season and, with the Curfews on course for a mid-table finish, Joe joined Aldershot Town for a fee of £4,000 in March 1998. However, he still finished that season as the Surrey club's top scorer. He scored just the once for the Shots that season, but that solitary goal meant he became the first player to score for and against Aldershot Town – while with Chertsey – in the same season.

By the start of the 1998–99 season, Joe's all-round game had improved and he scored 25 goals in all competitions, including five at Bishop's Stortford in September 1998 – a club first – and he nearly equalled that record in the home return later in the season. A slight dip in form saw Joe join Billericay Town on loan in the December as part of the deal that brought Leon Gutzmore to the Rec. Even though he continued to score goals on his return to the Rec, he looked a shadow of the player that the Rec faithful once knew.

Joe scored a solitary goal the following season before joining Chesham United for £3,500 in December 1999, scoring just twice more as third place in the Isthmian League Premier Division was secured (seven points behind the second-placed Shots). This signalled a time in Joe's career where injury was commonplace, and his goals dried up.

Joe had spells (some very brief) at several Isthmian League clubs plus Southern League Eastern Division side Erith and Belvedere before retiring in the summer of 2005. It is not known what Joe did immediately following his retirement, but he did have a spell as reserve-team manager at Waltham Forest during the 2007–08 season.

Ricky Newman — Midfielder

Born: 5 August 1970, Guildford.

Aldershot Town FC record:

Debut:	v Gravesend and Northfleet (h), Conference National, 12 August 2006.
Appearances:	69 + 14
Goals:	2

Playing career:

Crystal Palace (from trainee, January 1988), Maidstone United (2ML, February 1992), Millwall (July 1995), Reading (2ML, March 2000), Reading (July 2000), Brentford (June 2005), Aldershot Town (July 2006).
Ricky has made 359 Football League appearances, scoring 13 goals.

Club honours:

Division One (Crystal Palace 1993–94), Hampshire Senior Cup (Aldershot Town 2007), Setanta Shield (Aldershot Town 2008), Conference Premier (Aldershot Town 2007–08).

Ricky is a tough-tackling defensive midfielder whose no-nonsense approach has made him a valuable part of all the sides he has played for. Unfortunately, it has also had the adverse effect of earning him several suspensions. Ricky began as a trainee at Crystal Palace and signed full professional forms in January 1988. He was a regular in the reserves and was later loaned to Maidstone United, where he made his professional debut against Northampton Town in March 1992. He made his first appearance for Palace against Everton in January 1993 in the inaugural FA Premier League season, making one further appearance that season as the club were relegated.

The following season, Ricky played just under a dozen games as the Eagles came straight back up as Division One champions. Unfortunately, 1994–95 saw them go straight back down again, and Ricky was a member of the Palace side that was beaten by Manchester United in that season's FA Cup semi-final replay. He also helped the club reach the semi-finals of the League Cup that season.

In July 1995 Millwall paid £500,000 to bring Ricky to the Den, and he missed only a handful of games as they suffered relegation from Division One. The next season saw the club struggle through severe financial problems, but Ricky and a number of other players stayed faithful to the club when it would have been easy for them to walk away. Ricky played in Millwall's first appearance in a Wembley Final as they went down to a last-minute Wigan Athletic goal in the 1999 Football League Trophy.

Ricky joined Reading in July 2000 and had marshalled the midfield masterfully in all but five of the club's League games when, in April 2001, disaster struck – he damaged his cruciate ligament against Walsall and was out of action for nearly 18 months. After two more seasons at the Madejski Stadium, Ricky left and joined Brentford in June 2005. He was a virtual ever present after his October debut, and third place in League One was secured before the club lost the resultant Play-off semi-final to Swansea City.

Ricky was released by Brentford at the end of the season and came to Aldershot Town as a trialist, soon impressing enough to be offered a contract. He made his debut on the opening day of 2006–07 and was promptly sent off, although the red card was later rescinded. Later that season, he played in the FA Cup third-round defeat at Blackpool – the furthest the club had ever gone in the competition.

Ricky has always 'given his all' for the Shots, as well as showing his versatility by ably deputising in the centre of defence. He missed the start of the 2007–08 season as a result of a knee operation but then played an important part in the club reaching the FA Trophy semi-finals, where they lost to Ebbsfleet United. He captained the side to victory over Rushden and Diamonds in the Setanta Shield Final and played in more than half of the season's League games as the Shots were crowned Conference Premier champions. A couple of weeks after the end of the season, Ricky was given the role of player-coach at the Rec, with his main remit being to run the reserve side.

Andy Nunn — Utility

Born: 24 March 1965, Burton-on-Trent.

Aldershot Town FC record:

Debut:	as substitute v Hertford Town (a), Isthmian League Division Three, 10 October 1992.
Last appearance:	v Worthing (a), Isthmian League Full Members' Cup second round, 2 February 1999.
Appearances:	100 + 21
Goals:	8

Playing career:

Farnham Town (April 1983), Wokingham Town (January 1987), Holbeach United (February 1989), Wokingham Town (dual registered, April 1989), Sutton Rovers (August 1989), Wokingham Town (November 1989), Farnham Town (August 1991), Sutton Rovers (October 1991), Mablethorpe Athletic (September 1992), Aldershot Town (October 1992).

Club honours:

Isthmian League Division Three (Aldershot Town 1992–93).

Post-playing coaching/management career:

Youth-team manager of Aldershot Town (summer 1996), reserve-team manager of Aldershot Town (summer 1997), reserve-team manager of Farnborough Town (August 1999), manager of Farnham Town (June 2000).

Andy is the son-in-law of ex-Aldershot Town groundsman Dave Tomlinson. He is also the brother-in-law of Dave's two sons – ex-Shots player Chris and Football League referee Steve. He started out as a left-back at Farnham Town before moving into midfield and then onto the wing.

In January 1987 Andy moved to Wokingham Town, where he played as a striker, scoring on his debut against Thatcham Town. He was also part of the side that reached the FA Trophy semi-final in 1987–88 before leaving in November and moving up to Lincolnshire to play for United Counties League side Holbeach United. He was a member of the side that reached the last 16 of the FA Vase in 1988–89 and was also dual registered with former club Wokingham for the last month of the season.

Over the next three seasons, Andy had a couple of spells elsewhere before signing for Aldershot Town in October 1992. During his time at the Rec, Andy worked for the Royal Mail and was North Hampshire's version of the 'Flying Postman' – a nickname famously attributed to Coventry City's John Williams around the same time. His first two seasons with the Shots saw successive promotions achieved before he picked up an achilles injury in January 1996, which forced him into semi-retirement. Strangely, this had a positive consequence, as it facilitated a move into management – he was appointed manager of the Shots' youth team prior to the start of the 1996–97 season and had three successful seasons in the job. His last two seasons in that role were combined with managing the Shots' reserve side.

Having made just six more appearances for the Shots during his semi-retirement, Andy finally hung up his boots in the summer of 1999 and became reserve-team manager at neighbouring Farnborough Town. In June 2000 he returned to Farnham as manager and stayed at the Memorial Ground until he resigned in September 2003. Andy is currently Aldershot Town's head groundsman (a position he assumed in April 2006), having previously been on his father-in-law's groundstaff.

Chris Nurse — Midfielder/Winger

Born: 7 May 1984, Croydon.

Aldershot Town FC record:

Debut:	v Tamworth (h), Conference National, 13 August 2005.
Appearances:	1

Playing career:

Kingstonian (summer 2002), Sutton United (February 2004), Kingstonian (1ML, September 2004), Dulwich Hamlet (1ML, December 2004), Colchester United (trial, July 2005), Aldershot Town (M, August 2005), Bristol Rovers (trial, September 2005), Moor Green (October 2005), Hinckley United (May 2006), Tamworth (September 2007).

Chris is the younger brother of ex-Stevenage Borough forward Jon Nurse. He started as a youth player at Kingstonian, where he was a regular in the reserves, but made less than a dozen first-team appearances before joining Sutton United in February 2004. Chris helped push the club to the runners'-up spot behind Canvey Island in that season's Isthmian League Premier Division.

The following season, Chris was in and out of the Us' side and had various loan spells before he joined Aldershot Town on a monthly contract in August 2005. However, his stay at the Rec was very brief, as he left to study at Birmingham University shortly after playing in the opening game of the 2005–06 season. Chris trialled at Bristol Rovers before joining Moor Green in the October and played in over half of the club's League games as they achieved their best-ever finish of ninth in the Conference North.

That summer, he joined divisional rivals Hinckley United, where he (again) helped a club achieve a best-ever League position – the Knitters finished in fourth spot and lost the subsequent Play-off Final to Farsley Celtic by the odd goal in seven, with the winner coming by way of a last-minute penalty. Chris left Leicester Road in September 2007 to join Tamworth in a deal that took Lambs midfielder Kyle Storer in the opposite direction. Chris ended the season having scored six goals in 22 appearances as the Lambs finished in 15th spot in the Conference North.

John Nutter — Left-back/Midfielder

Born: 13 June 1982, Taplow.

Aldershot Town FC record:

Debut:	v Enfield (h), Isthmian League Premier Division, 18 August 2001.
Last appearance:	as substitute v Hereford United (a), Conference Play-off semi-final second leg, 3 May 2004.
Appearances:	46 + 33
Goals:	6

Playing career:

Blackburn Rovers (trainee, July 1998), Wycombe Wanderers (trainee, January 2001), Aldershot Town (May 2001), St Albans City (1ML, February 2002), Gravesend and Northfleet (1ML, November 2002), Grays Athletic (1ML,

January 2003), Grays Athletic (June 2004), Stevenage Borough (June 2006), Gillingham (November 2007). John has made 25 Football League appearances, scoring one goal.

Representative honours:
England National Game XI (three caps).

Club honours:
Hampshire Senior Cup (Aldershot Town 2002, 2003 [unused substitute in both Finals]), Isthmian League Premier Division (Aldershot Town 2002–03), Isthmian League Charity Shield (Aldershot Town 2003), Conference South (Grays Athletic 2004–05), FA Trophy (Grays Athletic 2005, 2006; Stevenage Borough 2007).

John is a left-back/midfielder who began as a trainee at Blackburn Rovers. He joined Wycombe Wanderers on the same basis in January 2001, joining Aldershot Town that summer. His ability to defend coupled with a confidence when dribbling made him a crowd favourite. Scoring a 40-yard screamer against Purfleet at the Rec during the 2001–02 season also helped.

John's progress was supplemented with loan spells and these bore fruit, as he helped the Shots win the Isthmian League Premier Division in 2002–03. He was a playing substitute in the club's first-ever Conference game against Accrington Stanley on the opening day of the following season, as well as being in the sides that lost to Hednesford Town in that season's FA Trophy semi-finals and to Shrewsbury Town in the Conference Play-off Final.

In June 2004 John moved to Grays Athletic and was an integral part of the side that completed the Conference South and FA Trophy double that season. The following season, he performed consistently and was part of the side that retained the FA Trophy by beating Woking. Shortly after the Final, John made his debut for the England National Game XI against the Republic of Ireland. He played two further internationals (against Wales and Scotland) before following manager Mark Stimson from Grays to Stevenage Borough in June 2006.

In November 2007 John's desire to play at a higher level (there were suggestions that he could do so quite comfortably) came to fruition when he joined Gillingham on a month's loan, becoming one of ex-Stevenage boss Mark Stimson's first signings in the process. This move became permanent, with the joint fee for John and his Stevenage teammate Adam Miller being a reported £65,000. John played 24 games and scored one goal in the 2007–08 season as relegation from League One was endured by virtue of a 22nd-place finish.

Damilola Odimosu — Left-back/Right-back

Born: 23 March 1990, Camden Town.

Aldershot Town FC record:

Debut:	as substitute v Eastleigh (a), Hampshire Senior Cup quarter-final, 15 March 2007.
Appearances:	0 + 1

Playing career:
Aldershot Town (youth), Grays Athletic (youth).

Damilola was a youth-team player when he made his sole first-team appearance for the Shots. He left the Rec in July 2007 and joined the youth set-up at Grays Athletic.

Magnus Okuonghae — Centre-back

Born: 16 February 1986, Dingim, Nigeria.

Aldershot Town FC record:

Debut:	v Weymouth (a), Conference National, 15 August 2006.
Last appearance:	v St Albans City (a), Conference National, 19 August 2006.
Appearances:	2

Playing career:
Fulham (youth), Norwich City (youth trial), Leicester City (youth trial), Rushden and Diamonds (from trainee, July 2005), Bishop's Stortford (1ML, November 2004, and 1ML, April 2005), Gillingham (trial, July 2006),

Aldershot Town (NC, July 2006), St Albans City (NC, August 2006), Crawley Town (January 2007), Dagenham and Redbridge (May 2007), Weymouth (1ML, February 2008).
Magnus has made 34 Football League appearances, scoring one goal.

Magnus's career began in the youth team at Fulham, and a move to the youth set-up at Rushden and Diamonds came in January 2003. He made his senior debut as a last-minute substitute against Colchester United in November 2003 before a couple of loan spells at Bishop's Stortford.

Magnus signed full professional forms at Nene Park in July 2005 and made 21 League appearances that season, in the side that finished rock bottom of the Football League. Rushden's relegation led to Magnus leaving, and he found his way to the Rec in July 2006 via a trial at Gillingham. However, his stay was brief and, following just two appearances, he signed for St Albans City.

The turn of the year saw him move on to Crawley Town then Football League new boys Dagenham and Redbridge, where he was an unused substitute for their season's opener against Stockport County. The move did not quite work out as Magnus had hoped, and he struggled to hold down a starting place at Victoria Road so was loaned to Weymouth in February 2008. The Daggers only just avoided dropping straight back out of the Football League, and Weymouth avoided the drop from the Conference Premier by finishing 18th.

Darren O'Neill — Right-back

Born: 12 June 1968, Kingston-upon-Thames.

Aldershot Town FC record:

Debut: v Egham Town (h), Isthmian League Division Two, 21 August 1993.
Last appearance: v Wokingham Town (h), Isthmian League Division One, 16 December 1995.
Appearances: 55 + 1

Playing career:
Weybridge Town, Wokingham Town (July 1989), Crawley Town (June 1992), Aldershot Town (June 1993), Kingstonian (August 1994), Wealdstone (March 1995), Aldershot Town (August 1995), Bracknell Town (December 1995), Walton and Hersham (January 1999), Staines Town (February 1999; left March 1999).

Darren was a tall right-back who spent the early part of his career at Weybridge Town before joining Wokingham Town in July 1989 and playing a part in achieving a runners'-up spot (behind Slough Town) in that season's Isthmian League Premier Division.

He played for Crawley Town in the 1992–93 season, and it was from there that Darren joined Aldershot Town in June 1993. The club enjoyed a successful second season in existence as he helped the club reach the FA Vase quarter-final and gain promotion from Isthmian League Division Two. Unfortunately for Darren, the arrival of right-backs Stewart Mitchell and Simon Turner in August 1994 signalled the end of his time at the Rec, and he was sold to Kingstonian for £3,000 (a Shots record at the time).

He then had a brief spell at Wealdstone before returning to the Rec in August 1995 but made less than a dozen appearances before joining Bracknell Town four months later. He spent just over three years at Larges Lane before leaving in January 1999, having month-long spells at Walton and Hersham and Staines Town, leaving the latter in March 1999. No further details of Darren's career are known, although it is believed that he has spent some time living in Belgium.

Curtis Osano — Right-back/Centre-back/Midfielder

Born: 8 March 1987, Nakuru, Kenya.

Aldershot Town FC record:

Debut: v York City (a), Conference National, 6 October 2006.
Last appearance: v Crawley Town (h), Conference National, 13 January 2007.
Appearances: 11 + 1

Playing career:
Reading (from scholar, July 2006), Aldershot Town (3ML, October 2006), Woking (3ML, January 2007), Rushden and Diamonds (SLL, July 2007).

Curtis can play in central-midfield, at right-back or as a centre-back and is surprisingly quick for such a big man. He was a scholar at Reading and made his senior debut as an extra-time substitute in an FA Cup third-round replay tie against West Bromwich Albion in January 2006. His performances in the reserve side led to him signing a full professional contract six months later, and he then joined Aldershot Town on a three-month loan deal in October 2006 to gain first-team experience.

Curtis put in some solid performances at the Rec before returning to Reading. Two weeks after his last Shots appearance, he made his second senior appearance for the Royals (again as a substitute in an FA Cup tie) before spending the rest of the season on loan at Woking.

In July 2007 Curtis joined Rushden and Diamonds on a season-long loan and played against the Shots in the 2008 Setanta Shield Final. He also missed just four Conference Premier games as the Diamonds finished the campaign in 16th place.

Dave Osgood — Midfielder/Right-back

Born: 6 June 1967, Rustington-on-Sea.

Aldershot Town FC record:

Debut:	v Clapton (h), Isthmian League Division Three, 22 August 1992.
Last appearance:	as substitute v Carshalton Athletic, FA Trophy second qualifying round, 8 November 1997.
Appearances:	152 + 15 (ninth in all-time top 10)
Goals:	38 (10th in all-time top 10)

Playing career:

Brentford (schoolboy), Maidenhead United (summer 1982), Windsor and Eton (summer 1984), Maidenhead United (September 1985), Windsor and Eton (summer 1986), Farnborough Town (October 1988), Basingstoke Town (September 1989), Newbury Town (summer 1990), Windsor and Eton (1990–91 season), Burnham (August 1991), Maidenhead United (February 1992), Aldershot Town (August 1992), Bracknell Town (3ML, February 1996), Bracknell Town (summer 1996), Basingstoke Town (March 1997), Aldershot Town (October 1997), Wrecclesham (December 1997; player-manager from summer 1998), Bracknell Town (July 1999).

Club honours:

Isthmian League Division Three (Aldershot Town 1992–93), Hampshire Senior Cup (Basingstoke Town 1997).

Dave, a midfield hard man, is the nephew of the late ex-Chelsea and England striker Peter Osgood and the cousin of ex-Shots 'keeper Steve Osgood. His early career consisted of schoolboy football at Brentford plus two spells at both Maidenhead United and Windsor and Eton before he signed for Farnborough Town in October 1988.

Dave's ability to distribute a defence-splitting pass greatly contributed to Boro's promotion to the Conference for the first time in the club's history at the end of the 1988–89 season. He later moved to Basingstoke Town, Newbury Town and Windsor again before moving on to Burnham and returning to Maidenhead. He joined Aldershot Town in August 1992, and his hard-tackling style coupled with his ability to lead by example made him the ideal choice to be the first-ever Shots captain. Dave duly wore the armband and the number-eight shirt in the club's first-ever game against Clapton, and his importance to the side was confirmed by the fact he missed just three of the 51 games (in all competitions) that were played in that Isthmian League Division Three-winning season. He also contributed 12 goals during the campaign, with his celebrations seeing him climb the East Bank fencing on more than one occasion.

Dave was a regular inclusion in the Shots side over the next two seasons, and he captained the team that reached the FA Vase quarter-final and gained promotion from Isthmian League Division Two in 1993–94. He also led them to a commendable fourth place in their first-ever season in Isthmian League Division One.

Dave's involvement during the 1995–96 season was far more limited than in the previous three seasons, and he spent the last three months of the campaign at Bracknell Town. The summer saw him leave the Rec and sign permanently at Larges Lane before having return spells at both Basingstoke (where he won the Hampshire Senior Cup in 1997) and Aldershot and then dropping into local league football at Wrecclesham in December 1997. He was player-manager at Riverdale for the 1998–99 season and returned to newly relegated Bracknell after the season's end.

Dave brought experience to Larges Lane during a time of change and consolidation, and his performances in a season that saw the club finish ninth were rewarded by him winning Player of the Year in 2000. Dave retired in November 2001 and currently runs his own carpentry and roofing business.

Steve Osgood **Goalkeeper**

Born: 20 January 1962, Bracknell.

Aldershot Town FC record:

Debut: v Hendon (a), Isthmian League Cup third round, 15 December 1992.

Appearances: 1

Playing career:

Chelsea (youth), Portsmouth (from apprentice, April 1979), Farnborough Town (November 1984), Newbury Town (April 1986), Aldershot FC (February 1989), Harrow Borough (1ML, March 1989), Chertsey Town (3ML, June 1989), Burnham (3ML, December 1990), Andover (3ML, January 1991), Fleet Town (1ML, March 1991), Molesey (6ML, September 1991), Fleet Town (April 1992), Grays Athletic (August 1992), Molesey (6ML, September 1992), Windsor and Eton (2MDRL, October 1992), Aldershot Town (STL, December 1992), Wokingham Town (February 1993), Farnborough Town (August 1993), Leatherhead (November 1993), Hampton (January 1994), Wokingham Town (August 1994), Dorking (player-manager) (June 1996).

Steve has made six Football League appearances.

Steve was a youth-team player at Chelsea before becoming an apprentice at Portsmouth and signing full professional forms in April 1979. However, he never made the first team at Fratton Park and eventually left in November 1984 to play for Farnborough Town, where he made three appearances as the Isthmian League Division One title was won.

Steve went on to play for Newbury Town for nearly three years before arriving at Aldershot FC in February 1989, making his professional debut against Fulham in the April. He was not first choice at the Rec and the fact that the club had no reserve side meant that he had to be loaned out to several clubs in order to get match practice. The club's plight towards the end of the 1991–92 season saw Steve play five League games, including their last-ever game at Cardiff City, before finishing the season at Fleet Town. He later joined Grays Athletic, Windsor and Eton and Aldershot Town on a short-term loan. His sole appearance back at the Rec was actually the first-ever instance of cousins playing in the same game for the club.

Steve then played for a handful of clubs before making a foray into management at Dorking in June 1996. However, Steve's time at the Meadowbank Stadium was made difficult by financial problems, so it was no real surprise that the club were relegated from Isthmian League Division Two at the end of his first season. Unfortunately, they fared no better in 1997–98 and he left in November 1998. Steve currently runs a door security company in Bracknell and can list the funerals of Charlie and Reggie Kray as occasions for which he has provided staff.

Andy Pape — Goalkeeper

Born: 22 March 1962, Hammersmith.

Aldershot Town FC record:

Debut: v Lymington and New Milton (a), FA Cup fourth qualifying round, 16 October 1999.
Last appearance: v Hitchin Town (a), Isthmian League Premier Division, 3 April 2001.
Appearances: 78

Playing career:

Queen's Park Rangers (from apprentice, July 1980), Wimbledon (1ML, November 1980), Charlton Athletic (January 1981), Ikast FS (Denmark, August 1981), Feltham (February 1983), Crystal Palace (February 1983), Harrow Borough (August 1983), Enfield (July 1985), Barnet (August 1991), Dagenham and Redbridge (STL, September 1992), Woking (STL, October 1992), Harrow Borough (6ML, November 1992), Enfield (player-coach, September 1993), Sutton United (February 1999), Aldershot Town (October 1999), Harrow Borough (August 2002), Sutton United (September 2002).
Andy has made 41 Football League appearances.

Representative honours:

FA XI, Isthmian League XI, England Semi-Professional XI (15 caps), Civil Service UK XI.

Club honours:

Isthmian League Premier Division (Harrow Borough 1983–84; Enfield 1994–95), Alliance Premier League (Enfield 1985–86), FA Trophy (Enfield 1988), Middlesex Senior Cup (Enfield 1989, 1991, 1998; Harrow Borough 1993), Hertfordshire Senior Cup (Barnet 1993), Middlesex Charity Cup (Harrow Borough 1993), Hampshire Senior Cup (Aldershot Town 2000).

Post-playing coaching/management career:

Assistant manager-goalkeeping coach at Hendon (February 2005).

Andy was a vastly experienced 'keeper who began his career as a schoolboy at Queen's Park Rangers, making his senior debut (and sole appearance) against Charlton Athletic in April 1980 while still an apprentice. He signed full professional forms three months later and had spells at many clubs, including Charlton Athletic, Denmark's Ikast FS, where he took part in the 1982 Intertoto Cup, Crystal Palace and Harrow Borough, where he quickly matured into a reliable and commanding last line of defence. He was a key member of the side that reached the FA Cup second round in 1983–84, and his first season at Earlsmead culminated in him having an Isthmian League Premier Division title-winners' medal. However, in order to avoid any potential financial hardship, the club declined the resultant promotion into the Alliance Premier League (an early incarnation of the Conference).

Andy's performances continued to improve, and this led to him making his England Semi-Professional XI debut as a substitute against Wales in March 1985. He eventually won 15 international caps, which currently puts him in joint-fifth place in the all-time list, along with Antone Joseph, Paul Shirtliff and Brian Thompson.

Andy eventually made the step up into the Alliance Premier League when he signed for newly promoted Enfield in July 1985. At the time they were a force to be reckoned with, and Andy was central to them winning the League and reaching the FA Trophy semi-finals in 1985–86 and beating Telford (in a replay) to win the FA Trophy in 1988. Andy remained at Southbury Road through their subsequent struggles, and he was instrumental in the club nearly bouncing straight back up, but they had to settle for the runners'-up spot (behind Redbridge Forest) in the Isthmian League Premier Division.

In August 1991 Andy finally returned to the Football League when Barnet paid £10,000 to bring him in as cover for future Shots 'keeper Gary Phillips, who had been injured in a League Cup tie against Brentford. Andy played in all but six of the Bees' League games that season as they reached the Division Four Play-off semi-finals before losing to Blackpool. The following season, however, was a different story, and his only first-team football came during loan spells elsewhere.

Andy returned to Enfield in September 1993 as player-coach and was instrumental in making them one of the strongest non-League sides around, winning the Premier Division title in 1994–95; however, they were denied their rightful promotion due to the Conference committee being dissatisfied with the club's finances. Cup giant-killings were also a speciality of the Es during that period, and Cardiff City, Torquay United and Peterborough United were all dispatched in the FA Cup.

In February 1999, having racked up an amazing club record of 570 appearances, Andy left Southbury Road and joined Sutton United. He missed the start of the 1999–2000 season due to an operation on a troublesome achilles tendon, but he subsequently signed for Aldershot Town in the October. The wealth of experience that Andy brought with him helped the club finish that season as runners-up to Dagenham and Redbridge in the Isthmian League Premier Division. His Shots career was ended by a broken shoulder sustained in the League game at Hitchin Town in April 2001, and he subsequently retired that summer.

Andy came out of retirement in August 2002, but he continued to be plagued by his shoulder injury and so played what was to be his last game in January 2003 for Sutton. Andy remained hopeful of playing again, but it was not to be and he retired that summer. The injury has subsequently required three operations to fix.

In February 2005 Andy took on the role of assistant manager/goalkeeping coach with Gary McCann at Hendon, a position he stayed in for 12 months before departing Claremont Road. Andy has not been involved in the game since and currently works for Her Majesty's Revenue and Customs.

Adam Parker — Midfielder

Born: 14 July 1975, Aldershot.

Aldershot Town FC record:

Debut: v Grays Athletic (a), Isthmian League Premier Division, 15 September 2001
Last appearance: v Cheshunt (a), Isthmian League Cup second round, 19 November 2002.
Appearances: 40 + 14
Goals: 13

Playing career:
Hatfield Town (July 1990), Stevenage Borough (summer 1993), Barnet (trial, January 1994), Luton Town (trial, February 1994), Hitchin Town (September 1995), Aldershot Town (September 2001), Boreham Wood (2ML, November 2002), Hitchin Town (March 2003), Braintree Town (December 2003), St Albans City (February 2004), Thurrock (December 2004), Billericay Town (1ML, September 2005), Hitchin Town (DR, February 2006), AFC Hornchurch (June 2006), Hitchin Town (DR, October 2006), Chesham United (DR, September 2007).

Representative honours:
Isthmian League XI, Middlesex Wanderers (only Aldershot Town player to do so).

Club honours:
Hertfordshire Senior Cup (Hitchin Town 1997), Hertfordshire Charity Cup (Hitchin Town 2000), Hampshire Senior Cup (Aldershot Town 2002), Isthmian League Premier Division (Aldershot Town 2002–03), Isthmian League Premier Division Play-off Final (St Albans City 2004), Isthmian League Division One North (AFC Hornchurch 2006–07), Berks and Bucks Senior Cup (Chesham United 2008).

Adam is an attacking midfielder who arrived at the Rec with a good goalscoring reputation, having scored 99 goals in six seasons at Hitchin Town. He started out at Hatfield Town as a 15-year-old before signing for Stevenage Borough in the summer of 1993. He forced his way into the Stevenage side during their first-ever season in the Conference (1994–95) and played in just under half of the games during that campaign.

In September 1995 Adam began his affinity with Hitchin Town, and his regular goalscoring led to him winning the Player of the Year award at Top Field in 1997 and 2000. The 1999–2000 season saw a club-best progression in the FA Trophy as the Canaries reached the fifth round before losing to Forest Green Rovers. Adam was appointed captain the following season and finished as top scorer (28 goals).

Adam's combative style of play often led to him falling foul of referees, and that was never more evident than when he earned the unusual distinction of being sent off while playing both against and for Aldershot Town within the space of seven days! His dismissal in the latter game earned him the unenviable accolade of becoming the only Shots substitute to be sent off on his debut.

Adam made valuable contributions to various midfield battles, and his strike rate of 12 goals in 39 appearances in the 2001–02 season was reasonable for a midfielder. However, he did not play as regularly the following season – 15 appearances and one goal – and was loaned out, rejoining Hitchin in March 2003. But Adam failed to reproduce the form he showed in his first spell at the club, and subsequently had spells at Braintree Town, St Albans City and Thurrock.

The following season saw him loaned to Billericay Town early on, but he then missed the next four months due to injury. In February 2006 Adam dual registered back at Hitchin before leaving Thurrock that summer. He signed for AFC Hornchurch in the June but was unable to command a regular place by October and so dual registered back at Top Field. However, he made just a handful of appearances before playing his last game in a Hitchin shirt in February 2007. His goal tally for the club currently stands at 110, but who is to say this will not be added to in the future?

Another dual-registration move came in September 2007 when Adam joined Southern League Division One Midlands side Chesham United, and it was with the Generals that he played the majority of his football. With his appearances limited due to suspensions, Adam proceeded to score six goals in all competitions for Chesham as they finished in sixth place in the League, missing out on the Play-offs on goal difference, and beat Wycombe Wanderers to win the Berks and Bucks Cup.

Kevin Parkins — Right-back

Born: 12 December 1960, Plymouth.

Aldershot Town FC record:

Debut: v Clapton (h), Isthmian League Division Three, 22 August 1992.
Last appearance: v Clapton (h), Isthmian League Cup preliminary round, 7 September 1993.
Appearances: 44
Goals: 1

Playing career:

Horsham YMCA (summer 1981), Windsor and Eton (NC, November 1983), DSC Arminia Bielefeld (Germany, summer 1988), Windsor and Eton (October 1989), Aldershot Town (August 1992), Camberley Town (September 1993), Fleet Town (October 1993).

Representative honours:

British Army (200+ games, several as captain), Combined Services (50+ games).

Club honours:

Sussex League Division Two (Horsham YMCA 1982–83), Isthmian League Division Three (Aldershot Town 1992–93), Wessex League (Fleet Town 1994–95).

Kevin was an uncompromising defender who was in the army for the duration of his non-League career, with work commitments making his appearances sporadic. Having played for Horsham YMCA (and won the Sussex League

Division Two title in 1982–83), Kevin moved on to Windsor and Eton and got a chance of FA Cup glory in November 1983 in their second-round tie against AFC Bournemouth. Unfortunately, the south coast side triumphed and progressed to play Manchester United in round three.

Kevin later played for DSC Armenia Bielefeld in Germany and was voted Army Player of the Year in 1988. However, the year ended in disappointment when he broke his leg in the October during an inter-corps match, which resulted in him missing the remainder of the season. Despite this, he remained involved within the army football set-up and coached his unit team (10Tpt Regt RCT) to the Army Cup in 1989. He later spent nearly three seasons back at Windsor, during which he served in the Gulf War in 1990 before signing for Aldershot Town in August 1992.

Kevin wore the number-two shirt in the club's first-ever League game against Clapton, and his fitness levels and competitiveness made him one of the first names on the team sheet. He played solidly throughout the season and contributed greatly to the winning of the Isthmian League Division Three title before having a brief spell at Camberley Town and then signing for Fleet Town. Again, he performed consistently and was a member of the side that won the Wessex League in 1994–95 before leaving and subsequently retiring in the summer of 1996. He left the army in 2001 after 22 years' service and currently lives in Canada, where he works as a plumber.

Andy Parr — Midfielder

Born: 8 October 1966, Reading.

Aldershot Town FC record:

Debut:	v Leyton Pennant (h), Isthmian League Division One, 30 September 1995.
Last appearance:	as substitute v Wokingham Town (h), Isthmian League Division One, 24 April 1997.
Appearances:	91 + 4
Goals:	8

Playing career:

Reading (youth), West Ham United (from apprentice, October 1984), Farnborough Town (summer 1986), Marlow (September 1986), Woking (August 1987), Chertsey Town (summer 1988), Woking (July 1989), Sutton United (June 1992), Kingstonian (October 1992), Newbury Town (August 1993), Aldershot Town (September 1995), Reading Town (August 1997), AFC Wallingford (November 1998).

Representative honours:

England Schoolboys, FA XI.

Club honours:

Isthmian League Cup (Woking 1991), Surrey Senior Cup (Woking 1991), Isthmian League Premier Division (Woking 1991–92), Isthmian League Charity Shield (Woking 1991), Combined Counties Division (AFC Wallingford 2001–02).

Post-playing coaching/management career:

Assistant manager of Wantage Town (May 2005).

Andy was an experienced and versatile central-midfielder who started out as a youth player at Reading, where he captained the Under-15 side. He later joined West Ham United as an apprentice and signed professional forms in October 1984 but never made a senior appearance. He appeared for Farnborough Town, Marlow, Woking, Chertsey Town and Woking again, where he helped the club gain promotion from Isthmian League Division One (as runners-up to Wivenhoe Town) in 1989–90. Unfortunately, Andy missed the Cards' best-ever FA Cup run in 1990–91 as a result of serving a 12-month prison sentence for theft and fraud. However, he did play a part in the winning of the Isthmian League Cup and Surrey Senior Cup double that season.

Having served his time, Andy carried on where he had left off but, following Woking's promotion, was reportedly unable to commit to the travelling that would have been involved in playing Conference football and so left Woking that summer and subsequently played for Sutton United and Kingstonian.

A month after joining the Ks, Andy was involved in FA Cup controversy during the 9–1 thrashing by Peterborough United in a first-round replay. The Ks 'keeper (Adrian Blake) was struck by a coin thrown from the crowd early on in the match, and Andy (who certainly was not the tallest of players!) went in goal following Blake's substitution. The FA later ordered the game to be replayed, and the Posh scraped a 1–0 win.

Andy signed for Newbury Town in August 1993, and his eye for a pass plus his ability to hold the ball when necessary helped the club to attain a club-best progression to the FA Vase quarter-finals and also win the Isthmian League Division Two title in 1993–94. Unfortunately, the momentum did not continue, and Andy joined Aldershot Town in September 1995 following the club's demise.

Aldershot were part way through establishing themselves in Isthmian League Division One, and Andy helped them attain fifth and seventh-place finishes during his two seasons with the club. In August 1997 he left and went on to play for Reading Town and AFC Wallingford, where he helped the latter finish as runners-up to Cove in the Combined Counties League in 2000–01 before going one better and securing the title in 2001–02.

It is not known what Andy did playing-wise after that title win, but it is known that he became assistant manager to David Crowdy at Wantage Town in May 2005. He has also played Sunday league football – he captained Theale to the Reading Senior League and FA Sunday Cup double in 1991–92 (scoring in the Final) and later played for Reading Irish. In January 2006 Andy was arrested at Sydney Airport 'on suspicion of importing a border-controlled drug under section 307.2 of the Australian Criminal Code Act 1995'. In August of that year, he was convicted and sentenced to five and a half years in prison.

Grant Payne — Forward

Born: 25 December 1975, Woking.

Aldershot Town FC record:

Debut: v Enfield (a), Isthmian League Premier Division, 13 November 1999.
Last appearance: v Havant and Waterlooville (at Southampton FC), Hampshire Senior Cup Final, 1 May 2002.
Appearances: 66 + 13
Goals: 31

Playing career:
Wimbledon (from apprentice, July 1992), Woking (3ML, January 1995), Woking (1ML, October 1996), Cambridge United (trial, summer 1997), Woking (July 1997), Aldershot Town (November 1999), Woking (July 2002), Kingstonian (February 2003), Westminster Casuals (summer 2004; player-assistant manager from summer 2005; player-manager from August 2007).

Representative honours:
Isthmian League XI.

Club honours:
Isthmian League Charity Shield (Aldershot Town 1999), Hampshire Senior Cup (Aldershot Town 2002), Kingston and District League Division One (Westminster Casuals 2004–05), Surrey Junior Cup (Westminster Casuals 2005), Teck Senior Cup (Westminster Casuals 2005), Kingston and District League Premier Division (Westminster Casuals 2005–06).

Grant was a stocky striker whose tremendous goalscoring rate was complemented by a great first touch. He began his footballing life as an apprentice at Wimbledon and signed full contract forms in the summer of 1992. He was sent on a three-month loan to Woking in January 1995 and, having scored on his debut against Bromsgrove Rovers, went on to score five goals during that spell, eventually signing permanently in July 1997. He spent the next two seasons tormenting the hell out of opposing defenders, with his strength plus ability to run straight through on goal enabling him to score 19 goals in 1997–98 and follow that up with nine in 1998–99.

Grant joined Aldershot Town in November 1999 for a then record fee for the Shots of £20,000. He made an explosive start, scoring four goals on his debut – to date, he is the only Shots player to score three or more on their debut. He then followed that up with a hat-trick in his second game (an Isthmian League Cup tie against Abingdon Town) 10 days later. But his time at the Rec was hampered by a knee injury; in fact, the injury kept him out of action completely from February 2000, by which time he had already scored 16 goals in 18 games, until the end of January 2001. He was not really injury-free until the 2001–02 season – a season during which he played 49 of his 79 games for the Shots, scoring 15 more goals.

During the summer of 2002 the Shots signed Lee Charles and Roscoe D'Sane, which meant that Grant would be pushed down the forwards' pecking order. There were also concerns about his long-term fitness, so it was no surprise when he opted to return to Woking. However, he was reportedly still struggling with the injury he had sustained while with the Shots, and his season yielded just two goals before he signed for Kingstonian in February 2003.

Grant scored nine goals in just over a season at Kingsmeadow before dropping down into the Kingston and District League with Westminster Casuals in the summer of 2004. His obvious class showed immediately and, amazingly, he scored in every Casuals game bar one in 2004–05, finishing the season with 53 goals from 28 games! His goals contributed in no small way to the winning of the Kingston and District League Division One title plus the Surrey Junior Cup and Teck Senior Cup that season. Unsurprisingly, Grant was that season's Player of the Year. He took up the role of player-assistant manager with the club in the summer of 2005 and proceeded to score 35 goals (including six hat-tricks) in the 2005–06 season as the Casuals won the Premier Division title, and 18 goals in 2006–07 as they finished runners-up to Maori Park in that same division.

Grant became player-manager of the Casuals in the summer of 2007 as the club moved into the Surrey South Eastern Combination League Intermediate Division Two, and he contributed 17 goals in a season that saw them finish fourth.

Andy Pearce — Centre-back

Born: 20 April 1966, Bradford-on-Avon.

Aldershot Town FC record:

Debut:	v Lymington and New Milton (a), FA Cup fourth qualifying round, 16 October 1999.
Last appearance:	v Basingstoke Town (a), Isthmian League Premier Division, 11 January 2000.
Appearances:	14

Playing career:

Wednesbury Town, Stourbridge, Halesowen Town, Coventry City (May 1990), Sheffield Wednesday (June 1993), Wimbledon (November 1995), Heart of Midlothian (trial, summer 1999), Stoke City (trial, summer 1999), Aldershot Town (NC, October 1999).

Andy has made 147 FA Premier League and Football League appearances, scoring seven goals.

Andy was a 6ft 4in colossus of a centre-back who played non-League football for West Midlands sides before First Division Coventry City paid £15,000 to take him into the Football League in May 1990. He had to wait until the following March to make his debut against Leeds United but then played in all bar one of Sky Blues' remaining games that season.

Andy's aerial strength made him a danger at both ends of the pitch and contributed to him being a regular in the side over the next two seasons, even though fans' opinions about him were divided. In June 1993 he joined Sheffield Wednesday for a fee of £500,000. However, his appearances were limited, and he decided to leave in search of first-team football. Wimbledon paid £600,000 to take him down South, but his time at Selhurst Park was not very productive. He made just seven appearances during the 1995–96 season and then, inexplicably, never played for the club again.

Following his eventual release in the summer of 1999, he trialled at Heart of Midlothian and Stoke City before signing for Aldershot Town, reportedly in preference to Kidderminster Harriers, in October 1999. Andy's signing came as a surprise to many and, in truth, his performances during his three months with the Shots were disappointing. He retired almost unnoticed just after the turn of the year, and his current whereabouts are unknown.

Michael Pearson — Forward

Born: 5 October 1982, Frimley.

Aldershot Town FC record:

Debut:	v Slough Town (a), Isthmian League Full Members' Cup first round, 24 October 2000.
Last appearance:	as substitute v Chesham United, Isthmian League Premier Division, 18 April 2001.
Appearances:	2 + 2
Goals:	1

Playing career:

Reading (youth), Aldershot Town (youth), Farnborough Town (youth), Aldershot Town (summer 2000), Basingstoke Town (summer 2001), Fleet Town (August 2002), Hartley Wintney (January 2003).

Michael began as a youth player at Reading before playing the same level of football at Aldershot Town and Farnborough Town (where he also played in the reserves). The Boro reserve side folded in the summer of 2000, so Michael returned to the Rec and was immediately offered a full contract. He scored on his Shots debut and made three further appearances before leaving the Rec and going on to play for Basingstoke Town, Fleet Town and Hartley Wintney. Details of his post-Hartley Wintney career are unknown.

Steve Perkins — Midfielder

Born: 25 April 1975, Southport.

Aldershot Town FC record:

Debut:	as substitute v Harrow Borough (a), Isthmian League Premier Division, 1 March 2003.
Last appearance:	as substitute v Bashley (at Southampton FC). Hampshire Senior Cup Final, 8 May 2003.
Appearances:	7 + 8
Goals:	1

Playing career:
Burscough (youth), Crediton United, Plymouth Argyle (February 1997), Stevenage Borough (September 1997), Welling United (1ML, September 1997), Woking (October 1998), Dagenham and Redbridge (June 2002), Aldershot Town (NC, February 2003), Gravesend and Northfleet (August 2003), Welling United (July 2005), Hayes and Yeading United (August 2007).
Steve has made four Football League appearances.

Representative honours:
British Universities, Isthmian League XI, FA XI, Middlesex Wanderers, FA England Futsal.

Club honours:
Isthmian League Premier Division (Aldershot Town 2002–03), Hampshire Senior Cup (Aldershot Town 2003).

Steve is a midfielder who is comfortable playing on the right or in the centre and is the son of ex-Burscough boss Russ Perkins. His career began in the youth set-up at Burscough before progressing on to Western League side Crediton United. Some impressive performances led to Second Division Plymouth Argyle taking a chance on him in February 1997. He made just four appearances for Argyle before joining Conference outfit Stevenage Borough in September 1997. Almost as soon as he had arrived at Broadhall Way, he was loaned to fellow Conference side Welling United. Following his return to Boro, he was part of the side that took FA Premier League side Newcastle United to a replay in the FA Cup fourth round.

Steve's next stop was Woking, who paid £10,000 to take him to Kingfield in October 1998. He quickly established himself as a regular in the side but was unfortunate that his time at Kingfield coincided with one of the club's least successful periods. However, he did perform consistently well and showed his versatility by occasionally playing in the right wing-back position.

Steve represented British Universities in the World Student Games in China in 2001 (along with Woking teammates Matthew Hayfield and Nick Roddis), and he signed for Dagenham and Redbridge in June 2002. He moved on to Aldershot Town the following February, helping with the final (successful) push towards the Isthmian League Premier Division title.

Summer 2005 saw Steve move to Welling United after a spell at Gravesend and Northfleet, and he was part of the side beaten by Grays Athletic in the quarter-finals of the 2006–07 FA Trophy, equalling the club's best-ever run in the competition. Having been appointed as captain at Hayes and Yeading United, he led them to 13th place in the League and was rewarded for his efforts by being voted 2008 Player of the Year. Aside from playing the 11-a-side version of the game, Steve has often been part of the England FA Futsal squad, a five-a-side version of football using a smaller ball.

James Peters — Forward

Born: 13 April 1982, Frimley.

Aldershot Town FC record:

Debut:	as substitute v Walton and Hersham (a), Isthmian League Cup first round, 12 September 2000.
Last appearance:	v Forest Green Rovers (a), Conference Challenge Cup Southern Section quarter-final, 15 February 2005.

Appearances: 3 + 2
Goals: 3

Playing career:
Aldershot Town (youth), Ash United (October 2002), Hartley Wintney (October 2003), Ash United (March 2004), Aldershot Town (trial, February 2005).

James was a youth-team player when he made his senior debut for the Shots during the 2000–01 season. He scored two extra-time goals in an Isthmian League Full Members' Cup tie at Slough Town later that season before leaving the Rec in October 2002 and going on to play for Ash United and Hartley Wintney.

James briefly returned to Aldershot as a trialist during the 2004–05 season and scored the only goal in a Conference Challenge Cup third-round tie against Exeter City before finishing the season as the club's top scorer with 31 goals.

Mark Peters — Defender

Born: 6 July 1972, St Asaph.

Aldershot Town FC record:
Debut: v Canvey Island (h), FA Cup first round, 13 November 2004.
Appearances: 1

Playing career:
Manchester City (from trainee, July 1990), Norwich City (August 1992), Peterborough United (August 1993), Mansfield Town (September 1994), Rushden and Diamonds (June 1999), Leyton Orient (September 2003), Aldershot Town (1ML, November 2004), Aldershot Town (trial, July 2005), Cambridge United (player-coach, August 2005).
Mark has made 235 Football League appearances, scoring 12 goals.

Representative honours:
Wales Youth, Wales Under-21s (three caps), Wales B.

Club honours:
Conference (Rushden and Diamonds 2000–01), Division Three (Rushden and Diamonds 2002–03).

Mark is a commanding defender with a wealth of experience in the lower leagues. He started as a trainee at Manchester City and signed full professional forms in July 1990. While at Maine Road, he played in the 1989 FA Youth Cup Final but was unable to get into the first team and so moved on to Norwich City, leaving there for the same reason.

He joined First Division Peterborough United, who were eventually relegated, and then Mansfield Town, where he matured into a steady and assured defender over the course of five injury-ridden seasons. He sustained a triple fracture of his tibia and fibula in March 1996 (against Hartlepool United), which required nine operations and kept him out of action until November 1997. The fact that Mark returned from that injury at all is testament to his strength and determination, so it was understandably frustrating when his injury jinx continued in 1997–98, causing him to miss about four months of the season.

Mark eventually moved on to Rushden and Diamonds and had a successful time there, being called-up for the Wales Semi-Professional XI (he was an unused substitute in their game against England in February 2001) and assisting in winning the Conference title, thus bringing League football to Nene Park for the first time in the club's history.

The form of Barry Hunter and Andy Edwards plus the emergence of youngster John Dempster at the start of the 2003–04 season saw him frozen out at Rushden, and he joined Leyton Orient. He went to the Shots on loan in November 2004, having played just three times for the Os that season, and it was hoped that his experience would be influential. Unfortunately, those hopes were dashed when he injured his toe during his sole appearance. He immediately returned to Brisbane Road but played no more games that season and was released the following summer.

Mark briefly reappeared at the Rec as a pre-season trialist in July 2005, but an offer from Cambridge United (newly relegated from the Football League) to become their player-coach and captain meant that his participation in the Conference National would be away from the Rec.

Mark was instrumental in the Us starting the 2007–08 season with a 12-game unbeaten run (their best-ever start to a season), and this contributed to the club eventually finishing as runners-up to the Shots and qualifying for the end-of-season Play-offs, where they eventually lost to Exeter City in the Final. Shortly after that defeat, Mark was one of the players released from the Abbey Stadium and at the time of writing is still without a club.

Gary Phillips — Goalkeeper

Born: 20 September 1961, St Albans.

Aldershot Town FC record:

Debut: v Maidenhead United (h), Isthmian League Division One, 13 December 1997
Last appearance: v Basingstoke Town (at Southampton FC), Hampshire Senior Cup Final, 5 May 1999.
Appearances: 78

Playing career:
Watford (schoolboy), Southampton (schoolboy), Watford (schoolboy), Birmingham City (trial, December 1977), Brighton & Hove Albion (NC, January 1978), Chalfont St Peter (March 1978), West Bromwich Albion (May 1978), Barnet (January 1981), Brentford (December 1984), Reading (August 1988), Barnet (1ML, March 1989), Hereford United (1ML, September 1989), Barnet (player-groundsman, December 1989; player-manager from July 1993), Enfield (1ML, December 1991), Aylesbury United (player-coach, June 1995; player-manager from October 1995), Aldershot Town (December 1997), Aylesbury United (player-coach, June 1999; player-manager from October 1999), Boreham Wood (player-manager, October 2000), Stevenage Borough (February 2001), Chesham United (March 2001), Hemel Hempstead Town (player-manager, July 2001).
Gary has made 290 Football League appearances.

Representative honours:
South East Schools, FA XI, Middlesex Wanderers, England Semi-Professional XI (1 cap).

Club honours:
Hertfordshire Senior Cup (Barnet 1991), Conference (Barnet 1990–91), Berks and Bucks Senior Cup (Aylesbury United 1997, 2000), Isthmian League Division One (Aldershot Town 1997–98), Isthmian League Cup (Aldershot Town 1999), Hampshire Senior Cup (Aldershot Town 1999).

Post-playing coaching/management career:
Assistant manager of Stevenage Borough (February 2002), reserve-team manager of Barnet (July 2005), goalkeeping coach at Grays Athletic (March 2007), assistant manager of Grays Athletic (January 2008).

Gary was a very experienced 'keeper and is the son of ex-Bishop's Stortford forward Derek Phillips. 'Sumo', as he is affectionately known, played schoolboy football before trialling at Birmingham City in the hope of being offered an apprenticeship, but they opted for Tony Coton instead. He eventually signed a full professional contract for West Bromwich Albion on his 17th birthday.

Gary began his love affair with Barnet in January 1981 when a reported £12,500 fee took him away from The Hawthorns. During his time at Underhill, he made his sole appearance for the England Semi-Professional XI (against Gibraltar in April 1982) and was voted Player of the Year in 1982 and 1984. A fee of £5,000 took Gary to Brentford in December 1984, and by August 1988 Gary's worth had increased to the point where Reading parted with £15,000 to take him to Elm Park. However, by the turn of the year, he was loaned out before making a permanent return to Barnet in December 1989 in the unusual role of player-groundsman.

Gary's near six seasons back at Underhill were certainly not dull! He was an ever present in 1990–91 as the Bees won the Conference title, then appeared in Barnet's first-ever Football League match against Crewe Alexandra, and one could have been excused for concluding that the Bees were determined to adopt an entertaining approach to both attacking and defending, as they lost the game 7–4!

The 1992–93 season was one of triumph through adversity, as the club suffered financial problems and lost manager Barry Fry to Southend United. And in the midst of an uncertain summer for Barnet, who were nearly expelled from the League and lost the bulk of their promotion-winning squad as a result of a tribunal nullifying their contracts, Gary was given the role of player-manager and had to hastily assemble a completely new squad.

Gary ended his association with Barnet in the summer of 1995, by which time he had rightly attained 'legend' status, to become player-coach at Aylesbury United, later becoming player-manager. He then moved on to Aldershot Town, becoming a firm favourite with the Shots faithful as a result of his fantastic sense of humour and his solid performances.

Having helped the Shots win the Isthmian League Division One title in 1997–98 and the Hampshire Senior Cup and Isthmian League Cup double in 1999, Gary returned to Aylesbury as a coach. However, the playing bug soon bit, and he was back between the sticks again three months later. Gary assumed the role of player-manager and stayed in that role till May 2000 when, following the Ducks' relegation from the Isthmian League Premier Division, he reverted to simply managing the side.

Gary went on to play for Boreham Wood, Stevenage Borough and Chesham United. In July 2001 he took on the role of player-manager at Isthmian League Division Two side Hemel Hempstead Town but resigned just four months later, as a raft of injuries to key players saw the team pick up just 13 points from their first 17 games.

Gary went on to fill various management roles at a number of clubs, as well as coaching at Grays Athletic. Gary has always loved coaching and has, at various points in his career, had stints coaching at Colchester United, Luton Town, Queen's Park Rangers – where he worked with future Shots legends Gary Waddock and Nikki Bull – Southend United and Wycombe Wanderers, as well as working at Les Cleevely's goalkeeping academy.

Kevin Phillips — Goalkeeper

Born: 27 July 1975, Gloucester.

Aldershot Town FC record:

Debut: v Horsham (a), Isthmian League Division Three, 27 February 1993.
Last appearance: v Thame United (h), Isthmian League Division Three, 10 April 1993.
Appearances: 5

Playing career:
Swindon Town (trainee), Aldershot Town (1ML, February 1993).

Kevin was a teenage 'keeper who began his career as a trainee at Swindon Town. He joined the Shots on a one-month loan in February 1993 and did very well, conceding just two goals in his five appearances. No further information is known about Kevin.

Lewis Phillips — Left-back/Midfielder

Born: 26 September 1990, Aldershot.

Aldershot Town FC record:

Debut: v Basingstoke Town (h), Hampshire Senior Cup quarter-final, 19 February 2008.
Appearances: 1
Goals: 1

Playing career:
Aldershot Town (youth), Camberley Town (2ML, March 2008).

Representative honours:
Hampshire Under-18s.

Lewis progressed from the Shots' Under-16 side and made a scoring debut for the first team while still a member of the youth side. Shortly after his debut, he joined Camberley Town on loan for the rest of the 2007–08 season.

Kieron Philpott — Midfielder

Born: 21 December 1976, Brighton.

Aldershot Town FC record:

Debut: as substitute v Bishop's Stortford (a), FA Cup second qualifying round, 4 October 1998.
Last appearance: v Worthing (a), Isthmian League Full Members' Cup second round, 2 February 1999.

Appearances: 4 + 9
Goals: 1

Playing career:
Aldershot Town (NC, September 1998), Chertsey Town (February 1999), Dorking (November 1999).

Representative honours:
British Universities.

Nothing is known of midfielder Kieron's pre-Aldershot Town career, other than he was at university prior to suddenly appearing at the Rec in September 1998. He moved to Chertsey Town in February 1999 and then Dorking in November of that year. Kieron was still playing for Dorking at the end of the 2006–07 season, but it is not known if he had been there continuously since joining from Chertsey. No information pertaining to his subsequent career is known.

James Powell — Right-back/Midfielder

Born: 30 September 1989, Peterborough.

Aldershot Town FC record:
Debut: v Eastleigh (a), Hampshire Senior Cup quarter-final, 15 March 2007.
Appearances: 1

Playing career:
Aldershot Town (youth), Cove (1ML, March 2008).

James can play as a right-back or a right-sided midfielder and was a member of the Shots' youth team when making his sole appearance for the senior side. He started the 2007–08 season at the Rec but missed a couple of months due to injury before moving to Cove on loan near the end of the season.

Jim Power — Goalkeeper

Born: 4 March 1976, Guildford.

Aldershot Town FC record:
Debut: as substitute v Selsey (h), FA Cup preliminary round, 26 August 1995.
Last appearance: v Wembley (h), Isthmian League Division One, 16 September 1997.
Appearances: 2 + 1

Playing career:
Fulham (trainee, July 1992), Dorking (September 1994), Aldershot Town (August 1995).

Jim was a trainee at Fulham and played for Dorking before joining Aldershot Town in August 1995. A broken leg restricted him to just three appearances for the Shots in a little over two seasons, and he left in October 1997. It is believed that he gave up playing shortly afterwards, but nothing else is known about him thereafter.

Paul Priddy — Goalkeeper

Born: 11 July 1953, Isleworth.

Aldershot Town FC record:
Debut: v Bromley (h), Isthmian League Cup semi-final second leg, 8 April 1999.
Appearances: 1

Playing career:
Hayes (August 1971), Maidenhead United (January 1972), Brentford (summer 1972), Wimbledon (summer 1974), Brentford (September 1975), Tooting and Mitcham (summer 1977), Wimbledon (October 1978), Oxford City (summer 1979), Hayes (summer 1980), Brentford (August 1981), Wimbledon (summer 1982), Hampton (player-assistant manager, summer 1983), Aldershot Town (NC, April 1999).

Paul has made 123 Football League appearances.

Representative honours:
Isthmian League XI.

Club honours:
Southern League Premier Division (Wimbledon 1974–75).

Post-playing coaching/management career:
Goalkeeping coach at Aldershot Town (summer 1994).

Paul is a highly respected goalkeeping coach who has been at the Rec since the summer of 1994, which means that he has worked under every manager the club has had. He played his early football at Hayes and Maidenhead United before signing as a professional at Brentford in the summer of 1972.

Having spent a couple of seasons with the struggling club, Paul joined Wimbledon and was involved in the winning of the Southern League Premier Division in 1974–75. Unfortunately, the form of Dickie Guy prevented him from being involved in the legendary FA Cup run that saw them beat First Division Burnley before losing by a single goal to the mighty Leeds United in a fourth-round replay.

Paul then returned to Griffin Park before playing for Tooting and Mitcham, Wimbledon and Oxford City, with return spells at Hayes (where he won the Sportsman of the Year award in 1980–81) and Brentford. He spent the 1982–83 season back at Wimbledon as cover for Dave Beasant before joining Hampton as player-assistant manager in the summer of 1983. Unfortunately, his career was ended that November after he sustained an injury in his only game for the Beavers, which necessitated the removal of his spleen.

In April 1999 Paul donned his gloves one last time in order to help the Shots out of a crisis – they were set to face Bromley in an Isthmian League Cup semi-final second-leg tie without a recognised 'keeper, so Paul was signed as a non-contract player and helped the Shots to a 2–1 extra-time victory. At the end of the game, Paul rightly left the pitch to a standing ovation. The appearance gave Paul a place in the record books as the oldest-ever Shots player (aged 45 years and 270 days). In addition to his excellent work at Aldershot, Paul used to run his own goalkeeping school and has coached at Walton and Hersham, Crystal Palace, Brentford and AFC Wimbledon.

Mark Pritchard — Forward

Born: 23 November 1985, Tredegar.

Aldershot Town FC record:

Debut:	v Gravesend and Northfleet (h), Conference National, 12 August 2006.
Last appearance:	v Fleet Town (at AFC Bournemouth), Hampshire Senior Cup Final, 5 May 2007.
Appearances:	6 + 24
Goals:	4

Playing career:
Swansea City (from trainee, July 2005), Merthyr Tydfil (1ML, March 2005), Aldershot Town (August 2006), Newport County (trial, July 2007), Llanelli (July 2007).
Mark has made four Football League appearances.

Representative honours:
Wales Under-18s, Wales Under-21s (four caps).

Club honours:
Hampshire Senior Cup (Aldershot Town 2007), Welsh Premier League (Llanelli 2007–08), Welsh League Cup (Llanelli 2008).

Mark was originally a trainee at Swansea City and was loaned to Merthyr Tydfil shortly before he signed full professional forms in July 2005. He went on to win caps for the Welsh Under-18s and Under-21s (scoring on his debut) and was released by Swansea at the end of the 2005–06 season, coming to the Rec as a pre-season trialist.

Mark soon impressed enough to earn himself a contract but found that his first-team opportunities were limited, and even when he did play he did not produce his pre-season form consistently. He played and scored for the Shots as they were beaten by Blackpool in the FA Cup third round in January 2007 before being released at the end of the season.

Mark trialled at Newport County before signing for Welsh Premier League side Llanelli, where his 16 goals in 41 appearances helped capture the Welsh Premier League title and the Welsh League Cup (they beat Rhyl in the Final) in 2007–08. He also experienced Cup disappointment that season, as the Reds were beaten by Newport County in the FAW Premier League Cup Final and lost to Bangor City in a fiery Welsh Cup Final that saw three dismissals.

Lee Protheroe — Right-back

Born: 5 November 1975, Edmonton, London.

Aldershot Town FC record:

Debut: v Sutton United (h), Isthmian League Premier Division, 19 August 2000.
Last appearance: v Havant and Waterlooville (at Southampton FC), Hampshire Senior Cup Final, 1 May 2002.
Appearances: 85 + 9
Goals: 13

Playing career:
Ridgeway Rovers (youth), Walthamstow Pennant (August 1994), St Margaretsbury (January 1995), Ruislip Manor (August 1995), Yeading (June 1996), Enfield (July 1998), Aldershot Town (May 2000), Canvey Island (June 2002), Gravesend and Northfleet (3ML, November 2003), Gravesend and Northfleet (June 2004), Margate (2ML, March 2006), Margate (July 2006), Chelmsford City (summer 2007).

Representative honours:
FA XI.

Club honours:
Hampshire Senior Cup (Aldershot Town 2002), Isthmian League Premier Division (Canvey Island 2003–04; Chelmsford City 2007–08).

Lee is a right-back and something of a dead-ball specialist. Having played for Chingford-based youth side Ridgeway Rovers, he spent his formative years in non-League sides before moving into the Isthmian League with Ruislip Manor and Yeading.

During his time at the Warren, Lee developed into a skilful defender who often looked as though he could easily play at a higher level. In July 1998 Enfield paid £5,000 to bring him to Southbury Road, where he was later part of the side that beat Chesterfield in the 1999–2000 FA Cup first round before losing to Preston North End in a second-round replay. Lee was also voted the Es Player of the Year that season.

In May 2000 he joined Aldershot Town and scored on his debut. Over the course of the next two seasons, his consistency of performances plus an admirable 13 goals helped the Shots to consecutive top-four finishes in the Isthmian League Premier Division.

Lee left the Rec in June 2002 and went on to play for Canvey Island and Gravesend and Northfleet, where he played a part in the club's best-ever progression in the FA Trophy as they reached the quarter-finals in 2004–05 before losing to Slough Town. Lee signed for Margate but left after a season, joining Chelmsford City.

The 2007–08 season yielded the Isthmian League Premier Division title for the Clarets, although Lee's participation in the campaign was briefly interrupted by a groin operation, which kept him out for a few weeks.

Mark Pye — Midfielder

Born: 29 February 1968, Hammersmith.

Aldershot Town FC record:

Debut: as substitute v Harrow Borough (a), Isthmian League Premier Division, 22 August 2000.
Last appearance: as substitute v Heybridge Swifts (a), Isthmian League Premier Division, 5 May 2001.
Appearances: 27 + 6

Playing career:
West Ham United (YTS), Queen's Park Rangers (trial, summer 1986), North Greenford United (summer 1989),

Harrow Borough (July 1990), Enfield (July 1992), Slough Town (July 1995), Hayes (July 1997), Chesham United (July 1998), Hendon (October 1998), Slough Town (February 1999), Aldershot Town (July 2000), Boreham Wood (trial, July 2001), Aylesbury United (July 2001), Yeading (trial, August 2001), Harrow Borough (September 2001), Hendon (October 2001), Carshalton Athletic (March 2002), Enfield (July 2003), Staines Town (August 2003), Boreham Wood (September 2004).

Representative honours:
FA XI.

Club honours:
Isthmian League Premier Division (Enfield 1994–95), Isthmian League Division One South (Carshalton Athletic 2002–03).

Mark was a fiercely competitive central-midfielder whose style of play led him to endure many a suspension. He began as a YTS player with West Ham United and had spells elsewhere before signing for Enfield in July 1992. His determination was one of the driving forces behind the Es enjoying top-three finishes in the Isthmian League Premier Division in his first two seasons. Mark's participation in a third tilt at the title brought the ultimate success, as the 1994–95 Championship was won by a margin of 14 points from Slough Town.

Despite Enfield being denied promotion by the Conference amid concerns over the club's financial structure, Mark still managed to get into the division by way of a £5,500 move to Slough Town, who were promoted in Enfield's place. Unfortunately, the move was not as successful as had been hoped, and Mark then had spells at a handful of clubs before signing for Aldershot Town in July 2000 and helping to achieve a fourth-place finish in the Isthmian League Premier Division.

Club spells followed before Mark returned to Harrow, where he would achieve infamy in a game against the Shots in September 2001. At the end of this game, he kicked out at Shots boss George Borg and was subsequently arrested, charged with assault and later sentenced to do 200 hours' community service. He was immediately sacked by Harrow and re-signed for Hendon the following month but was released a week later due to fan displeasure at his signing.

Mark went on to appear for Carshalton Athletic, Enfield, Staines Town and Boreham Wood before retiring three months later. He currently works as a black cab driver in London.

Dan Read — Forward

Born: 27 May 1990, Frimley.

Aldershot Town FC record:

Debut:	as substitute v Hamble ASSC (a), Hampshire Senior Cup third round, 4 December 2007.
Appearances:	0 + 1

Representative honours:
Hampshire Under-18s.

Playing career:
Aldershot Town (youth).

Dan is a forward who scored 24 goals for Shots in 32 youth-team games during the 2006–07 season. He won that season's youth-team Player of the Year award and then averaged nearly a goal a game for the youth side in 2007–08, making his sole first-team appearance in that season's Hampshire Senior Cup.

Paul Read — Midfielder

Born: 13 September 1981, Frimley.

Aldershot Town FC record:

Debut:	v Brading Town (h), Hampshire Senior Cup second round, 1 November 2001.
Last appearance:	as substitute v Corinthian-Casuals (h), Isthmian League Cup third round, 27 February 2002.

Appearances:	1 + 2
Goals:	1

Playing career:
Chelsea (youth), Fulham (May 1998), Queen's Park Rangers (trial, summer 2001), Grimsby Town (trial, summer 2001), Aldershot Town (NC, October 2001), Chertsey Town (3ML, March 2002), Chertsey Town (September 2002), Hampton and Richmond Borough (October 2002), Kingstonian (July 2006), Fleet Town (September 2006).

Paul is a central-midfielder who began playing youth-team football at Chelsea. He joined Fulham in May 1998 but was released three years later without making a first-team appearance. Having trialled at Queen's Park Rangers and Grimsby Town, he joined Aldershot Town on a non-contract basis in October 2001 and scored on his debut the following month.

Paul made two more appearances for the Shots before going on to play for Chertsey Town, Alwyns Lane and Hampton and Richmond Borough, where he stayed until April 2003, after which he took a break from the semi-pro game. Unfortunately, Paul sustained a knee injury while playing local Sunday league football during this break, and the severity of the injury was such that he was out of the game for three years.

Paul made a return to the game with Kingstonian in July 2006 but moved to Fleet Town a couple of months later. He sustained an ankle injury in the summer of 2007, and any chances of him playing in the 2007–08 season disappeared when complications set in with the injury. However, he does hope to play again in 2008–09 after he returns from a coaching assignment in the States. Paul currently teaches at a college in Surrey, and his responsibilities include managing their football team, who play in the English Colleges Football Association League.

Tim Read — Goalkeeper

Born: 23 June 1971, Shoreham.

Aldershot Town FC record:

Debut:	v Clapton (h), Isthmian League Division Three, 22 August 1992.
Last appearance:	v Northwood (h), Isthmian League Division Three, 31 October 1992.
Appearances:	16

Playing career:
Worthing (from youth, April 1989), Woking (June 1990), Tottenham Hotspur (trial, November 1990), Bognor Regis Town (3ML, October 1991), Aldershot Town (2ML, August 1992), Baldock Town (1ML, 1992–93 season), Chesham United (1ML, December 1994), Worthing (December 1995; left September 1997).

Club honours:
Isthmian League Cup (Woking 1991), Surrey Senior Cup (Woking 1991), Isthmian League Division Three (Aldershot Town 1992–93), FA Trophy (Woking 1995 [unused substitute]).

Tim began playing in the youth team at Worthing before signing a full contract in April 1989. He joined Woking for a fee of £7,500 (still a record for a player departing Woodside Road) in June 1990, and his early season form was such that he trialled at Tottenham Hotspur. He was then part of the Woking side that reached the fourth round of the 1990–91 FA Cup, where they admirably lost 1–0 to First Division Everton, and the side that won that season's Isthmian League Cup and Surrey Senior Cup.

Following little playing action at Woking, Tim joined Aldershot Town in the summer of 1992 on a two-month loan and wore the 'keeper's jersey in the club's first-ever game against Clapton. His time at the Rec ended in the November when Mark Watson was signed from Camberley Town and, having returned to Kingfield, he was then loaned out to Baldock Town and Chesham United.

In December 1995 Tim returned to Worthing, where he endured relegation from the Isthmian League Premier Division at the end of the season. Tim retired in September 1997 and currently works as an area manager for a national bank.

Karl Ready — Centre-back

Born: 14 August 1972, Neath.

Aldershot Town FC record:

Debut:	v Enfield (a), Isthmian League Premier Division, 4 September 2002.
Last appearance:	v Hayes (h), Isthmian League Premier Division, 12 November 2002.
Appearances:	16
Goals:	1

Playing career:
Queen's Park Rangers (from trainee, August 1990), Motherwell (July 2001), Aldershot Town (NC, August 2002), Wycombe Wanderers (trial, July 2003), Aylesbury United (July 2003), Crawley Town (August 2003; player-coach from November 2003), Farnborough Town (trial, July 2004).
Karl has made 262 FA Premier League, Football League and Scottish Premier League appearances, scoring 13 goals.

Representative honours:
Wales Schoolboys, Wales Under-21s (six caps, one goal), Wales B (two caps), Wales full international (five caps).

Club honours:
Isthmian League Premier Division (Aldershot Town 2002–03), Southern League Cup (Crawley Town 2004), Southern League Premier Division (Crawley Town 2003–04).

Karl was a solid centre-back whose strength and consistency enabled him to spend 11 years at Queen's Park Rangers. Karl became part of history in the 1992–93 season when QPR were one of the 22 founder members of the FA Premier League, finishing fifth that season. Among bouts of disappointment including relegation in his time at QPR, Karl won the Player of the Year award twice and made his full international debut in Wales' 0–0 draw with the Republic of Ireland in February 1997. His last appearance for Wales came against Tunisia in June 1998 and he also captained the B side.

Towards the end of the 2000–01 season, QPR went into administration, which eventually led to Karl being released and joining Motherwell. Unfortunately, he found himself in a familiar situation, as he played in all but two of the club's League games in a season, in which they were dogged by financial problems. He was one of a number of players released in the summer of 2002, and he subsequently joined Aldershot Town and immediately brought an air of invincibility to the Shots' defence.

Karl was a popular signing with the Shots fans and enhanced this by scoring against local rivals Farnborough Town in a County Cup tie in the October. Karl was released by the Shots a couple of months after that goal, and it is believed that he took a break from the game for the remainder of the season.

Having trialled at Wycombe Wanderers, he later signed for Aylesbury United before joining Crawley Town. He then became player-coach at the Broadfield Stadium and was a major factor in the club winning the Southern League Premier Division and League Cup double that season. Karl retired in the summer of 2004 and is believed to be running a property development company.

Stephen Reed — Left-back

Born: 18 June 1985, Barnstaple.

Aldershot Town FC record:

Debut: v Accrington Stanley (a), Conference National, 20 September 2005.
Last appearance: v AFC Bournemouth (a), LDV Vans Trophy first round, 18 October 2005.
Appearances: 5 + 1

Playing career:
Plymouth Argyle (youth), Yeovil Town (September 2002), Forest Green Rovers (1ML, October 2004), Woking (1ML, August 2005), Aldershot Town (1ML, September 2005), Torquay United (2ML, March 2006), Torquay United (May 2006), Tiverton Town (1ML, February 2007), Weston-Super-Mare (1ML, March 2007), Cambridge United (May 2007).
Stephen has made 34 Football League appearances.

Stephen is a young left-back and an expert at set-pieces. Having played youth-team football at Plymouth Argyle, he moved to Yeovil Town in September 2002. Finding his chances in the Glovers' first team limited, Stephen had loan spells before coming to Aldershot Town on a similar basis in September 2005 to cover for the injured Darren Barnard. Although Stephen fitted in well, he did not play as much as had been expected due to Darren's quick recovery.

He was loaned out to Torquay United at the tail end of the season before being released by Yeovil that summer. The Shots were reportedly one of a number of clubs interested in his signature, but he opted to return to Plainmoor on a permanent basis. Unfortunately, the move did not quite work out, and he saw out the season on loan at Tiverton Town and Weston-Super-Mare.

Following Torquay's relegation out of the Football League at the end of the season, Stephen joined Cambridge United and made 38 appearances as they finished the 2007–08 season as runners-up to the Shots in the Conference Premier and then lost to Exeter City in the Play-off Final.

Matt Rees — Centre-back

Born: 2 September 1982, Swansea.

Aldershot Town FC record:

Debut: v Halifax Town (h), Conference, 11 October 2003.
Last appearance: v Colchester United (a), FA Cup second round, 6 December 2003.
Appearances: 11

Playing career:
Millwall (from trainee, April 2000), Aldershot Town (1ML, October 2003), Dagenham and Redbridge (1ML, January 2004), Swansea City (1ML, March 2004), Crawley Town (August 2004), Newport County (November 2004), Port Talbot Town (December 2004).
Matt has made three Football League appearances, scoring one goal.

Representative honours:
Wales Under-21s (four caps).

Matt is a commanding centre-back who began his footballing life as a trainee at Millwall. He signed full professional forms in April 2000 and captained the reserves but never played for the first team; however, he won all of his Wales Under-21 caps while with the Lions and was unlucky not to gain full honours.

Following loan spells at Conference sides Aldershot Town (in October 2003) and Dagenham and Redbridge (in January 2004), Matt joined Swansea City on a one-month loan in March 2004 and was released by Millwall that summer. He had short stints at Crawley Town and Newport County before signing for League of Wales side Port Talbot Town in December 2004. Matt was later appointed captain and was part of the Steelmen's side beaten by TNS in the 2006 Welsh Challenge Cup Final. They also had good runs in the FAW Welsh Cup, reaching the semi-finals in 2005–06.

Matt missed just four League games during the 2007–08 season, and his leadership was influential in Port Talbot finishing the season in fourth spot in the Welsh Premier League.

Martin Reeves — Midfielder/Forward

Born: 9 July 1981, Birmingham.

Aldershot Town FC record:

Debut: v York City (a), Conference National, 6 February 2005.
Last appearance: v Exeter City (h), Conference Challenge Cup third round, 8 February 2005.
Appearances: 2

Playing career:

Leicester City (from trainee, November 2000), Hull City (2ML, March 2003), Northampton Town (June 2003), Shrewsbury Town (trial, January 2005), Aldershot Town (NC, January 2005), Rushden and Diamonds (trial, March 2005), Nuneaton Borough (March 2005), Hucknall Town (December 2006), Brackley Town (October 2007).
Martin has made 31 FA Premier League and Football League appearances, scoring one goal.

Martin could play as a box-to-box midfielder or as a forward and started his career as a trainee at Leicester City. He signed full professional forms in November 2000 but did not make many appearances and later joined Hull City on loan.

Following his release from the Walkers Stadium, Martin joined Northampton Town and was part of the side that reached that season's Division Three Play-off semi-finals, where they lost to Mansfield Town. The following season, he found himself 'surplus to requirements' at Northampton and went on to join Aldershot Town in January 2005. However, his stay at the Rec was short, and he trialled at Rushden and Diamonds before joining Nuneaton Borough, for whom he played in the Conference North Play-off semi-final defeat against Altrincham.

The following season, Martin was instrumental in Nuneaton equalling their best-ever progression in the FA Cup as they reached the third round before losing in a replay to Middlesbrough. Indeed, their draw in the original tie was seen by many as one of the greatest-ever shock FA Cup results. That season also saw the club reach the Play-off semi-finals for a second successive season, but they tasted defeat again as Droylsden won by the only goal of the game.

Martin was troubled by injuries during the 2006–07 season which, coupled with the arrival of Jay Denny, saw him leave Liberty Way to sign for fellow Conference North side Hucknall Town, for whom he scored in his first two games. Martin joined Brackley Town in October 2007 and helped them finish the 2007–08 Southern League Premier Division season in eighth spot.

Scott Rendell — Forward

Born: 21 October 1986, Ashford, Middlesex.

Aldershot Town FC record:

Debut: as substitute v Yeading (h), Isthmian League Charity Shield, 19 August 2003.
Last appearance: v Winchester City (at AFC Bournemouth), Hampshire Senior Cup Final, 27 April 2005.
Appearances: 6 + 7
Goals: 4

Playing career:

Aldershot Town (youth), Reading (academy, January 2004), Aldershot Town (3ML, February 2005), Forest Green Rovers (5ML, August 2005), Hayes (2ML, March 2006), Crawley Town (August 2006), Cambridge United (May 2007), Peterborough United (3ML, February 2008), Peterborough United (May 2008).
Scott has made 10 Football League appearances, scoring three goals.

Representative honours:

Hampshire Youth.

Club honours:

Isthmian League Charity Shield (Aldershot Town 2003).

Scott started out as a youth player with the Shots and made a scoring debut against Yeading in the 2003 Isthmian League Charity Shield. In doing so, he set a double record by becoming the club's youngest-ever goalscorer (16 years and 302 days), as well as the youngest-ever scoring debutant. He joined Reading's academy in January 2004 but never got a chance to play in the first team and returned to the Rec on a three-month loan in February 2005, scoring a further three goals in 12 games.

Scott later joined Forest Green Rovers on loan and scored on his debut against Cambridge United, with that goal being significant in that it was their first-ever as a professional club. He then had loan spells at Hayes and Crawley Town, before making a permanent move to Crawley. He then joined Cambridge United in May 2007. In February 2008 (and with him having reportedly rejected an £80,000 move to League Two side Rochdale in the January transfer window), Cambridge rejected a six-figure bid for his services from near-neighbours Peterborough United. By this time, Scott had scored 19 goals in 34 appearances for the Us and handed in a transfer request, which resulted in him eventually joining Peterborough on loan until the end of the season, with a view to a permanent move.

Scott made his Football League debut against Macclesfield Town and finished the 2007–08 season with three goals in 10 appearances for the Posh as they gained promotion. Scott's parent club finished the season in the runners'-up spot in the Conference Premier (15 points behind the Shots). Towards the end of May 2008, Scott's move to London Road was, as expected, made permanent.

Jon Richards — Centre-back/Forward

Born: 3 October 1974, Southend.

Aldershot Town FC record:

Debut: as substitute v Oxford City (a), Isthmian League Full Members' Cup first round, 17 December 1996.

Appearances: 0 + 1

Playing career:

Fulham (W, from trainee, July 1993), Aldershot Town (November 1993), Fleet Town (2ML, March 1997), Fleet Town (summer 1997), Molesey (January 1999), Chesham United (summer 2001), Chertsey Town (October 2001), Fleet Town (January 2002), Ash United (November 2003).

Jon was equally at home as a centre-back or centre-forward and began as a trainee at Fulham. He joined Aldershot Town in November 1993 but sustained a horrendous knee injury in training and did not make his debut (and sole appearance) until December 1996!

He had spells at Fleet Town and then Molesey, but his versatility could not prevent the Walton Road outfit being relegated from Isthmian League Division One at the end of the 1998–99 season. He eventually left Molesey in the summer of 2001 and had short spells at Chesham United and Chertsey Town before returning to Fleet and helping them secure the runners'-up spot in the Wessex League, thus gaining promotion to the Southern League Eastern Division.

Unfortunately, the following season yielded a bottom-three finish, and Jon moved on to Ash United before retiring in the summer of 2004. He is currently a partner in a local security supply firm and plays for the Fleet Town veterans' side.

Sean Ridgway — Midfielder

Born: 10 December 1986, Paddington.

Aldershot Town FC record:

Debut: v Basingstoke Town (a), Hampshire Senior Cup quarter-final, 14 January 2006.

Last appearance: v East Cowes Victoria Athletic (h), Hampshire Senior Cup second round, 31 October 2006.

Appearances: 2

Playing career:

Luton Town (trainee), Rushden and Diamonds (trainee, November 2004), Dunstable Town (1ML, March 2005), Aldershot Town (6ML, November 2005), Chesham United (2MDRL, February 2006), Aldershot Town (June 2006), Hayes (1ML, September 2006), Crawley Town (January 2007), Stafford Rangers (January 2007), Hayes (March 2007), King's Lynn (trial, August 2007), Manly United (Australia, October 2007).

Representative honours:

Republic of Ireland Under-18s.

Sean is a holding central-midfielder and the son of ex-Luton Town coach Mark Ridgway. He began life as a trainee at Luton Town before moving on to Rushden and Diamonds and making a sole loan appearance for Dunstable Town before joining Aldershot Town on a six-month loan in November 2005. He was a regular in the reserves before making his first-team debut a couple of months later. Sean also played that season on dual-registration forms for Southern League Premier Division side Chesham United.

Sean signed permanently for the Shots in June 2006 after being released by Rushden, but was loaned out to Hayes shortly afterwards and later joined Crawley Town and Stafford Rangers before rejoining Hayes on a permanent basis in March 2007. Once again, Sean could not secure a first-team place and made just a handful of appearances before being allowed to leave Church Road in the summer. He subsequently trialled at King's Lynn but was not offered a contract. A family connection then took him out to Australia, where he played for New South Wales Premier League side Manly United for a few months. On his return to the UK, Sean took a break from the game and is currently without a club.

Jake Robinson — Forward

Born: 23 October 1986, Brighton.

Aldershot Town FC record:

Debut: v Barnet (a), Conference National, 26 February 2005.
Last appearance: v Basingstoke Town (h), Hampshire Senior Cup semi-final second leg, 5 April 2005.
Appearances: 10
Goals: 4

Playing career:

Brighton & Hove Albion (from trainee, December 2003), Aldershot Town (1ML, February 2005).
Jake has made 118 Football League appearances, scoring 12 goals.

Jake is a pacy striker whose career began as a trainee at Brighton & Hove Albion. He is Brighton's youngest-ever goalscorer (16 years and 355 days) – an accolade he earned in a Football League Trophy game against Forest Green Rovers in October 2003 (only his second game for the club). Later that season, he played a handful of League games as the Seagulls were promoted from League One via victory in the Play-off Final against Bristol City.

Jake joined Aldershot Town on a month's loan in February 2005 and made a scoring debut before going on to score in four of his first five Shots games. On leaving the Rec, he had become widely regarded as one of the Shots' best-ever loan signings. The following season, he established himself in the first team at the Withdean but scored just once in a struggling side, as the club were relegated from the Championship by virtue of their rock-bottom finish.

The following season, they fared only slightly better by finishing 18th, with Jake scoring 12 goals in all competitions. In 2007–08 Jake played 39 games in all competitions but scored just five goals as the Seagulls finished seventh in League One and narrowly missed out on the Play-offs.

Darren Robson — Midfielder

Born: 18 November 1969, Woolwich.

Aldershot Town FC record:

Debut: v Hendon (a), Isthmian League Premier Division, 14 August 1999.
Last appearance: v Whitchurch United, Hampshire Senior Cup second round, 2 November 1999.
Appearances: 10 + 7
Goals: 1

Playing career:

Petersfield United, Andover, Waterlooville, Basingstoke Town (1988–89 season), Gosport Borough (1989–90 seasons), Southwick (1990–91 season), Worthing (July 1991), Farnborough Town (June 1995), Aldershot Town (June 1999), Kingstonian (November 1999), Newport (Isle of Wight, November 1999), Basingstoke Town (December 1999), Bashley (March 2000), Gosport Borough (June 2003), Alton Town (February 2006), Fareham Town (trial, July 2006), Alton Town (August 2006), Christchurch City United (November 2006), Hamble ASSC (2006–07 season), Paulsgrove (2007–08 season).

Club honours:

Isthmian League Division Two (Worthing 1992–93).

Darren was a creative, attacking midfielder and is the son of ex-Worthing manager John Robson. He spent his formative years at clubs including Petersfield United and Basingstoke Town, where his distribution of the ball coupled with his ability to score important goals helped secure the runners'-up spot behind Staines Town in Isthmian League Division One in 1988–89.

His performances during that season caught the eye of Gosport Borough, who parted with £3,250 to bring him to Privett Park, but the club struggled amid management changes and numerous player departures and ended the season being relegated out of the Southern League Premier Division.

Darren endured another relegation with Southwick (from Isthmian League Division One) at the end of the 1990–91 season before moving to Worthing that summer, where he was the joint winner of the 1992 Player of the Year award with Gary Penhaligon. He was a member of the side that won the Isthmian League Division Two title in 1992–93 (becoming only the second club to win it twice) and the side that finished runners-up to Boreham Wood in Division One in 1994–95. Darren joined Farnborough Town in June 1995, and his ability to create something from nothing in midfield greatly assisted the club in finishing in the top 10 in the Conference twice and progressing to the FA Cup first round in his first three seasons at Cherrywood Road.

That summer saw Darren join Aldershot Town, and a sensational strike against Rushden and Diamonds in a pre-season friendly suggested that he would be a major player in the upcoming season. That assumption seemed to be well-founded, as he made an excellent start to the season. His form tailed off, though, and he left the Rec in the November, having short spells at several clubs before signing for Bashley in March 2000 and then rejoining Gosport in June 2003.

Darren's influence from the middle of the park contributed to top-four finishes in the Wessex League and Wessex League Division One in the next two seasons. Darren subsequently played for a number of clubs, the most recent being Paulsgrove, who achieved a fourth-place finish in the Hampshire League Division One in 2007–08.

Nick Roddis — Midfielder

Born: 18 February 1973, Rotherham.

Aldershot Town FC record:

Debut: v Hitchin Town (a), Isthmian League Premier Division, 17 August 2002.
Last appearance: as substitute v Forest Green Rovers (h), Conference, 1 November 2003.
Appearances: 48 + 3
Goals: 2

Playing career:

Nottingham Forest (trainee, June 1989), Mansfield Town (July 1991), Grantham Town (1ML, November 1992), Eastwood Town (August 1993), Grantham Town (October 1993), Boston (November 1993), Yeading (March 1995), Hayes (June 1996), Woking (June 2000), Margate (December 2001), Aldershot Town (August 2002), Crawley Town (trial, July 2004), AFC Wimbledon (September 2004), St Albans City (player-coach, November 2004), Slough Town (player-assistant manager, June 2007), Alton Town (January 2008).

Representative honours:

British Universities (captain), Isthmian League, FA XI, England Semi-Professional XI (six caps [one as captain], one goal).

Club honours:

Isthmian League Premier Division (Aldershot Town 2002–03), Hampshire Senior Cup (Aldershot Town 2003), Hertfordshire Senior Cup (St Albans City 2005).

Nick is a ball-winning central-midfielder whose tough-tackling style of play often got him into trouble with referees. He spent his early career in the Midlands before signing for Boston, Yeading and then Hayes (newly promoted to the Conference) in June 1996. In his four seasons at Church Road, he was an integral part of the sides that reached the FA Trophy quarter-finals in 1997–98, where they lost to Cheltenham Town, and the FA Cup second round in 1999–2000, where they were beaten in a replay by Hull City.

Nick joined Woking in June 2000 and performed well enough to make his England Semi-Professional XI debut against Holland in March 2001. However, a few months later he upset both the club and its fans when he decided to attend the World Student Games instead of playing in the opening game of the 2001–02 season. This led to a public spat with the club that ultimately resulted in him leaving and signing for Margate, marking his debut by getting sent off.

Nick joined Aldershot Town in August 2002 and was a regular member of the side that completed the Isthmian League Premier Division and County Cup double that season. In 2003–04 he played in the club's first-ever Conference game against Accrington Stanley before getting injured against Forest Green Rovers at the start of the November, missing the rest of the season. He left the Rec in the summer of 2004 when the Shots turned full-time, due to the fact that his position as a teacher offered him better job security.

Nick then trialled at Crawley Town and had a short spell at AFC Wimbledon before taking up the role of player-coach at St Albans City in November 2004. His combative nature was inspirational in attaining the runners'-up spot (behind Weymouth) in the Conference South in 2005–06 and gaining promotion via a subsequent Play-off Final victory over Histon.

Nick left St Albans in May 2007 after being told that he would not be considered for the manager's position, and he joined Slough Town as player-assistant manager to Darren Wilkinson. However, he left just five months later (along with Wilkinson) after the Rebels won just three of their first 21 games in the Southern League Division One South and West. In January 2008 Nick joined Wessex League Premier Division side Alton Town, where he teamed up again with his ex-Shots teammate Jason Chewins, but made just two appearances before leaving. No information pertaining to his career or current whereabouts is known.

Jim Rodwell — Centre-back

Born: 20 November 1970, Lincoln.

Aldershot Town FC record:

Debut: v Accrington Stanley (h), Conference, 10 August 2003.
Last appearance: v Tamworth (a), Conference, 18 October 2003.
Appearances: 11 + 2

Playing career:

Lincoln City (youth), Darlington (trainee, July 1987), Nettleham (March 1989), Sabah (Malaysia, June 1989), Bury (March 1990), Boston (October 1990), Boston United (trial, summer 1992), Bedworth United (August 1992), Hednesford Town (June 1993), Nuneaton Borough (November 1993), Halesowen Town (September 1995), Birmingham City (trial, May 1996), Leeds United (trial, May 1996), Rushden and Diamonds (May 1996), Dagenham and Redbridge (1ML, January 2002), Boston United (February 2002), Farnborough Town (August 2002), Crawley Town (trial, July 2003), Worcester City (trial, July 2003), Aldershot Town (NC, July 2003), Tamworth (December 2003), Havant and Waterlooville (January 2004).
Jim has made 13 Football League appearances.

Club honours:

Northamptonshire Senior Cup (Rushden and Diamonds 1999), Conference (Rushden and Diamonds 2000–01; Boston United 2001–02).

Post-playing coaching/management career:

Caretaker manager of Boston United (February 2004), director of football at Boston United (March 2004), executive chairman of Bolton United (March 2006).

Jim was a big, strong centre-back who started out as a youth player at Lincoln City, becoming a trainee at Darlington in July 1987 and signing full professional forms in January 1989. Over the next four and a half years, he played for a handful of clubs, including Sabah in Malaysia, before signing for Halesowen Town in the Premier Division, where he was a mainstay of the team's back four as the runners'-up spot was secured behind Rushden and Diamonds. His performances that season brought him to the attention of a host of clubs and he eventually joined Rushden. The fee of £40,000 was the highest fee paid between two non-League sides during the 1996–97 season, and is still Halesowen's record sale.

Jim had a successful time at Rushden, attaining successive top finishes and helping to fulfil the quest for Football League status with the winning of the 2000–01 Conference title, as well as a Player of the Year award. Interestingly, he became a TV star in February 2002 when finishing third in a one-off television show to find Britain's brainiest footballer. Later that month he signed for Boston United, and the solidity of his partnership with future Shot Ray Warburton played no small part in securing that season's Conference title.

Jim went on to play for Farnborough Town and trialled at Crawley Town and Worcester City. At the end of July 2003, having turned down the chance of a coaching role in the States with Dallas Sidekicks, he signed for

Aldershot Town and played in their first-ever Conference game against Accrington Stanley. He went on to make 13 appearances for the Shots before brief spells at Tamworth and Havant and Waterlooville preceded his retirement in February 2004.

Shortly after hanging up his boots, Jim returned to Boston United as caretaker manager – a position he held until Steve Evans returned to the York Street hot seat in March 2004. He then became director of football at Boston, but the club was declining and was unfortunate to be suffering financial difficulties by the summer of 2005.

Jim made the step up to the role of executive chairman in March 2006 and was firmly ensconced in that role when Boston took the unpopular decision to enter administration in May 2007. He left the Pilgrims in July 2007 when Chestnut Homes acquired the club from Lavaflow Limited, a company in which he was a shareholder. Jim currently works as a consultant within the football industry.

Lee Rogers — Midfielder

Born: 19 December 1977, Reading.

Aldershot Town FC record:

Debut: as substitute v Croydon (h), FA Trophy first qualifying round, 18 October 1997.
Last appearance: as substitute v Thame United (a), Isthmian League Division One, 25 April 1998.
Appearances: 4 + 8

Playing career:
Reading (trainee, November 1994), Aldershot Town (August 1997), Staines Town (August 1998).

Lee was originally a trainee at Reading before joining Aldershot Town in August 1997. He played in just five of the Shots' League games that season (when they won the Isthmian League Division One title) before leaving to join Staines Town. Nothing is known about Lee's subsequent career.

Michael Ruffles — Midfielder

Born: 18 October 1982, Frimley.

Aldershot Town FC record:

Debut: v Walton and Hersham (a), Isthmian League Cup first round, 12 September 2000.
Last appearance: v Slough Town (a), Isthmian League Full Members' Cup first round, 24 October 2000.
Appearances: 2

Playing career:
Mytchett Athletic (youth), Aldershot Town (August 2000), Wokingham Town (September 2001), Hartley Wintney (2002–03 season), Godalming Town, Bracknell Town (July 2006), Godalming Town (September 2006).

Michael is a midfielder who came to the Rec from local youth side Mytchett Athletic. He performed well enough in the Shots' youth team to be offered a full contract in August 2000 and made his senior debut the following month. He left the Rec in the summer of 2001 and spent a month at Wokingham Town.

It is not known where Michael played immediately after that, but he did reappear at Hartley Wintney in the latter part of the 2002–03 season before having spells with Godalming and Bracknell Town. His second spell at Godalming ended in the summer of 2007, but no details are known about his subsequent career.

Andy Russell — Centre-back

Born: 23 March 1965, Crowthorne.

Aldershot Town FC record:

Debut: v Billericay Town (h), Isthmian League Division One, 13 August 1994.
Last appearance: v Kingstonian (at Aldershot Town FC), Isthmian League Cup Final, 6 May 1996.
Appearances: 48 + 3
Goals: 4

Playing career:
Reading (youth), Bracknell Town (May 1985), Wycombe Wanderers (January 1989), Woking (June 1989), Kingstonian

(July 1992), Hayes (3ML, January 1994), Aldershot Town (July 1994), Wokingham Town (July 1996), Hampton (March 1998), Sandhurst Town (summer 1998), Ash United (summer 2001), Finchampstead (summer 2002).

Representative honours:
FA XI, Isthmian League XI.

Club honours:
Isthmian League Cup (Woking 1991), Surrey Senior Cup (Woking 1991), Isthmian League Charity Shield (Woking 1991), Isthmian League Premier Division (Woking 1991–92).

Andy was a commanding centre-back and is the older brother of Scott Russell and the younger brother of Marc Russell, both of whom are ex-Reading apprentices. His leadership qualities have enabled him to enjoy spells as captain at every club he has played for. Having played youth-team football at Reading, Andy joined Bracknell Town in May 1985. Despite Andy's game improving noticeably year-on-year, the Robins' third season was a complete contrast to the previous two, as they struggled and finished in the bottom four.

Andy then had a short spell at Wycombe Wanderers before joining Woking in June 1989, and he became the mainstay of the back four during what turned out to be the most successful period of his career. Highlights include finishing as runners-up to Wivenhoe Town in Isthmian League Division One, reaching the FA Cup second round (where they lost to Cambridge United) in 1989–90 and winning the Isthmian League Premier Division title in 1991–92.

Andy then appeared for Kingstonian and Hayes before joining Aldershot Town in July 1994 for a fee of £1,500. His dominance in the air meant he was effective at both ends of the pitch. Andy's calmness when the ball was at his feet made him a very useful asset, and he helped the club achieve two top-five finishes in Isthmian League Division One.

Andy left the Rec in the summer of 1996 and went on to play for several clubs until he retired in January 2004, but instead of taking it easy he decided to play local rugby! Andy currently runs his own business designing, fitting and furnishing offices.

Mark Russell — Goalkeeper

Born: 9 February 1975, Kingston-Upon-Thames.

Aldershot Town FC record:

Debut:	v Hendon (a), Isthmian League Premier Division, 14 August 1999.
Last appearance:	v Fisher Athletic (London, a), FA Cup third qualifying round, 2 October 1999.
Appearances:	13

Playing career:
Kingstonian, Dorking, Windsor and Eton (August 1994), Hampton (November 1994), Aldershot Town (June 1999), Fleet Town (October 1999), Hampton and Richmond Borough (July 2000), Yeading (December 2001), Banstead Athletic (February 2002), Chessington and Hook United (summer 2003).

Club honours:
Middlesex Charity Cup (Hampton 1998), Aldershot Senior Cup (Fleet Town 2000).

Mark had played for several clubs before joining Hampton, where he would forge his reputation, in November 1994. He improved season-by-season and helped the club achieve promotion from Isthmian League Division Two in 1995–96. This was followed by a very creditable fourth-place finish the following season and then promotion into the Premier Division in 1997–98, with the latter being accompanied by the winning of the Middlesex Charity Cup. He also attained personal glory by winning the 1995, 1997 and 1999 Player of the Year awards at the Beveree.

Mark joined Aldershot Town in June 1999 following a host of outstanding performances for Hampton. However, he struggled to replicate that form and left somewhat acrimoniously in October 1999, with his departure being sealed by his reported failure to turn up for a Full Members' Cup game at Bromley. One positive that can be taken from his move to Fleet Town is that the Shots received a £3,000 fee (Fleet's record buy) for a player who had cost nothing.

Things got worse for Mark, as Fleet struggled for the entire season and finished rock bottom of the Southern League Eastern Division. He then had a number of club spells, but it is not known what he did for the 2002–03 season. However, it is known that he joined Combined Counties Premier League side Chessington and Hook United in the summer of 2003 and that he was voted the club's Player of the Year in 2004 and 2005 as they finished third in the League. Mark retired in the summer of 2006, but nothing is known of his current whereabouts.

Emmanuel Sackey — Midfielder/Right-back/Centre-back

Born: 1 February 1988, Hackney.

Aldershot Town FC record:

Debut: as substitute v Christchurch (h), Hampshire Senior Cup second round, 27 November 2007.

Last appearance: v Basingstoke Town (h), Hampshire Senior Cup quarter-final, 19 February 2008.

Appearances: 1 + 2

Playing career:

Wimbledon (schoolboy), Charlton Athletic (academy), Cheltenham Town (academy), Dagenham and Redbridge (summer 2004), Southend United (February 2005), Gravesend and Northfleet (summer 2005), Hayes/Hayes and Yeading United (March 2006), Aldershot Town (trial, 2006–07 season), Aldershot Town (trial, summer 2007), Aldershot Town (trial, October 2007), Aldershot Town (NC, November 2007), Waltham Forest (December 2007), Northwood (February 2008), Enfield Town (March 2008).

Representative honours:

England Schoolboys.

Emmanuel is a versatile player and is the cousin of England rugby player Paul Sackey. He played schoolboy football at Wimbledon and then played in the academies at Charlton Athletic and Cheltenham Town. In the summer of 2004 he joined Dagenham and Redbridge, where he played for the reserves and in minor Cup competitions, and it was a similar story at Southend United and Gravesend and Northfleet.

In March 2006 he joined Hayes and captained their reserve side during the 2006–07 season. He also made a handful of appearances for the Shots' reserve side during that season, and he returned to the Rec as a trialist that summer, trialling again in the reserves once the season got under way.

In November 2007 he was released by Hayes and Yeading United and joined the Shots as a non-contract player while also signing for Isthmian League Division One North side Waltham Forest. Behind the scenes, changes at Wadham Lodge in February 2008 led to several players (including Emmanuel) leaving, and he subsequently joined divisional rivals Northwood and then Enfield Town the following month, while continuing to play for Aldershot's reserves.

Enfield Town finished the 2007–08 season in 12th spot in the League, as well as qualifying for the Middlesex Charity Cup Final, where they were due to face Hillingdon Borough. However, a waterlogged pitch caused the game to be postponed, with the decision being taken to 'hold it over' until the start of the following season.

Will Salmon — Utility

Born: 25 November 1986, Basingstoke.

Aldershot Town FC record:

Debut: as substitute v Locksheath (h), Hampshire Senior Cup third round, 2 December 2003.

Last appearance: as substitute v Forest Green Rovers (a), Conference Challenge Cup Southern Section quarter-final, 15 February 2005.

Appearances: 0 + 3

Playing career:

Aldershot Town (from youth, August 2005), Fleet Town (SLL, August 2005), Fleet Town (SLL, August 2006), AFC Wimbledon (June 2007), Fleet Town (3ML, February 2008).

Representative honours:

Hampshire Youth.

Club honours:

Russell Cotes Cup (Fleet Town 2007, 2008).

Will is a player who is comfortable at right-back, centre-back or in central-midfield. He made his senior debut for the Shots while still a member of the youth team, and his continued good form in the reserves led to him signing full contract forms in August 2005.

Oddly, he never made another first-team appearance at the Rec and spent the entire 2005–06 and 2006–07 seasons on loan at Fleet Town. In the latter season, his confidence in the tackle and excellent distribution contributed to the club finishing fifth in the Isthmian League Division One South and to Will winning both the Supporters' and Players' Player of the Year awards.

Will was released by Aldershot in the summer of 2007 and immediately snapped up by ex-Shots boss Terry Brown at AFC Wimbledon. However, he struggled to hold down a regular first-team place at Kingsmeadow and returned to Fleet on a four-month loan in February 2008. Following his arrival at Calthorpe Park, he helped claim the runners'-up spot in Southern League Division One South and West (four points behind Farnborough), was involved in the resultant Play-off semi-final loss to Uxbridge and also played in the Russell Cotes Cup Final victory over New Milton Town, and the defeat to Tadley Calleva in the North Hants Cup Final.

While Will was at Calthorpe Park, AFC Wimbledon (whose season finished before Fleet's) released him, and it is believed that he is still considering his options concerning another club.

Ryan Scott — Midfielder

Born: 27 December 1986, Aldershot.

Aldershot Town FC record:

Debut:	v Newport (Isle of Wight, h), Hampshire Senior Cup third round, 30 November 2004.
Last appearance:	v Halifax Town (a), Conference Premier, 19 April 2008.
Appearances:	52 + 31
Goals:	3

Playing career:
Aldershot Town (from youth, December 2005), Farnborough (May 2008).

Representative honours:
Aldershot, Farnborough and District Schoolboys.

Club honours:
Conference Premier (Aldershot Town 2007–08).

Ryan is an energetic central-midfielder and the cousin of ex-Farnborough Town defender Sean Hankin. He initially appeared for the Shots' first team while still a member of the youth team and finished the 2004–05 season as youth team Player of the Year.

Ryan's performances and continued improvement the following season impressed boss Terry Brown so much that he signed full contract forms in December 2005, and his strength in the challenge and ability to create openings helped establish him in the first team over the next two seasons.

In a three-week period in 2007 Ryan set two club records: in March, he became the youngest-ever captain (aged 20 years and 78 days) when he wore the armband in the Hampshire Senior Cup quarter-final against Eastleigh; the following month, he acquired the unenviable distinction of receiving the fastest-ever red card when he was dismissed just 67 seconds after coming on as a substitute in a League match against Exeter City!

Ryan was a member of the Shots side that lost in the FA Cup third round at Blackpool in January 2007 before suffering the misfortune of breaking his leg in the final League match of the season at Altrincham. He was expected to miss the entire 2007–08 season because of post-operative complications, but his determination allowed him to make his comeback ahead of schedule in February 2008. He played a handful of games before the season's end but was released shortly after the campaign finished, subsequently joining neighbours Farnborough.

Stuart Searle — Goalkeeper

Born: 27 February 1979, Wimbledon.

Aldershot Town FC record:

Debut:	v Sutton United (h), Isthmian League Charity Shield, 6 December 1999.

Last appearance: v Heybridge Swifts (a), Isthmian League Premier Division, 5 March 2001.
Appearances: 20

Playing career:
Tooting and Mitcham (youth), Wimbledon (from trainee, June 1996), Woking (July 1997), Carshalton Athletic (July 1998), Crawley Town (September 1999), Aldershot Town (November 1999), Molesey (3ML, February 2000), Carshalton Athletic (3ML, January 2001), Carshalton Athletic (July 2001), Barnet (NC, July 2005), Basingstoke Town (November 2005), Chelsea (player-youth-team coach, July 2007), Walton and Hersham (DR, July 2007).

Club honours:
Isthmian League Charity Shield (Aldershot Town 1999), Isthmian League Division One South (Carshalton Athletic 2002–03).

Stuart is a 'keeper who has a great command of his area and who started out as a youth player at Tooting and Mitcham. Having played in their first team at the age of 16, he went on to become a trainee at Wimbledon and signed full professional forms in June 1996, going on to play for Woking and Carshalton Athletic. Despite playing in a team that finished in the bottom three in the Isthmian League Premier Division, Stuart put in some good performances.

After a short spell at Crawley Town, Stuart signed for Aldershot Town in November 1999 (to replace the recently departed Mark Russell) as understudy to Andy Pape. Unfortunately, he made just four appearances in his first season at the Rec and was loaned out to Molesey to get some much-needed match experience. He fared slightly better in 2000–01 by making 16 appearances but was loaned out to former club Carshalton Athletic before moving to Colston Avenue permanently in the summer for £2,500.

Carshalton had just been relegated after 24 years in the Isthmian Premier Division and a fast-improving Stuart inspired the club to a sixth-place finish. They won the Isthmian League Division One South title in 2002–03 and went into the newly formed Conference South the following season.

Stuart remained at Carshalton for the start of the 2005–06 season and signed for Barnet on a non-contract basis, where he spent the next three months playing for the Bees' reserves. In November 2005 he left Carshalton and joined Basingstoke Town, but the club endured the loss of several key players as well as long-time manager Ernie Howe, which resulted in consecutive bottom-four finishes in the Conference South.

A few eyebrows were raised in July 2007 when FA Premier League big guns Chelsea signed Stuart on a one-year full-time reserve contract. At the time, he was working at the club's academy as well as at former Shots 'keeper Les Cleevely's goalkeeping academy, and his move into the big time meant he had to resign from the latter job. However, he did sign dual-registration forms to allow him to play for Walton and Hersham, managed by Les, in the Isthmian League Division One South, and he made 15 League appearances as the Swans finished the 2007–08 season in 10th spot.

Aside from his playing, Stuart has built up a reputation as a well-respected goalkeeping coach, and he has worked at Wimbledon's academy and in America.

Joe Sebo — Defender/Midfielder

Born: 19 April 1980, Chertsey.

Aldershot Town FC record:
Debut: v Worthing (a), Isthmian League Full Members' Cup second round, 2 February 1999.
Appearances: 1

Playing career:
Camberley Town (from youth), Aldershot Town (youth), Fleet Town (March 1999), Camberley Town (August 2000), Wokingham Town (October 2001), Chertsey Town (January 2002), Egham Town (2001–02 season), Westfield (2002–03 season), Ash United (March 2006).

Joe can play as a defender or midfielder and was originally a youth player at Camberley Town before joining Aldershot Town's youth team. Having made his sole appearance for the Shots, he went on to play for Fleet Town, Camberley again, Wokingham Town, Chertsey Town and Egham Town. Joe signed for Combined Counties side Westfield during the 2002–03 season, but it is not known how long he stayed there. However, it is known that he signed for Ash United in March 2006 and left there in the summer of 2007. Joe reportedly runs a soccer coaching school.

Neil Selby — Forward

Born: 12 March 1974, Reading.

Aldershot Town FC record:

Debut: as substitute v Merstham (h), FA Cup first qualifying round, 14 September 1996.
Last appearance: v Hampton (h), Isthmian League Division One, 22 October 1996.
Appearances: 2 + 6

Playing career:
Southampton (trainee, July 1990), Havant Town (July 1992), Waterlooville (August 1993), Aldershot Town (August 1996), Wokingham Town (November 1996), Chertsey Town (July 1998), Aylesbury United (July 1999), Boreham Wood (December 1999), Staines Town (September 2001), Bracknell Town (July 2003), Godalming and Guildford (4ML, September 2004), Sandhurst Town (September 2006).

Club honours:
Gosport War Memorial Cup (Havant Town 1993), Isthmian League Division One (Boreham Wood 2000–01), Berks and Bucks Senior Trophy (Sandhurst Town 2007).

Neil is an experienced and free-scoring forward who, having been a trainee at Southampton, signed for Havant Town in July 1992. He finished the 1992–93 season as the club's top scorer (19 goals) and then joined local rivals Waterlooville, where he continued to trouble opposing defences and was the club's top scorer in 1993–94 (18 goals) and 1994–95 (23 goals).

Neil came to the Rec in August 1996 having been courted by Shots manager Steve Wigley for some time. However, considering the amount of effort that had gone into getting him, it was rather surprising that he was allowed to sign for Wokingham Town (albeit for a fee/profit of £2,000) a mere two months after arriving. Neil's ability to conjure a goal out of nothing enabled him to stand out in a struggling side, but he could not prevent relegation from Isthmian League Division One in 1997–98. It was also little comfort to him that he was the club's top scorer (20 goals) and Player of the Year that season.

Neil then joined Chertsey Town in July 1998 and was the top scorer in Isthmian League Division One in 1998–99 (26 goals), as well as being voted the Curfews' Player of the Year. Following a brief stint at Aylesbury United, he signed for Boreham Wood in December 1999 and endured a complete contrast in fortunes during his near two seasons at Meadow Park. In 1999–2000 the club were relegated from the Isthmian League Premier Division but won the Division One title in 2000–01. Unfortunately, Neil played very little part in that Championship-winning season due to an achilles injury, and he dropped back down to Division One in September 2001 to sign for Staines Town. Unsurprisingly, he finished as top scorer in both 2001–02 (13 goals) and 2002–03 (14 goals) – two seasons in which the club struggled in the lower reaches of the table.

Neil went on to play for Bracknell Town, Godalming Town and Sandhurst Town, where he finished the 2006–07 season as top scorer (14 goals). He had a quieter 2007–08 season, scoring seven goals in 31 appearances, 20 of which were as a substitute, as the Fizzers finished 16th in the Combined Counties League Premier Division.

James Sharp — Left-back/Centre-back

Born: 2 January 1976, Reading.

Aldershot Town FC record:

Debut: v Maidenhead United (h), Isthmian League Full Members' Cup second round, 5 December 1995.
Last appearance: v Eastleigh (a), Hampshire Senior Cup second round, 3 January 1996.
Appearances: 3

Playing career:
Aldershot FC (apprentice, 1991–92 season), Reading (youth), Florida Tech (US), Aldershot Town (November 1995), Marlow, Wokingham Town (September 1997), Andover (summer 1999), Hartlepool United (August 2000), Falkirk (July 2003), Brechin City (3ML, February 2005), Torquay United (July 2005), Wycombe Wanderers (trial, July 2006), Shrewsbury Town (M, August 2006), Rochdale (August 2006), Airdrie United (June 2007).

Club honours:
Scottish League Division Two (Brechin City 2004–05).
James has made 148 Football League and Scottish League appearances, scoring five goals.

James began his footballing career as an apprentice forward at the 'old' Aldershot FC during the 1991–92 season and appeared in the youth and reserve sides. He then played in the youth team at Reading before going out to the States to study, during which time he played for Florida Tech and was selected for the 1994 Sunshine State All-Conference Team.

On his return to the UK he signed for Aldershot Town and made three senior appearances in the 1996–97 season, having played some games in the reserves. He later played for Marlow and Wokingham Town before joining Andover in the summer of 1999, and it was his maturing performances during the forthcoming season (in which the club finished third in the Wessex League) that started to alert clubs higher up the pyramid of his potential.

In what could be described as a strange move, James joined Division Three side Hartlepool United in August 2000 and made his debut against Lincoln City on the opening day of the 2000–01 season. He increased his value by scoring the last-gasp winner in the penultimate League game of the season against Kidderminster Harriers to secure the club's place in the Play-off semi-finals, where they lost to Blackpool. The disappointment of that loss was slightly softened for James, as he won the Player of the Year award.

The 2001–02 season was to end early for James – he was substituted in a League match against Plymouth Argyle in the November (for tactical reasons) and did not play again until the summer of 2003, when he signed for Falkirk. He was a regular inclusion during his first season with the Bairns but made just four appearances in 2004–05 as they won the Division One title. Interestingly, James was still a title-winner that season, as he played as a loanee in the last 13 games for Division Two champions Brechin City.

James moved back to England in the summer of 2005 when he joined Torquay United. He was appointed as captain and stood out in a struggling side; however, he was one of several players to leave Plainmoor that summer. He later played for Shrewsbury Town and Rochdale later that month. Scottish Division One outfit Airdrie United were interested in signing him in 2007–08, but FIFA's 'three clubs' rule prevented him playing for another club that season. He duly signed for the Diamonds in June 2007 and was appointed as captain but played just nine times before sustaining knee and achilles tendon injuries. James left Broomfield Park in January 2008 and reportedly moved back to the Reading area, but no further information is known about him.

Alastair Shaw — Midfielder

Born: 6 December 1983, Frimley.

Aldershot Town FC record:

Debut:	as substitute v Hendon (h), Isthmian League Cup second round, 14 February 2002.
Last appearance:	as substitute v Braintree Town (a), Isthmian League Premier Division, 18 April 2002.
Appearances:	0 + 2

Playing career:
Aldershot Town (youth).

Alastair was a midfielder and was a member of the Shots' youth side when making his two senior appearances. He was released in the summer of 2002 due to his educational commitments, and no details of his subsequent career are known.

Tony Shields — Midfielder

Born: 4 June 1980, Londonderry.

Aldershot Town FC record:

Debut:	v Tamworth (a), Conference, 18 October 2003.
Last appearance:	v Exeter City (a), Conference, 13 March 2004.
Appearances:	18 + 1

Playing career:
Omagh Town (schoolboy), Norwich City (schoolboy), Peterborough United (from trainee, July 1998), Stevenage Borough (1ML, January 2002), Derry City (1ML, February 2002), Aldershot Town (initially on 3ML, October

2003), Waterford United (March 2004), Omagh Town (August 2004), Limavady United (August 2005), Finn Harps (January 2007).
Tony has made 123 Football League appearances, scoring three goals.

Representative honours:
Republic of Ireland Youth, Republic of Ireland Under-21s.

Club honours:
League of Ireland Division One Promotion/Relegation Play-off (Finn Harps 2007).

Tony is a tenacious central-midfielder with a propensity for collecting yellow and red cards. He played schoolboy football before joining Peterborough United's youth team, signing full professional forms in July 1998. His most successful season at London Road came in 1999–2000 when he played in 24 of the club's League games as they were promoted from Division Three via a Play-off Final win over Darlington.

Tony later had loan spells at Stevenage Borough and Derry City (his hometown club) before joining Aldershot Town on a three-month loan deal in October 2003. It was reported that he was looking to return to his native Ireland at the end of the spell, but he fitted into the Shots' midfield and performed so well that he changed his plans and signed permanently in January 2004. However, the move did not quite work out as both parties had hoped and, after collecting two red cards (including one in his last appearance), Tony left.

Cork City were reportedly interested in his signature, but he signed instead for their League of Ireland rivals Waterford United, later playing for Omagh Town, Irish Premier League side Limavady United and most recently League of Ireland Division One side Finn Harps. He was Harps' captain in 2007–08 as they finished runners-up to Cobh Ramblers in the division and then beat Waterford United in the two-leg Play-off to gain promotion to the Premier Division. At the time of writing, Finn Harps currently sit in 10th place in the League of Ireland Premier Division; the season runs from March to November.

Jason Short — Defender/Midfielder

Born: 18 February 1986, Aldershot.

Aldershot Town FC record:
Debut: as substitute v Brockenhurst (h), Hampshire Senior Cup second round, 21 October 2003.
Last appearance: v Winchester City (at AFC Bournemouth), Hampshire Senior Cup Final, 27 April 2005.
Appearances: 6 + 2

Playing career:
Aldershot Town (youth, August 2003), Chertsey Town (6ML, August 2004), Cove (3ML, February 2005), Camberley Town (6ML, August 2005), Badshot Lea (January 2006), Camberley Town (July 2007), Badshot Lea (March 2008).

Club honours:
Hellenic League Supplementary Cup (Badshot Lea 2006).

Jason is a competitive defender-cum-midfielder who made all of his appearances in the senior side while a member of the Shots' youth team. He was loaned out to various clubs before leaving the Rec in January 2006 and signing for Hellenic League Division One East side Badshot Lea, where he was one of several ex-Shots youngsters who helped Badshot Lea attain a third-place finish in 2006–07, thus gaining promotion to the Premier Division for the first time in the club's history.

That summer, Jason made a permanent return to Camberley Town, where he stayed until March 2008 then re-signed for Badshot Lea. The club were losing finalists in the Aldershot Senior Cup Final, but Jason did not play in the defeat to Fleet Town as a result of being Cup-tied, having played for Camberley Town earlier in the competition.

Paul Shrubb — Right-back/Midfielder

Born: 1 August 1955, Guildford.

Aldershot Town FC record:
Debut: v Hertford Town (a), Isthmian League Division Three, 10 October 1992.

Last appearance: v Malden Vale (h), Isthmian League Division Two, 19 April 1994.
Appearances: 29 + 2

Playing career:
Fulham (from apprentice, August 1972), Hellenic (South Africa, June 1975), Brentford (March 1977), Aldershot FC (August 1982), Woking (player-coach, August 1987), Dorking (player-coach, August 1989), Leatherhead (player-coach, August 1990), Fleet Town (player-coach, January 1991), Cove (player-coach, August 1991), Aldershot Town (player-joint assistant manager, October 1992).
Paul has made 357 Football League appearances, scoring 13 goals.

Representative honours:
Guildford and District Schools.

Club honours:
Isthmian League Division Three (Aldershot Town 1992–93).

Post-playing coaching/management career:
Assistant manager of Aldershot Town (January 1995), coach at Hampton (summer 1997), assistant coach at Kingstonian (July 2000), scout for Charlton Athletic (August 2001).

Paul is one of life's gentlemen and has been very popular with the fans wherever he has played. He is also part of the unique band of players to have played for both Aldershot sides. Paul joined Fulham as an apprentice on his 15th birthday and captained the youth team. He attended England youth trials but was unsuccessful and signed full professional forms at Craven Cottage in August 1972. However, he made just one appearance before being released on FA Cup Final Day in 1975.

Bobby Moore, who captained the Cottagers in the aforementioned Final, then persuaded Paul to go out to South Africa that summer, where he signed for Cape Town side Hellenic. Paul returned home to the UK after a couple of seasons, but Hellenic refused to release his registration. A six-month wrangle followed, during which time he trained with Brentford, who were managed by Bill Dodgin Jnr (his boss at Fulham). Following the intervention of the FA, Paul's registration was finally released and he was free to sign for the Bees. During his time at Griffin Park, Paul was involved in promotion to Division Three in 1977–78 and went on to make 182 Football League appearances.

Paul signed for Aldershot FC in August 1982 and made his debut against Tranmere Rovers in the opening game of the 1982–83 season, immediately bringing a sense of calmness to the Shots side. He was a member of the side that achieved a club-best progression in the League Cup in 1984–85, when they drew with Division One Norwich City at a fog-bound Rec before losing the replay at Carrow Road.

Paul has the unique distinction of wearing every shirt number from one to 11 while at Brentford and Aldershot FC, and many Shots fans can recall the game where he donned the number-one jersey for the Shots – a League match at Swindon Town in March 1986 when 'keeper David Coles was stretchered off with a broken leg.

Paul's 1986–87 season was curtailed by an arm injury sustained in training, but he was a regular until the end of November in a season that culminated in promotion via victory over Wolverhampton Wanderers in the Division Four Play-off Final. Having made 174 Football League appearances for the Shots, Paul left to take up the post of player-coach at Woking, where he helped achieve successive third-place finishes in Isthmian League Division One. He subsequently adopted the same role at various clubs before joining the 'new' Shots as player-joint assistant manager a couple of months into their inaugural season.

Paul's experience was a noticeable factor in the club winning the 1992–93 Isthmian League Division Three title, and he was also involved in the run to the FA Vase quarter-finals and a second successive promotion the following season. In January 1995 he became player-caretaker manager at the Rec following Steve Wignall's departure, and he can lay claim to having a 100 per cent managerial record as victory was attained in the only game for which he was in charge (against Berkhamsted Town)! As is documented elsewhere in this book, the Shots fans also have Paul to thank for the fact that the legendary Jason Chewins did not leave the Rec earlier than he did!

Following Steve Wigley's arrival as boss at the Rec, Paul decided to retire and, as Keith Baker had already departed, he took on the role of assistant manager in his own right. He left the Rec along with Wigley in the summer of 1997 and subsequently worked in coaching roles before moving into his current role as a scout for Charlton Athletic.

Tim Sills — Forward

Born: 10 September 1979, Romsey.

Aldershot Town FC record:

Debut: v Accrington Stanley (h), Conference, 10 August 2003.
Last appearance: v Canvey Island (h), Conference National, 24 January 2006.
Appearances: 112 + 14
Goals: 51 (sixth in all-time top 10)

Playing career:

Millwall (youth), Camberley Town (July 1997), Basingstoke Town (March 1999), Staines Town (1ML, September 2000), Kingstonian (January 2002), Aldershot Town (May 2003), Oxford United (January 2006), Hereford United (June 2006), Torquay United (June 2007).
Tim has made 49 Football League appearances, scoring three goals.

Representative honours:

England Semi-Professional XI (one cap), Middlesex Wanderers.

Club honours:

Aldershot Senior Cup (Camberley Town 1998).

Tim is a powerful and energetic player and is one of the few forwards who can defend ably too. The younger brother of ex-Camberley Town defender Julian Sills, he began his football career as a youth-team player at Millwall. Having decided to combine his studies with football, he moved to Camberley Town in July 1997 and his 23 goals helped the club finish fourth in Isthmian League Division Three (missing promotion by four points), as well as enabling him to finish the season as joint top scorer along with ex-Shot Ian Jopling. Tim was later a member of the Camberley sides that reached the FA Cup first round in 1998–99 and the FA Vase fifth round.

Tim remained at Krooner Park until March 1999 when, having scored 43 goals in 76 appearances, he joined Basingstoke Town with brother Julian for a joint fee of £3,000. He made an immediate impact at the Camrose, scoring in the first five minutes of his debut against Bishop's Stortford, and he went on to be the club's top scorer in 1999–2000 (15 goals) and 2000–01 (23 goals).

Tim moved to Kingstonian in March 2002 following a loan spell there and scored 33 goals in 64 games, making him their top scorer in 2002–03 (25 goals). He also won the Player of the Year award, as well as winning his sole England National XI cap against Belgium in February 2003. Three months later, Tim became Aldershot Town's first signing as a Conference club, with controversy regarding his Ks contract surrounding his arrival at the Rec.

Tim's debut came in Aldershot's first-ever Conference game against Accrington Stanley in August 2003, and he scored the first goal in a 2–0 victory, thus becoming the club's first-ever scorer in said League. He was also a member of the side that lost to Hednesford Town in that season's FA Trophy semi-finals. Aside from the aggregate defeat, the second leg of that tie will be remembered for Tim finishing the game in goal following Nikki Bull's dismissal, with all of the permitted substitutes having been used. He later endured end-of-season heartache when he was a playing substitute as the Shots lost the 2004 Conference Play-off Final to Shrewsbury Town.

Tim's magnificent scoring rate and all-round game brought him many admirers from further up the footballing pyramid, and both Grimsby Town and Bristol Rovers were reported to be the main clubs interested in signing him in the summer of 2004. However, following the club's transition to full-time professional status, he resigned from his job in the Tussauds Group and stayed loyal to the Shots, top-scoring in 2004–05 (18 goals) as the club reached the Play-off semi-finals. In fact Tim scored both goals in the 2–0 home victory over Scarborough in the final game of the 'regular' season, confirming the Shots' fourth-place finish before they went on to lose to Carlisle United.

In January 2006 the pull of the Football League became too great for Tim to ignore, and he signed for Oxford United for £50,000. Despite that move, he still finished the 2005–06 season as the Shots' top scorer (11 goals). Unfortunately, he scored just once in 13 appearances for a struggling Oxford side and went on to play for Hereford United, where he found it no easier, and Torquay United. Here, he had a more fruitful 2007–08 season goal-wise, scoring 21 in all competitions. However, this achievement was tainted by disappointment in both the Conference Premier and the FA Trophy. At the end-of-season National Game Awards, Tim won the Goal of the Season award for his scissor-kick in the home game against Histon in January.

Daniel Simmonds — Midfielder/Forward

Born: 22 November 1989, Frimley.

Aldershot Town FC record:

Debut:	v Rushden and Diamonds (h), Conference Premier, 17 November 2007.
Appearances:	1 + 1

Representative honours:
Hampshire Under-18s.

Playing career:
Aldershot Town (youth), Camberley Town (3ML, February 2008).

Club honours:
Conference Premier (Aldershot Town 2007–08).

Daniel was a regular goalscorer for the Shots' youth team, which eventually enabled him to break into the first team during the 2007–08 season. He also had a three-month loan spell at Camberley Town later that season.

Ian Simpemba — Defender

Born: 28 March 1983, Dublin.

Aldershot Town FC record:

Debut:	v Kidderminster Harriers (a), Conference National, 18 March 2006.
Last appearance:	v Southport (a), Conference National, 29 April 2006.
Appearances:	10

Playing career:
Wycombe Wanderers (from scholar, July 2001), Woking (3ML, October 2002), Woking (1ML, September 2003), Crawley Town (July 2004), Aldershot Town (2ML, March 2006), Lewes (July 2006), Havant and Waterlooville (May 2008).
Ian has made 20 Football League appearances, scoring two goals.

Representative honours:
FA Youth, Republic of Ireland Under-17s, Republic of Ireland Under-18s, Republic of Ireland Under-19s.

Club honours:
Southern League Championship Trophy (Crawley Town 2004), Conference South (Lewes 2007–08).

Ian is a solid defender who was a scholar at Wycombe Wanderers. He signed full professional forms in July 2001 and was loaned to Woking before playing the second half of 2003–04 for Wycombe, which saw them relegated from Division Two. This prompted a clear-out that saw Ian move to Crawley Town in July 2004 for a fee that, although undisclosed, is listed as a record buy for the Sussex club.

Towards the end of 2005–06, he found it hard to claim a place in the Crawley side and so was loaned out to the Shots, later signing for Lewes, where he helped equal a club-best progression to the FA Cup first round in both 2006–07 (losing to Darlington) and 2007–08 (beaten by Mansfield Town).

Ian played 49 times in all competitions and scored six goals for Lewes as they secured the 2007–08 Conference South title. He scored against Weston-Super-Mare in the last game of the season before opting to stay in the division and become Havant and Waterlooville's first summer signing in May 2008.

Jamie Slabber — Forward

Born: 31 December 1984, Enfield.

Aldershot Town FC record:

Debut:	v Crawley Town (h), Conference National, 9 April 2005.

Last appearance: as substitute v Carlisle United (a), Conference National, Play-off semi-final second leg, 6 May 2005.
Appearances: 2 + 3
Goals: 1

Playing career:
Tottenham Hotspur (from scholar, January 2002), AB Copenhagen (Denmark, 1ML, March 2004), Swindon Town (2ML, December 2004), Aldershot Town (NC, March 2005), Bristol Rovers (trial, July 2005), Grays Athletic (July 2005), Oxford United (1ML, November 2006), Stevenage Borough (January 2007), Rushden and Diamonds (trial, July 2007), Havant and Waterlooville (July 2007).
Jamie has made 10 FA Premier League and Football League appearances.

Representative honours:
England Under-18s, England Under-20s, England National Game XI (1 cap).

Club honours:
FA Trophy (Grays Athletic 2006 [unused substitute]; Stevenage Borough 2007 [unused substitute]).

Jamie is a striker whose career began as a scholar at Tottenham Hotspur, where he signed professional forms in December 2001. He injured his foot during the 2003–04 season and joined Danish side AB Copenhagen on a three-month loan in March 2004 in order to give him some matches to aid his recovery. He later had a two-month loan spell at Swindon Town before joining Aldershot Town in March 2005 and will always be part of club folklore, after scoring the last-minute header that sent the second leg of the 2005 Play-off semi-final against Carlisle United into extra-time.

Jamie was unable to secure a contract at the Rec and so left to trial elsewhere, signing permanently at Grays Athletic in July 2005. Jamie was part of the Grays side knocked out of the FA Cup by Mansfield Town at the second-round stage in 2005–06 – the furthest the club has ever progressed – and his early-season form earned him his sole appearance for the England National Game XI against Belgium (in the November) – a game that contributed to the winning of the 2005–06 European Challenge Trophy. Jamie's 13 goals – scored as a result of a great partnership with ex-Shot Aaron McLean – and performances helped Grays finish that season in third place in the Conference National and as FA Trophy winners.

The following season both club and player struggled, and Jamie went on to appear at Oxford United, Stevenage Borough and Havant and Waterlooville, where he was part of the 2007–08 side that won national acclaim for their best-ever FA Cup run, during which they knocked out League Two side Notts County and (at the time of the game) League One leaders Swansea City before losing at Liverpool in round four. The Anfield game will long be remembered, not only because the Hawks were by no means disgraced but for the fact that they led the Mighty Reds not once but twice before losing 5–2! Jamie made 32 appearances in all competitions but netted just three times that season as the Hawks attained seventh place in the Conference South.

Gary Smart — Right-back

Born: 29 April 1964, Totnes.

Aldershot Town FC record:
Debut: v Purfleet (a), Isthmian League Premier Division, 22 August 1998.
Last appearance: v Altrincham (h), FA Trophy fourth round, 6 February 1999.
Appearances: 34 + 1

Playing career:
Wokingham Town (January 1988), Oxford United (July 1988), Woking (trial, July 1994), Stevenage Borough (August 1994), Chertsey Town (December 1994), Chesham United (March 1995), Hayes (January 1996), Slough Town (March 1996), Aldershot Town (June 1998), Oxford City (February 1999), Leighton Town, Windsor and Eton (October 2000).
Gary has made 175 Football League appearances.

Representative honours:
FA XI.

Details of Gary's early career are unknown, but it is known that he signed for Wokingham Town in January 1988 and that his performances facilitated a move to Oxford United that summer. He made his Football League debut against AFC Bournemouth in September 1988 and would later be part of the Oxford sides that shocked First Division Chelsea in the FA Cup third round in 1990–91 and that avoided relegation from Division Two in 1991–92 by just two points.

Having not been involved at all during the 1993–94 season, Gary left the Manor Ground and played for several teams. He joined Slough Town in March 1996 and was a member of the 1997–98 side that progressed to the FA Cup first round (where they lost to Cardiff City) and were beaten by Southport in the FA Trophy semi-finals.

Gary joined Aldershot Town that summer but suffered a loss of form as the season went on. This prompted public criticism from manager George Borg and ultimately led to him taking on the role of player-coach at Oxford United and then playing for Leighton Town before joining Windsor and Eton in October 2000.

Gary's experience helped the Royalists to finish the season as runners-up to Tooting and Mitcham United in Isthmian League Division Two, but the following season saw them endure a complete reversal of fortune and finish rock bottom of Division One. Gary retired in the summer of 2002, and no further information about him is known.

Dean Smith — Right-back

Born: 13 August 1986, Islington.

Aldershot Town FC record:

Debut:	v Gravesend and Northfleet (h), Conference National, 12 August 2006.
Last appearance:	v Rushden and Diamonds (h), Setanta Shield Final, 3 April 2008.
Appearances:	60 + 11

Playing career:
Chelsea (from academy, August 2003), Aldershot Town (June 2006).

Club honours:
Hampshire Senior Cup (Aldershot Town 2007), Setanta Shield (Aldershot Town 2008), Conference Premier (Aldershot Town 2007–08).

Dean is an attacking right-back who, having signed full professional forms at Stamford Bridge in August 2003, was a regular in Chelsea's reserve side in 2005–06. He joined Aldershot Town in June 2006 and made an excellent start to his Shots career, which resulted in him being rewarded with a contract extension a couple of months later.

Dean was a member of the Shots side that reached the FA Cup third round in 2006–07, losing at Blackpool, and ended the season as winners in the Hampshire Senior Cup. A combination of a loss of form and injuries restricted his appearances the following season, but he still played his part in the Shots reaching the FA Trophy semi-finals and winning the Setanta Shield. He put in a memorable performance in the latter game when he bravely played on despite being injured and having moved across to an unfamiliar centre-back role as a result of an injury to Dave Winfield. Unfortunately, Dean was released at the end of the 2007–08 season and, at the time of writing, has not found another club.

Tyron Smith — Midfielder/Defender

Born: 4 August 1986, Frimley.

Aldershot Town FC record:

Debut:	v Yeading (h), Isthmian League Charity Shield, 19 August 2003.
Last appearance:	v Winchester City (at AFC Bournemouth), Hampshire Senior Cup Final, 27 April 2005.
Appearances:	17 + 13
Goals:	2

Playing career:
Aldershot Town (from youth, August 2003), Wimbledon (trial, 2003–04 season), Farnborough Town (June 2005), Basingstoke Town (June 2007), Maidenhead United (May 2008).

Club honours:
Isthmian League Charity Shield (Aldershot Town 2003), Hampshire Senior Cup (Farnborough Town 2006; Basingstoke Town 2008).

Tyron is yet another graduate from the Shots' youth team. He signed a full contract at the Rec in August 2003 and made his senior debut later that month. However, he spent much of the 2003–04 season playing for Wimbledon's youth and reserve sides (with fellow Shots youngster Luke Walker) when Shots commitments allowed.

Tyron always looked confident when selected for the Shots' first team, even when dealing with more experienced opponents. However, in the summer of 2005 he was deemed not to have a future at the Rec and so joined neighbouring Farnborough Town, where he was involved in the club finishing third in the Conference South in 2005–06 before losing to Histon in the Play-off semi-final.

The following season, in which Tyron was a virtual ever present, was one of financial turmoil for the club and ended in a creditable 11th-place finish. However, the club's problems snowballed to the point where they went out of business in the summer, and Tyron subsequently signed for Basingstoke Town, where he played in the team that beat Farnborough to win the 2008 Hampshire Senior Cup. He moved to Maidenhead United in May 2008.

Louie Soares — Midfielder/Winger/Right-back

Born: 8 January 1985, Reading.

Aldershot Town FC record:

Debut: v Gravesend and Northfleet (h), Conference National, 12 August 2006.
Appearances: 83 + 18
Goals: 13

Playing career:

Reading (from trainee, July 2004), Tamworth (2ML, February 2005), Bristol Rovers (1ML, April 2005), Barnet (July 2005), Aldershot Town (May 2006).
Louie has made 21 Football League appearances, scoring one goal.

Representative honours:

Barbados full international (three caps, one goal).

Club honours:

Hampshire Senior Cup (Aldershot Town 2007), Setanta Shield (Aldershot Town 2008 [unused substitute]), Conference Premier (Aldershot Town 2007–08).

Louie is the older brother of Crystal Palace midfielder Tom Soares and started out as a trainee at Reading. He signed full professional forms at the Madejski Stadium in July 2004 before being loaned out to Tamworth and Bristol Rovers. Following his release by Reading, Louie trialled successfully at Barnet and played in around half of their 2005–06 League games, as well as in their defeat at Manchester United in the League Cup third round.

He signed for Aldershot Town in May 2006, and his form at the beginning of the season saw him quickly rewarded with a contract extension in the September. Later that season, he was a member of the side that were beaten by Blackpool in the FA Cup third round before going on to achieve two Shots player 'firsts' in the space of five days in January 2007: he made his full international debut for Barbados against Trinidad and Tobago (the first time a Shots player had won full international honours); then scored his first international goal against Martinique (the first time a Shots player had scored at full international level).

Louie's form dipped during the early part of the 2007–08 season, but he still managed to be selected by Barbados for a CONCACAF region qualifier for the 2010 World Cup. As the season went on, Louie's form picked up and he was a member of the Shots side that reached the FA Trophy Semi-Finals. He was also an unused substitute in the Setanta Shield Final and played an active part in the run-in to the winning of the Conference Premier title. Shortly after the season's end, Louie signed a new two-year deal at the Rec.

Matt Somner — Utility defender/Midfielder

Born: 8 December 1982, Isleworth.

Aldershot Town FC record:

Debut: v Halifax Town (a), Conference National, 20 August 2005.
Last appearance: v Southport (a), Conference National, 29 April 2006.

Appearances:	38 + 2
Goals:	2

Playing career:
Brentford (from trainee, July 2001), Cambridge United (December 2004), Aldershot Town (trial, July 2005), Bristol Rovers (NC, August 2005), Aldershot Town (August 2005), Notts County (June 2006).
Matt has made 176 Football League appearances, scoring three goals.

Representative honours:
Wales Under-21s (two caps).

Matt is a combative defender-cum-midfielder and, although right-footed, his versatility has often seen him play on the left side of the park. He made his debut for Brentford as a substitute against Swansea City in May 2001 while still a trainee and signed full professional forms that summer. It was during the 2003–04 season that Matt's continued good form won him both of his Wales Under-21 caps. By December 2004, having appeared just twice, it was clear that he was not part of boss Martin Allen's plans at Griffin Park. This led to him being loaned to Cambridge United in December 2004, and his ability to play virtually anywhere in midfield or defence paved the way for the move to become permanent two months later.

Unfortunately, Matt's talents could not prevent Cambridge being relegated out of the Football League at the end of the season. He briefly trialled at the Rec in pre-season and signed permanently after playing just one League game with Bristol Rovers. Although the club endured their worst-everl finish within a division (13th), Matt performed superbly and was reportedly watched by several Football League sides over the course of the season. This eventually resulted in him joining League Two side Notts County in June 2006, and he would later be part of an historic FA Cup run in 2007–08 – but it was not County's. The Magpies were one of two Football League sides disposed of by Havant and Waterlooville during their historic progression to round four.

Matt made 16 League appearances for the Magpies that season, the last of which was at the start of December. Therefore, it came as no surprise when he was released at the end of the season and it is believed that he is still without a club.

Nick Sowden **Midfielder**

Born: 22 June 1984, Aldershot.

Aldershot Town FC record:

Debut: v Hampton and Richmond Borough (a), Isthmian League Premier Division, 22 October 2002.
Last appearance: v Hendon (a), Isthmian League Premier Division, 1 May 2003.
Appearances: 4 + 2

Playing career:

Badshot Lea (youth, 2000–01 season), Aldershot Town (from youth, August 2002), Metropolitan Police (2ML, December 2002), Metropolitan Police (summer 2003), Badshot Lea (summer 2004), Bisley (December 2005), Godalming Town (2005–06 season), Badshot Lea (March 2006), Ash United (summer 2007).

Club honours:

Hellenic League Supplementary Cup (Badshot Lea 2006).

Nick progressed from the Shots' youth team, having previously played for Badshot Lea during the 2000–01 season as a 16-year-old, and signed full contract forms in August 2002. He made a handful of first-team appearances and had a loan spell at Metropolitan Police before departing the Rec and returning to Imber Court on a permanent basis in the summer of 2003.

Nick subsequently played for Badshot Lea, Bisley and Godalming Town before returning to Badshot Lea in March 2006 and helping them gain promotion to the Hellenic League Premier Division in 2006–07. With that task successfully completed, Nick joined Ash United in the summer of 2007 and made 48 appearances in all competitions in a season that saw the club finish 15th in the Combined Counties League Premier Division.

Calvin Sparshatt **Goalkeeper**

Born: 17 November 1981, Portsmouth.

Aldershot Town FC record:

Debut: v Worthing (a), Isthmian League Full Members' Cup second round, 2 February 1999.
Last appearance: v Walton and Hersham (a), Isthmian League Cup first round, 12 September 2000.
Appearances: 2

Playing career:
Havant and Waterlooville (youth), Aldershot Town (youth), Havant and Waterlooville (August 2002), Fleet Town (October 2003), Salisbury City, Brockenhurst (January 2006).

Calvin was part of the Havant and Waterlooville youth team before joining the same set-up at Aldershot Town. Having been one of several youth players to play for the Shots' first team, Calvin returned to Westleigh Park in August 2002 before playing for Fleet Town, Salisbury City and Brockenhurst. Information pertaining to Calvin's later career and current whereabouts is not known.

Oliver Squires — Midfielder

Born: 15 September 1980, Harrow.

Aldershot Town FC record:

Debut:	as substitute v Chesham United (a), Isthmian League Premier Division, 11 September 1999.
Appearances:	0 + 1

Playing career:
Millwall (youth), Watford (from trainee, October 1997), Norwich City (trial, January 1999), Aldershot Town (NC, September 1999), Chertsey Town (October 1999), Aylesbury United (November 1999), Wealdstone (trial, August 2000), Harrow Borough (September 2000), St Albans City (September 2000), Grays Athletic (January 2001), Barking and East Ham United (March 2001).

Oliver played youth-team football at Millwall before becoming a trainee at Watford and signing full professional forms in October 1997. He played regularly for the reserves but never made a first-team appearance while at Vicarage Road.

Oliver trialled at Norwich City before being released by Watford and joining Aldershot Town as a non-contract player in September 1999. Oliver went on to play for a number of clubs, experiencing relegation with Aylesbury United and spending just over two and a half years with Barking and East Ham United. In November 2003, Oliver retired due to business commitments and currently works as a property consultant.

Steve Stairs — Forward

Born: 6 May 1968, Fareham.

Aldershot Town FC record:

Debut:	v Clapton (h), Isthmian League Division Three, 22 August 1992.
Last appearance:	v Ruislip Manor (a), Isthmian League Division One, 6 February 1995.
Appearances:	116 + 10
Goals:	75 (joint-third in all-time top 10)

Playing career:
Farnham Town (summer 1984), Kingsway Olympic (Australia, June 1989), Farnham Town (June 1990), Aldershot Town (August 1992), Basingstoke Town (February 1995), Hampton (November 1996), Chertsey Town (March 1997), Sandhurst Town (January 2000; player-assistant manager from summer 2004).

Club honours:
Combined Counties League (Farnham Town 1990–91, 1991–92), Dan Air Elite Cup (Farnham Town 1992), Combined Counties Premier Challenge Cup (Farnham Town 1992), Isthmian League Division Three (Aldershot Town 1992–93), Hampshire Senior Cup (Basingstoke Town 1996), Southern Combination Cup (Chertsey Town 1998; Sandhurst Town 2003), Aldershot Senior Cup (Sandhurst Town 2001, 2006), Berks and Bucks Senior Trophy (Sandhurst Town 2007).

Post-playing coaching/management career:
Assistant manager of Sandhurst Town (summer 2007).

Steve was a strong, brave and powerful forward, and is the son of ex-Farnham Town right-back Graham Stairs and nephew of ex-Farnham midfielder Dennis Stairs. Having helped Farnham attain four consecutive top-five finishes in the Combined Counties League (1985–86 to 1988–89), Steve embarked on a trip to Australia in the summer of 1989, where he and a friend joined Western Australian Super League side Kingsway Olympic. That part of Steve's career led to several publications erroneously listing him as 'an Australian forward'.

When Steve returned to the UK, he rejoined Farnham and was part of the all-conquering side that won the Combined Counties League title in 1990–91 and completed the Combined Counties treble for the first time (League title, Dan Air Elite Cup and Premier Challenge Cup) in 1991–92. He was also the club's top scorer in the latter season (28 goals).

Following the well-documented demise of Farnham, Steve joined Aldershot Town in August 1992 and wore the number-nine shirt in their first-ever game against Clapton, scoring twice. That season he scored 26 league goals and top scored with 32 in all competitions, helping the Shots win the Isthmian League Division Three title.

The following season, he became the first Shots player to score four goals in a game, doing so against Gosport Borough in the FA Vase in October 1993. That match was part of a campaign that would see the Shots reach the quarter-finals of the competition. Steve scored 20 League goals that season (29 in all competitions), which contributed greatly to securing a second successive promotion.

The 1994–95 season saw Steve score 14 goals in 27 games before leaving to join Basingstoke Town in the February, and he went on to help them achieve two top-10 finishes and a Hampshire Senior Cup Final victory. A brief spell at Hampton preceded a relatively unsuccessful time at Chertsey Town, before he departed for Combined Counties League side Sandhurst Town in January 2000. Steve was Fizzers' top scorer in 2000–01 (18 goals) and has helped the club win several pieces of silverware, as well as attaining consecutive top-six finishes from 2002–05. The latter season also saw Sandhurst achieve a club-best progression to the FA Vase third round before losing to AFC Newbury.

In January 2007 Steve broke his tibia and fibula after coming on as a substitute in a match against North Greenford United. Strangely, he was playing as a stand-in goalkeeper at the time due to Sandhurst's regular 'keeper being sent off. After a couple of operations, Steve decided to retire from playing but stayed on at Sandhurst as assistant manager to Peter Browning, and the duo led the Fizzers to 16th spot in the Combined Counties League Premier Division in 2007–08. Away from football, Steve works as an independent mortgage adviser.

Simon Stapleton — Midfielder

Born: 10 December 1968, Oxford.

Aldershot Town FC record:

Debut:	v Purfleet (a), Isthmian League Premier Division, 22 August 1998.
Last appearance:	v Locksheath (h), Hampshire Senior Cup third round, 1 December 1998.
Appearances:	14 + 2
Goals:	1

Playing career:

Portsmouth (from apprentice, December 1986), Bristol Rovers (July 1988), Wycombe Wanderers (August 1989), Slough Town (June 1996), Rushden and Diamonds (January 1997), Stevenage Borough (December 1997), Aldershot Town (June 1998), Witney Town (February 1999), Freeland (2002–03 season).

Simon has made 54 Football League appearances, scoring three goals.

Representative honours:

England Semi-Professional XI (one cap).

Club honours:

Berks and Bucks Senior Cup (Wycombe Wanderers 1990), Bob Lord Trophy (Wycombe Wanderers 1992), Conference (Wycombe Wanderers 1992–93), FA Trophy (Wycombe Wanderers 1991, 1993).

Post-playing coaching/management career:

Coach at Maidenhead United (January 2005), joint assistant manager of Freeland.

Simon was a holding midfielder who began his footballing life at Portsmouth. However, he never made the first team and left to join Bristol Rovers in July 1988. He made five appearances for Rovers before dropping down into the Conference with Wycombe Wanderers in August 1989.

In his seven seasons with Wycombe, he made over 250 appearances and matured into a confident and talented player capable of an array of passes. Simon's ability to direct play from midfield helped the club defeat Kidderminster Harriers to win the FA Trophy in 1991 and to finish as Conference runners-up in 1991–92, only losing out to Colchester United on goal difference. He also played a major part in them completing the 'ultimate' non-League double in 1992–93, when they defeated Runcorn in the FA Trophy Final and won the Conference title. That season also saw Simon make his only appearance for the England Semi-Professional XI against Wales. He appeared in the Chairboys' first-ever Football League match in August 1993 and helped the club attain a fourth place finish, which gave them entry into the Play-offs.

Simon eventually departed and played for Slough Town, Rushden and Diamonds and Stevenage Borough, where he had a successful stint before joining Aldershot Town in June 1998. However, Simon struggled with an achilles tendon injury, which meant that he never reproduced his early-career form. He had a brief spell playing at Southern League Southern Division side Witney Town before retiring in the summer of 1999.

It is not known what Simon did immediately after his retirement, but he did resume playing at Witney Premier League side Freeland during the 2002–03 season and was still playing there in the 2006–07 season. In between, he has been a coach at Maidenhead United and has, at various times, fulfilled the roles of youth development officer, club development officer, Under-7s manager, treasurer and joint assistant manager at Freeland.

Dave Stephenson — Centre-back

Born: 27 September 1969, Lewisham.

Aldershot Town FC record:

Debut:	v Leyton Pennant (h), Isthmian League Division One, 7 February 1998.
Last appearance:	v Uxbridge (h), Isthmian League Division One, 7 March 1998.
Appearances:	5

Playing career:

Croydon, Dorking, Tooting and Mitcham United, Croydon, Malden Vale (1993–94 season), Hendon (August 1994), Chesham United (November 1996), Dulwich Hamlet (June 1997), Aldershot Town (1ML, February 1998), Hampton (July 1998), Chesham United (December 1998).

Club honours:

Isthmian League Division One (Chesham United 1996–97).

Very little is known about Dave's early career, other than that he had two spells at Croydon and also played for Tooting and Mitcham, Malden Vale and Hendon, where he won the Player of the Year award in 1996. He joined Chesham United in November 1996, and his ability both in the air and on the floor were major factors in helping the club win the Isthmian League Division One title in 1996–97. He then moved to Dulwich Hamlet, from where he joined Aldershot Town on loan in February 1998.

Dave quickly became the fans' favourite at the Rec, to the point where his exit from the pitch when substituted in the final game of his loan spell was greeted by a standing ovation. He had a short spell at Hampton before returning to Chesham in December 1998, where he played an important role in achieving a third-place finish in the Isthmian League Premier Division in 1999–2000. Dave left the Meadow in September 2000, and no details of his subsequent career or current whereabouts are known.

Dominic Sterling — Centre-back

Born: 8 July 1976, Isleworth.

Aldershot Town FC record:

Debut:	v Hitchin Town (a), Isthmian League Premier Division, 17 August 2002.
Last appearance:	v Shrewsbury Town (at Stoke City FC), Conference Play-off Final, 16 May 2004.
Appearances:	89 + 10
Goals:	2

Playing career:

Wimbledon (youth), Ruislip Manor (summer 1993), Hayes (summer 1995), Wealdstone (October 1996), Hayes (July 2000), Aldershot Town (July 2002), Canvey Island (June 2004), Maidenhead United (May 2006).

Club honours:
Isthmian League Division Three (Wealdstone 1996–97), Isthmian League Premier Division (Aldershot Town 2002–03), Hampshire Senior Cup (Aldershot Town 2003), Southern League Premier Division Play-off Final (Maidenhead United 2007).

Dominic is a centre-back who is strong in the tackle and dominant in the air. He started in Wimbledon's youth team before playing for Ruislip Manor, Hayes and Wealdstone, where his game started to improve. He was an important part of the sides that won the Isthmian League Division Three title in 1996–97 and that gained a second successive promotion in 1997–98. The 1998–99 season was to end in frustration for club and player as they were denied their rightful place in the Premier Division due to the fact that Edgware Town's ground, where the Stones were ground-sharing, did not meet the grading criteria necessary for promotion. It was, therefore, little comfort to Dominic that he won that season's Player of the Year award.

Dominic's performances coupled with his confidence when bringing the ball out of defence had brought him to the attention of several clubs, and Conference outfit Hayes eventually paid £1,500 for him in July 2000. He won the Player of the Year award in his first season, but his second season ended in disappointment as the club were relegated.

Dominic signed for Aldershot Town in July 2002 and was a rock-like presence in the back four as the Isthmian League Premier Division title was secured in his first season at the Rec. He played in the club's first-ever Conference game in August 2003 and was in the sides that lost to Hednesford Town in the FA Trophy semi-finals and that took Shrewsbury to extra-time and penalties in that season's Conference Play-off Final.

Dominic left the Rec in June 2004 after the Shots turned full-time, as he was unwilling to give up his job as a civil servant. He then spent two seasons at Canvey Island but left after financial problems forced the club to take voluntary demotion to Isthmian League Division One North. This would have been a waste of Dominic's talents, so it was no surprise that he was offered that chance to play at a higher level by Southern League Premier Division side Maidenhead United in May 2006. It proved to be a good move, as the Magpies equalled a club-best progression to the FA Cup first round, and the season culminated in promotion to the Conference South via a Play-off Final victory over Team Bath.

Dominic was part of the Maidenhead side that again reached the FA Cup first round in 2007–08, but this time they were victims of a giant-killing as they were beaten by Horsham. The Magpies endured a season of struggle in the League, but a good end-of-season run eventually ensured their participation in the Conference South for at least one more season, as they finished in 17th place.

Anthony Straker — Left-back

Born: 23 September 1988, Ealing.

Aldershot Town FC record:

Debut:	v Kidderminster Harriers (a), Conference Premier, 11 August 2007.
Appearances:	55 + 1
Goals:	1

Playing career:
Crystal Palace (youth), Yeovil Town (trial, March 2007), Brentford (trial, July 2007), Millwall (trial, July 2007), Weymouth (trial, July 2007), Aldershot Town (July 2007).

Representative honours:
England Under-18s.

Club honours:
Setanta Shield (Aldershot Town 2008), Conference Premier (Aldershot Town 2007–08).

Anthony is a left-back who possesses pace and the ability to deliver a pin-point cross. He was originally a youth player at Crystal Palace but never made a first-team appearance. He then trialled elsewhere before signing for Aldershot Town in July 2007.

In January 2008 Anthony was selected by Barbados for an upcoming CONCACAF region qualifier for the 2010 World Cup (but did not play), and his continued good form was rewarded the following month when he signed a contract extension to the end of the 2009–10 season. He was a member of the Shots side that was beaten by

Ebbsfleet United in the FA Trophy semi-final, but that was forgotten a few days later when he scored a long-range wonder goal, with his wrong foot, against Woking in the Setanta Shield semi-final. He followed that by helping the club win the Final and the Conference Premier title before his season ended on a slightly sour note, sent off in the last minute of the final game at Rushden and Diamonds.

Jimmy Sugrue — Midfielder

Born: 1 January 1974, Hammersmith.

Aldershot Town FC record:

Debut: v Abingdon Town (a), Isthmian League Division One, 18 March 1995.
Last appearance: as substitute v Sutton United (h), FA Cup third qualifying round, 13 October 2001.
Appearances: 158 + 42 (fifth in all-time top 10)
Goals: 44 (ninth in all-time top 10)

Playing career:

Fulham (trainee, July 1990), Dorking, Kingstonian (December 1992), Aldershot Town (March 1995), Hayes (February 1996), Aldershot Town (October 1996), Carshalton Athletic (trial, July 2000), Sutton United (trial, July 2000), Croydon (August 2000), Chelmsford City (December 2000), Dulwich Hamlet (December 2000), Aldershot Town (July 2001), Bracknell Town (November 2001), St Albans City (November 2001), Billericay Town (March 2002), Bishop's Stortford (August 2002), Staines Town (July 2003), Berkhamsted Town (September 2003).

Club honours:

Isthmian League Premier Division (Hayes 1995–96), Isthmian League Division One (Aldershot Town 1997–98), Isthmian League Cup (Aldershot Town 1999), Hampshire Senior Cup (Aldershot Town 1999, 2000).

Jimmy was a tenacious, terrier-like midfielder who was loved by the Shots faithful. The fact that he is the only player to have had three separate permanent spells with the Shots is proof that the affection was a two-way street. His first stint at Aldershot was a one-month loan in March 1995, and he scored on his debut. Jimmy's combative nature and will to win immediately endeared him to the fans, and it was no surprise that his move subsequently became permanent.

What Jimmy lacked in height, he more than made up for with his determination, although it often got him into trouble with match officials. Unfortunately, he paid the price for his on-the-field indiscipline when Shots boss

Steve Wigley sold him to Hayes for a then Shots record £3,000 in February 1996, following three dismissals that season. He ended the season with an Isthmian League Premier Division-winners' medal but never really settled at Church Road.

In a surprising move, Wigley brought Jimmy back to the Rec in November 1996 in return for Hayes recouping £2,000 of their outlay. He won that season's Player of the Year award even though he played in less than half of the games, indicating how popular he was with the Shots fans. Over the course of the next three seasons, he was an integral part of the Shots sides that won the Isthmian League Division One title in 1997–98 – to which he contributed a personal-best 11 goals, as well as being one of the goalscorers who clinched the title – and the side that completed the Isthmian League Cup and Hampshire Senior Cup double in 1998–99, beating Boreham Wood and Basingstoke Town respectively.

The following season, he helped the Shots reach the FA Cup second round for the first time (where they lost to Exeter City) and finish as runners-up to Dagenham and Redbridge in the Isthmian League Premier Division.

Jimmy left the Rec in the summer of 2000 and had stints at several clubs, including Chelmsford City and Dulwich Hamlet. He returned to the Rec in July 2001 but made just five substitute appearances before being released in the November.

Apart from making enough appearances and scoring enough goals to give him to a place in the all-time top 10 for both, Jimmy's six red cards afford him the unenviable record of the most sendings off in an Aldershot Town career. Following his final departure from the Rec, he played one game for Bracknell Town and then signed for St Albans City before playing for various other clubs and subsequently retiring in 2003 due to a troublesome knee injury. Jimmy currently works as a storeman in the motor trade in Devon.

Hassan Sulaiman — Utility

Born: 26 September 1985, Lambeth.

Aldershot Town FC record:

Debut:	v Tamworth (h), Conference National, 13 August 2005.
Last appearance:	as substitute v Southport (a), Conference National, 29 April 2006.
Appearances:	13 + 16
Goals:	1

Playing career:

Arsenal (trainee, July 2002), Wigan Athletic (trainee, summer 2004), Peterborough United (trial, July 2005), Aldershot Town (August 2005), Slough Town (December 2006), Aldershot Town (trial, December 2006), Aldershot Town (trial, February 2007), Crawley Town (March 2007), St Albans City (July 2007).

Hassan is primarily a right-back but has also played as a midfielder and a forward. He played in the colts and youth teams at Arsenal before signing as a trainee but never quite made the grade and was released from Highbury in the summer of 2004. He then joined Wigan Athletic, where he was a regular in the reserves, but left 12 months later.

Following a trial at Peterborough United, Hassan joined Aldershot Town as a pre-season trialist and was offered a contract in August 2005. He broke into the side early in the season as a result of an injury to Tarkan Mustafa, but he was never a regular. However, he will be remembered for his only goal in the red and blue – a cracking strike at Forest Green Rovers in December 2005. This match itself will be remembered for taking over two and a half hours to complete due to two floodlight failures!

Hassan left the Rec in the summer of 2006, underwent two operations on a troublesome groin and then signed for Slough Town in December 2006. He returned to the Rec as a trialist in reserve games twice during the season and had a brief spell at Crawley Town before signing for St Albans City in July 2007. However, the 2007–08 Conference South season would prove to be one of struggle for the Saints, and Hassan made 36 appearances and scored twice as they finished the campaign in 19th place, just one above the drop zone.

Andy Sullivan — Midfielder/Forward

Born: 16 June 1979, Frimley.

Aldershot Town FC record:

Debut:	v Bromley (a), Isthmian League Full Members' Cup first round, 26 October 1999.
Appearances:	1

Playing career:
Southampton (trainee, August 1995), Fulham (trial, March 1997), Farnborough Town (August 1997), Wokingham Town (1ML, February 1998), Reading (trial, October 1998), Kingstonian (December 1998), Hayes (August 1999), Aldershot Town (NC, October 1999), Kingstonian (November 1999), Staines Town (July 2000), AFC Wimbledon (August 2002), Carshalton Athletic (August 2004), Whyteleafe (October 2004), Bracknell Town (March 2007), Fleet Town (July 2007), Cove (August 2007).

Club honours:
Combined Counties League Premier Division (AFC Wimbledon 2003–04), Combined Counties Premier Challenge Cup (AFC Wimbledon 2004).

Representative honours:
Aldershot, Farnborough and District Schoolboys, Hampshire County Schools, England Schoolboys.

Andy can play as a midfielder, a winger or a forward and began his football career as a schoolboy at Southampton. He was offered a scholarship at the FA Coaching Centre at Lilleshall but decided to turn it down in order to concentrate on his schooling, later signing as a trainee at The Dell. He then had a trial at Fulham in the latter days of Mickey Adams's managerial reign, but his departure signalled the same fate for Andy. Following that disappointment, spells at Farnborough Town, Wokingham, Kingstonian and Hayes preceded Andy joining Aldershot Town in October 1999, but he was on the move again a month later when he returned to Kingstonian, where he mainly played in the reserves.

Andy then had a couple of seasons at Staines Town before joining the newly formed AFC Wimbledon in August 2002, and he was an integral part of the side that finished in an admirable third place in their inaugural season in the Combined Counties League. The following season, he helped the Dons secure the Combined Counties League Premier Division and Combined Counties Premier Challenge Cup double.

Unfortunately, Andy suffered an injury that summer, which resulted in him leaving Kingsmeadow. He played for Carshalton Athletic and Whyteleafe but suffered cruciate ligament and cartilage injuries in April 2005 that would put him out of the game for nearly two years. Once recovered, Andy signed for Bracknell Town, Fleet Town and Cove, leaving the last of these in October 2007. He is currently taking a break from playing due to work commitments. However, he is hoping to rejoin Bracknell in time for the 2008–09 season.

Toby Sumner — Midfielder

Born: 20 October 1981, Aldershot.

Aldershot Town FC record:

Debut:	v Slough Town (a), Isthmian League Premier Division, 2 May 2000.
Last appearance:	v Walton and Hersham (a), Isthmian League Cup first round, 12 September 2000.
Appearances:	6 + 1

Playing career:
Reading (trainee, July 1998), Aldershot Town (March 2000), Basingstoke Town (December 2000), Fleet Town (1ML, February 2005), Cove (March 2005), Winchester City (August 2005), Ash United (August 2006).

Club honours:
Hampshire Senior Cup (Aldershot Town 2000), Wessex League Division One (Winchester City 2005–06).

Toby is an energetic midfielder who started out as a trainee at Reading. He joined Aldershot Town in March 2000 and played in the Hampshire Senior Cup-winning side shortly afterwards. He left the Rec to join divisional and county rivals Basingstoke Town in December 2000 and helped in the attainment of a third-place finish in the Isthmian League Premier Division that season (five points and a single place ahead of the Shots).

In August 2002 Toby severely injured his knee in a League match against Canvey Island and took six months to recover, which effectively ended his season. He helped the Stoke achieve their best-ever progression in the FA Trophy in 2003–04 when they reached the third round (before losing to King's Lynn) but played just a handful of games in 2004–05 before being released and signing for Cove in March 2005.

Toby moved to Winchester City that summer and was a part of the side that won the Wessex League

Division One title before moving on to Ash United, where he made just two appearances in 2007–08 before leaving at the start of 2008. It is believed that Toby did not play for any other club that season.

Graham Sutton — Left-back

Born: 6 January 1975, Ascot.

Aldershot Town FC record:

Debut: v DCA Basingstoke (h), Hampshire Senior Cup second round, 2 November 1993.
Last appearance: as substitute v Bracknell Town (h), Isthmian League Cup preliminary round, 23 August 1994.
Appearances: 6 + 3

Playing career:

Portsmouth (trainee, July 1991), Aldershot Town (August 1993).

Graham was a young left-back who began as a trainee at Portsmouth. He joined Aldershot Town in August 1993 and was a member of the side that reached that season's FA Vase quarter-finals. He was released due to his educational commitments in September 1994, and nothing is known about his subsequent career.

Chris Swan — Centre-back

Born: 23 November 1978, Johannesburg, South Africa.

Aldershot Town FC record:

Debut: as substitute v Croydon (h), Isthmian League Cup first round, 11 December 2001.
Last appearance: v Brockenhurst (h), Hampshire Senior Cup quarter-final, 10 January 2002.
Appearances: 1 + 1

Playing career:

Camberley Town (2000–01 season), Aldershot Town (NC, December 2001), Christchurch City United (playing October 2005), Brockenhurst (October 2005).

Chris was a big, strong South African-born defender, who was in the Queen's Regiment of the British Army. Very little is known about Chris, apart from the fact that he played a couple of games for Camberley Town in 2000–01 before embarking on tours of duty in Northern Ireland and Bosnia. He then appeared for the Shots in two minor Cup games during the 2001–02 season and performed very well but left shortly afterwards.

Chris seems to have disappeared off the footballing radar after that and does not reappear until the 2005–06 season, when he played for Wessex League Division One sides Christchurch City United and Brockenhurst, leaving the latter club in January 2006. No further information pertaining to Chris is known.

Rob Symes — Midfielder/Forward

Born: 27 February 1988, Lambeth.

Aldershot Town FC record:

Debut: as substitute v Fleet Town (h), Hampshire Senior Cup third round, 10 January 2006.
Appearances: 0 + 1

Playing career:

Arsenal (youth), Reading (youth), Aldershot Town (youth), Guildford City (November 2006), Cove (March 2007), Badshot Lea (August 2007).

Representative honours:

Hampshire Youth.

Rob played youth-team football at Arsenal and Reading before joining the Shots, where he was a member of the youth side when making his sole appearance for the first team. He joined Guildford City in November

2006 but made just one appearance before joining Cove in March 2007. He then moved on to Badshot Lea, whom he helped reach 11th place in their first-ever season in the Hellenic League Premier Division in 2007–08.

Eric Talbot — Goalkeeper

Born: 6 January 1974, Springfield, Massachusetts, USA.

Aldershot Town FC record:

Debut: v Boreham Wood (a), Isthmian League Premier Division, 10 April 1999.
Last appearance: v Chesham United (h), Isthmian League Premier Division, 29 April 1999.
Appearances: 5

Playing career:
Sacramento Scorpions (US, 1997), Banstead Athletic, Woking, Hayes, Aldershot Town (NC, March 1999), Hendon (trial, summer 1999), Crawley Town (August 1999), Harrow Borough (September 1999), Carshalton Athletic (November 1999), Tooting and Mitcham United (February 2000), Aylesbury United (March 2000), Chesham United (August 2000), Hampton and Richmond Borough (September 2000), Central Coast Mariners (Australia, trial, September 2001).

Club honours:
Isthmian League Cup (Aldershot Town 1999 [unused substitute]).

Eric was an American-born 'keeper, who played for Sacramento Scorpions in his homeland before coming to play in the UK. He joined Aldershot Town on a non-contract basis in March 1999 as cover for Gary Phillips and was actually one of seven 'keepers used that season. He left the Rec that summer and trialled at Hendon before having short spells at Crawley Town and a handful of Isthmian League sides.

Eric joined Hampton and Richmond Borough in September 2000 and was part of the side that was knocked out of that season's FA Cup by Barnet at the first-round stage and the side that finished the season in ninth place in the Isthmian League Premier Division. He later trialled at Central Coast Mariners in Australia, but no further information on his career is known.

Steve Talboys — Midfielder

Born: 18 September 1966, Bristol.

Aldershot Town FC record:

Debut: v Bishop's Stortford (h), Isthmian League Premier Division, 13 February 1999.
Last appearance: v Basingstoke Town (at Southampton FC), Hampshire Senior Cup Final, 5 May 1999.
Appearances: 13 + 1
Goals: 2

Playing career:
Bristol Rovers (schoolboy and youth), Longwell Green Sports (summer 1982), Forest Green Rovers (summer 1983), Mangotsfield United (summer 1984), Bath City (summer 1985), Trowbridge Town (summer 1986), Gloucester City (November 1987), Birmingham City (trial), AFC Bournemouth (trial), Swansea City (trial), Wimbledon (January 1992), Watford (July 1996), Boreham Wood (January 1998), Kingstonian (March 1998), Sutton United (September 1998), Aldershot Town (February 1999), Carshalton Athletic (September 1999), Hampton and Richmond Borough (December 1999), Gloucester City (March 2000), Staines Town (July 2000). Steve has made 31 FA Premier League and Football League appearances, scoring one goal.

Representative honours:
FA XI.

Club honours:
Southern League Midland Division (Gloucester City 1988–89), Gloucestershire Senior Cup (Gloucester City 1991 [unused substitute]), Isthmian League Cup (Aldershot Town 1999), Hampshire Senior Cup (Aldershot Town 1999).

Steve started his footballing life as a forward but matured into a strong and experienced midfielder with the ability to score goals. Having played schoolboy and youth-team football at Bristol Rovers (where he acquired the nickname 'Sticksie' due to him having skinny legs) and local league football for Longwell Green Sports, he played for Forest Green Rovers and Mangotsfield United.

In the summer of 1985 he made the step up to the Alliance Premier League (the forerunner of the Conference) with Bath City and was part of the side that reached the second round of that season's FA Cup, where they lost to Peterborough United. This was followed by just over a season at Trowbridge Town before he moved to Gloucester City. This was where Steve's abilities really came to the fore and where, having scored on his debut against Moor Green, he was part of the side that won the Southern League Midland Division in 1988–89. The following season he was the Player of the Year at Meadow Park, and his performances led to various club trials, which came to nothing.

In January 1992 Division One outfit Wimbledon paid Gloucester £10,000 to take Steve to South London. However, he had to wait nearly a year to make his Dons debut, doing so against Norwich City in an FA Premier League match in December 1992. Injuries limited him to just 31 League and Cup appearances for Wimbledon in his four and a half years there, although he did captain the reserve side while at Selhurst Park.

In July 1996 he moved to Watford, but a combination of injuries and a reported fall-out with manager Kenny Jackett meant that he played just six games for the Hornets before dropping back into non-League and having short spells at Boreham Wood, Kingstonian and Sutton United. In February 1999 Steve joined Aldershot Town and his class was immediately evident, as he helped the club complete the Isthmian League Cup and Hampshire Senior Cup double that season.

Short club spells preceded him joining Staines Town in July 2000, and he went on to captain the side before retiring in September 2003. Steve became an associate director of a company involved in insurance settlements for professional sportsmen and women.

Stuart Tanfield — Midfielder/Winger

Born: 18 April 1981, Ascot.

Aldershot Town FC record:

Debut: as substitute v Enfield (h), Isthmian League Premier Division, 5 April 2003.
Last appearance: as substitute v Eastleigh (h), Hampshire Senior Cup quarter-final, 27 January 2004.
Appearances: 4 + 8

Playing career:

Swindon Town (schoolboy), Ascot United (August 1999), Romsey Town (DR, October 2001), Fareham Town (August 2002), Wokingham Town (October 2002), Aldershot Town (March 2003), Chertsey Town (4ML, January 2004), Basingstoke Town (July 2004), Hayes (October 2004), Bracknell Town (July 2005), Windsor and Eton (July 2006), Uxbridge (August 2007), Bracknell Town (November 2007).

Club honours:
Isthmian League Charity Shield (Aldershot Town 2003).

Stuart is a talented midfielder whose speed also allows him to play out on the wing. His early career consisted of playing schoolboy football at Swindon Town before playing for three seasons at Reading Senior League side Ascot United. He also spent part of the 2001–02 season dual registered with Hampshire League Division One side Romsey Town to coincide with his studies. After a brief spell at Fareham Town, Stuart joined Wokingham Town in October 2002 and, despite leaving to join Aldershot Town in March 2003, he still finished the season as their joint top scorer with John Finnieston (15 goals).

Stuart looked to have a promising future with the Shots when he started on the left wing in their first-ever Conference match against Accrington Stanley in August 2003, but it was not to be. After just nine more appearances in all competitions plus four months spent on loan at Chertsey Town, he moved on to Basingstoke Town in August 2004. He quickly moved on to Hayes, where he played a part in them reaching the FA Trophy fourth round before being knocked out by Eastwood Town and finishing in a mid-table position in the inaugural season of the Conference South.

Stuart then had spells elsewhere before returning to Bracknell in November 2007 in the hope that he could help turn their fortunes around. At the time of his rejoining, the Robins had attained just three points from their opening 11 Southern League Division One South and West games. The season did not get much better as relegation was avoided by just two points!

Nathan Tapley — Defender/Midfielder

Born: 28 September 1979, Haslemere.

Aldershot Town FC record:

Debut:	as substitute v Bishop's Stortford (a), Isthmian League Premier Division, 5 September 1998.
Last appearance:	as substitute v Hitchin Town (a), Isthmian League Cup first round, 8 September 1998.
Appearances:	0 + 2

Playing career:
Aldershot Town (NC, from youth, August 1998), Yeading (3ML, October 1998), Yeading (summer 1999), Camberley Town (September 2000), Egham Town (March 2001), Chertsey Town (August 2001), Wokingham Town (September 2001), Egham Town (January 2002), Dulwich Hamlet (July 2005), Ash United (September 2005), Banstead Athletic (DR, October 2005), Guildford City (player-coach, November 2006), Liphook United (player-coach, summer 2007).

Nathan can play in defence or midfield and made his two appearances for the Shots on a non-contract basis, having previously been in the youth team. During his last season at the Rec, he was loaned to Yeading before signing permanently at the Warren in the summer of 1999. He then played briefly for Camberley Town, Egham Town, Chertsey Town and Wokingham Town before returning to Egham in January 2002. That season, he helped push the club to a sixth-place finish in Isthmian League Division Three, which eventually gave them promotion to the Isthmian League Division One South, following restructuring of the League. A creditable 10th-place finish followed in 2002–03, but the club then struggled and had successive bottom-three finishes. Nathan then left Egham and played for Dulwich Hamlet, Ash United and Banstead Athletic.

Over the last few seasons, Nathan has been working on his coaching badges as well as running his own soccer school, and he has put his knowledge into practice in the role of player-coach at both Guildford City and Liphook United, with the latter club finishing fourth in the Surrey County Intermediate League Western Premier Division in 2007–08.

Jamie Taylor — Forward

Born: 16 December 1982, Crawley.

Aldershot Town FC record:

Debut:	as substitute v Hitchin Town (a), Isthmian League Premier Division, 17 August 2002.
Last appearance:	as substitute v Accrington Stanley (a), Conference, 13 December 2003.
Appearances:	12 + 25
Goals:	12

Playing career:
Broadbridge Heath (summer 2000), Horsham (August 2001), Crawley Town (trial, July 2002), Aldershot Town (July 2002), Horsham (1ML, February 2003), Crawley Town (1ML, April 2003), Carshalton Athletic (1ML, December 2003), Oakwood (February 2004), AFC Wimbledon (March 2004), Horsham (October 2004), Woking (NC, December 2006), Dagenham and Redbridge (March 2007), Grays Athletic (2ML, February 2008), Grays Athletic (May 2008).
Jamie has made 12 Football League appearances, scoring one goal.

Representative honours:
Sussex FA XI.

Club honours:
Sussex Floodlight Cup (Horsham 2002), Isthmian League Premier Division (Aldershot Town 2002–03), Southern League Cup (Crawley Town 2003), Isthmian League Charity Shield (Aldershot Town 2003), Combined Counties League Premier Division (AFC Wimbledon 2003–04), Combined Counties Premier Challenge Cup (AFC Wimbledon 2004).

Jamie is a diminutive, pacy and prolific forward who started playing for Sussex County League Division Two side Broadbridge Heath. His 17 goals during the 2000–01 season helped the club attain a fifth-place finish in the League and prompted neighbours Horsham to bring him into the Isthmian League in August 2001. It proved to be a good move for both club and player, as he top scored with 35 goals in 37 games in all competitions, with 24 of those goals helping the club finish as runners-up to Lewes in Isthmian League Division Two and secure promotion. Further personal honour came Jamie's way when he won that season's Player of the Year award.

He trialled at both Crawley Town and Aldershot Town that summer, but it was the Shots who took the plunge and signed him, and a scoring debut suggested that he would be a part of great things to come. Unfortunately for Jamie, his two seasons at the Rec came at a time when a number of more experienced forwards were also at the club, which limited his opportunities. It also appeared that defenders at Isthmian League Premier Division level were better equipped to cope with the threat he posed than defenders he had come up against previously. He played in 21 of the Shots' League games that season, making just four starts and scoring four times as the Premier Division title was won.

The following season saw Jamie score five goals in just eight appearances for the Shots as well as being loaned to Carshalton Athletic before leaving the Rec in February 2004. He played briefly for Sussex County League Division Two side Oakwood before joining AFC Wimbledon in March 2004, where he scored six goals in 13 games to help secure the Combined Counties League Premier Division and Combined Counties Premier Challenge Cup double.

Jamie started the 2004–05 season at Kingsmeadow but moved back to Horsham in the October. He went on to score many goals for the Hornets, finishing as top scorer in 2004–05 (26) and 2005–06 (28), and helping them to success. Conference side Woking made an approach for Jamie in December 2006 and he opted to venture into full-time football with the Surrey side, despite being offered an improved deal to stay at Queen Street.

Across all his spells at Horsham Jamie scored 108 goals in 178 games. His goals rather dried up at Kingfield – scoring once in 11 appearances – but that did not stop Conference champions-elect Dagenham and Redbridge signing him the following March. He later joined Grays Athletic on loan in February 2008. The move worked out well, as he ended up scoring nine goals in 16 games, which played no small part in the club finishing 10th in the Conference Premier. Although Jamie returned to his parent club at the end of the loan, he had made such an impression at the 'other' Recreation Ground that he joined Grays permanently in the summer.

Anthony Thirlby — Midfielder

Born: 4 March 1976, Berlin, Germany.

Aldershot Town FC record:

Debut:	v Berkhamsted Town (a), Isthmian League Division One, 9 December 1997.
Last appearance:	v Maidenhead United (h), Isthmian League Division One, 13 December 1997.
Appearances:	2

Playing career:
Exeter City (from trainee, July 1994), Bideford (August 1996), Tiverton Town (September 1996), Dorchester Town (November 1996), Torquay United (February 1997), Barnstaple Town (August 1997), Woking (trial, December 1997), Aldershot Town (December 1997), Tiverton Town (January 1998), Dorchester Town (January

1998), Fleet Town (February 1998), Windsor and Eton (February 1999), AFC Newbury (October 1999), Millbrook (August 2000), Plymouth Parkway (August 2002).
Anthony has made 42 Football League appearances, scoring two goals.

Representative honours:
Northern Ireland Youth.

Anthony started as a trainee at Exeter City and signed full professional forms in July 1994. He made his debut for the Grecians as a substitute against Lincoln City on the opening day of the 1994–95 season and went on to play in 27 of their League games (scoring twice) in a season that saw them finish rock bottom of the Football League. He went on to have brief non-League spells before Torquay United brought him back into League football in February 1997. Following a bottom-four finish, he left Plainmoor and had a short spell at Western League Premier Division side Barnstaple Town.

Anthony played as a trialist for Woking a few days before joining Aldershot Town in December 1997, but he failed to make an impression at the Rec and subsequently had brief return stints at Tiverton and Dorchester before joining Fleet Town in February 1998. He later helped Windsor and Eton to a fifth-place finish in Isthmian League Division Two (in 1998–99), played for Wessex League side AFC Newbury and had two seasons at South Western League side Millbrook.

Anthony finished his career at fellow South Western League side Plymouth Parkway, where he was a member of the sides that finished as runners-up in the George Gillin Trophy in 2002–03 and the Devon Premier Cup in 2003–04 and 2004–05. Anthony retired in the summer of 2005 and currently works as an operations director for a company providing litho printing and artwork services.

Bradley Thomas — Centre-back

Born: 29 March 1984, Forest Gate.

Aldershot Town FC record:

Debut:	v Accrington Stanley (a), Conference, 13 December 2003.
Last appearance:	v Dagenham and Redbridge (h), Conference, 1 January 2004.
Appearances:	5
Goals:	1

Playing career:
Millwall (youth), Leyton Orient (youth), Peterborough United (from scholar, July 2003), Kettering Town (1ML, August 2003), Aldershot Town (1ML, December 2003), Heybridge Swifts (1ML, March 2004), Sutton United (1ML, August 2004), Welling United (1ML, October 2004), Weymouth (January 2005), Eastleigh (September 2005), Yeovil Town (January 2006), Tamworth (4ML, August 2006), Boston United (3ML, January 2007), Crawley Town (June 2007).
Bradley has made 11 Football League appearances, scoring two goals.

Representative honours:
England Under-19s, Jamaica Under-23s.

Bradley is a young centre-back who, having played youth-team football at Millwall and Leyton Orient, joined Peterborough United's youth set-up before signing full professional forms in July 2003. However, he never made a first-team appearance for the Posh, and the only first-team football he played in the whole of the 2003–04 season was during one-month loan spells at Kettering Town, Aldershot Town and Heybridge Swifts.

During his loan spell at the Rec he endeared himself to the fans, scoring the only goal in a victory at title-chasing rivals Stevenage Borough. Bradley started the 2004–05 season with loan spells, moving permanently to Weymouth in February 2005. However, he departed the Wessex Stadium a month into the 2005–06 season for a short spell at Eastleigh before joining Yeovil Town, where he had loan spells elsewhere before joining Crawley Town in June 2007. He was unfortunate to suffer a broken leg in an early-season friendly against Tottenham Hotspur, which kept him out until the new year.

Once recovered, Bradley went on to play in just under half of the club's League games in the 2007–08 season as they finished in 15th spot in the Conference Premier, following a six-point deduction for 'financial irregularities'. They also lost the Sussex Senior Cup Final to Brighton & Hove Albion.

Julian Thompson — Forward

Born: 9 April 1982, Accra, Ghana.

Aldershot Town FC record:

Debut: as substitute v Brading Town (h), Hampshire Senior Cup second round, 1 November 2001.
Last appearance: as substitute v Cheshunt (a), Isthmian League Cup second round, 19 November 2002.
Appearances: 1 + 3
Goals: 1

Playing career:

Aldershot Town (youth), Leatherhead (March 2003), Hayes (August 2004), Leatherhead (August 2005), Walton and Hersham (December 2007).

Julian is a lively young forward who was a consistent scorer for the Shots' youth team, having previously played Sunday football in South London. His pace and ability to strike a ball from distance make him a constant threat, so it was unsurprising that he scored on his Shots debut before leaving to play for Leatherhead, Hayes, Leatherhead (again) and then Walton and Hersham. Julian's nine goals in 16 League games in the 2007–08 season helped the Swans finish in 10th spot in the Isthmian League Division One South.

Paul Thompson — Goalkeeper

Born: 21 June 1972, Eastleigh.

Aldershot Town FC record:

Debut: v Hampton (h), Isthmian League Cup second round, 17 November 1992.
Appearances: 1

Playing career:

Swindon Town (trainee, June 1988), Shrewsbury Town (trial), Wrexham (trial), Farnborough Town (August 1990), Aldershot Town (1ML, November 1992), Salisbury (December 1992), Westbury United, Hungerford Town (August 1995), Oxford City (1996–97 season), Hungerford Town, Devizes Town (March 1999), Mangotsfield United (November 2000), Oxford City (August 2001), Devizes Town (August 2001), Chippenham Town (July 2002), Mangotsfield United (October 2002), Cirencester Town (July 2003), Frome Town (3ML) (December 2004), Weston-Super-Mare (August 2005), Llanelli (NC, November 2005), Devizes Town (player-manager, May 2006), Hungerford Town (March 2008).

Club honours:

Southern League Southern Division (Salisbury 1992–93), Western League Division One (Devizes Town 1999–2000), Hellenic League Challenge Cup (Hungerford Town 2008).

Paul is a very experienced 'keeper who has chipped in with a few goals throughout his career, due to being a penalty taker. He began as a trainee at Swindon Town but never appeared for the first team. Following trials at Shrewsbury Town and Wrexham, he joined Farnborough Town in August 1990 and made a handful of appearances in the side that won the Southern League Premier Division that season.

Finding his opportunities limited at Cherrywood Road, primarily because of the excellent form of John Power, Paul joined Aldershot Town on loan in November 1992. This move came about because the recently recruited Mark Watson was Cup-tied, and the Shots had no recognised 'keeper for an upcoming Isthmian League Cup tie.

Over the next few seasons, Paul played for Salisbury (where he won the Southern League Southern Division in 1992–93), Westbury United, Hungerford (two spells) and Oxford City before joining Devizes in March 1999, little knowing that he would go on to become a cult hero at Nursteed Road. By the time he arrived, the club were well on their way to achieving a fourth-place finish in the Western League Division One that season. However, he was very much a part of the side that won the League title in 1999–2000 before he departed for Mangotsfield United in November 2000, where his 12 goals(!) helped attain a fifth-place finish in the Southern League Western Division.

He briefly returned to Oxford City before rejoining Devizes in August 2001, helping the club finish the season in fifth place in the Western League Premier Division – their highest position to date. He joined local rivals Chippenham Town for a fee of £2,500 in July 2002, but his time at Hardenhuish Park was short-lived as a reported bust-up with boss Tommy Saunders led to him moving to former club Mangotsfield United for £1,500 three months later. Paul performed well and helped the club attain a top-six finish in the Southern League Western Division before spending the 2003–04 season with Cirencester Town, where he played a major part in the Centurions gaining promotion to the Southern League Premier Division.

The 2004–05 season saw Paul loaned out to Frome Town before signing for Conference South side Weston-Super-Mare in the 2005–06 campaign. He also appeared once for Llanelli (in the first leg of a Welsh League Cup semi-final against Port Talbot Town) in that latter season. May 2006 saw Paul return to Devizes as player-manager, but he tendered his resignation at the end of the 2006–07 season.

Despite a reported offer to become goalkeeping coach at Southern League Premier Division new boys Swindon Supermarine, Paul was persuaded to stay at Nursteed Road, but a persistent knee injury limited his appearances in the 2006–07 and 2007–08 seasons. He resigned from his position in March 2008 and returned to Hungerford solely in a playing capacity. He helped the Crusaders finish the season in third place in the Hellenic League Premier Division and then beat Almondsbury Town to win the Hellenic League Challenge Cup.

Brian Tinnion — Midfielder

Born: 23 February 1968, Stanley.

Aldershot Town FC record:

Debut:	v Gravesend and Northfleet (h), Conference National, 12 November 2005.
Last appearance:	v Exeter City (h), Conference National, 2 January 2006.
Appearances:	10
Goals:	1

Playing career:

Newcastle United (from apprentice, February 1986), Bradford City (March 1989), Bristol City (March 1993; player-manager from June 2004), Cheltenham Town (trial, October 2005), Aldershot Town (NC, November 2005), Weston-Super-Mare (February 2006), Team Bath (player-coach, January 2007).
Brian has made 635 Football League appearances, scoring 60 goals.

Representative honours:

England Youth.

Club honours:

FA Youth Cup (Newcastle United 1985), Football League Trophy (Bristol City 2003).

Brian was a very experienced and accomplished left-sided midfielder of whom ex-Newcastle United boss Jack Charlton was once quoted as saying 'If Brian had an extra two yards of pace, he'd play for England.' Affectionately known as the 'Tinman', Brian's career began as an apprentice with Newcastle and, having been a member of their FA Youth Cup-winning side in 1985, he signed pro forms for the Magpies on his 18th birthday. He made his senior debut against Everton in April 1987 and was later part of the side that was relegated from Division One at the end of the 1988–89 season. However, by the time that relegation was confirmed, Brian had already joined Bradford City in a £150,000 move, and he went on to play for Bristol City, who paid £180,000 to bring him to Ashton Gate. His sweet left foot and composure in the centre of the park contributed to him being immensely popular with the City fans.

In his 12 years with the club, he was an integral part of sides that experienced both joy and despair. In 1993–94 the Robins reached the FA Cup fifth round, after Brian scored the only goal in a shock third-round win at Liverpool. They also suffered relegation from Division One twice (in 1994–95 and 1998–99), as well as enduring triple Play-off disappointment, losing in the Division Two semi-finals in 1997 (to Brentford) and 2003 (to Cardiff City) and to Brighton & Hove Albion in the Division Two Final in 2004. Sandwiched in between all of that was a promotion as runners-up to Watford in Division Two in 1997–98, a defeat by Stoke City in the 2000 Football League Trophy Final plus victory over Carlisle United in the 2003 Final of the same competition. There was even time for City to finish one place and five points outside the Division Two Play-offs in 2001–02!

Brian took on the role of player-manager at Ashton Gate in the summer of 2004 and steered the club to a seventh-place finish in League One, missing the Play-offs by a single point. Following a trial at Cheltenham Town, he joined Aldershot Town in November 2005, where he became popular with the fans in a short space of time. He surprisingly left the Rec the following February and joined Conference South side Weston-Super-Mare.

In January 2007 he joined Team Bath as player-coach and helped them to the runners'-up spot behind Bath City in that season's Southern League Premier Division. Brian retired in the summer of 2007 and is currently running his own soccer schools in the UK and Spain.

Chris Tomlinson — Centre-back

Born: 10 July 1970, Aldershot.

Aldershot Town FC record:

Debut:	v Clapton, Isthmian League Division Three, 22 August 1992.
Last appearance:	as substitute v Farnborough Town (h), Hampshire Senior Cup fourth round, 18 January 1994.
Appearances:	53 + 2
Goals:	8

Playing career:

Aldershot FC (apprentice, summer 1986), Canterbury City (1ML, November 1991), Whitstable Town (1ML, January 1992), Aldershot Town (June 1992), Wokingham Town (March 1994), Egham Town (summer 1994), Clevedon Town (summer 1995), Forest Green Rovers (December 1995), Truro City (summer 1997), Falmouth Town (summer 1998), Aldershot Town Reserves (1998–2001), Holsworthy (summer 2002), Hertford Town (August 2003), Hullbridge Sports (summer 2006).

Chris has made two Football League appearances.

Representative honours:

British Universities, Cornwall FA XI.

Club honours:

Isthmian League Division Three (Aldershot Town 1992–93), Southern League Southern Division (Forest Green Rovers 1996–97), South Western League (Truro City 1997–98; Falmouth Town 1999–2000), Cornwall Senior Cup (Truro City 1998), South Western Charity Cup (Falmouth Town 2000).

Chris was a skilful centre-back who was very capable of running with the ball at his feet – a skill he demonstrated on more than one occasion in the near 500 non-League appearances that he made. He is the son of ex-Aldershot Town groundsman Dave Tomlinson, as well as the brother of referee Steve and the brother-in-law of ex-Shot Andy Nunn.

Chris had an innate desire to play for his home-town club and took the first step towards this as a schoolboy at Aldershot FC. He signed apprentice forms in the summer of 1986 and later registered as a non-contract player. He was loaned out before making his Football League debut as a substitute against Lincoln City in March 1992, and his only other appearance for the 'old' club came in their last-ever game at Cardiff City, six days after his debut. In the aforementioned game at Ninian Park, Chris earned the distinction of being the last-ever Aldershot FC player to be booked! He also has the honour of being the first-ever player to be registered with Aldershot Town and wore the number-five shirt in the club's first-ever game against Clapton – a game in which he and Brian Lucas earned the unique distinction of becoming the first players to play competitively for both Aldershot clubs. That Championship-winning season, Chris played in 42 games in all competitions and scored seven goals, with the majority of those coming from open play as opposed to the centre-back's staple diet of set-pieces.

Chris's appearances the following season were limited, but he still played an active enough part in the Shots gaining a second successive promotion, as well as playing in the early stages of the run that saw them reach the FA Vase quarter-finals.

Following spells elsewhere, Chris joined Forest Green Rovers in December 1995 and played an important part in them winning the Southern League Southern Division in 1996–97. That summer, he joined Truro City, who were managed by ex-Aldershot FC defender Leigh Cooper, and scored a last-minute goal in the final game of the 1997–98 season against Falmouth Town that won the South Western League title. Ironically, he then joined Falmouth and played for just over half a season, missing the last three months with a facial injury. The following season, he scored the winning goal in Town's penultimate game of the season to virtually secure the League title.

Chris studied at Kent University, and as well as playing for Aldershot Town's reserves during his holidays (1998–2001) he also won a double blue (boxing and football). In addition to that, he won the university Boxer of the Year and Footballer of the Year awards in 2001. He also represented British Universities at boxing and football (the only person to do so).

Chris took a break from the game in 2001–02 before joining South Western League side Holsworthy and then Hertford Town, where he helped the club to successive top-four finishes in Isthmian League Division Two (in 2003–04 and 2004–05), as well as equalling a club-best FA Vase third-round progression in his first season at Hertingfordbury Park. He spent the 2006–07 season captaining Essex Senior League side Hullbridge Sports before retiring at the season's end. He is currently headmaster of a school in Essex and was, at one time, the second-youngest headmaster in the country (aged 35).

Leon Townley — Defender

Born: 16 February 1976, Epping.

Aldershot Town FC record:

Debut: v Enfield (h), Isthmian League Premier Division, 18 August 2001.
Last appearance: v Braintree Town (a), Isthmian League Premier Division, 18 April 2002.
Appearances: 39 + 4
Goals: 1

Playing career:
Tottenham Hotspur (from trainee, July 1994), Leyton Orient (trial, July 1997), Brentford (September 1997), Slough Town (August 1999), Boreham Wood (trial, July 2001), Aldershot Town (July 2001), St Albans City (July 2002), Windsor and Eton (November 2002), Boreham Wood (initially on 1ML, September 2004), Hitchin Town (October 2005), Debden Sports (summer 2006).
Leon has made 16 Football League appearances, scoring two goals.

Representative honours:
Essex Schools, Isthmian League XI.

Club honours:
Romford Charity Cup (Debden Sports 2007), Skip Attwood Trophy (Debden Sports 2007), Romford and District Premier League (Debden Sports 2006–07).

Leon's career began as a trainee at Tottenham Hotspur, with him signing full professional forms in July 1994. He was an unused substitute for Spurs during their Intertoto Cup campaign in the summer of 1995 before trialling at Leyton Orient and then joining Brentford for a fee of £55,000 in September 1997. He made his senior debut against Wycombe Wanderers that same month, but the season was to end in disappointment as the club were relegated from Division Two.

Leon suffered relegation with Slough Town before trialling at Boreham Wood. He signed for Aldershot Town in July 2001 and played in the majority of games that season as a third-place finish in the Isthmian League Premier Division was achieved. Unfortunately, he missed out on the Hampshire Senior Cup Final win that season despite playing in some of the earlier rounds.

Leon left the Rec in the summer of 2002 and had a short spell at St Albans City before joining Windsor and Eton (initially on loan) in November 2002. While at Stag Meadow, he was a member of the sides that achieved a club-best FA Trophy fifth-round progression in 2002–03 and finished third in Isthmian League Division One South the following season.

Leon then played for Boreham Wood (signing permanently after an initial loan) and Hitchin Town before joining his brother Ross at Romford and District Premier League side Debden Sports in the summer of 2006. The 2006–07 season would see the Townley brothers play a major part in Debden winning the Romford Charity Cup, Skip Attwood Trophy and Romford and District Premier League treble. Following the success of the previous season, Debden played in Hertfordshire Senior County League Division One in 2007–08 and finished fifth, with Leon scoring seven goals in all competitions.

Jason Tucker — Midfielder/Defender

Born: 3 February 1973, Isleworth.

Aldershot Town FC record:

Debut: v Bognor Regis Town (h), Isthmian League Division One, 17 August 1996.
Last appearance: v Berkhamsted Town (h), Isthmian League Division One, 2 May 1998.

Appearances: 29 + 4
Goals: 10

Playing career:
Chelsea (trainee), Aldershot FC (from apprentice, July 1991), Yeading (March 1992), Chertsey Town (October 1992), Aldershot Town (August 1996), Enfield (October 1996), Aldershot Town (January 1998), Chertsey Town (July 1998), Aylesbury United (September 1998), Bishop's Stortford (October 1998), Yeading (February 1999), Hayes (March 2000), Boreham Wood (September 2000), Yeading (November 2000; player-coach from December 2001), Hanwell Town (August 2002), Yeading (August 2003), Hanwell Town (summer 2004), North Greenford United (November 2006), Hanwell Town (December 2006).
Jason has made seven Football League appearances.

Club honours:
Isthmian League Associate Members' Trophy (Chertsey Town 1994), Isthmian League Cup (Chertsey Town 1994), Isthmian League Division One (Aldershot Town 1997–98), Isthmian League Division One North (Yeading 2003–04).

Jason is an intelligent attacking midfielder and yet another ex-Aldershot FC player. He started as a trainee at Chelsea and, on his release from Stamford Bridge in the summer of 1990, signed as an apprentice for Aldershot FC. He captained the youth team, where his performances led to him making his first-team debut as a substitute against Halifax Town in the final game of the 1990–91 season before signing full professional forms in July 1991. The last of Jason's seven Football League appearances came in the club's last-ever game at Cardiff City in March 1992, and he then saw the season out at Yeading.

Jason joined Chertsey Town in October 1992, and his dominance of the midfield plus his ability to weigh in with some important goals helped the club finish as runners-up to Newbury Town in Isthmian League Division Two in 1993–94, securing promotion along with the third-placed Shots, as well as winning that season's Isthmian League Cup and Associate Members' Trophy double. Jason then helped the Curfews gain a second successive promotion in 1994–95, when their superior goal difference enabled them to claim third place ahead of the Shots.

Jason joined Aldershot Town in August 1996 for a fee of £1,500 and announced his arrival by scoring a hat-trick in only his second appearance – the first away game of the 1996–97 season at Uxbridge. He went on to score seven goals in his first 14 games that season but strangely was allowed to join Enfield for a then record fee for the Shots of £5,000 two months after arriving.

Having helped the Es finish as runners-up to Yeovil Town in the Isthmian League Premier Division in 1996–97, Jason returned to the Rec in January 1998 and played his part in winning that season's Isthmian League Division One title, although this time round he made more goals than the three he scored. He took part in the early stages of the 1998–99 pre-season but then left for a short return to Chertsey, from where he went on to have short spells at various clubs including Yeading, before signing for the Ding for a third time in November 2000.

When Johnson Hippolyte took sole charge of Yeading in December 2001, Jason took up a player-coach role until the summer of 2002, when he started his association with Spartan South Midlands League Premier Division side Hanwell Town. Jason then returned to The Warren for a fourth spell in August 2003 where, combining his playing duties with managing the reserve team, he helped lift the 2003–04 Isthmian League Division One North title.

Jason rejoined Hanwell in the summer of 2004 and won the Player of the Year award in 2005 and 2006. The Geordies played in the Spartan South Midlands League Premier Division in 2007–08, and Jason made 25 appearances, scoring nine times as the club finished ninth. Away from football, Jason is a pub landlord at The Greyhound in Kew.

Mark Turkington — Midfielder

Born: 31 January 1964, Aldershot.

Aldershot Town FC record:
Debut: as substitute v Northwood (a), Isthmian League Division Three, 16 January 1993.
Last appearance: as substitute v Waterlooville (a), Hampshire Senior Cup third round, 2 February 1993.
Appearances: 2 + 2

Playing career:
Chelsea (from apprentice, summer 1981), Charlton Athletic (May 1982), Maidenhead United (February 1983), Woking (February 1983), Leatherhead (April 1983), Farnborough Town (summer 1983), Woking (July 1990), Slough Town (September 1990), Farnborough Town (February 1992), Aldershot Town (January 1993), Farnborough Town (summer 1993).

Representative honours:
Isthmian League XI.

Club honours:
Isthmian League Division One (Farnborough Town 1984–85), Hampshire Senior Cup (Farnborough Town 1984, 1986), Isthmian League Division Three (Aldershot Town 1992–93), Southern League Premier Division (Farnborough Town 1993–94).

Post-playing coaching/management career:
Joint manager of Farnborough Town Reserves (with Simon Read, January 1996 to May 1996).

Mark was an attacking midfielder who started out as an apprentice at Chelsea and signed full professional forms in the summer of 1981. He then played for several clubs before joining Farnborough Town in the summer of 1983. He made an immediate impact by scoring three goals in his first four games and went on to score 14 goals that season, helping them win the Hampshire Cup in 1984 and the Isthmian League Division One title in 1984–85 (scoring 23 goals in 31 games in all competitions), as well as scoring the winning goal in the 1986 Hampshire Cup Final.

Mark briefly rejoined Woking before getting another crack at the Conference with newly promoted Slough Town in September 1990. That was the Rebels' first-ever season in the division, and they struggled, finishing in the bottom four. The following season was slightly worse, and Mark returned to Farnborough in February 1992 before joining Aldershot Town in January 1993. Unfortunately, the move did not work out, and he returned to Farnborough that summer and helped the club achieve promotion back to the Conference by winning the 1993–94 Southern League Premier Division.

Mark carried on playing until December 1995, when he decided to retire. By the time he hung up his boots, he had become one of only two players to make over 400 appearances for Farnborough (the other being Brian Broome), and he is second in their all-time appearance-makers list, having played 419 times for them. During that time, he scored an impressive 97 goals.

Following his retirement, he was joint manager of Farnborough's reserve side with Boro scoring legend Simon Read from January to May 1996. Mark is not currently involved with any football club and works in the financial services industry.

John Turner — Forward

Born: 12 February 1986, Harrow.

Aldershot Town FC record:

Debut:	as substitute v Forest Green Rovers (h), Conference National, 26 November 2005.
Last appearance:	v Forest Green Rovers (a), Conference National, 31 December 2005.
Appearances:	4 + 1

Playing career:
Aston Villa (youth), Cambridge United (from scholar, December 2003), Rushden and Diamonds (trial, October 2005), Scunthorpe United (trial, November 2005), Aldershot Town (1ML, November 2005), Rushden and Diamonds (January 2006), Grays Athletic (July 2006), Braintree Town (1ML, October 2006), Bishop's Stortford (3ML, January 2007), King's Lynn (May 2007).
John has made 75 Football League appearances, scoring 10 goals.

Representative honours:
England Schoolboys.

Club honours:
Southern League Premier Division (King's Lynn 2007–08).

John was yet another loan signing who delivered very little during his time at the Rec. He was originally a youth player with Aston Villa before moving to Cambridge United in August 2002, making his debut as a substitute and scoring the last-minute winner against Exeter City the following April. He played one more game that season before signing full professional forms at the Abbey Stadium in December 2003, and he went into the club's history books in March 2004 when he scored their 2,000th Football League goal against Cheltenham Town. Just prior to the end of the 2004–05 season, and with their relegation already confirmed (ending 35 years as a Football League club), Cambridge went into administration and were deducted 10 points.

John had scored 13 goals in 91 games for Cambridge before trialling at Rushden and Diamonds and Scunthorpe United and spending a month on loan with the Shots. He then joined Rushden permanently in January 2006 and encountered déjà vu as the club were relegated out of the Football League, with him having scored just once in 11 games. John went on to appear for Grays Athletic, Braintree Town, Bishop's Stortford and King's Lynn, where his seven goals in 34 League games helped the Linnets win the 2007–08 Premier Division title.

Simon Turner — Right-back/Centre-back

Born: 2 May 1976, Reading.

Aldershot Town FC record:

Debut: v Heybridge Swifts (h), Isthmian League Division One, 5 November 1994.
Last appearance: v Newport (Isle of Wight, a), FA Cup first qualifying round, 13 September 1997.
Appearances: 34 + 6

Playing career:

Aldershot FC (youth), Oxford United (trainee, July 1992), Aldershot Town (August 1994), Wokingham Town (October 1997), Bracknell Town (December 2001), Woodley Town (May 2002), Wokingham Town (March 2004), Woodley Town (2005–06 season).

Simon was a very capable defender who could play as a right-back or a centre-back. He was a youth player at Aldershot FC during the 1991–92 season before signing as a trainee at Oxford United in July 1992. He returned to the Rec in August 1994 when signing for Aldershot Town, but had to wait nearly three months to make his debut. Unfortunately (and despite his obvious talent), Simon was never a regular in the Shots side that tried so hard to get out of Isthmian League Division One, so he moved on to divisional rivals Wokingham Town in October 1997. During his time at Finchampstead Road, he matured into a solid presence in the back four and captained the side in the 1999–2000 and 2000–01 seasons. Towards the end of Simon's time at the club they were already on a downward spiral, with his final full season there ending in a rock-bottom finish in (and relegation from) Isthmian

League Division Two. In December 2001 he joined Berkshire rivals Bracknell Town and helped the club to a fourth-place finish in Isthmian League Division Three, which qualified them for promotion to the newly formed Division One South. He then joined Reading League Senior Division side Woodley Town in May 2002 and was a member of the team that was relegated at the end of the 2002–03 season before making a brief return to Wokingham in their last-ever season. It is not known what Simon did for the 2004–05 season, but he reappeared at Woodley in the 2005–06 season. No further details pertaining to Simon's career or current whereabouts are known.

Phil Turrell — Centre-back/midfielder

Born: 12 October 1986, Portsmouth.

Aldershot Town FC record:

Debut: as substitute v Newport (Isle of Wight, h), Hampshire Senior Cup third round, 30 November 2004.
Appearances: 0 + 1

Playing career:
Portsmouth (youth trial), Havant and Waterlooville (youth), Aldershot Town (youth), Havant and Waterlooville (December 2004), Fleet Town (summer 2005), Liss Athletic (October 2005), Moneyfields (August 2006).

Representative honours:
Hampshire Youth (captain).

Phil can play in defence or midfield and, following a youth trial at Portsmouth, played in the Havant and Waterlooville youth side. He joined the youth set-up at the Rec in the summer of 2004 and made his sole first-team appearance six months later. He returned to Westleigh Park in December 2004 before going on to play for Fleet Town, Liss Athletic and Moneyfields. In January 2007 Phil gave up playing due to work commitments.

Stuart Udal — Defender

Born: 8 January 1972, Epsom.

Aldershot Town FC record:

Debut: v Clapton, Isthmian League Division Three, 22 August 1992.
Last appearance: v Maidenhead United (a), Isthmian League Division One, 3 May 1997.
Appearances: 203 + 33 (fourth in all-time top 10)
Goals: 4

Playing career:
Aldershot FC (youth), Brentford (youth), Tongham (summer 1991), Ash United (October 1991), Aldershot Town (August 1992), Havant Town (June 1997), Staines Town (July 1998), Egham Town (December 1999), Basingstoke Town (trial, summer 2000), Ash United (player-assistant manager, summer 2003; player-manager from August 2005).

Club honours:
Isthmian League Division Three (Aldershot Town 1992–93).

Stuart was a fully committed and uncompromising defender and is the cousin of Hampshire and England cricketer (and Aldershot Town fan!) Shaun Udal. He played youth-team football at the 'old' club and Brentford before playing for local sides Tongham and Ash United. He signed for Aldershot Town in August 1992 and wore the number-four shirt in their first-ever game against Clapton. A month into the season, Stuart showed he could do more than just defend by scoring a spectacular long-range goal in the dying minutes against Petersfield United at the Rec. In his five seasons at the Rec, he was a regular member of the sides that won the Isthmian League Division Three title in 1992–93 and that reached the FA Vase quarter-finals and gained a second successive promotion in 1993–94. He also won the supporters' Player of the Year award in 1995 before eventually leaving the Rec and going on to play for Havant Town (in their last-ever season before amalgamating with Waterlooville), Staines Town, Egham Town and Basingstoke Town (trial). In the summer of 2001, Stuart took a break from football due to work commitments, returning in the summer of 2003 to become player-assistant manager to Tony Calvert at Ash. That partnership lasted until the summer of 2004 when Tony left Shawfields Road and Stuart reverted to being a player. However, Terry Eames (Calvert's successor) left in December 2004 and Stuart took on the role of joint player-manager with Danny Rolfe. The following summer, Stuart assumed sole control of team affairs and led the club to successive top-four finishes in the Combined Counties League Premier Division. He stepped down from his post (and retired) at the end of the 2006–07 season due to work and family commitments and currently runs his own company involved in landscape gardening, conservatories and general building work.

Simon Ullathorne — Midfielder/Forward

Born: 19 November 1970, Goole.

Aldershot Town FC record:

Debut:	v Aylesbury United (h), Isthmian League Premier Division, 19 February 2000.
Last appearance:	v Stevenage Borough (h), FA Trophy third round, 13 January 2001.
Appearances:	32 + 3
Goals:	3

Playing career:
Windscale United, Workington, Cleator Moor Celtic, Croydon, Gravesend and Northfleet (December 1991), Sittingbourne (August 1994), Gloucester City (February 1995), Hastings Town (August 1995), Cambridge City (July 1997), Crawley Town (January 1998), King's Lynn (trial, July 1998), St Albans City (February 2000), Aldershot Town (February 2000), Purfleet (March 2001), Dover Athletic (August 2001), Welling United (September 2001), Slough Town (October 2001), Horsham (August 2003), Eastbourne Borough (October 2003), Sidley United (March 2005), Tilbury (March 2005), Margate (trial, July 2005), Dagenham and Redbridge (trial, July 2005), Maidenhead United (trial, July 2005), Aveley (March 2006).

Club honours:
Southern League Southern Division (Gravesend and Northfleet 1993–94), Sussex Senior Cup (Hastings Town 1996), Sussex Floodlight Cup (Crawley Town 1999), Hampshire Senior Cup (Aldershot Town 2000).

Simon was a well-travelled midfielder-cum-forward. Having spent the early part of his career in his native North of England, his work brought him 'down south'. He played for Croydon before joining Gravesend and Northfleet, where he was part of the sides that were relegated from the Southern League Premier Division in 1991–92 and regained their place by way of winning the Southern Division title two seasons later. Spells at Sittingbourne and Gloucester City preceded a move to Hastings Town in August 1995, where he helped win the Sussex Senior Cup in 1996 as well as earning himself the Player of the Year award that season. Simon then played for Cambridge City, Crawley Town and King's Lynn (on trial) before joining St Albans City in February 2000. He made his Saints debut against Aldershot Town before, ironically, making his debut for the Shots a week later! That season, he played in 20 games and scored twice as the Shots attained runners'-up spot behind runaway leaders Dagenham and Redbridge in the Isthmian League Premier Division and won the Hampshire Senior Cup.

After leaving the Rec towards the end of the 2000–01 season, Simon had short spells at Purfleet, Dover Athletic and Welling United before joining Slough Town, where he spent nearly two years. He left the Rebels in the summer of 2003 and played for a handful of other clubs without seeming to settle anywhere, with his cause not being helped by the fact that he missed most of the 2004–05 season due to injury. Simon trialled at a few clubs in the summer of 2005 and then 'disappeared' until the tail end of the 2005–06 season, when he signed for Aveley. It is believed that he left there at the end of the season, but no further information about his career or current whereabouts is known.

Ashley Vincent — Forward

Born: 26 May 1985, Oldbury.

Aldershot Town FC record:

Debut:	v Cambridge United (a), Conference National, 19 November 2005.
Last appearance:	v Grays Athletic (h), FA Trophy first round, 17 December 2005.
Appearances:	4

Playing career:
Wolverhampton Wanderers (scholar), Cheltenham Town (May 2004), Aldershot Town (1ML, November 2005).
Ashley has made 93 Football League appearances, scoring seven goals.

Club honours:
League Two Play-off Final (Cheltenham Town 2006).

Ashley was a scholar at Wolverhampton Wanderers, but made no first-team appearances for the Midlanders. He joined Cheltenham Town in May 2004 and made his debut as a substitute against Southend United on the opening day of the 2004–05 season. In November 2005 he came to the Rec, but disappointed in his four loan appearances. Ashley returned to Whaddon Road and helped the Robins push towards a fifth-place finish in League Two that season and played in their subsequent Play-off Final victory over Grimsby Town. Unfortunately, his progression was halted somewhat as he sustained a cruciate ligament injury in August 2006 that caused him to miss the rest of the 2006–07 season. Ashley played in 37 of the Robins' League One games in the 2007–08 season, but only scored twice as they finished in 19th place, avoiding relegation by three points.

Adi Viveash — Defender

Born: 30 September 1969, Swindon.

Aldershot Town FC record:

Debut:	v Hartlepool United (a), FA Cup second round, 4 December 2004.
Last appearance:	v Forest Green Rovers (a), Conference National, 1 January 2005.
Appearances:	7

Playing career:
Swindon Town (from trainee, July 1988), Reading (1ML, January 1993), Reading (1ML, January 1995), Barnsley (1ML, August 1995), Walsall (initially on 1ML, October 1995), Reading (July 2000), Oxford United (2ML, September 2002), Swindon Town (July 2003), Kidderminster Harriers (1ML, March 2004), Kidderminster Harriers (1ML, August 2004), Aldershot Town (M, December 2004), Cirencester Town (January 2005).
Adi has made 372 FA Premier League and Football League appearances, scoring 19 goals.

Post-playing coaching/management career:
Manager of Cirencester Town (May 2007).

Adi is a cultured defender (although he was originally a forward!) who began his footballing life as a trainee at Swindon Town. He signed full pro forms in July 1988 but had to wait until September 1990 to make his senior debut, coming on as a substitute against Middlesbrough. He played in an unfamiliar midfield role in that game and was (strangely) substituted 40 minutes after coming on. During his time at the County Ground, he experienced a combination of highs and lows. He played just five times in the side that gained promotion to the FA Premier League via victory over Leicester City in the Division One Play-off Final in 1993. The following season saw Swindon relegated at the end of their one and only season in the FA Premier League, but Adi played no part in that campaign. The 1994–95 season brought mixed fortunes as the Robins reached the League Cup semi-finals (where they lost to Bolton Wanderers) and suffered their second successive relegation. During that time, he had two loan spells at Reading and spent a month temporarily at Barnsley. Following a reported falling-out with Swindon boss Steve McMahon, Adi joined Walsall on a month's loan in October 1995, with his ability to lead from the back facilitating the move becoming permanent at the end of the term.

In his near five seasons at the Bescot Stadium, he attained 'legend' status and was an ever present during the 1996–97 season. He was also involved in successive Football League Trophy Final defeats (against AFC Bournemouth in 1998 and Millwall in 1999), a promotion from Division Two (as runners-up to Fulham) in 1998–99 and an immediate relegation from Division One in 1999–2000.

Adi left the Saddlers in the summer of 2000 and joined Reading, whom he helped reach the Division Two Play-off Final in 2001 (where they lost, ironically, to Walsall). Club and player fared better the following season when the Royals were promoted as runners-up to Brighton & Hove Albion in Division Two. Adi found it hard to get into the Reading side during the 2002–03 season and spent two months on loan at Oxford United. On returning to the Madejski Stadium, he played a handful of games at the tail end of the season as the Royals reached the Division One Play-off semi-finals, although he played no part in the two-legged loss to Wolverhampton Wanderers.

In the summer of 2003 he rejoined Swindon Town, but sustained an injury against Chesterfield in the October which kept him out of action until the following March when, unable to get back into the Robins' side, he joined Kidderminster Harriers on a one-month loan. He played just one more League game for Swindon that season as the Division Two Play-offs were reached, but played no part in either leg of the semi-final defeat (on penalties) to Brighton. Adi started the 2004–05 season back on loan at Kidderminster before being released by Swindon.

He joined Aldershot Town in December 2004, but made just seven appearances before joining Cirencester Town, who were enjoying their first-ever season in the Southern League Premier Division. The addition of Adi to their squad helped push the side to a very creditable seventh-place finish at the end of the season. Unfortunately, the club struggled through the 2005–06 and 2006–07 seasons and finished in the bottom five in both seasons. Adi retired from playing at the end of the 2006–07 season and, having attained his UEFA A licence, took over the managerial reins at the Corinium Stadium. Player shortages forced him to play sporadically during the 2007–08 season, but his on and off-field efforts couldn't prevent the club from being relegated by way of their 21st-place finish.

Dale Walker — Goalkeeper

Born: 2 May 1975, Aldershot.

Aldershot Town FC record:

Debut: v Horsham (a), Isthmian League Associate Members' Trophy first round, 17 February 1993.

Last appearance: v Worthing (a), Isthmian League Associate Members' Trophy second round, 24 February 1993.

Appearances: 3

Playing career:

Aldershot FC (YTS, summer 1991), Bass Alton (SLL, summer 1991), Aldershot Town (summer 1992), Newcastle United (M, July 1993), Egham Town (3ML, September 1993), Bass Alton Town (summer 1994), Cove (summer 1995), Aldershot Town Reserves (February 1996), Fleet Town (November 1996), Alton Town Bass (January 1997), Ash United (summer 1997), Basingstoke Town (November 1997), Whitley Bay (July 1999).

Representative honours:

West Surrey Boys League XI.

Club honours:

Isthmian League Division Three (Aldershot Town 1992–93).

Post-playing coaching/management career:

Goalkeeping coach at Ashington (January 2003).

Dale is an ex-Aldershot FC YTS player and the son of ex-Bass Alton midfielder Pat Walker. While at the 'old' club, he went on a season-long loan to Bass Alton in the summer of 1991 and had the rare distinction of playing with his father in a League match against New Street during the 1991–92 season.

Following the demise of the 'old' club, Dale followed his heart and signed for the newly formed Aldershot Town, and his excellent performances for the youth team thrust him into the first-team fray in February 1993. He had an excellent first couple of games against Horsham and Hertford Town, keeping clean sheets on both occasions. At the time of his debut he was the youngest-ever player to pull on a Shots shirt, aged 17 years and 291 days old. He was also the first-ever youth-team player to make it into the senior team.

FA Premier League new boys Newcastle United beckoned for Dale in July 1993, when he was offered a trial at St James' Park. Fortune intervened shortly afterwards, as the Magpies experienced problems with obtaining a work permit for Brad Friedel, which resulted in Dale being given a monthly deal. During his time in the North East, he made several appearances for the reserves, often being picked ahead of future first-teamer Steve Harper. Sadly, Dale sustained a back injury and Newcastle eventually signed Mike Hooper, meaning that Dale returned South to Egham Town on a three-month loan in the September, eventually leaving the Rec in the summer of 1994 to join Bass Alton Town.

Dale then had various spells before returning to the renamed Alton Town Bass in January 1997, where he

again played in a game with his father. Ironically, New Street were again the opposition as they had been six seasons previously. Following a brief spell at Ash United, Dale signed for Basingstoke Town in November 1997 and later missed the bulk of the 1998–99 season with a back injury.

In the summer of 1999 Dale relocated to the North East and signed for Northern Premier League Division One outfit Whitley Bay. He was unfortunate to pick up a double ankle injury and injuries to metatarsals in both feet shortly after arriving at Hillheads Park. His last game came in October 1999, when he gallantly played the last 10 minutes of a game against Witton Albion with broken bones in his foot! Unsurprisingly, these injuries forced Dale into retirement.

In January 2003 he became goalkeeping coach at Northern League Division Two side Ashington and was on the coaching staff when the club won the League title and were runners-up in the League Cup in 2003–04.

In October 2006 Dale came out of retirement for a month to take up the role of player-caretaker manager of Ashington following the resignation of Peter Johnson, before eventually leaving in January 2007. Dale has had a variety of off-field interests, including running his own goalkeeping school and working at the Swindon Town School of Excellence, and he currently runs his own industrial supplies company just outside Newcastle.

Luke Walker — Forward

Born: 16 July 1986, Basingstoke.

Aldershot Town FC record:

Debut:	as substitute v Heybridge Swifts (a), Isthmian League Premier Division, 15 February 2003.
Last appearance:	as substitute v Gravesend and Northfleet (h), Conference National, 12 November 2005.
Appearances:	0 + 6
Goals:	1

Playing career:

Tadley Town (summer 2001), Queen's Park Rangers (youth trial, 2001), Aldershot Town (from youth, summer 2003), Wimbledon (trial, 2003–04 season), Chertsey Town (SLL, August 2004), Cove (2ML, March 2005), Camberley Town (SLL, August 2005), Overton United (March 2006), Tadley Calleva (summer 2006).

Club honours:

Isthmian League Charity Shield (Aldershot Town 2003), North Hampshire Senior Cup (Tadley Calleva 2007, 2008), Persona Cup (Tadley Calleva 2007), Wessex League Division One (Tadley Calleva 2007–08).

Luke is a skilful forward who played in Tadley Town's reserve side as a 15-year-old. He then had a youth trial at Queen's Park Rangers before coming to the Rec where, having scored regularly in the youth and reserve teams, he made three substitute appearances during the 2002–03 season. He was the youngest-ever Shots player, aged 16 years and 213 days when making his debut.

Luke signed full contract forms in the summer of 2003 and, in addition to making two further substitute appearances and scoring once for the Shots, spent the 2003–04 season playing for Wimbledon's youth and reserve sides with Shots teammate Tyron Smith.

After loan spells plus one more substitute appearance for the Shots, Luke joined Wessex League Division Three side Overton United in March 2006. A move to Division Two side Tadley Calleva came that summer, and the season was to produce two winners' medals for Luke – the North Hampshire Senior Cup – Luke scored twice in the Final against Andover – and the Persona Cup.

Luke had a phenomenal 2007–08 season, scoring 30 goals in 39 League appearances as the Wessex League Division One title was won. Unfortunately, Calleva were denied promotion as a result of failing to meet the Wessex League's ground grading criteria. He also scored the only goal of the game as Fleet Town were defeated in that season's North Hants Cup Final.

Nathan Wallace — Defender/Midfielder

Born: 15 July 1981, Basingstoke.

Aldershot Town FC record:

Debut:	v Worthing (a), Isthmian League Full Members' Cup second round, 2 February 1999.
Appearances:	1

Playing career:

Basingstoke Town (youth), Aldershot Town (youth), Basingstoke Town (March 2000), Staines Town (August 2001), Basingstoke Town (November 2001).

Nathan was a youngster who could play in defence or midfield. He played in the youth team at Basingstoke Town and Aldershot Town, making his sole appearance for the Shots while in their youth side, before returning to The Camrose in March 2000. He had a brief spell at Staines Town at the start of the 2001–02 season before returning to Basingstoke in November 2001, staying there until October 2003. No information pertaining to Nathan's subsequent career or current whereabouts is known.

Ben Walshe — Midfielder/Winger

Born: 24 May 1983, Hammersmith.

Aldershot Town FC record:

Debut: v Purfleet (h), Isthmian League Premier Division, 7 December 2002.
Last appearance: v Bishop's Stortford (h), Isthmian League Premier Division, 4 January 2003.
Appearances: 6

Playing career:
Queen's Park Rangers (from trainee, July 2000), Aldershot Town (1ML, December 2002), Gravesend and Northfleet (7ML, September 2003), Luton Town (trial, August 2004), St Albans City (August 2004), Fisher Athletic (London, June 2005), St Albans City (December 2005), St Albans City (October 2006), Wealdstone (January 2007), Richmond SC (Australia, May 2007), Doveton (Australia, 2007), St Albans City (January 2008). Ben has made two Football League appearances.

Club honours:
Conference South Play-off Final (St Albans City 2006).

Ben can play on the left side of midfield or on the wing and began as a youngster at Queen's Park Rangers, making his debut as a substitute in April 2001 against Stockport County. He joined Aldershot Town on a month's loan in December 2002 before returning to Loftus Road, where his professional career was prematurely ended as a result of an injury sustained in only his second appearance (against Chesterfield) in February 2003.

Following a loan spell at Gravesend and Northfleet, Ben trialled with Luton Town before beginning an association with St Albans City in August 2004. He was part of the side that finished as runners-up to Weymouth in the Conference South in 2005–06 and that was promoted via the resultant Play-off Final victory over Histon.

At the end of the season, he took some time out of the game to concentrate on his burgeoning acting career – he has appeared in the Sky One TV football drama *Dream Team* – before returning to Clarence Park in October 2006. Three months later, he joined Wealdstone but played just twice.

In the summer of 2007 Ben embarked on a trip to Australia, where he played for Richmond SC and Doveton before returning to his spiritual home in January 2008. He then departed Clarence Park again a month later, and no details about his subsequent career are known.

Ray Warburton — Centre-back

Born: 7 October 1967, Rotherham.

Aldershot Town FC record:

Debut: v Grays Athletic (a), Isthmian League Premier Division, 11 January 2003.
Last appearance: v Winchester City (at AFC Bournemouth), Hampshire Senior Cup Final, 27 April 2005.
Appearances: 95 + 3
Goals: 5

Playing career:
Rotherham United (from apprentice, October 1985), York City (August 1989), Northampton Town (February 1994), Rushden and Diamonds (October 1998), Boston United (March 2002), Aldershot Town (January 2003). Ray has made 297 Football League appearances, scoring 21 goals.

Representative honours:
Isthmian League XI.

Club honours:
Division Three Play-off Final (Northampton Town 1997), Conference (Rushden and Diamonds 2000–01; Boston United 2001–02), Isthmian League Premier Division (Aldershot Town 2002–03).

Post-playing coaching/management career:
Under-15s/16s manager of Northampton Town (July 2006).

Ray was a brave, strong and intelligent centre-back who possessed a wealth of experience in both League and non-League football. The fact he led by example contributed to him being immensely popular among the fans of the clubs that he played for.

He started out as an apprentice at his home-town club, Rotherham United, and signed full professional forms in October 1985 but made just eight appearances in all competitions before leaving for York City in August 1989. While at Bootham Crescent, Ray played a major part in helping the club gain promotion from Division Three by beating Crewe Alexandra on penalties in the 1993 Play-off Final. However, injury restricted his appearances and he was loaned out to Northampton Town in February 1994 and signed permanently (for a fee of £35,000) a month later.

Due to his arrival so late in the season, Ray was powerless to stop the Cobblers finishing rock bottom in Division Three, but the club were reprieved from relegation due to the fact that Conference champions Kidderminster Harriers' ground was deemed unsuitable. He captained Northampton to a fourth-place finish in Division Three in 1996–97 and then led them to victory over Swansea City in the subsequent Play-off Final.

Cobblers fans were stunned when Ray was allowed to move to local rivals Rushden and Diamonds for £60,000 in October 1998. The following season he was an integral part of the Diamonds side that took Division One side Sheffield United to an FA Cup third-round replay (in which the Blades triumphed on penalties), the side that was defeated by Sutton United in the FA Trophy quarter-finals and the side that finished as runners-up to Kidderminster Harriers in the Conference. Ray was voted the 2001 non-League Player of the Year after he helped achieve the dream of entry into the Football League in 2000–01, when he was a mainstay in the defence as the Conference title was won.

Two months later he moved to Boston United, where he formed a solid partnership with the recently signed Jim Rodwell, with whom he had played at Rushden, and the pair helped the Pilgrims achieve promotion into the Football League that season. Ray made the defining contribution to winning that Conference title by coming on as a second-half substitute against Hayes in the final game of the season and scoring with his first touch – a towering header. The Hayes 'keeper that day was Nikki Bull, who Ray would team up with less than a year later at the Rec.

In January 2003 Ray joined Aldershot Town and played in 14 League games before picking up an injury at Canvey Island in the April and missing the run-in to the winning of the Isthmian League Premier Division. He played in the club's first-ever Conference game in August 2003 and was a member of the side that lost to Hednesford Town in the FA Trophy semi-finals that season.

Ray narrowly missed out on achieving three promotions from the Conference in four years when the Shots were beaten in the Play-off Final by Shrewsbury Town. Unsurprisingly, he won the supporters' Player of the Year award but then suffered a groin injury against Accrington Stanley in mid-October 2004, which caused him to miss the next three months of the season. However, he returned to play his part in reaching the Play-offs for the second successive season, although his involvement in the last month or so was mainly from the subs' bench. Indeed, in the two-leg semi-final itself he was an unused substitute.

Ray's strength, heart and commitment to the cause contributed to him becoming an Aldershot Town legend, but it was unsurprising that he decided to retire that summer. A worthwhile footnote to his time at the Rec is the marked improvement that youngsters Will Antwi, Brett Johnson and Chris Giles all made while playing alongside him.

In the summer of 2006 Ray returned to Northampton to take up the role of manager of the Under-15s/16s side. A year later, he was named on a list of Northampton legends that was produced as part of the PFA's centenary celebrations.

Marc Ward — Centre-back

Born: 27 November 1986, East Ham.

Aldershot Town FC record:

Debut: v Forest Green Rovers (a), Conference Challenge Cup Southern Section quarter-final, 15 February 2005.

Appearances: 1

Playing career:

Millwall (youth), Aldershot Town (1ML, February 2005), Dagenham and Redbridge (trial, July 2005), Waltham Forest (July 2005), Thurrock (June 2006).

Club honours:

Essex Senior Cup (Waltham Forest 2006).

Marc was a strong, young centre-back and a member of Millwall's youth team when he made his sole loan appearance for the Shots in February 2005. Following his release by the Lions in the summer of 2005, he played as a trialist for Dagenham and Redbridge against Waltham Forest in a pre-season friendly and impressed the Forest management sufficiently to earn himself a move to Wadham Lodge. He followed manager Hakan Hayrettin to Thurrock in June 2006 but was released in January 2007. No further information is known about Marc's career.

Mark Ward — Forward

Born: 27 January 1982, Sheffield.

Aldershot Town FC record:

Debut: as substitute v Bedford Town (h), Isthmian League Premier Division, 9 February 2002.
Last appearance: v Grays Athletic (h), Isthmian League Premier Division, 23 February 2002.
Appearances: 3 + 1
Goals: 1

Playing career:
Sheffield United (from apprentice, July 2000), Aldershot Town (1ML, February 2002), Ossett Albion (trial, July 2002), Stocksbridge Park Steels (August 2002), Belper Town (September 2002), Boston United (trial, October 2002), Lincoln City (March 2003), Belper Town (summer 2003), Worksop Town (1ML, October 2003), Hucknall Town (October 2003), Eastwood Town (1ML, September 2004), Frickley Athletic (March 2006), Grantham Town (December 2006), Bradford Park Avenue (February 2007), Stocksbridge Park Steels (July 2007).
Mark has made two Football League appearances.

Representative honours:
Sheffield Colleges, England Under-18s.

Club honours:
Northern League Premier Division (Hucknall Town 2003–04).

Mark began his footballing life as an apprentice at his local club, Sheffield United, where he signed full professional forms in July 2000. Two League appearances followed before he came to the Rec on a disappointing month's loan in February 2002.

Mark was released by the Blades in the summer of 2002 and spent the majority of the remainder of his career 'doing the rounds' in the Northern League, which included a transfer to Hucknall Town in October 2003 for a four-figure fee. He played in over half of the club's League games that season – with the majority of his appearances from the bench – as the Northern League Premier Division title was won but, frustratingly, he did not score a single goal.

Following a month's loan at Eastwood Town, Mark joined Frickley Athletic in March 2006 and helped with the club's final push towards the runners'-up spot behind Blyth Spartans in the Northern Premier League Premier Division. Part-way through the following season, he joined Grantham Town and then Bradford Park Avenue, scoring on his debut against former club Belper.

In July 2007 Mark rejoined Stocksbridge Park Steels and proceeded to score three goals in 46 games as the Steels finished fifth in the Northern Premier League Division One South. They then lost the resultant Play-off semi-final to Sheffield FC.

Mark Wardell — Midfielder

Born: 15 August 1989, Tooting.

Aldershot Town FC record:

Debut: v Eastleigh (a), Hampshire Senior Cup quarter-final, 15 March 2007.
Appearances: 1

Playing career:
Aldershot Town (youth), AFC Wimbledon (summer 2007), Redbridge (1ML, November 2007).

Mark was a member of the Shots' youth team when he made his sole first-team appearance in the 2006–07 season. He then joined AFC Wimbledon in the summer of 2007 and made two substitute appearances before being loaned to Isthmian League Division One North side Redbridge in November 2007. After he returned to Kingsmeadow, Mark did not make another appearance for the Dons, who finished the season being promoted from the Isthmian League Premier Division.

Phil Warner — Right-back

Born: 2 February 1979, Southampton.

Aldershot Town FC record:

Debut: v York City (h), Conference National, 14 August 2004.
Last appearance: v Exeter City (h), Conference Challenge Cup Southern Section third round, 8 February 2005.
Appearances: 26 + 1

Playing career:

Southampton (from trainee, May 1997), Brentford (6ML, July 1999), Cambridge United (May 2001), Eastleigh (January 2003), Aldershot Town (July 2004), Eastbourne Borough (3ML, February 2005), Eastbourne Borough (June 2005), Havant and Waterlooville (July 2006), Bognor Regis Town (1ML, March 2008).
Phil has made 40 FA Premier League and Football League appearances.

Club honours:

Wessex League (Eastleigh 2002–03).

Phil was a schoolboy and trainee at Southampton, signing full professional forms in May 1997. He made six appearances in the 1998–99 season and went on a six-month loan to Brentford in July 1999, playing 14 games before returning to The Dell. He did not add to his tally of Saints games and, following his release at the end of the 2000–01 season, signed for Cambridge United. Unfortunately, Phil suffered relegation there, but he joined Eastleigh in January 2003 and helped the Hampshire side win that season's Wessex League title and attain a commendable fourth-place finish in the Southern League Eastern Division in 2003–04.

Phil joined Aldershot Town in July 2004, having impressed Terry Brown in the Shots' Hampshire Senior Cup quarter-final tie against Eastleigh the previous season, and he looked as if he had a great deal of promise. However, once the season started he struggled to perform consistently and was loaned to Eastbourne Borough, making the move permanent in the summer. In 2005–06, his only season at Priory Lane, he was part of the Borough side that reached the FA Cup first round for the first time in the club's history before losing in a replay to Oxford United.

In July 2006 Phil moved to fellow Conference South side Havant and Waterlooville and was part of the Hawks' sides that finished in fourth place in the League in 2006–07 and beat Notts County and Swansea City to reach the FA Cup fourth round (before losing at Liverpool) in 2007–08. He spent the last few weeks of that season on loan at fellow Conference South side Bognor Regis Town ,as part of the deal that took the Rocks striker Luke Nightingale to Westleigh Park. Phil was released by the Hawks at the end of the campaign and, at the time of writing, it is believed he is without a club.

Russell Watkinson — Winger

Born: 3 December 1977, Epsom.

Aldershot Town FC record:

Debut: v Altrincham (h), FA Trophy fourth round, 6 February 1999.
Last appearance: as substitute v Billericay Town (h), Isthmian League Premier Division, 21 August 1999.
Appearances: 16 + 8

Playing career:

Woking (youth), Farnborough Town (2ML, November 1995), Fleet Town (summer 1996), Southampton (September 1996), Millwall (2ML, March 1998), Kingstonian (August 1998), Colchester United (trial, November 1998), Aldershot Town (February 1999), Chesham United (September 1999), Hampton and Richmond Borough (trial, August 2000).
Russell has made two FA Premier League appearances.

Club honours:

Isthmian League Charity Shield (Kingstonian 1998), Isthmian League Cup (Aldershot Town 1999), Hampshire Senior Cup (Aldershot Town 1999).

Russell was a fleet-of-foot winger who played in Woking's youth team before going on a two-month loan to Farnborough Town, where he was restricted to just two appearances in the 1995–96 Hampshire Senior Cup. He joined Fleet Town but quickly made a move to FA Premier League side Southampton in September 1996. His only three appearances for the Saints came from the bench later that month.

Following a two-month loan at Millwall, Russell joined Kingstonian in August 1998, making his debut in the Isthmian League Charity Shield victory over local rivals Sutton United. He made three further appearances before trialling at Colchester United and then joining Aldershot Town (in February 1999), where he was part of the side that won the Isthmian League Cup and Hampshire Senior Cup that season. He then played for Chesham United before trialling at Hampton and Richmond Borough in the summer of 2000. No further information pertaining to Russell's playing career is known, but he currently runs his own soccer school.

Mark Watson **Forward**

Born: 28 December 1973, Birmingham.

Aldershot Town FC record:

Debut:	v Enfield (h), Isthmian League Premier Division, 18 August 2001.
Last appearance:	as substitute v Boreham Wood (a), Isthmian League Premier Division, 27 April 2002.
Appearances:	31 + 15
Goals:	15

Playing career:

Local football, Sutton United (August 1993), West Ham United (May 1995), Leyton Orient (1ML, September 1995), Cambridge United (1ML, October 1995), Shrewsbury Town (1ML, February 1996), AFC Bournemouth (May 1996), Welling United (July 1997), Sutton United (March 1998), Woking (May 2000), Chesham United (November 2000), Aldershot Town (May 2001), Sutton United (August 2002), Lewes (November 2003), Bromley (March 2004), Metropolitan Police (February 2005), Worthing (July 2005), Kingstonian (September 2005), Sutton United (February 2006), Worthing (October 2006), Margate (July 2007).

Mark has made 22 FA Premier League and Football League appearances, scoring four goals.

Club honours:

Surrey Senior Cup (Sutton United 1995, 1999, 2003), Isthmian League Cup (Sutton United 1998), Isthmian League Premier Division (Sutton United 1998–99), Hampshire Senior Cup (Aldershot Town 2002 [unused substitute]).

Mark is a stocky and powerful forward who, having played local football, joined Isthmian League Premier Division outfit Sutton United in August 1993. His performances over the next two seasons led to a move into the professional game with FA Premier League side West Ham United, who paid £50,000 for his services. Unfortunately, the move did not work out as Mark would have hoped, and his sole appearance for the Hammers consisted of 13 minutes as a substitute against Queen's Park Rangers in the penultimate League game of the 1995–96 season.

Prior to that, Mark had been loaned out before AFC Bournemouth paid £100,000 to take him to Dean Court in May 1996. Having scored just twice in 16 games for the Cherries, he was released in the summer of 1997 and joined Welling United before rejoining Sutton the following March and scoring five goals to help the Us finish third in the Isthmian League Premier Division and win the League Cup.

Despite missing two months of the 1998–99 season through injury, Mark was Sutton's top scorer (32 goals) as the Premier Division title and Surrey Senior Cup were won. He top scored again in 1999–2000 (11 goals) as the club reached the FA Trophy semi-finals and suffered an immediate relegation from the Conference after a rock-bottom finish. However, he managed to stay in the Conference by way of an £8,000 move to Woking but lasted just six months at Kingfield, during which time he scored once in 14 appearances before joining Chesham United.

Mark moved to Aldershot Town in May 2001 and scored on his debut but then spoiled the occasion by earning the unfortunate distinction of becoming the first Shots debutant to be sent off. He went on to score 15 goals that season as third place in the Isthmian League Premier Division was secured.

In August 2002 he returned to Sutton, where his 18 goals in all competitions helped the club finish in sixth place in the Isthmian League Premier Division. He also scored his 100th goal for the Us in their Surrey Senior Cup Final win against Kingstonian that season. Mark then had various spells elsewhere before returning to Gander Green Lane for a fourth spell in February 2006. It is not known what he did immediately after he left that summer. Mark re-signed for Worthing in October 2006 but left after a month, and it is believed that he did not play again that season.

In July 2007 Mark signed for Margate after a successful pre-season trial and scored just once in 11 appearances before leaving in January 2008. No information relating to Mark's subsequent career or current whereabouts is known.

Mark Watson — Goalkeeper

Born: 23 August 1967, Basingstoke.

Aldershot Town FC record:

Debut: v Tring Town (h), Isthmian League Division Three, 7 November 1992.
Last appearance: v Molesey (h), Isthmian League Division One, 15 October 1996.
Appearances: 142

Playing career:

Arsenal (schoolboy), Southampton (schoolboy and youth), Plymouth Argyle (youth), Reading (youth), Hartley Wintney, Camberley Town (summer 1991), Aldershot Town (November 1992), Basingstoke Town (October 1996), Colchester United (NC, November 1996), Fleet Town (December 1996), Aldershot Town (March 1997), Banstead Athletic (March 1997), Walton and Hersham (August 1999), Banstead Athletic (October 1999), Fleet Town (January 2000), Wokingham Town (September 2001), Banstead Athletic (August 2002), AFC Totton (summer 2003), Lymington and New Milton/New Milton Town (August 2004).

Representative honours:

Hampshire Youth.

Club honours:

Isthmian League Division Three (Aldershot Town 1992–93), Wessex League Division One (Lymington and New Milton 2004–05).

Mark is an experienced 'keeper who commands his area very well and is renowned as an excellent shot-stopper. Having played as a schoolboy for both Arsenal and Southampton, he joined Plymouth Argyle as a youth player in the summer of 1983 and went on to Reading, where he shattered his hand nearly two years later – an injury that signalled the end of his time at Elm Park.

Following his release in the summer of 1985, Mark took a year out of football before playing for Hartley Wintney and Camberley Town. He joined Aldershot Town in November 1992, with the £1,000 paid for his services being the first fee the Shots had paid for a player. He made 25 appearances in all competitions that season as the Isthmian League Division Three title was secured. The form of Phil Burns restricted Mark to just three appearances in the 1993–94 season, but he was a regular again the following two seasons as successive top-five finishes in Isthmian League Division One were achieved, together with creditable runs in both the Isthmian League Cup and Hampshire Senior Cup.

Mark left the Rec in October 1996 and had short spells elsewhere before making a non-playing return to the Shots then joining Banstead Athletic in March 1997. After another couple of spells, he rejoined Fleet Town in January 2000. The club finished in fourth spot in the Wessex League in 2000–01, and Mark attained personal glory that season by winning the Player of the Year award.

Mark joined Lymington and New Milton in August 2004 and his first season there was a successful one. He played a key role in the winning of that season's Wessex League Division One title, thus gaining promotion to Isthmian League Division One. They also achieved a club-best progression to the FA Cup fourth qualifying round, where they lost in a replay to Woking, and the FA Vase fifth round, where thy were defeated by Bury Town. Mark's season was then completed by him being a joint winner of the Player of the Year award along with Chris Smith and Paul Towler.

Following great financial upheaval and the loss of a majority of their playing staff, renamed New Milton Town voluntarily dropped down to the Wessex League Premier Division. Mark made four more League appearances but then left the club. No further details pertaining to his career or current whereabouts are known.

Matthew Watson — Left-back / Goalkeeper

Born: 9 March 1983, Chertsey.

Aldershot Town FC record:

Debut: v Newport (Isle of Wight (a), Hampshire Senior Cup second round, 2 November 2000.
Appearances: 1

Playing career:

Crystal Palace (youth), Aldershot Town (youth), Hartley Wintney (August 2003), Frimley Green (January 2004), Cove (August 2006). Frimley Green (August 2007).

Representative honours:

Aldershot and District Schools, Hampshire Youth.

Matthew is unique in that he is equally comfortable playing at left-back or as a goalkeeper, having done so for all of his clubs to date! He played youth-team football at Crystal Palace and Aldershot Town before joining Hartley Wintney in August 2003. He then had just over two seasons at Frimley Green, with the latter seeing the club relegated from the Combined Counties Premier League due to ground grading issues.

Matthew spent the 2006–07 season at Cove before returning to Frimley Green in August 2007, helping the club finish the 2007–08 Combined Counties League Division One season in sixth place.

Steve Watson — Midfielder

Born: 23 December 1971, Croydon.

Aldershot Town FC record:

Debut: v York City (h), Conference National, 14 August 2004.
Last appearance: v Grays Athletic (h), Conference National, 17 April 2006.
Appearances: 62 + 3
Goals: 4

Playing career:

Crystal Palace (youth), Farleigh Rovers (summer 1991), Whyteleafe (summer 1992), Croydon (summer 1993), Sutton United (October 1995), Farnborough Town (July 1999), Stevenage Borough (February 2003), Aldershot Town (July 2004), AFC Wimbledon (June 2006).

Representative honours:

Combined Counties League XI, Isthmian League XI, England Semi-Professional XI (three caps).

Club honours:

Isthmian League Full Members' Cup (Sutton United 1996), Isthmian League Cup (Sutton United 1998; Farnborough Town 2000), Surrey Senior Cup (Sutton United 1999), Isthmian League Premier Division (Sutton United 1998–99; Farnborough Town 2000–01), Isthmian League Charity Shield (Farnborough Town 2001).

Steve's tough-tackling and uncompromising style of play has made him a valuable member of various sides throughout his career. At Crystal Palace from the age of nine, he was offered an apprenticeship when he was 16 years old but turned it down. He subsequently left Selhurst Park and turned his back on the game for nearly four years before returning with Combined Counties League side Farleigh Rovers in the summer of 1991 and then Croydon in the summer of 1993.

Although Croydon were relegated from Isthmian League Division One at the end of his first season, Steve's ability to win a tackle helped him stand out in a struggling side. Both club and player improved the following season as a club-best FA Vase fourth-round progression was achieved together with a seventh-place League finish.

Steve made the step up to the Isthmian League Premier Division in October 1995 when Sutton United paid £6,000 for him, and his game improved year-on-year. He soon gained a reputation as a midfield 'hard man' and was instrumental in Sutton attaining successive third-place finishes in the Premier Division (in 1996–97 and 1997–98) before captaining them to the Premier Division title in 1998–99. That season, he scored 14 goals and also won the Player of the Year award.

Steve joined Farnborough Town and was made captain in 2000–01 when the Isthmian League Premier Division was won. He also skippered the side the following season and made his England Semi-Professional XI debut as a substitute against the USA in March 2002. He was joint captain (with Tony Pennock) in the 2002–03 season, as well as being an integral part of the Boro side that achieved a club-best progression to that season's FA Cup fourth round, losing to Arsenal in a 'home' tie that was controversially switched to Highbury.

Shortly after that game, Steve was one of a number of players to follow boss Graham Westley to Stevenage Borough, where he was immediately named as captain. After just over a season at Broadhall Way, he signed for Aldershot Town and was named as captain for the forthcoming 2004–05 season. He arrived at the Rec knowing that he would have to work harder than many incoming players to win over the Shots fans, due to the fact that he had played for Graham Westley at both Farnborough Town and Stevenage Borough. However, his combative style of play, coupled with the fact that he scored on his debut against York City, greatly reduced the time it took the Rec faithful to change their minds. He made a huge contribution as the Shots reached the Play-offs for a second successive season and won the 2005 Player of the Year award. However, he missed chunks of the 2005–06 season due to a hip injury, which coincided with the Shots having their worst-ever season in terms of League position.

Steve left the Rec in the summer of 2006 and joined AFC Wimbledon, where another season took its toll on his hip. He retired from 'regular' football in the summer of 2007 but went on to captain the Bromley veterans' side during the 2007–08 season, with the campaign culminating in victory over Whyteleafe in the Isthmian League Veterans' Cup Final. When not donning his boots, Steve runs his own building company.

Dan Weait — Goalkeeper

Born: 12 July 1987, Ascot.

Aldershot Town FC record:

Debut:	v Brockenhurst (h), Hampshire Senior Cup second round, 1 November 2005.
Last appearance:	v Cambridge United (h), Conference National, 8 April 2006.
Appearances:	3 + 1

Playing career:

Southampton (youth), Basingstoke Town (youth), Leicester City (trial, summer 2005), Aldershot Town (August 2005).

Dan is a former Southampton youth 'keeper who joined Aldershot Town in August 2005. Prior to joining the Shots, he spent the 2004–05 season at North Hampshire rivals Basingstoke Town and had a brief trial at Leicester City.

Dan made his Shots debut in a Hampshire Senior Cup second-round tie against Brockenhurst in November 2005, but it is probably his last appearance for which he will be remembered. In what was to be his only League appearance, Dan came on as a half-time substitute for the injured Nikki Bull against Cambridge United and finished the game on the wrong end of a 3–1 scoreline, with the Shots having led 1–0 at the break. Dan was released at the end of that season, and no further information is known about his career.

Neil Webb **Midfielder**

Born: 30 July 1963, Reading.

Aldershot Town FC record:

Debut:	v Whyteleafe (h), Isthmian League Division One, 21 September 1996.
Last appearance:	v Worthing (h), Isthmian League Division One, 12 April 1997.
Appearances:	36
Goals:	6

Playing career:

Reading (from apprentice, November 1980), Portsmouth (July 1982), Nottingham Forest (June 1985), Manchester United (June 1989), Nottingham Forest (November 1992), Swindon Town (1ML, October 1994), Exeter City (trial, July 1996), Grimsby Town (July 1996), Aldershot Town (September 1996), Rotherham United (trial, April 1997), Weymouth (player-manager, June 1997), Merthyr Tydfil (NC, November 1999), West Reading (NC, March 2001), Reading Town (player-manager, June 2001), Thame United (NC, April 2006).

Neil has made 456 FA Premier League and Football League appearances, scoring 114 goals.

Representative honours:

England Youth, Football League XI, England Under-21s (three caps), England B (four caps), England full international (26 caps, four goals).

Club honours:

Division Three (Portsmouth 1982–83), Football League Cup (Nottingham Forest 1989; Manchester United 1992 [unused substitute]), Full Members' Cup (Nottingham Forest 1989), FA Cup (Manchester United 1990), European Cup-Winners' Cup (Manchester United 1991 [unused substitute]).

Neil is the son of ex-Reading centre-forward Douggie Webb and the father of Hereford United midfielder Luke and Reading youth-team player Josh. He made his Reading debut while still an apprentice against Mansfield Town in February 1980 and became the Royals' youngest-ever League goalscorer when he netted against Swindon Town in August of that year, aged 17 years and 31 days. He signed full professional forms at Elm Park two months later and went on to make 72 League appearances and score 22 goals for the club before a fee of £83,000 took him to fellow Division Three side Portsmouth in July 1982. It proved to be a good move for club and player, as Neil missed just four League games and scored eight goals as Pompey won the Division Three title in 1982–83.

With each passing season, Neil was getting better and attracting favourable press coverage, which led to him stepping up to Division One in June 1985 when Brian Clough's Nottingham Forest paid £250,000 for his services. In his four seasons at the City Ground, he developed into one of the best midfielders in the country, as well as being part of the Forest sides that finished third in the League in 1987–88 and 1988–89, beat Luton Town to win the League Cup in 1989 and beat Everton that same season to win the Full Members' Cup.

Neil's time at Forest also brought him international recognition – he made his England debut as a substitute against West Germany in September 1987 and, in doing so, became the 1,000th player to be capped by the country. He also played in the European Championship Finals in West Germany in 1988.

Neil joined Manchester United in June 1989 for a fee of £1.5 million but was unfortunate to snap his achilles tendon against Sweden in a World Cup qualifier three months later – an injury that would eventually contribute to ending his professional career. He recovered sufficiently to help United win that season's FA Cup, and it was from his near 50-yard pass that Lee Martin scored the only goal of the replay against Crystal Palace. He was a member of the England squad that finished fourth in the 1990 World Cup Finals in Italy before helping the Reds reach the European Cup-Winners' Cup Final in 1991 (he was an unused substitute for the defeat of Barcelona). United were also runners-up in that season's League Cup, losing to Sheffield Wednesday.

The 1991–92 season saw United finish as runners-up to Leeds United in the League title race and beat Neil's former club, Nottingham Forest, to win the League Cup (again, Neil was an unused substitute). But the summer brought disappointment for Neil when he was part of the England squad knocked out at the first-round stage of the European Championship Finals in Sweden. Finding himself third choice behind Paul Ince and Bryan Robson, he rejoined Nottingham Forest in November 1992 for £800,000, but it was not a happy return as the club were relegated from the FA Premier League at the end of that season by virtue of a rock-bottom finish. A further achilles injury would limit Neil to just 30 League appearances in nearly four seasons back at the City Ground.

Neil was loaned to Swindon Town during the 1994–95 season before eventually being released by Forest in the summer of 1996, having made a total of 176 League appearances and scoring 50 goals in his two spells. Following a trial at Exeter City and a short spell at Grimsby Town, Neil surprisingly joined Aldershot Town in September 1996, where he linked up with his friend and ex-Nottingham Forest teammate Steve Wigley (Shots boss at the time).

Having amassed a wealth of experience in the professional game, Neil was often unfairly derided for seemingly failing to adapt to the level of football at which he was now playing. A lot of this criticism centred on him playing balls that his teammates simply were not expecting but which would have been gleefully received by players at a higher level.

After seven months at the Rec, Neil trialled at Rotherham United and then took on the role of player-manager at Southern League Southern Division Weymouth, where he lasted just 70 days before resigning in the September. He later became player-manager of Combined Counties League side Reading Town but resigned in the November after a run of poor results, and he subsequently retired.

In April 2006 Neil came out of retirement and signed for Southern League Division One West side Thame United, with his signing reportedly being made to highlight the fact that the club had been evicted from their ground. After a sole appearance against Dunstable Town, he retired again. His media work has included local radio and being the English football correspondent for the Canadian Score TV network programme *Sportsworld*. Neil's latest honour is to have been voted into Reading's best-ever XI in 2007.

Louis Wells — Goalkeeper

Born: 22 February 1982, Hillingdon.

Aldershot Town FC record:

Debut: v East Cowes Victoria Athletic (h), Hampshire Senior Cup second round, 31 October 2006.
Appearances: 6 + 1

Playing career:
Local football, Hayes (summer 2005), Aldershot Town (trial, April 2006), Aldershot Town (June 2006), Maidenhead United (August 2007), Uxbridge (March 2008).

Club honours:
Hampshire Senior Cup (Aldershot Town 2007).

Having played local league football, Louis joined Hayes in the summer of 2005 and played mostly in the reserves, although he did manage seven first-team games during 2005–06. He trialled with Aldershot Town in April 2006 before signing permanently two months later, but he found that the excellent form of Nikki Bull restricted his appearances almost entirely to Hampshire Senior Cup matches. He played six times in that competition, including the Final victory over Fleet Town in 2007, as well as making a solitary League appearance as a substitute.

Louis left the Rec in the summer of 2007 in search of first-team football and successfully trialled at Maidenhead United, where he was part of the side that reached the FA Cup first round for the first time in 45 years in 2007–08. Unfortunately, that achievement was tainted by the Magpies being the victims of a giant-killing, as they were knocked out by Isthmian League Premier Division side Horsham.

It did not get much better for Louis after that, as he was unable to command a regular first-team place at York Road and was released in March 2008. He joined Southern League Division One South and West side Uxbridge shortly afterwards and helped them secure a fifth-place League finish, thus qualifying them for the Play-offs. However, having disposed of Fleet Town in the resultant semi-final, the Reds then lost the Play-off Final to Oxford City.

Rob Westell — Midfielder

Born: 28 September 1984, Reading.

Aldershot Town FC record:

Debut: as substitute v Yeading (h), Isthmian League Charity Shield, 19 August 2003.
Last appearance: v Eastleigh (h), Hampshire Senior Cup quarter-final, 27 January 2004.
Appearances: 3 + 3

Playing career:
Wycombe Wanderers (schoolboy and youth), Queen's Park Rangers (youth), Aldershot Town (youth), Burnham (3ML, November 2003), Basingstoke Town (1ML, February 2004), Frimley Green (2ML, April 2004), Basingstoke Town (August 2004), Bracknell Town (October 2004), Cove (2004–05 season), Badshot Lea (January 2005).

Club honours:
Isthmian League Charity Shield (Aldershot Town 2003), Hellenic League Supplementary Cup (Badshot Lea 2006).

Rob is a skilful attacking midfielder who played as a schoolboy and youth player at Wycombe Wanderers before going on to be a member of the youth set-up at Queen's Park Rangers and Aldershot Town. He made all of his six first-team appearances for the Shots during the 2003–04 season and also had loan spells before the season's end. Short stints at Bracknell Town and Cove followed before Rob signed for Badshot Lea in January 2005. He was one of several ex-Shots youngsters who helped the club win the Hellenic League Supplementary Cup in 2006 and gain promotion to the Hellenic League Premier Division in 2006–07. He then helped the club attain a creditable 11th-place finish and reach the Aldershot Senior Cup Final, where they lost to Fleet Town, in 2007-08.

Darren Wheeler — Midfielder/Winger/Striker

Born: 6 February 1984, Guildford.

Aldershot Town FC record:

Debut:	v Walton and Hersham (a), Isthmian League Cup first round, 12 September 2000.
Last appearance:	v Slough Town (a), Isthmian League Full Members' Cup first round, 24 October 2000.
Appearances:	2

Playing career:
Swindon Town (youth), Leicester City (youth), Wolverhampton Wanderers (youth), Portsmouth (youth), Farnham Town (youth), Mytchett Athletic (youth), Aldershot Town (youth), Mytchett Athletic (youth), Hartley Wintney (summer 2002), Godalming and Guildford (summer 2004), Aldershot Town (trial, January 2005), Crawley Town (trial, January 2005), Yeovil Town (trial, January 2005), Weymouth (February 2005), Chippenham Town (2ML, January 2006), Eastleigh (June 2006), Mangotsfield United (August 2007), Farnborough (November 2007).

Club honours:
Conference South (Weymouth 2005–06), Southern League Division One South and West (Farnborough 2007–08).

Darren is a quick and skilful left-footed player who can play in a variety of positions. He played youth-team football for a number of professional sides but was unfortunate to pick up an ankle injury when he looked certain to be given a place at Portsmouth's academy. He then joined Farnham Town's youth set-up before moving on to Mytchett Athletic and then the Shots, for whom he made his two first-team appearances during the 2000–01 season.

Darren left the Shots midway through the 2001–02 season and, having returned to play in Mytchett Athletic's youth team, was then involved in a bizarre incident while playing against the Shots. He was sent off in that game but refused to leave the field of play and was later given a whopping 148-day ban! Once he had served his ban, he played and trialled at various clubs, including Aldershot Town, and joined Weymouth in February 2005. However, he could not hold down a regular place at the Wessex Stadium during the 2005–06 season and so spent the tail end of the season on loan at Chippenham Town. Darren helped the Bluebirds reach the Southern League Premier Division Play-off Final (which they lost to Bedford Town) before returning to Weymouth and playing in their last three League games of the season as the Conference South title was won.

In June 2006 Darren signed for Eastleigh and played steadily until he found himself pushed down the pecking order following the arrival of Damian Scannell and Ellis Green. He joined Southern League Premier Division side Mangotsfield United for an undisclosed fee. However, his stay there lasted just three months before he signed for the newly formed Farnborough FC, where his 15 goals in all competitions assisted in the winning of the 2007–08 Southern League Division One South and West title. The season ended on a losing note, as they lost the Hampshire Senior Cup Final to Basingstoke Town, but that dissappointment was offset by Darren being voted Player of the Year.

Ryan Williams — Winger

Born: 31 August 1978, Sutton-in-Ashfield.

Aldershot Town FC record:

Debut:	v Crawley Town (h), Conference National, 5 September 2005.
Last appearance:	v Halifax Town (a), Conference Premier, 19 April 2008.
Appearances:	79 + 5
Goals:	21

Playing career:

Mansfield Town (trainee, June 1995), Tranmere Rovers (August 1997), Chesterfield (November 1999), Hull City (June 2001), Bristol Rovers (October 2003), Forest Green Rovers (1ML, December 2004), Aldershot Town (1ML, August 2005), Aldershot Town (January 2006), Weymouth (May 2008).

Ryan has made 201 Football League appearances, scoring 22 goals.

Representative honours:

England Youth.

Club honours:

Hampshire Senior Cup (Aldershot Town 2007), Setanta Shield (Aldershot Town 2008 [unused substitute]), Conference Premier (Aldershot Town 2007–08).

Ryan is a tricky, diminutive winger who started out as a trainee at Mansfield Town in June 1995 and made his debut against Leyton Orient in January 1996. He was due to sign full professional forms at Field Mill in August 1997 but Tranmere Rovers 'nipped in' and paid £70,000 for him; however, a broken foot limited him to just five appearances in a little over two seasons at Prenton Park. Ryan joined Chesterfield on a three-month loan in November 1999, signing permanently at the end of the term for a fee of £85,000, and his near two seasons at Saltergate certainly were not dull, including relegation, promotion and a second successive regional semi-final spot in the Football League Trophy in 2000–01.

In June 2001 Hull City paid £150,000 for Ryan's services, and his first season at Boothferry Park looked as though it would bring him his second successive promotion as the Tigers occupied the promotion and Play-off places for most of the campaign. However, they underwent a massive turnaround in form following manager Brian Little's departure in the February and eventually finished in 11th place. Ryan was on familiar territory when suffering defeat to Huddersfield Town in the Northern Area semi-finals of the Football League Trophy.

In October 2003 Ryan joined Bristol Rovers and later Forest Green Rovers on a one-month loan, during which he ran the Shots' defence ragged in two League matches over the Christmas period. Ryan was then a regular inclusion back in the Bristol side and played in the defeat by Southend United in the Southern Area Final of that season's Football League Trophy.

By the start of the 2005–06 season, it was obvious that Ryan was not in boss Ian Atkins's plans, and he joined Aldershot Town on a one-month loan in August 2005. He made an immediate impact by scoring with a superb free-kick on his debut against Crawley Town in a televised game at the Rec, but then he picked up an injury against Accrington Stanley at the end of the following month, which saw him return to the West Country.

After two months recovering from his injury, Ryan made four more substitute appearances for Rovers before being released. He rejoined the Shots on a permanent basis in January 2006 and finished the season with seven goals to his name. The following season, he scored 14 goals in 57 appearances (playing in every League game) and was the part of the sides that were beaten by Blackpool in the FA Cup third round and that won the Hampshire Senior Cup.

In July 2007 Ryan tore an anterior cruciate ligament in a pre-season friendly against Crystal Palace and was expected to miss the entire season. However, he worked tremendously hard and returned to action in the reserves the following March. He was then an unused substitute in the Setanta Shield Final triumph over Rushden and Diamonds the following month before making his only appearance of the season in the penultimate away League match at Halifax Town. Ryan left the club shortly after the season's end and subsequently became Weymouth's first summer signing.

Paul Wilson — Defender/Midfielder

Born: 26 September 1964, Forest Gate.

Aldershot Town FC record:

Debut:	v Carshalton Athletic (a), Isthmian League Premier Division, 10 October 1998.
Last appearance:	as substitute v Boreham Wood (h), Isthmian League Premier Division, 7 November 1998.
Appearances:	2 + 1

Playing career:

West Ham United (youth), Billericay Town, Barking (August 1987), Barnet (March 1988), Aldershot Town (1ML, October 1998), Boston United (September 2000).

Paul has made 263 Football League appearances, scoring 24 goals.

Representative honours:

FA XI.

Club honours:

Bob Lord Trophy (Barnet 1989), Conference (Barnet 1990–91).

Post-playing coaching/management career:

Reserve-team manager at Barnet, assistant coach at Barnet (February 2002), assistant manager of Barnet (April 2003).

Paul was an experienced, committed and tough-tackling midfielder who could also play as a full-back. He is regarded by many at Barnet as a legend and played close on 600 games for the Bees, 263 of which make him the holder of the club record for Football League appearances. Paul played youth-team football at West Ham United before dropping into the non-League game. He started his love affair with Barnet in March 1988 and helped them beat Hyde United to win the Bob Lord Trophy in 1989. He missed just one League game in 1989–90 as Barnet finished as runners-up in the Conference, and promotion to the Football League finally came in 1990–91 by virtue of victory over Fisher Athletic on the last day of the season. That season also saw the club equal their best-ever progression as a non-League club in the FA Cup, when they bowed out in the third round to Second Division Portsmouth, having beaten Division Four side Northampton Town in the previous round.

Paul made his Football League debut as a substitute against Doncaster Rovers in September 1991 and went on to play 25 times as the Division Three Play-off semi-finals were reached. He then missed the bulk of the 1992–93 season because of injury, playing just nine times as the club battled off-the-field problems to gain promotion via a third-place finish. Following that promotion, several players left Underhill but Paul stayed and was the mainstay of the new team that emerged.

Unfortunately, the 'new look' Barnet were relegated at the end of the 1993–94 season and then had three barren seasons, during which Paul was a virtual ever present. Club and player then sampled Division Three Play-off semi-final disappointment twice in three seasons – they lost to Colchester United in 1997–98 (Paul only played in the second leg) and Peterborough United in 1999–2000 (when Paul only played in the first leg). In between, he played three games on loan at Aldershot Town during the 1998–99 season.

Paul finally left Underhill in September 2000 and joined Conference side Boston United before a knee injury ended his career in January 2002. He then returned to Underhill to take on the role of reserve-team manager and then assistant coach. In April 2003 Paul became Barnet boss Martin Allen's assistant before financial constraints led to him leaving that summer. It is not known what Paul did after this, nor is any information available pertaining to his current whereabouts.

Dave Winfield — Centre-back

Born: 24 March 1988, Aldershot.

Aldershot Town FC record:

Debut:	v Forest Green Rovers (a), Conference Challenge Cup Southern Section quarter-final, 15 February 2005.
Appearances:	55 + 20
Goals:	3

Playing career:
Aldershot Town (from youth, August 2005), Chertsey Town (3ML, March 2005), Staines Town (2ML, February 2006).

Representative honours:
Hampshire Youth.

Club honours:
Hampshire Senior Cup (Aldershot Town 2007), Setanta Shield (Aldershot Town 2008), Conference Premier (Aldershot Town 2007–08).

Dave is a towering, 6ft 3in centre-back, who made his Shots debut while still a member of the youth team. He was loaned out to Chertsey Town at the tail end of the 2004–05 season before returning to the Rec and signing full contract forms in August 2005. He then missed a proportion of the 2005–06 season with a toe injury, and was loaned to Staines Town in February 2006 to help with his recovery.

By the start of the 2007–08 season, Dave had bulked up and matured into a solid defender, whose confidence and ability belied his age. In February 2008 he signed a contract extension to the end of the 2009–10 season before helping the Shots reach the FA Trophy semi-finals and win the Setanta Shield. Dave picked up a knee injury in the latter game and missed the remainder of the Conference Premier title-winning season.

Jeff Wood — Forward

Born: 8 March 1964, Bermondsey.

Aldershot Town FC record:

Debut:	v Whyteleafe (a), Isthmian League Division One, 11 November 1995.
Last appearance:	v Wokingham Town (a), Isthmian League Division One, 4 May 1996.
Appearances:	33 + 3
Goals:	15

Playing career:
West Ham United (youth), Greenwich Borough (February 1983), Crawley Town (July 1983), Wimbledon (trial, 1985), Dartford (June 1986), Bishop's Stortford (December 1986), Harlow Town (August 1988), Purfleet (January 1991), Barking (October 1992), Aldershot Town (November 1995), Ford United (July 1996), Leyton (July 2001).

Representative honours:
Inner London Schools Under-18s, Essex FA XI (three appearances, six goals).

Club honours:
London Spartan League Cup (Greenwich Borough 1983), Southern Counties Combination Cup (Crawley Town 1984), Hertfordshire Senior Cup (Bishop's Stortford 1987), Isthmian League Division Two North (Harlow Town 1988–89), East Anglian Cup (Harlow Town 1990), Isthmian League Division Two (Purfleet 1991–92), Isthmian League Associate Members' Trophy (Purfleet 1992; Leyton 2003), Essex Senior League (Ford United 1996–97; Leyton 2001–02), London Senior Cup (Ford United 1998), Isthmian League Division Three (Ford United 1998–99), Essex Thameside Trophy (Ford United 1999), Gordon Brasted Memorial Trophy (Leyton 2002).

Jeff was a prolific marksman who went for England Under-18 trials while a youth-team player at West Ham United but was unsuccessful. Following his release from Upton Park he had a brief spell at London Spartan League side Greenwich Borough, during which he scored six goals in 15 games. Jeff joined Crawley Town, whom he fired to the runners'-up spot behind RS Southampton in the Southern League Southern Division in 1983–84 and to victory in that season's Southern Counties Combination Cup Final.

Jeff trialled at Wimbledon before leaving Crawley, having scored 65 goals in 160 games, joining their newly relegated divisional rivals Dartford for a fee of £3,000 in June 1986. Jeff scored 12 goals in 24 games for the Darts but was allowed to leave Watling Street just six months later, when Isthmian League Premier Division outfit Bishop's Stortford paid £1,500 for him.

With only the 1987 Hertfordshire Senior Cup to show for his 19 goals in 40 games at Rhodes Avenue, Jeff joined Harlow Town in August 1988 and it was here that his career really took off. His first season at Hammarskjold Road yielded the Isthmian League Division Two North title and the Player of the Year trophy, as well as seeing him set two club scoring records – he scored in 12 consecutive League games (also an Isthmian League record) and finished the season with 44 goals. When he left for Purfleet in March 1991, he had scored 80 goals in 140 games.

Jeff was an integral part of the Purfleet side that won the Isthmian League Division Two title and the Associate Members' Trophy in 1991–92, scoring the winning goal in the Final against Egham Town. Unsurprisingly, he finished the season as the club's top scorer (32 goals). He went on to score 41 goals in 80 appearances for Purfleet before joining Barking in October 1992. In just over three years at Mayesbrook Park, he was Player of the Year in 1993 and 1995 and top scored between 1992–95, with 14, 27 and 44 goals respectively.

Jeff scored a total of 93 goals in 170 games for the Blues before joining Aldershot Town for a fee of £2,000 in November 1995. Unsurprisingly, he scored on his Shots debut and went on to bag 15 goals in 36 games in his only season at the Rec. Amazingly, he also managed to finish that season as Barking's joint-top scorer with Tim Hope, scoring seven goals, despite having only played for them in the first three months of the campaign.

Jeff left the Rec in July 1996 for an undisclosed fee and signed for Ford United, who were managed by his former Barking boss Dennis Elliott. The goals and honours kept coming as the Essex Senior League title was secured in his first season at Oakside. He also finished the season as Ford and the Essex Senior League's top goalscorer with 53 goals, as well as winning that season's Player of the Year award. Jeff fondly relates the story that Elliott had told the club's board of directors that Jeff would get them 50 goals that season, but Jeff did not find that out until after the season had ended! He was again Ford's Players of the Year and top scorer in 1997–98, with 33 of his 48 goals also winning him the Isthmian League Division Three Golden Boot. The 1998–99 and 1999–2000 seasons saw him top score again, with 49 and 45 goals respectively, as well as winning the Isthmian League Division Three title plus two more Player of the Year awards! In five seasons with the Motormen, Jeff scored a staggering club record 197 goals in 200 games, which facilitated three promotions.

In September 2000 Jeff retired due to 'toe fusing' complications, which arose from a foot fracture. It is thought that he may well have picked up this injury during his time at the Rec, but he played on unaware of it. In the end, the injury required two operations to correct. Jeff had recovered sufficiently to come out of retirement and sign for Essex Senior League side Leyton in July 2001, and his 16 goals helped them to win the 2001–02 title and earned him the Player of the Year award.

The 2002–03 season saw him top score yet again, with his 26 goals winning him yet another Player of the Year award, as well as helping the Lilywhites finish runners-up to Cheshunt in Isthmian League Division Two. However, they did beat the champions to win that season's Associate Members' Trophy. Leyton again finished runners-up in the League the following season, this time to Yeading in Isthmian League Division One North.

Jeff retired that summer, having scored 44 goals in 130 appearances for Leyton, bringing his career total to an amazing 578 goals from 998 games! Jeff currently works as a senior project manager in UK Government.

Paul Wooller — Centre-back

Born: 29 July 1970, Chertsey.

Aldershot Town FC record:

Debut:	v Berkhamsted Town (a), Isthmian League Division One, 19 April 1997.
Last appearance:	v Billericay Town (a), Isthmian League Division One, 14 October 1997.
Appearances:	7 + 1
Goals:	1

Playing career:

Horsell (summer 1986), Woking (summer 1987), Leatherhead (January 1989), Crawley Town (summer 1989), Leatherhead (summer 1990), Crystal Palace (trial, April 1991), Egham Town (October 1992), Wokingham Town (summer 1994), Basingstoke Town (January 1996), Fleet Town (summer 1996), Aldershot Town (April 1997), Walton and Hersham (November 1997), Bisley Sports (summer 1998), Old Guildfordians (summer 2004), Bisley (summer 2005), Old Guildfordians (summer 2006).

Club honours:

Sussex Senior Cup (Crawley Town 1990).

Paul started his career as a 16-year-old at local league side Horsell before signing for neighbouring Isthmian League Division One side Woking and having a short spell at Leatherhead. He joined Crawley Town together with Jerry Alleyne in the summer of 1989 for a combined fee of £2,000, and his only season at Town Mead yielded the Sussex Senior Cup and a back injury that was to plague him throughout the rest of his career.

Paul rejoined Leatherhead in the summer of 1990 and performed well enough to earn himself a trial at Crystal Palace and win the Tanners' Player of the Year award in 1991. He was named captain at Fetcham Grove for the 1991–92 season and led the club to a fourth-place finish in Isthmian League Division Two, missing promotion by five points. He played at various clubs before signing for Aldershot Town in April 1997, playing in two of the remaining League games that season plus six the following term before picking up a leg injury that signalled the end of his Shots career.

After an extremely brief spell at Walton and Hersham, for whom he played approximately seven minutes of a reserve game before injury caused him to be substituted, Paul retired in October 1997 due to a combination of his back and leg injuries. He came out of retirement in the summer of 1998 and played for Bisley Sports for the next six seasons, playing an important part in the club's progression from the Surrey County League to the Hellenic League Division One East.

A family connection took him to Amateur Football Combination League Intermediate Division South side Old Guildfordians for the 2004–05 season, and he helped the club to the runners'-up spot behind Wandsworth Borough, thus gaining promotion to the Senior Division Three South. The 2005–06 season saw Paul back at renamed Bisley before he returned to Old Guildfordians in the summer of 2006. The club finished in sixth place in Senior Division Three South in both 2006–07 and 2007–08, with Paul missing just four games in the latter season.

Craig Wright — Defender/Winger

Born: 7 November 1972, Rinteln, Germany.

Aldershot Town FC record:

Debut:	v Kingsbury Town (a), Isthmian League Cup first round, 22 September 1992.
Last appearance:	v East Thurrock United (a), Isthmian League Division Three, 3 October 1992.
Appearances:	2

Playing career:

Aldershot FC (apprentice, summer 1989), Aldershot Town (summer 1992), Alabama University (US, October 1992).

Club honours:

Isthmian League Division Three (Aldershot Town 1992–93).

Craig could play as a defender or a winger and was an apprentice at the 'old' Aldershot FC, where he captained the youth team and appeared regularly in the reserves. He looked to have a great future ahead of him before a knee ligament injury forced him to retire from the professional game during the 1990–91 season at the age of 18. He joined the 'new' club in the summer of 1992 but played just twice before departing the Rec to study in America, where it is believed he played for Alabama University. No further information pertaining to Craig is known.

Lloyd Wye — Defender

Born: 14 May 1967, Wokingham.

Aldershot Town FC record:

Debut:	v Chertsey Town (a), Isthmian League Division One, 16 August 1997.
Last appearance:	v Uxbridge (a), Isthmian League Division One, 27 September 1997.
Appearances:	10 + 1

Playing career:

Southampton (schoolboy), Woking (from youth, summer 1983), Brentford (trial, July 1987), Wanganui Athletic (New Zealand, May 1992), Woking (November 1992), Wanganui Athletic (New Zealand, March 1993), Woking (November 1993), Aldershot Town (August 1997), Welling United (October 1997), Kingstonian (October 1997), Westfield (February 1998), Staines Town (March 1998), Farnborough Town (September 1998), Staines Town (August 2000), Molesey (November 2000), Walton and Hersham (player-coach/assistant manager, January 2003),

Windlesham United (DR, January 2004), Bisley (player-coach, October 2006), Guildford City (player-assistant manager, June 2007).

Representative honours:
Surrey Youth, FA XI, Isthmian League XI.

Club honours:
Isthmian League Division Two South (Woking 1986–87), Isthmian League Cup (Woking 1991; Farnborough Town 2000), Surrey Senior Cup (Woking 1991, 1994, 1996), Isthmian League Charity Shield (Woking 1991), Isthmian League Premier Division (Woking 1991–92; Kingstonian 1997–98), New Zealand Central League (Wanganui Athletic 1992), FA Trophy (Woking 1994, 1995, 1997), Championship Shield (Woking 1994), Isthmian League Division One (Aldershot Town 1997–98), Hellenic League Division One East (Bisley 2006–07).

Lloyd is an experienced player who, along with his older brother Shane (they are often erroneously described as twins), played a big part in establishing Geoff Chapple's Woking side as a force to be reckoned with in the 1980s and 1990s. Lloyd had played as a schoolboy at Southampton before becoming a youth player at Woking, playing in the Cards' first team as a 16-year-old. He became involved at Kingfield at a time when the club were in decline, reaching their lowest-ever point in 1984–85 when they were relegated to Isthmian League Division Two South. However, the appointment of ex-player Chapple as manager and Lloyd's undoubted ability were two of the main factors in the club moving upwards from there. Indeed, Lloyd developed into a major and steadying influence in Cards' progression over the nine seasons that made up his first spell with the club.

Woking finished in third place in 1985–86 before Lloyd experienced double joy the following season, as the club won the Division Two South title and he won the Player of the Year trophy. Successive third-place finishes in Division One came in 1987–88 and 1988–89 (Lloyd was captain in the latter season) before promotion to the Premier Division was achieved in 1989–90, by virtue of finishing runners-up to Wivenhoe Town. Lloyd was part of the Woking team that reached the fourth round of the FA Cup in 1990–91, famously beating West Bromwich Albion before losing narrowly to Everton. The club also won the Isthmian League Cup and Surrey Senior Cup double that season. Lloyd's last contribution in his first spell at Kingfield was to play a central role in the winning of the Premier Division title (with an 18-point cushion over Enfield), thus gaining promotion to the Conference for the first time in the club's history.

In the summer of 1992 Lloyd went out to New Zealand to play for Central League side Wanganui Athletic and left with a Championship medal. He played part of the 1992–93 season back at Woking before returning to New Zealand in the March, safe in the knowledge that their Conference safety was assured. He returned to Woking in November 1993 and was part of the sides that won the FA Trophy in 1994, 1995 (becoming only the second team to retain the trophy) and 1997. The Cards also finished in third in the Conference in 1993–94 and followed that up with a runners'-up spot to Macclesfield Town in 1994–95 and to Stevenage Borough in 1995–96. That season also saw the club reach the FA Cup third round, where they lost to Swindon Town, and they took FA Premier League Coventry City to a replay at the same stage of the competition in 1996–97 before being defeated by the odd goal in three.

In August 1997 Lloyd left Kingfield (having made 509 appearances) and signed for Aldershot Town. However, his stay at the Rec only lasted a couple of months before he joined ex-Woking boss Chapple at Kingstonian, via a brief stint at Welling United. In four months at Kingsmeadow Lloyd helped the club establish themselves in a strong position from which they went on to win that season's Isthmian League Premier Division title. He played elsewhere before joining Farnborough Town in September 1998, where he endured a rock-bottom finish in the Conference in 1998–99 before helping attain victory in the Isthmian League Cup Final the following season.

Following a brief return to Staines, Lloyd joined Molesey in November 2000 and stayed there until March 2002, when he decided to take some time out of the game. He was bitten by the football bug again in January 2003 and took on the dual role of player-coach/assistant manager to his former Woking teammate Laurence Batty at Walton and Hersham. He remained in this role until January 2004, when he dual registered with Surrey Intermediate League side Windlesham United for the remainder of the season.

In October 2004 he again took on the role of player-coach/assistant manager to Alan Dowson at Stompond Lane, and the duo guided the Swans to promotion from Isthmian League Division One at the end of the 2004–05 season. That season also saw the club equal a club-best FA Trophy fourth-round progression before they bowed out to Stamford in a replay. The 2005–06 season would see the Swans equal their best-ever Premier Division placing as they finished in ninth position.

Following Dowson's resignation in September 2006, Lloyd took over the running of team affairs before moving to Bisley as player-coach the following month, with his experience contributing greatly to the Surrey side winning the 2006–07 Hellenic League Division One East title. In June 2007 Lloyd moved to Guildford City to become player-assistant manager to his former Woking teammate Scott Steele, and they led the club to finish the season as runners-up to Merstham in the Combined Counties League Premier Division. Confirmation of the excellent job that the management duo had done lies in the fact that City finished the 2006–07 season one place off the bottom of the League!

Roy Young — Forward

Born: 28 October 1973, Romsey.

Aldershot Town FC record:

Debut: v Aylesbury United (h), Isthmian League Cup quarter-final, 21 February 1995.
Last appearance: v Boreham Wood (at Slough Town FC), Isthmian League Cup Final, 3 May 1999.
Appearances: 138 + 36 (eighth in all-time top 10)
Goals: 75 (joint-third in all-time top 10)

Playing career:
Portsmouth (from apprentice, July 1992), Colchester United (trial, summer 1994), Weymouth (1ML, November 1992), Poole Town (August 1994), Stockport County (2ML, January 1995), Aldershot Town (February 1995), Billericay Town (1ML, February 1999), Bognor Regis Town (1ML, March 1999), Bognor Regis Town (summer 1999), Bashley (March 2000).

Representative honours:
Hampshire Youth.

Club honours:
Isthmian League Division One (Aldershot Town 1997–98), Isthmian League Cup (Aldershot Town 1999).

Roy was a free-scoring forward who began his career as an apprentice with Portsmouth. He signed full professional forms in July 1992 and was then loaned to Weymouth before being released in the summer of 1994. He subsequently trialled at Colchester United before signing for Poole Town and then having another crack at the pro game by way of a two-month loan at Stockport County.

Roy became Aldershot Town boss Steve Wigley's first signing when he joined in February 1995 for £2,000 and finished the season having scored 10 goals in 19 appearances as the Shots finished in a creditable fourth place in their first season in Isthmian League Division One. He developed a good working relationship with Wigley and later worked for him at his soccer school. Roy's power and predatory instincts resulted in him scoring 10 goals in 21 games in the 1995–96 season before top scoring in 1996–97 (15 goals).

That summer, Wigley departed the Rec to take on a role within the youth set-up at Nottingham Forest, and Roy took on sole responsibility for the running of the aforementioned soccer school. He top scored again in 1997–98 (27 goals), which contributed substantially to the winning of the Division One title. In fact, Roy was one of the Shots goalscorers (the other being Jimmy Sugrue) in the 2–0 victory over Staines Town at the Rec in mid-April that clinched the Division One title.

Roy found himself pushed down the pecking order in the 1998–99 season as Joe Nartey and Leon Gutzmore were often picked ahead of him, and he was loaned out towards the end of the season. However, he did finish the season as a winner, having played in the Shots' Isthmian League Cup Final triumph over Boreham Wood.

Roy eventually left the Rec in the summer of 1999 and joined Bognor on a permanent basis, but his appearances at Nyewood Lane were limited by hamstring injuries. He moved on to Southern League Eastern Division side Bashley in March 2000 and played there until his troublesome hamstrings forced him to retire in November 2001. Roy currently works as the manager of a couple of petrol stations in Southampton.

ALDERSHOT TOWN MANAGERS

Steve Wignall

Born: 17 September 1954, Liverpool.
Managerial tenure: 23 May 1992 to 12 January 1995.
First game: v Clapton (h), Isthmian League Division Three, 22 August 1992.
Last game: v Barking (a), Isthmian League Division One, 7 January 1995.

Managerial honours at ATFC:
Isthmian League Division Three Manager of the Month (August/September 1992; October 1992; December 1992), Isthmian League Division Three Manager of the Year (1993), Isthmian League Division Two Manager of the Month (November 1993; March 1994).

P	W	D	L	Win Rate
146	97	24	25	66.43%

A centre-back, Steve started his career as a junior at Liverpool. In March 1972 he joined Doncaster Rovers and made his Football League debut in a Division Four fixture at home to Crewe Alexandra in November 1972. The following season he featured against Liverpool in the FA Cup third round. Rovers drew 2–2 at Anfield in front of 31,483 spectators, and 22,499 saw the replay at Belle Vue (then Doncaster's home) which Bill Shankly's side won 2–0. In total, Steve made 130 appearances for Rovers, scoring a solitary goal in a 3–2 victory against Swansea City in March 1975.

In September 1977 Steve joined Colchester United for £5,000. The Essex club gained promotion from Division Four that season and established themselves in Division Three, finishing eighth in 1977–78. They reached the fifth round of the FA Cup the following season before losing 1–0 at home to Manchester United the same evening that Aldershot were seconds away from reaching the quarter-final of the competition against Shrewsbury Town. After making 281 appearances for the Us and scoring 22 goals, he moved to Brentford in August 1984. Two seasons at Griffin Park saw a further 67 appearances and two goals.

In September 1986 an £8,000 fee brought Steve to Aldershot FC. With the side having collected just one point from their opening three matches, he made his Shots debut at home to Lincoln City in September 1986. The 4–0 victory was watched by just 1,443 spectators. The season proved to be possibly the most successful in the history of Aldershot FC, as promotion to Division Three was secured via Play-off victories over Bolton Wanderers and Wolverhampton Wanderers. Len Walker's side also reached the Southern Area Final of the Associate Members' Cup and the FA Cup fourth round. Steve made 55 appearances that season and scored a vital goal at Swindon Town in the Associate Members' Cup semi-final as the Shots reversed a 2–0 deficit to win 3–2 at the County Ground. In total, Steve made 199 appearances for Aldershot, scoring seven goals. He remained on the coaching staff at the Rec, where he assisted caretaker manager Ian McDonald until the demise of AFC in March 1992.

With the formation of Aldershot Town, Steve was appointed the first manager of the club in June 1992 after McDonald had been appointed reserve-team manager of Millwall. He had just one player on his books at the time – the groundsman's son Chris Tomlinson.

There was no indication of what league the new club would be in. Indeed, Steve made a phone call to chairman Terry Owens while on holiday in Majorca to ascertain what division Aldershot had been accepted into. He was told Diadora (Isthmian League) Division Three. Having played under influential managers such as Brian Clough, Frank McLintock and John Docherty, he knew what was required.

When the new club made their inaugural competitive debut at home to Clapton on 22 August 1992, Steve, together with assistant manager Keith Baker, had assembled a squad comprising primarily of local players on next-to-nothing wages. Indeed, the first season's total playing and management budget was just £44,163. Victory in the first 10 matches sent the team on their way to success, with the attendances matching the work being undertaken on the pitch. The Division Three title was won by 18 points, and Aldershot were back on the map. An attendance of 5,951 watched the Hampshire Senior Cup semi-final against neighbours Farnborough Town at the Rec.

The following season saw a further promotion and success in the FA Vase, where the Shots were finally eliminated from the Wembley-bound competition at the quarter-final stage after three matches against Greater Manchester-based Atherton Laburnum Rovers.

The manner that Steve went about his first managerial job started to alert other clubs. Not only did he establish first-team success, but he had a talent of ensuring the playing side of the club was structured from junior level upwards to enable the opportunity for future development of players, too. In January 1995 Steve's former club Colchester United made an approach, as they were aiming to appoint a manager to replace George Burley. Steve and his family had always had an affinity with the Essex club, and it was an offer that could not be refused. A compensation fee was paid to Aldershot Town for the cancellation of the contract and the negotiations between the two clubs were first class.

During his time as manager of Aldershot Town, Steve's management record is such that 72.54 per cent of points available were achieved – a tremendous record. Steve built a similar platform at Layer Road. In four seasons at the Essex club, he led them to 10th, seventh (Play-off semi-finals), eighth and fourth in Division Three. A Play-off Final victory against Torquay United was secured in the1997–98 season. The Us also reached the Final of the Auto Windscreens Shield at Wembley in 1996–97, where they were narrowly defeated by Carlisle United. He left Colchester on 21 January 1999, believing, at the time, that he could take the club no further. After a brief spell at

Stevenage Borough during the 1999–2000 season, he became manager of another former club, Doncaster Rovers, in May 2000.

After stabilising a club that had finished bottom of the Football League in 1997–98 and 16th in the Conference in the previous two seasons, Steve provided a firm footing in his first season as the Yorkshire club finished ninth. He was surprisingly replaced in December 2001, with Rovers hovering around the top six in the table.

After a spell out of the game, Steve was appointed as manager of Southend United in April 2003 but was only in charge for 23 matches, having to dismantle and rebuild the squad that had been struggling in Division Three before his arrival. After recruiting new players, he was not given the time for the squad to settle before he was dismissed in November 2003. Steve has since been both assistant manager and first-team coach at Wivenhoe Town (taking a break in between the two roles) as well as starting his own property development business.

Paul Shrubb (Caretaker manager)

Managerial tenure: 13 January 1995 to 25 January 1995.
First/Last game: v Berkhamsted Town (h), Isthmian League Division One, 14 January 1995.

P	W	D	L	Win Rate
1	1	0	0	100%

For full details of Paul's career, see the A to Z of Aldershot Town Players section of this book.

Steve Wigley

Born: 15 October 1961, Ashton-Under-Lyne.
Managerial tenure: 26 January 1995 to 30 July 1997.
First game: v Maidenhead United (h), Isthmian Division One, 28 January 1995.
Last game: v Maidenhead United (a), Isthmian Division One, 3 May 1997.

Managerial honours at ATFC:
Isthmian League Division One Manager of the Month (April/May 1995).

P	W	D	L	Win Rate
135	72	25	38	53.33%

Steve started his playing career at his local club, Curzon Ashton, before being signed by Nottingham Forest in March 1981. A right-sided winger, he made his Football League debut as a 21-year-old against Arsenal in October 1982. His best season was in 1983–84 when he figured in 39 matches in all competitions as Brian Clough's side finished third in Division One and reached the semi-finals of the UEFA Cup before a controversial exit against Anderlecht. Steve is remembered for a vintage performance that season at Parkhead as Forest won 2–1 against Celtic after a goalless draw at the City Ground. In four seasons at Nottingham Forest, he made 82 Football League appearances, scoring two goals.

In October 1985 Steve joined Sheffield United where he made 28 appearances, scoring one goal. Ironically, in March 1987 he left Bramall Lane to join Birmingham City in a swap deal that saw Martin Kuhl move in the opposite direction. The pair were to become teammates at Portsmouth later in their careers before both having strong connections with Aldershot Town. Steve made 87 appearances for the Blues and scored four goals before joining Portsmouth in March 1989 after then manager Alan Ball decided to sign him following a demolition 45-minute performance at St Andrews against his future employers.

Steve remained at Fratton Park for four years, making 120 appearances and scoring 12 goals before teaming up again with Ball at Exeter City in August 1993 for his final Football League season. By the end of the 1993–94 season, he had made 23 appearances and scored one goal for the Devon club.

Steve joined Aldershot Town as manager in January 1995, signing as player-manager, although he never represented the Shots in a competitive match. He had actually featured against the Shots that season while playing for Bognor Regis Town, where he was combining football with a sales job.

In his first full season Steve took the club to the fringes of a promotion place, but with plenty to do. An excellent finale to the season saw six successive victories as the Shots finished level on points with Chertsey Town in third place, missing out on promotion on goal difference. In 1994–95, he took the club to the Final of the Isthmian League Cup, where they suffered a 4–1 defeat to Kingstonian at the Rec. They also reached the fourth qualifying round of the FA Cup in 1995–96 before losing to Ashford Town. After finishing fourth, fifth and seventh in his three seasons, Steve left the Rec in August 1997 to become director of youth development at Nottingham Forest under Paul Hart.

After serving his former club in a variety of roles, he became academy director at Southampton in 2001 and was appointed caretaker manager in February 2004 after the departure of Gordon Strachan. In August of that year, he became head coach at Southampton on a permanent basis after being appointed by then Saints chairman Rupert Lowe. He was relieved of his duties in December 2004 after just one victory, against arch-rivals Portsmouth, in his 14 League matches in charge. A season as reserve-team manager at Manchester City followed before Steve became assistant manager/first-team coach at the City of Manchester Stadium, with former Nottingham Forest colleague Stuart Pearce as manager. The pair departed the club at the end of the 2006–07 season.

As of May 2008 Steve is England Under-21s coach, again under the guidance of Pearce, and he is also the Football Association national coach with responsibility for young players between the ages of 17 and 21; a position that to which he was appointed in August 2007.

Andy Meyer, Mark Butler and Joe Roach (Joint caretaker managers)

Managerial Tenure: 1 August 1997 to 17 September 1997.
First Game: v Chertsey Town (h), Isthmian Division One, 16 August 1997.
Last Game: v Wembley (h), Isthmian Division One, 16 September 1997.

P	W	D	L	Win Rate
8	3	2	3	37.5%

Due to the timing of Steve Wigley's departure, the Shots started the 1997–98 season with the trio of reserve-team manager Andy Meyer, leading army football figure Joe Roach (one of the most capped army players of all time) and crowd favourite Mark Butler in joint charge of team affairs.
For full details of Mark's career, see the Players section of this book.

George Borg

Born: 11 May 1958, Hackney.
Managerial tenure: 18 September 1997 to 31 January 2002.
First game: v Croydon (h), Isthmian League Division One, 20 September 1997.
Last game: v Hitchin Town (h), Isthmian League Premier Division, 19 January 2002.

Managerial honours at ATFC:
Isthmian League Division One Manager of the Month (October 1997; February 1998), Isthmian League Division One Manager of the Year (1998), Isthmian League Premier Division Manager of the Month (December 1999; March 2000).

P	W	D	L	Win Rate
261	147	50	64	56.32%

A playing career that started at West Ham United and Millwall saw George released from the Den in May 1977 at the same time as former Aldershot FC player Terry Shanahan. He never made a Football League appearance for the South London side.

Of Maltese origin, George made his name as a no-nonsense, tough-tackling left full-back, and his career took in spells at Wycombe Wanderers, Maidstone United, Dartford, Dulwich Hamlet, Cape Town City in South Africa and Carolina Lightning in the United States. In Carolina, he played alongside Rodney Marsh and Bobby Moore. Furthermore, he can count Barry Fry and John Still as former managers.

An injury prevented George from continuing his playing career and he started his managerial career at Barking before a spell at Chelmsford City between November 1989 and October 1990. In 1990–91 George led Chesham United to the Isthmian League First Division Championship, having taken over when they were in a mid-table position. In the process, the Buckinghamshire club scored over 100 goals to reach the Premier Division for the first time in their history. In 1991 he took over as manager of Harrow Borough when they were bottom of the Isthmian League Premier Division and led them to safety before guiding them to an eighth-place finish the following season, as well as winning both the Middlesex Senior and Middlesex Charity Cups. He took over as assistant manager and coach of Enfield in 1993, and they finished as runners-up in the Isthmian Premier Division and reached the FA Cup first round and the FA Trophy semi-finals.

The following season George took over as manager at Southbury Road, and the Middlesex side won the Isthmian League Premier Division title, scoring 106 goals in the process. They also reached the FA Cup third round before losing to Leicester City at Filbert Street. Two seasons as runners-up, including a 25-match unbeaten run, followed before George became manager of Aldershot Town (bringing Stuart Cash with him as his assistant) in September 1997 after extensive negotiations.

In his first season he led the Shots to the Isthmian League Division One title despite the club languishing in mid-table upon his arrival. Indeed, attendances rose from 1,618 at his first match in charge to 4,289 for the final match of the season – a carnival day against Berkhamsted Town. The final eight matches of the season were won as the Shots were crowned champions by 11 points. George certainly produced a flair and charisma that, at the time, was a breath of fresh air to the Rec faithful. The following season 65 first-team matches were played. The Shots scored 53 goals at home (more than any other club in senior football) and also secured their first-ever Cup successes, winning the Hampshire Senior Cup at The Dell and the Isthmian League Cup (against Boreham Wood) at Slough Town within two days of each other. They were special times for the club, and the County Cup success against Basingstoke Town was a unique evening, as the Shots won with a goal in the final minute of injury-time despite playing with 10 players for most of the match.

In 1999–2000, a placing of second in the Isthmian League Premier Division followed with more Cup success, as a club record 9–1 victory over Andover secured the Hampshire Senior Cup. The club also reached the FA Cup first round for the first time, defeating Hednesford Town after a replay before eventually losing at Exeter City in round two. Two further FA Cup runs saw the only capacity crowd at the Rec since the club's inception in 1992 (7,500 against Brighton & Hove Albion) attend a first-round tie in November 2000, together with the *Match of the Day* cameras.

The following season, defeat was suffered in a first-round replay at Bristol Rovers. George had his own brand of leadership that proved extremely popular with the Shots faithful in the early years, although his determination to succeed finally succumbed in the 2001–02 season when, after the realisation that promotion was not to be, despondency and apathy crept in with the supporters. After a period of negotiations, George finally left the Rec by mutual consent in January 2002. However, the difficult and unnecessary final few months of his reign should not overshadow the contribution that he made to the progress of the club, especially in his early tenure. Since leaving the club, George has had spells as first-team coach at Billericay Town and manager of Hornchurch (appointed in September 2003), whom he led to the FA Cup second round in 2003–04 after defeating Darlington. He also enjoyed success at Braintree Town, whom he led to the Isthmian Premier Division title in 2005–06. There followed a narrow defeat to Salisbury City in 2007 in the Conference South Play-off Final.

After being relieved of his duties at Braintree in October 2007, George served as caretaker manager of Boreham Wood for a second time in February 2008 before he was given compassionate leave to look after his ill brother. He also passed his UEFA B licence in the Netherlands and has coached the USA Under-19s side.

Stuart Cash (Caretaker manager)

Managerial tenure: 1 February 2002 to 23 March 2002.
First game: v Croydon (a), Isthmian League Premier Division, 2 February 2002.
Last game: v Sutton United (h), Isthmian League Premier Division, 23 March 2002.

P	W	D	L	Win Rate
14	9	2	3	64.28%

For full details of Stuart's career, see the Players section of this book.

Terry Brown

Born: 5 August 1952, Hillingdon.
Managerial tenure: 24 March 2003 to 27 March 2007.
First game: v Newport (Isle of Wight, a), Hampshire Senior Cup semi-final second leg, 26 March 2002.
Last game: v Weymouth (h), 27 March 2007, Conference National.

Managerial honours at ATFC:
Isthmian League Premier Division Manager of the Month (August/September 2002; April/May 2003), Isthmian League Premier Division Manager of the Year (2003), non-League Club Directory Individual Merit Award (2003), Conference Manager of the Month (October 2003 [shared with two other managers]), Conference National Manager of the Month (November 2005).

P	W	D	L	Win Rate
284	145	52	87	51.05%

Having played local football, Terry started playing at his home-town club of Hayes as a 19-year-old forward and made his debut against Enfield in April 1971. He became a regular during the next season and featured in the FA Cup defeat of Bristol Rovers. He caught the attention of scouts from Fulham and Millwall and was selected for the FA Amateur XI. After two seasons, he briefly joined Sutton United and moved to Slough Town before rejoining Hayes in August 1977. He stayed at Church Road until October 1979 and made a total of 148 appearances and scored 45 goals across his two spells.

Terry then left for Wokingham Town, where he went on to become the Berkshire club's record goalscorer with 91 goals. He remained at Finchampstead Road in a variety of coaching capacities until he joined former club Hayes as manager in December 1993 (at a time when the club were struggling at the foot of the Isthmian League Premier Division). In 1995–96 they won the Premier Division, ironically finishing above George Borg's Enfield on goal difference. That season also saw Terry appointed as manager of the Isthmian League representative side, a role which he assumed in October 1995.

The years that followed in the Conference showed what could be achieved by an enthusiastic manager working on a low budget. Hayes achieved a club-best third-place finish in 1998–99, finishing six points below Cheltenham Town. Realising he would be unable to take Hayes any further, Terry applied for the vacancy at the Rec and, after 462 matches (featuring 722 goals) in charge of Hayes, he left Church Road to become manager of Aldershot Town in March 2002.

His arrival at the Rec started a five-year love affair with the Shots supporters. He immediately made his first crucial signing by keeping Stuart Cash as his assistant. George Borg's former assistant had steered the side through a rocky period as caretaker manager and the two struck up a firm relationship immediately; the Hampshire Senior Cup was secured in their first month together.

The following season Terry steered the club to the Isthmian League Premier Division title (by a 13-point margin), accumulating 105 points in the process. The victory at Canvey Island in April 2003 remains one of the most memorable in the club's short existence.

The Shots exceeded all expectations, securing an unlikely Play-off spot in 2003–04 by virtue of finishing fifth in the Conference together with recording the highest average attendance at the Rec since 1979. After a penalty shoot-out defeat of Hereford United in the semis, the Shots lost in another shoot-out to Shrewsbury Town in front of 19,216 spectators at the Britannia Stadium, Stoke. The season also saw the FA Trophy semi-finals reached and another FA Cup first-round placing.

In 2004–05, with the club having gone full-time, another Play-off position was achieved and penalty shoot-out heartbreak was again experienced with Carlisle United winning an epic encounter at Brunton Park. The Shots also reached the second round of the FA Cup and the Final of the Hampshire Senior Cup (where they lost to Winchester City). The 2005–06 season was a disappointment, as the club finished 13th in the Conference National. It was the first time an Aldershot Town side had finished in the lower half of a table as, for a variety of reasons, 47 players were used.

Terry's final season in charge saw the club reach the FA Cup third round for the first time in their history, but personal anxiety caused the respected West Londoner to resign his position to care for his wife, Susan, who had been diagnosed with leukaemia. Testament to his popularity, his farewell bid to Shots supporters in his final match against Weymouth in March 2007 was amid emotional scenes and a standing ovation from spectators and players alike after the final whistle.

After a short break from football, Terry teamed up with Stuart Cash again in May 2007 when he was appointed manager of the progressive AFC Wimbledon (Cash linked up as his assistant after a spell at Lewes). In Terry's first season at Kingsmeadow, promotion was achieved through a tense Play-off Final against Staines Town, where the Wombles won 2–1, with both goals scored in the final 10 minutes at Wheatsheaf Park to steer the club into the Conference South for the first time in their history.

Martin Kuhl (Caretaker manager)

Managerial tenure: 28 March 2007 to 16 May 2007.
First game: v Farnborough Town (h), Hampshire Senior Cup semi-final first leg, 29 March 2007.
Last game: v Fleet Town, Hampshire Senior Cup Final (at AFC Bournemouth), 5 May 2007.

P	W	D	L	Win Rate
11	5	3	3	45.45%

For full details of Martin's career, see the Players section of this book.

Gary Waddock

Born: 17 March 1962, Kingsbury.
Managerial Tenure: 19 July 2007 to date.
First Game: v Kidderminster Harriers (a), Conference Premier, 11 August 2007.

Managerial honours at ATFC:

Conference Premier Manager of the Month (September 2007).

P	W	D	L	Win Rate
63	43	10	10	68.25%

Gary was a hard-tackling midfielder who started his playing career at Queen's Park Rangers in 1979 and eventually made 203 appearances for the West London side, scoring eight goals, including two FA Cup Final appearances at Wembley as Rangers narrowly lost to Tottenham Hotspur after a replay in 1982. The following season, QPR went on to win the Division Two title and returned to English football's top division, where they finished the 1983–84 season in fifth spot, thus qualifying for the UEFA Cup before manager Terry Venables departed to take charge of Barcelona. However, a nasty injury threatened Gary's career and forced him to leave Rangers. Once recovered, insurance restrictions at the time prevented him resuming his career in the UK, so he joined Belgian side RSC Charleroi in the summer of 1987.

During his time in Belgium, Gary made 40 appearances and scored one goal. He returned to London in August 1989 and signed for Millwall, where he spent two seasons, during which he scored twice in 58 appearances. A return to QPR in December 1991 did not work out so, after a loan spell at Swindon Town (March 1992), Gary joined Bristol Rovers in November 1992 and played 71 times, scoring once. A move to Luton Town followed in September 1994 and his four years there yielded three goals in 153 appearances. His most successful season at Kenilworth Road was in 1996–97 when he made 39 League appearances as the Hatters finished third in Division Two before eventually missing out to Crewe Alexandra in the Play-off semi-finals.

In addition to a fine club career, Gary also made 21 appearances for the Republic of Ireland and netted three goals. He made his debut against Switzerland in April 1980 as an 18-year-old and featured against Argentina the same year in a 1–0 success in Dublin. His only appearance against England came in 1985 in a 2–1 defeat at Wembley. His final international appearance was in a goalless draw in Turkey in May 1990.

After his playing career ended Gary returned to QPR and teamed up with Ian Holloway. He was responsible for the youth and reserve teams before becoming caretaker manager when Holloway was initially given gardening leave in February 2006. With Alan McDonald assisting, QPR retained their place in the Championship by finishing in 21st spot (just one place above the relegation zone). He was appointed as manager on a permanent basis in June 2006, but the club were struggling due to off-field problems and a run of poor results saw Gary replaced by former colleague John Gregory just four months later.

After a break from the game, he was surprisingly appointed as manager of Aldershot Town in May 2007 despite having no previous experience of the Conference. However, he soon provided the Shots supporters with confidence by the way he conducted business, strengthening a squad that, by his own admission, included a number of fine players left by Terry Brown. Inserting his own brand and style and keeping Brown's former assistant Martin Kuhl, the Waddock-led Shots started the season strongly with a 2–1 victory at Kidderminster Harriers and eventually went on to achieve the finest season in the short history of Aldershot Town.

With expectation low at the start of the campaign, the Shots secured promotion to the Football League with the Blue Square-sponsored Conference Premier title and achieved the highest-ever points total of the competition in the process (101). A new divisional record of 31 wins was also established. Aldershot Town also won the Setanta Shield (the club's first piece of national silverware) by way of a penalty shoot-out victory over Rushden and Diamonds and reached the FA Trophy semi-finals before succumbing to eventual winners Ebbsfleet United over two legs.

It was a dream inaugural season for Gary, who became the man to realise the dreams of all Aldershot Town supporters and reach the Football League, which had been taken away from them on 25 March 1992. He will go down in history as the manager who guided the club into the League, but he is always conscious of praising the achievements made by the squad by virtue of a team effort.

Gary's achievements were formally recognised when he was named the Conference Premier Manager of the Year at the League's annual end-of-season awards, and further clarification came at the end of June 2008 when he signed a new three-year contract at the Rec, along with assistant Martin Kuhl.

ROLL OF HONOUR

Richard Adams
Richard Adshead
Christopher Amy
Andyshot
Mel Baird
Gina Balsdon
Richard Bartlett - Puerto Rico Shot
Liam Binfield
Phil Blackmore
David Bleach
Anthony Bonnici (Malta)
Bob Bowden
Bill Brade
Andy Bradley - Shetland Shot
Dave Brewer
Sid Broad
Tony Brooker
Nikki Bull
Steve Bull
Joe Burdfield
Nick James Matt Cansfield
Craig Campbell
Robin Carder
Grant Carroll
Patrick Carroll
Alan John Case
Steve 'Chappie' Chapman
Alan Chitson
Jae Clark
John Clark
Paul Clark
Andy Clarke
Martin Clarke
Alan Clarkson
Andrew Cleeve
Richard Clifford
Nick Collins
Rona Collins
Tim Cowden
James David Crawshaw
Terry Cull
Alastair Cunningham
Colin Cunningham
Levi Darch
Paul Darch
Peter Darch
Dave Davies
Harrison Dawson
Alexander Dobrev
Richard Dowding
David Dresch
Andy Duff
Andrew Duffett
Tony Eaton
Craig Edmondson
Barry John Elcombe
Sarah Lesley Elcombe
Craig Etherington
Neville Farrar
Damian Faulkner
David Frowen
Nick Fryer
Jeremy Garrett 1965
Steven Gibbs
Clive Girdler
Alan Glaum
Geoff Goddard
Derek Gosden
Lloyd Grassi
Jack Gray
Sam Gray
Stuart 'Musestar' Griffiths
Martin Harrington
Kevin Harris
Malcolm Harris
Nigel Harris
Nigel Harris
Simon Harvey
Mark Hatherley
Chris Hayes
Andy Hazeldine
Ray Hazeldine
Chris Heath
Chris Heath - Melbourne Red
David Hedgecock
Eggy Hepburn
Martin 'Tenerife's Mr.Shots' Hillyer
Terry Hillyer
Graham D Hocking
Neil S Hocking
Paul Hopkins
John Horlock
Jonathan Hubbard
Lesley Hubbard
Gary Hunt
Jon Jackson
Andy Jones
Chris Kane
Liam Kane
Dennis Keefe
Gary Kent
Slasher Kent
Martin Knott
Wayne Kercher - Taunton Red
Kevin Lambden
Paul Arthur Lambden
Andy Leete
Steve Levene
Carol Lewis
Daniel & Steve Lewis
David Little
Stuart Longden
Peter Looseley
Michael Lord
Brian MacLennan
Graham MacLennan
John Manby
Manc Bob
Dean Martin
Craig Matthews
Andy Meyer
John Miller
Liam Miller
Kelly Montgomery
Craig Morrow
Kevin Moseling
Andrew Mower
Julian Munday
Chris Munn
Bill Myles
Chris Myles
Pete Myles
Bill Nelson
Micky Nelson
Ryan Nelson

William Nelson
Graham Neves
John Orme
Chris Osborne
Sefton Owens
Des Paddock
Daniel Thomas Parmiter
Michael A Parry
Michael E Parry
Eric Pearce
Andy Permain
Graham Pether
Ian Pether
Nigel Pether
Malcolm Plumb
Joe Potterton
Kevin J. Powell
Nick Powell
David Price
Ed Price
Gareth Prior
Owen Prior
Richard Prior
Lisa Pugh
Mark Pugh
Andy Pusey
Rev Mike Pusey
Des Pyke
Dave Raney - Finchampstead Shop
Joseph Rapley
Samuel Rapley
Tont Ratycleft
Peter Richardson
James Rogers
John Rogers
Victoria Rogers
Chris Rowsell
Julian Saunders
Peter Saunders
Richard Scholfield
Martin Scott
Michael Scott
John Setterfield
Tim Setterfield
John Sharman
Nick Sharman
Dave Shearer
Stephen Shelley
Barry Smith
Carl Smith
David Smith
Robert Smith
Roland Smithies
Dougie Snape
Allen Soane
Roger Spencer
Vera Stanford
Simon Stead
Simon Stevens
Richard Stevens
Ian Stevenson - Lightwater Shot
Chris Stewart
Laura Stockley
Rob Stoker
Phil 'Stokesey' Stokes
Lauren Storey
John Sturt
Chris Sumner
Bill Taylor
Trevor Taylor
Mark Treadwell
Ray Treadwell
Barry Underwood
Jack Underwood
Tom Varley
Lenny Vee
Kevin Wallis
Peter Ward
Charlie Warley
South Warnborough Warrens
Chris Watts
Adrian Wells
Richard Wells
Andy White
Julian White 28 August 1999 RIP
Leighton Wicks
Sian Williams
Nigel Willoughby
Gerry Wiseman
The Wolf
Derek Wood
George Wooderson
Tim Woodman
Mark Worley
Riley Yarrow
Phil Yarney
The Sweet Family Cardiff